Search User Interfaces

This book focuses on the human users of search engines and the tool they use to interact with it: the search user interface. The truly worldwide reach of the Web has brought with it a new realization among computer scientists and laypersons of the enormous importance of usability and user interface design. In the last ten years, much has become understood about what works in search interfaces from a usability perspective, and what does not. Researchers and practitioners have developed a wide range of innovative interface ideas, but only the most broadly acceptable make their way into major Web search engines. This book summarizes these developments, presenting the state of the art of search interface design, both in academic research and in deployment in commercial systems.

Many books describe the algorithms behind search engines and information retrieval systems, but the unique focus of this book is specifically on the user interface. The intended audiences are industry professionals who are designing systems that use search interfaces as well as graduate students and academic researchers who investigate information systems.

Dr. Marti A. Hearst is a Professor in the School of Information at the University of California, Berkeley. She received B.A., M.S., and Ph.D. degrees in computer science from Univeristy of California Berkeley and was a member of the research staff of Xerox PARC from 1994 to 1997. Her research focuses on search user interfaces, computational linguistics, and information visualization. She is an Okawa Foundation Fellow and an IBM faculty Fellow and is a recipient of the NSF CAREER Grant, a Google faculty research grant, and more than $2 million in government research funding. She has advised and consulted for numerous search-related companies.

Search
User
Interfaces

Marti A. Hearst

University of California, Berkeley

 **CAMBRIDGE**
UNIVERSITY PRESS

CAMBRIDGE UNIVERSITY PRESS
Cambridge, New York, Melbourne, Madrid, Cape Town, Singapore,
São Paulo, Delhi, Dubai, Tokyo

Cambridge University Press
32 Avenue of the Americas, New York, NY 10013-2473, USA

www.cambridge.org
Information on this title: www.cambridge.org/9780521113793

First published 2009

Printed in the United States of America

A catalog record for this publication is available from the British Library.

Library of Congress Cataloging in Publication Data

Hearst, Marti.
Search user interfaces / Marti A. Hearst.
   p.   cm.
Includes bibliographical references and index.
ISBN 978-0-521-11379-3
1. Web search engines.   2. User interfaces (Computer systems)
3. Human-computer interaction.   I. Title.
TK5105.884.H43 2009
006.7'784–dc22   2009025735

ISBN 978-0-521-11379-3 Hardback

In memory of my mother, Jean.

Contents

Preface   *page* xi

1 The Design of Search User Interfaces   1

  1.1 Keeping the Interface Simple   1
  1.2 A Historical Shift in Search Interface Design   3
  1.3 The Process of Search Interface Design   5
  1.4 Design Guidelines for Search Interfaces   6
  1.5 Offer Efficient and Informative Feedback   7
  1.6 Balance User Control with Automated Actions   14
  1.7 Reduce Short-Term Memory Load   18
  1.8 Provide Shortcuts   22
  1.9 Reduce Errors   23
  1.10 Recognize the Importance of Small Details   25
  1.11 Recognize the Importance of Aesthetics in Design   26
  1.12 Conclusions   28

2 The Evaluation of Search User Interfaces   29

  2.1 Standard Information Retrieval Evaluation   30
  2.2 Informal Usability Testing   34
  2.3 Formal Studies and Controlled Experiments   36
  2.4 Longitudinal Studies   46
  2.5 Analyzing Search Engine Server Logs   47
  2.6 Large-Scale Log-Based Usability Testing (Bucket Testing)   49
  2.7 Special Concerns with Evaluating Search Interfaces   52
  2.8 Conclusions   63

3 Models of the Information Seeking Process   64

   3.1   The Standard Model of Information Seeking   64
   3.2   Cognitive Models of Information Seeking   66
   3.3   The Dynamic (Berry-Picking) Model   67
   3.4   Information Seeking in Stages   69
   3.5   Information Seeking as a Strategic Process   71
   3.6   Sensemaking: Search as Part of a Larger Process   80
   3.7   Information Needs and Query Intent   82
   3.8   Conclusions   90

4 Query Specification   91

   4.1   Textual Query Specification   91
   4.2   Query Specification via Entry Form Interfaces   101
   4.3   Dynamic Term Suggestions During Query Specification   105
   4.4   Query Specification Using Boolean and Other Operators 107
   4.5   Query Specification Using Command Languages   114
   4.6   Conclusions   118

5 Presentation of Search Results   120

   5.1   Document Surrogates   120
   5.2   KWIC, or Query-Oriented Summaries   122
   5.3   Highlighting Query Terms   128
   5.4   Addition Features of Results Listings   130
   5.5   The Effects of Search Results Ordering   135
   5.6   Visualization of Search Results   139
   5.7   Conclusions   139

6 Query Reformulation   141

   6.1   The Need for Reformulation   141
   6.2   Spelling Suggestions and Corrections   142
   6.3   Automated Term Suggestions   144
   6.4   Suggesting Popular Destinations   151
   6.5   Relevance Feedback   152
   6.6   Showing Related Articles (More Like This)   154
   6.7   Conclusions   156

7 Supporting the Search Process   157

   7.1   Starting Points for Search   157
   7.2   Supporting Search History   162

7.3 Supporting the Search Process as a Whole   164
7.4 Integrating Search with Sensemaking   168
7.5 Conclusions   173

8 Integrating Navigation with Search   174

8.1 Categories for Navigating and Narrowing   175
8.2 Categories for Grouping Search Results   177
8.3 Categories for Sorting and Filtering Search Results   180
8.4 Organizing Search Results via Table-of-Contents Views   182
8.5 The Decline of Hierarchical Navigation of Web Content   187
8.6 Faceted Navigation   188
8.7 Navigating via Social Tagging and Social Bookmarking   196
8.8 Clustering in Search Interfaces   199
8.9 Clusters vs. Categories in Search Interfaces   208
8.10 Conclusions   210

9 Personalization in Search   211

9.1 Personalization Based on Explicit Preferences   213
9.2 Personalization Based on Implicit Relevance Cues   221
9.3 Combining Implicit and Explicit Information   229
9.4 Searching over Personal Information   231
9.5 Conclusions   232

10 Information Visualization for Search Interfaces   234

10.1 Principles of Information Visualization   235
10.2 Techniques for Interactive Visualization   237
10.3 The Effects of Data Types on Information Visualization   238
10.4 The Difficulties with Visualizing Nominal Data   240
10.5 Visualization for Query Specification   247
10.6 Visualizing Query Terms Within a Large Document   252
10.7 Visualizing Query Terms Within Retrieval Results   254
10.8 Visualizing Faceted Navigation   267
10.9 Visualizing Search Results as Clusters and "Starfields"   273
10.10 3D Visualization in Search   278
10.11 Conclusions   280

11 Information Visualization for Text Analysis   281

11.1 Visualization for Text Mining   281
11.2 Visualizing Document Concordances and Word
     Frequencies   286

11.3 Visualizing Literature and Citation Relationships   294
11.4 Conclusions   296

12 *Emerging Trends in Search Interfaces*   297

12.1 Mobile Search Interfaces   297
12.2 Multimedia Search Interfaces   306
12.3 Social Search   317
12.4 A Hybrid of Command and Natural Language Search   322
12.5 Conclusions   323

Appendix: Additional Copyright Notices   325

Bibliography   329
Index   365
Author Index   375

Preface

Search is an integral part of peoples' online lives; people turn to search engines for help with a wide range of needs and desires, from satisfying idle curiousity to finding life-saving health remedies, from learning about medieval art history to finding video game solutions and pop music lyrics. Web search engines are now the second most frequently used online computer application, after email. Not long ago, most software applications did not contain a search module. Today, search is fully integrated into operating systems and is viewed as an essential part of most information systems.

Many books on information retrieval describe the *algorithms* behind search engines and information retrieval systems. By contrast, this book focuses on the human users of search systems and the tool they use to interact with them: the search *user interface*. Because of their global reach, search user interfaces must be understandable by and appealing to a wide variety of people of all ages, cultures, and backgrounds, and for an enormous variety of information needs.

The truly worldwide reach of the Web has brought with it a new realization among computer scientists and laypersons alike of the enormous importance of usability and user interface design. In the last ten years, much has become understood about what works in search interfaces from a usability perspective, and what does not. Researchers and practitioners have developed a wide range of innovative interface ideas, but only the most broadly acceptable make their way into major Web search engines. This book attempts to summarize these developments, presenting the state of the art of search interface design, both in academic research and in deployment in commercial systems.

This is a fast-changing field, and any attempt to summarize the state of the art will no doubt soon be proven obsolete. Nonetheless, certain principles and techniques seem to hold steady over the years, and there is much that is now known about search interfaces that should stand for at least the near future.

Book Overview

This book outlines the human side of the information seeking process and focuses on the aspects of this process that can best be supported by the user interface. It describes the methods behind user interface design generally, and search interface design in particular, with an emphasis on how best to evaluate search interfaces. It discusses research results and current practices surrounding user interfaces for query specification, display of retrieval results, grouping retrieval results, navigation of information collections, query reformulation, search personalization, and the broader tasks of sensemaking and text analysis. Much of the discussion pertains to Web search engines, but the book also covers the special considerations surrounding search of other information collections. The chapters are elaborated on in the following paragraphs.

The Design of Search User Interfaces (Chapter 1) introduces the ideas and practices surrounding user interface design generally, and search interface design in particular. It opens with an analysis of why Web search interfaces appear standardized and relatively simple compared to other interfaces and places modern search interfaces into a historical context. The remainder of the chapter is a summary of interface design guidelines as applied specifically to search interfaces. This chapter is intended to be useful for those people who do not have time to read the entire book but want to understand best practices and problems to avoid in the design of search user interfaces.

The Evaluation of Search User Interfaces (Chapter 2) is a companion to the chapter on design, as user-centered design requires tight-coupling with evaluation. The chapter summarizes the key methods for evaluating search interfaces: informal studies, formal studies, field studies, longitudinal studies, and large-scale log-based studies (also known as bucket testing). This is followed by advice about best practices and special considerations to keep in mind when evaluating search interfaces.

Models of the Information Seeking Process (Chapter 3) summarizes the theoretical models that have been proposed about how people seek information. These models are the foundation on which much of search interface design is based. These include the standard model, the cognitive model, the dynamic (berry-picking) model, information seeking as a strategic process (including cost-structure analysis and foraging theory), orienteering and incremental strategies, and the theory of sensemaking. This is followed by a discussion of information needs and query intent, including attempts to create taxonomies of searcher's information needs and intents, by manually and automatically analyzing queries and online behavior.

Query Specification (Chapter 4) is the first of a set of three chapters that describe interfaces to support the interlocked information seeking cycle of query specification, viewing of retrieval results, and query reformulation. This chapter summarizes both research and the state of current practice in search interface design for query specification, including textual queries, natural language questions, query specification forms, dynamic feedback, queries using Boolean and other operators, faceted queries, and command-based queries.

Presentation of Search Results (Chapter 5) is the second of three chapters on interface support for the standard information seeking cycle. This chapter summarizes research as well as the state of current practice for displaying search results pages. Topics include document surrogates, properties of results listings, summaries or extracts as used in search results, and user response to search results ordering.

Query Reformulation (Chapter 6) is the third of three chapters on interface support for the standard information seeking cycle. This chapter discusses the need for and frequency of query reformulation, followed by interface ideas that support reformulation from both research and the current state of practice. Specifically, these are spelling suggestions and corrections, automated suggestions for query refinement and expansion, suggesting popular destinations, relevance feedback, and suggesting related articles.

Supporting the Search Process (Chapter 7) is a capstone to the previous three chapters, describing interfaces that encompass and augment the full standard process of information seeking. Topics include interfaces to support finding starting points for search, using history and re-finding, and to support the sensemaking process that often accompanies but is broader than search.

Integrating Navigation with Search (Chapter 8) discusses interfaces to support the integration of browsing of information structures with directed search, primarily in information collections (as opposed to for the Web as a whole). Topics include using categories to sort, filter, and group search results; organizing results by table-of-contents-like views; faceted navigation; and automatically derived clusters for organizing search results. The chapter concludes with a discussion of the tradeoffs of using categories versus clusters for search results organization.

Personalization in Search (Chapter 9) explores the emerging area of using information about individual users to influence search results ordering, to create automated alert services, and to tailor information recommendations to users. There is intense interest in research and industry surrounding information personalization, although most attempts to personalize information are still short of their mark.

Information Visualization for Search Interfaces (Chapter 10) is the first of two closely related chapters on the use of information visualization in search and text analysis. This first chapter provides a brief introduction to the main principles and techniques used in visualization of abstract information (as opposed to scientific visualization, which renders real-world objects in visual form). It also discusses why visualization of nominal data – of which text is composed – is difficult to do effectively. It then describes some of the many attempts to use information visualization to improve query specification and display of retrieval results, as well as to give overviews of information collections. Unfortunately, in most cases, usability studies incorporating these visualizations find that in the best case they do not improve peoples' performance, and in the worse case they slow people down or cause them to make errors. That said, in many cases study participants find visualizations to be appealing, at least at first exposure if not for extended use.

Information Visualization for Text Analysis (Chapter 11) describes information visualization for text analysis, which seems to be a more successful application area for visualization of textual information. Although primarily of interest for analysts and specialists, as opposed to for everyday search use, these techniques are often creative in design and captivating to view.

Emerging Trends in Search Interfaces (Chapter 12) closes the book with a discussion of areas of search that are still relatively new but promise to be of increasing importance in the coming years. Topics include mobile search, multimedia search, social search, and a hybrid of command-based and natural language search.

There are a number of topics related to search that this book does not cover. These include interfaces for database systems, Search Engine Optimization (SEO), the role of advertising in search, spam detection and elimination, and ranking algorithms. This book assumes that the reader is familiar with the technical basics behind search engines and information retrieval, including crawling, indexing, ranking, Boolean queries, and PageRank. (For those who are not, see the Related Books section for suggested readings.)

This book is an update and expansion of a chapter written in 1998 for the book *Modern Information Retrieval*, Baeza-Yates and Ribeiro-Neto (Eds.), Addison Wesley, 1999. At that time, little was known definitively about which ideas result in usable search interfaces. In the intervening ten years, much has been learned. Thus, one goal of this book is to back up every statement with verification from the literature. This can be challenging when much of the knowledge is locked up in industry, but fortunately, a number of recent papers have appeared that share insights from the major Web search engines. (An exception is made for Chapter 1, which is intended to be a summary of best practices encapsulated into one chapter; unsupported statements made there are verified in later chapters.) Although a large proportion of the references are necessarily drawn from research from the last few years, readers are also exposed to early foundations and ideas.

Using This Book

This book has two intended primary audiences. The first is academic researchers, graduate students, and those teaching graduate-level courses in information retrieval, user interfaces, and other information management–related topics. The second intended audience is practitioners who design and build search interfaces. Although the book makes heavy use of academic references, an attempt has been made to keep the language and concepts approachable. Instructors may want to view this book as having two main parts, with Chapters 1–7 covering search interface fundamentals and Chapters 8–12 covering advanced topics.

The contents of this book are available online at `http://searchuser interfaces.com`. Updates to the subject matter presented in this book will appear at the Web site.

Related Books

For a nice introduction to the mathematical foundations and algorithms for search, geared primarily towards undergraduates, see *Introduction to Information Retrieval*, by Manning, Rhagavan, and Schütze, Cambridge University Press, 2008. For a more advanced research-oriented book on a wider range of topics related to search, see *Modern Information Retrieval, 2nd Edition*, by Baeza-Yates and Ribeiro-Neto (Eds.), Addison Wesley, 2009 (to appear).

For details on Web search algorithms, see *Mining the Web: Analysis of Hypertext and Semi Structured Data* by Chakrabarti, Morgan Kaufmann, 2002, and for details on link-based algorthms as well as general Web search algorithms, see *Google's PageRank and Beyond: The Science of Search Engine Rankings* by Langville and Meyer, Princeton University Press, 2006. For implementing search engines, see *Managing Gigabytes* by Witten, Moffat, and Bell, Morgan Kauffman, 1999, and *Lucene in Action* by Gospodnetic and Hatcher, Manning Publications, 2004.

To date, there is no other academic book that focuses on search user interfaces. The most closely related is *Information Seeking in Electronic Environments* by Marchionini, Cambridge University Press, 1995, which focuses on the search process rather than on interfaces for search. *Finding Out About: A Cognitive Perspective on Search Engine Technology and the WWW* by Rik Belew, Cambridge University Press, 2008, is a new edition of a book first published in 2000 and describes basic algorithms as well as some cognitive properties of search.

Books written by and for practioners include *Information Architecture for the World Wide Web, 3rd Edition* by Morville and Rosenfeld, O'Reilly Media, 2006, which describes design of information architecture, including two chapters on search, and *Designing Web Navigation, Optimizing the User Experience*, by Kalback and Gufstafson, O'Reilly Media, 2007, which discusses navigation design for Web sites.

A Note on Terminology

The words *user, searcher,* and *information seeker* are used interchangibly in this book to indicate a hypothetical or an actual person using a search system. Some authors object to the word *user,* both because they feel it reduces a person to what they are doing with a computer and because of its association with recreational drug use. Its use is, however, standard in the field and is convenient to write with, and so this book is a user user. By contrast, the word *participant* is used to refer to a person who voluntarily participates in a usability study.

This book also unapologetically uses the pronoun *they* and the possessive *their* to refer to the third person singular as a way to avoid making explicit (and unnecessarily distracting) gender distinctions.

Disclaimer

The author has been employed by, consulted for, and/or received research gifts or grants from the following institutions whose ideas, products, or projects are mentioned in this book: AltaVista, DeepDyve, Google, IBM, Microsoft, Powerset, (Xerox) PARC, University of California Berkeley, Yahoo, and Zvents. No compensation has been received or is expected in exchange for mentioning these organizations' products or ideas in this book.

Acknowledgments

I wish to thank the following people for commenting on this manuscript: Bob Glushko made extensive comments on an early draft that led to my writing a single chapter that can be read in isolation (the design chapter). I am grateful to Ben Shneiderman, who was generous with an extensive conversation about the visualization chapters. Daniel Russell provided invaluable feedback on the design, query specification, and results presentation chapters, and Dan Rose and Anne Aula provided detailed comments on the evaluation chapter. I am also grateful to Omar Alonso, Anne Aula, Stephen Few, Greg Linden, Gary Marchionini, Avi Rappoport, and Jamie Teevan for comments on other chapters.

I would like to thank the hundreds of former master's students who have taken my courses in User Interface Design, Information

Visualization, and Information Organization and Retrieval. The more than 50 projects I oversaw in the User Interface Design course were invaluable for deepening my understanding of how the interface design process unfolds, and the pitfalls as well as the successful paths toward good design. I also thank the former master's students, PhD students, and postdocs who worked with me on search interface research projects: Anna Divoli, Ame Elliott, Jennifer English, Melody Ivory, Kevin Li, Preslav Nakov, Ariel Schwartz, Rashmi Sinha, Emilia Stoica, Kirsten Swearingen, Michael Wooldridge, and Ka-Ping Yee.

I would like to thank the University of California, Berkeley, for granting me a sabbatical that allowed me to finish the writing of this book, Lauren Cowles at Cambridge University Press for acting as my editor and liaison to the publisher, and Ricardo Baeza-Yates and Berthier Ribiero-Neto, whose request for a chapter for the revision of *Modern Information Retrieval* led me to write an entire book.

Closer to home, I thank my brother Ed for persistently encouraging me to write a book, my sister Dor for inspiring me by finishing her first novel this year, my parents for surrounding me with books and a love of words and science, and Emmi for frequent play breaks. Finally, I thank Carl for being there throughout, in the best way possible.

1 The Design of Search User Interfaces

1.1. Keeping the Interface Simple

The job of the search user interface is to aid users in the expression of their information needs, in the formulation of their queries, in the understanding of their search results, and in keeping track of the progress of their information seeking efforts.

However, the typical search interface today is of the form type-keywords-in-entry-form, view-results-in-a-vertical-list. A comparison of a search results page from Google in 2007 to that of Infoseek in 1997 shows that they are nearly identical (see Figure 1.1). Why is the standard interface so simple? Some important reasons for the relative simplicity and unchanging nature of the standard Web search interface are:

- Search is a means towards some other end, rather than a goal in itself. When a person is looking for information, they are usually engaged in some larger task, and do not want their flow of thought interrupted by an intrusive interface.
- Related to the first point, search is a mentally intensive task. When a person reads text, they are focused on that task; it is not possible to read and to think about something else at the same time. Thus, the fewer distractions while reading, the more usable the interface.
- Since nearly everyone who uses the Web uses search, the interface design must be understandable and appealing to a wide variety of users of all ages, cultures and backgrounds, applied to an enormous variety of information needs.

Designers of Web search interfaces have learned that in order to be able to successfully serve their highly diverse user base, they must be very

1

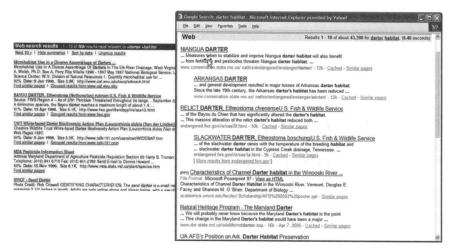

Figure 1.1. Search results listings from Infoseek in 1997 (left) and Google in 2007 (right). (Courtesy Jan Pedersen.)

careful about any complexity that they introduce. Almost any feature that a designer might think is intuitive and obvious is likely to be mystifying to a significant proportion of Web users.

To illustrate this point, despite the simplicity of the search results listings shown above, research suggests that even this spartan presentation is too complex for some people. A study of elderly users by Aula and Käki (2005) found that further simplifying the list of results reduced errors substantially. And research by Hargittai (2004) showed that some people do not understand even the very basics of keyword specification. Unlike most studies that involve university-educated participants exclusively, Hargittai obtained a random sample of 100 participants representative of the population of a county in New Jersey according to socio-economic factors. Hargittai (2004) found that, in addition to not really understanding keyword queries, many participants confused the address bar with the search entry form, and vice versa (the latter effect is common, as can be inferred from the fact that the most frequent queries for all search engines are `google` and `yahoo`). Some participants confused the syntax of the address bar with the syntax of query terms, placing spaces within URLs in the address form, as in `www.new york times.com` and `time warner.com`, or omitting all spaces from their keywords, resulting in queries like `presidentalcampaign2000`, `employmentopportunities`, and `fordescort`.

Another study by Muramatsu and Pratt (2001) with 14 participants found that most people had strong misconceptions about simple Boolean operations. When comparing search engines that automatically applied AND versus OR to query terms, some assumed the ANDing search engine indexed a smaller collection; most had no explanation at all. When receiving empty results for the query `to be or not to be`, two thirds could not explain this phenomenon in a way that remotely resembled stopword removal. For term order variation in queries (for example, `boat fire` vs. `fire boat`), two thirds did not expect the results to differ.

Although today's standard search is a big improvement in usability over older command-line based Boolean systems, there is evidence that keyword querying is not initially intuitive. In fact, the literature suggests that people who are new to using search engines tend to start by asking a natural language question (Bilal 2000; Schacter et al. 1998). Novice searchers must *learn* to expect that a query will not yield immediately usable results, and that they must scan search results lists, navigate through Web sites and read through Web pages to try to find the information they seek. A study by Pollock and Hockley (1997) found that, for novice searchers, the notion of iterative searching was unfamiliar. Some study participants assumed that if their first attempt failed then either they were incapable of searching or the system did not contain information relevant to their interest.

Given the difficulty that some users experience in using relatively simple interface elements, it is perhaps not surprising that attempts to improve search via more complex interfaces have for the most part not been widely adopted. There are, however, some successful innovations in search interfaces which are becoming widely used; some of these are discussed in the design guidelines sections below. First though, a historical interlude explains the evolution of search interfaces over time. This is followed by a brief summary of how interface design is done in practice, and then a discussion of design guidelines for search user interfaces.

1.2. A Historical Shift in Search Interface Design

The story of search user interfaces is complicated by a radical shift that occurred after the Web became a worldwide phenomenon. Before the Web, computerized information retrieval was usually done only by members of a narrow demographic: highly educated users, such as paralegals, librarians and other search intermediaries, and journalists. These people searched over highly specialized, high-quality, information-oriented text collections such as bibliographic records for university libraries, legal cases and opinions, and newswire articles. Often the providers of search access to these collections had monopolies on the content, and therefore did not feel the pressure of competition to provide improved interfaces for that content.

By contrast, the Internet is now accessed by 75% of the U.S. adult population, and 91% of those who use the Internet use Web search engines (Pew 2008b). The content of the Web differs from that of earlier systems in several important ways. Older systems usually did not allow search over full text; rather, the user could only search over titles and perhaps abstracts and other descriptive metadata. Search was usually used to find the name and location of a source containing this information, and then a physical paper copy would have to be obtained to see the full text. By contrast, most of what is available on the Web is the full text itself; the desired information is often immediately accessible.

The content available on the Web is vastly broader than that of older systems, and in addition to expository text, contains the equivalent of brochures and local newsletters, official information for companies and all kinds of organizations, information that can be used directly, such as guitar chords and knitting patterns, how-to information, hobbyist guides, and so on. The Web can be used to see the answers to questions, such as `what is the population of Madagascar`, directly. This was not usually possible in the older systems, which acted as gateways to more detailed information that was available only offline.

Older systems were developed before bitmapped (graphical) displays were commonplace, and so were based on command-line interfaces. These usually required complex combinations of operators – which had to be memorized – and Boolean syntax for query specification. Very few members of the lay public understand Boolean syntax and even fewer are willing to learn command languages. The lack of competitors with access to the content, plus an installed base of users who knew the old systems, probably slowed the adoption of modern user interface conventions. Another important difference between old and new search systems is that older retrieval systems often charged for use (in terms of number of queries issued, number of results returned, or amount of time used), whereas Web search has always been free of charge.

These contrasts – highly educated and trained users verses everyone as a user; high-quality, expensively edited expository text versus a huge variety and multiplicity of information types, search over document metadata (titles and abstracts) rather than over full text, TTY displays versus graphical displays, and expensive usage controlled by one provider versus free usage provided by a multiplicity of search providers – help explain the differences seen in search user interfaces before and after the Web. These differences will be revisited throughout this book.

1.3. The Process of Search Interface Design

An important quality of a user interface (UI) is its *usability*, a term which refers to those properties of the interface that determine how easy it is to use. Shneiderman and Plaisant (2004) identify five components of usability, restated by Nielsen (2003b) as:

- *Learnability:* How easy is it for users to accomplish basic tasks the first time they encounter the interface?
- *Efficiency:* How quickly can users accomplish their tasks after they learn how to use the interface?
- *Memorability:* After a period of non-use, how long does it take users to reestablish proficiency?
- *Errors:* How many errors do users make, how severe are these errors, and how easy is it for users to recover from these errors?
- *Satisfaction:* How pleasant or satisfying is it to use the interface?

How are interfaces designed in order to attain the goals of usability? Despite the newly recognized importance of usability and user interface design, it is nonetheless surprisingly difficult to design highly usable interfaces. The field that encompasses interface design, as well as understanding how people interact with information and technology, is called *Human–Computer Interaction*, or HCI (Shneiderman and Plaisant 2004). Among many other activities, this field has led to the development of a design technique called *user-centered design* whose goal is to lead to the development of usable designs.

In user-centered design, decisions are made based on responses obtained from target users of the system. (This is in contrast with standard software practice in which the designers assume they know what users need, and so write the code first and assess it with users later.) In user-centered design, first a *needs assessment* is performed in which the designers investigate who the users are, what their goals are, and what tasks they have to complete in order to achieve those goals. The next stage is a *task analysis* in which the designers characterize which steps the users need to take to complete their tasks, decide which user goals they will attempt to support, and then create scenarios which exemplify these tasks being executed by the target user population (Kuniavsky 2003; Mayhew 1999).

Once the target user goals and tasks have been determined, design is done in a design–evaluate–redesign cycle consisting of creating prototypes, obtaining reactions from potential users, and revising the designs based on those reactions. This sequence of activities often needs to be repeated several times before a satisfactory design emerges. Evaluation at this phase can often achieve useful results by testing with only a few participants, so the evaluation method used at this point in the design space is often referred to as "discount" usability testing (Nielsen 1989b). After a design is testing well in discount or informal studies, formal experiments comparing different designs and measuring for statistically significant differences can be conducted.

This iterative procedure is necessary because interface design is still more of a practice than a science. There are usually several good solutions within the interface design space, and the task of the designers is to navigate through the design space until reaching some "local optimum." The iterative process allows study participants to help the designers make decisions about which paths to explore in that space. Experienced designers often can begin the design near a good part of the solution space; less experienced designers need to do more exploration. Designing for an entirely novel interaction paradigm often requires more iteration and experimentation. Evaluation is part of every cycle of the user-centered design process. Because it is such an important topic, it receives a chapter of its own in this book (Chapter 2).

1.4. Design Guidelines for Search Interfaces

Researchers and practitioners in the field of Human–Computer Interaction have proposed dozens of sets of guidelines for successfully building user interfaces. Some authors have proposed guidelines for search interfaces specifically; an influential paper by Shneiderman et al. (1997) specifies eight design desiderata for search user interfaces generally (re-ordered below):

- Offer informative feedback.
- Support user control.
- Reduce short-term memory load.
- Provide shortcuts for skilled users.

- Reduce errors; offer simple error handling.
- Strive for consistency.
- Permit easy reversal of actions.
- Design for closure.

These guidelines provide good advice for search UI design. However, design guidelines can be difficult to follow, for a number of reasons. First, they are under-specified; they do not usually say *how* to achieve the guideline's goals. Second, meeting one guideline often conflicts with meeting another. For instance, in order to satisfy the consistency rule, if every results page must look identical, then an interface that shows query term suggestions in retrieval results must show a label stating "no feedback terms available" when it has no suggestions to make. This message would keep the interface consistent, but at the cost of distracting users with unnecessary information. Third, any list of guidelines is incomplete. For instance, the list above omits Nielsen's (1993) commonly stated guideline of "speak the user's language," which urges designers to adopt concepts and language familiar to users where possible. And finally, for any given interface, some guidelines will be superfluous.

Despite these drawbacks, the following sections elaborate in more detail about how some of these design guidelines should be applied to search interfaces. These guidelines and recommendations are informed by a study of the search interface literature, by cognitive considerations in search, and by a decade of experience designing such interfaces. The substance behind most of these is discussed in more detail in later chapters of this book.

It should be noted that these guidelines are specific to search interfaces; there are many other very important design guidelines for other aspects of interface design, and a number of excellent books to refer to for them (e.g., Cooper et al. 2007; Nielsen and Loranger 2006).

1.5. Offer Efficient and Informative Feedback

A bedrock principle of interface design is to provide the user with *feedback* about the status of the system and how that relates to the user's interactions with the system. A familiar example of interface feedback is the hourglass timer icon that is typically shown in a graphical operating system interface to indicate that the user has to wait while an application is launching or saving a large file.

Because the search task is so cognitively intensive, feedback about query formulation, about the reasons the particular results were retrieved, and about next steps to be taken is critically important. The subsections below describe important feedback indicators for search interfaces.

1.5.1. *Show Search Results Immediately*

Numerous studies show that an important search interface design principle is to show users some search results immediately after their initial query or navigation step (Hutchinson et al. 2006; Käki 2005a; Plaisant et al. 1997a). This information can be shown alongside other navigation aids, but at least a few initial results should be shown. This helps searchers understand if they are on the right track or not, and also provides them with suggestions of related words that they might use for query reformulation. Many experimental systems make the mistake of requiring the user to look at large amounts of helper information, such as query refinement suggestions or category labels, before viewing results directly. Information visualization interfaces that show documents as dots or icons in a two-dimensional space suffer from poor usability because the searcher cannot see the text of the titles and document surrogates (Granitzer et al. 2004; Hornbæk and Frøkjær 1999).

1.5.2. *Show Informative Document Surrogates; Highlight Query Terms*

Most search results listings today show a vertical list of results, each containing information about the document and why it was retrieved, such as the title, the URL, and a textual summary; this information is referred to as the *document surrogate*. The documents' *summaries* (also called *snippets*, *extracts*, and *abstracts*) are typically a few lines of text extracted from the retrieved documents.

An important form of feedback in search results listings is to include the terms from the query in the document surrogates in order to show how the retrieved document relates to the concepts expressed in the query. Early Web search interfaces showed the first few lines of the document in the summary, but today, summaries are designed to show the query terms in the context in which they occur in the document. Research shows that summaries are most informative if they contain the query terms shown in their context from the document (Tombros and Sanderson 1998; White et al. 2003a).

Query term proximity information can be quite effective at improving precision of searches (Clarke et al. 1996; Hearst 1996; Tao and Zhai 2007). According to a large study by Clarke et al. (2007), when possible, all the query terms should appear in the search result surrogate, but if all of the query terms are present in the title for the hit, they need not appear in the summary, which can then include other useful relevance information. Clarke et al. (2007) also found that query terms appearing in the URL can be a useful cue, but that length and complexity of the displayed URL should be reduced where possible.

It has also been shown that visually highlighting query terms can be a useful feature for search interfaces (Aula 2004; Landauer et al. 1993; Lesk 1997; Marchionini 1995). Term highlighting refers to altering the appearance of portions of text in order to make them more visually salient, or "eye-catching." Highlighting can be done in boldface, reverse video, by displaying a colored background behind each occurrence of a query term, assigning a different color to each term. This helps draw the searcher's attention to the parts of the document most likely to be relevant to the query, and to show how closely the query terms appear to one another in the text. However, it is important not to highlight too many terms, as the positive effects of highlighting will be lost (Kickmeier and Albert 2003).

There is an inherent tradeoff between showing long, informative summaries and minimizing the screen space required by each search hit. There is also a tension between showing fragments of sentences that contain all or most of the query terms and showing coherent stretches of text containing only some of the query terms. Research is mixed about how and when chopped-off sentences are preferred and when they harm usability (Aula 2004; Rose et al. 2007). Research also shows that different results lengths are appropriate depending on the type of query and expected result type (Guan and Cutrell 2007; Kaisser et al. 2008; Lin et al. 2003), although varying the length of results has not been widely adopted in practice.

Figure 1.2 shows a screenshot from the BioText interface for searching over bioscience literature in which several kinds of document surrogate information are used (Hearst et al. 2007). Figures extracted from the articles are shown alongside each search hit, query terms are highlighted (in title) and boldfaced (in abstract and full-text excerpt), and the user can vary how much information is shown in the text excerpts by selecting or deselecting checkboxes for showing the abstract and full-text excerpts.

Figure 1.2. Search results in the BioText system (Hearst et al. 2007), in which rich document surrogate information is shown, including figures extracted from the articles, query term highlighting and boldfacing, and an option to expand or shorten extracted document summaries. From http://biosearch.berkeley.edu. (See color plate 3.)

The figure shows a case in which the second word in the query appears in the body of the article, but not in the title or abstract.

1.5.3. *Allow Sorting of Results by Various Criteria*

Another effective form of feedback in the display of search results allows for the dynamic sorting of search results according to different ranking criteria (e.g., recency, relevance, author, price, etc.). An effective interface for displaying results sortable along several dimensions at once uses a sortable columns format, as seen in email search interfaces, some product search, and some bibliographic search (see Figure 1.3). With this view, users can sorting results according to different criteria, while being able to visually compare those criteria, because the changes are directly visible (Cutrell et al. 2006a; Reiterer et al. 2000). This kind of view is typically more effective than showing choices hidden behind drop-down menus.

	Size	Identifier	Title	Creator/Author (s)	Pub Date	Adopt-A-Doc
☐		US 4768152	Oil well bore hole surveying by kinematic navigation	Egli, W.H. , Vallot, L.C.	1988 Aug 30	-
☐		CA 972556	Apparatus for surveying bore holes	Templeton, F.E.	1975 Aug 12	-
☐		UCID-17852	BIFUR II, a program for calculating borehole gravity caused by two-dimensional structure	Hearst, J.R.	1978 Jul 13	Y
☐		CONF-8305265-	Present stand of coal deposit exploration techniques	Bonnet, M.	1984 Jan 01	-
☐		US 4406332	Rotary earth boring tool	Dismukes, N.B.	1983 Sep 27	-
☐	422 K	DOE/CE /15500--T2	Commercialization of atom interferometers for borehole gravity gradiometry. Quarterly report, January--March 1993	Clauser, J.F.	1993 May 01	-
☐	0 K	LA-UR-88-2351; CONF-8806193-1	The inverse-square law and quantum gravity	Nieto, M.M. , Goldman, T. , Hughes, R.J.	1988 Jan 01	-
☐	3 Mb	DOE/BC/14951--5	Integrated approach towards the Application of Horizontal Wells to Improve Waterflooding Performance. Annual report	Kelkar, M. , Liner, C. , Kerr, D.	1994 Jun 01	-
☐		US 4436168	Thrust generator for boring tools	Dismukes, N.B.	1984 Mar 13	-
☐		US 3993146	Apparatus for mining coal using vertical bore hole and fluid. [9 claims, magnetite slurry to dislodge and float coal]	Poundstone, W.N. , Miller, W.J.	1976 Nov 23	-
☐	2 Mb	COO-4715-1	Preliminary targeting of geothermal resources in Delaware. Progress report, July 15, 1978-July 14, 1979	Woodruff, K.D.	1979 Jul 01	-
☐		CA 1154429	Method and apparatus for forming lateral passageways	Dismukes, N.B.	1983 Sep 27	-

Figure 1.3. An example search results listing, on the query `bore hole gravity`, that allows sorting results listings columns representing bibliographic fields (author, title, date, etc.). From the Energy Citations Database published by the U.S. Department of Energy (DOE) Office of Scientific and Technical Information (OSTI), http://www.osti.gov/energycitations.

Grouping search results by categories is also an effective form of feedback, as discussed in the section below on integrating navigation and search.

1.5.4. *Show Query Term Suggestions*

After a user has issued a query, it has been shown useful to provide feedback in the form of automatically generated query term suggestions and refinements. These include spelling correction suggestions as well as suggestions of related or alternative query terms. The phrase *term expansion* is usually applied to tools that suggest alternative wordings. Usability studies are generally positive as to the efficacy of term suggestions when users are not required to make relevance judgements and do not have to choose among too many terms (Anick 2003; Bruza et al. 2000; Divoli et al. 2008; White et al. 2007). A study of session logs of the Dogpile Web search engine showed found that 8.4% of all queries were generated by the reformulation assistant provided (Jansen et al. 2007b). Figure 1.4 shows an example of a term expansion interface provided by Yahoo.

A related recent development in rapid and effective user feedback is an interface that suggests a list of query terms dynamically, *as the user types the query*, and that match the query or are semantically similar to it in some way. (This is sometimes referred to as *incremental search*.) For example, typing the letters `ba` on the Ask.com Web search engine shows

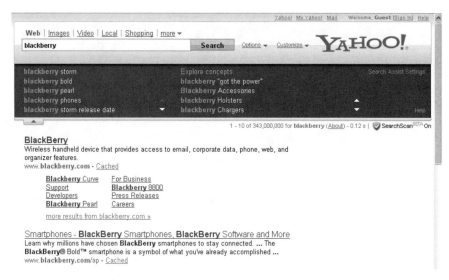

Figure 1.4. Example of an interface for showing two types of search assistance, from Yahoo. The left hand column shows suggestions dynamically as the user types their query. These suggestions usually match the prefix characters of the query. The right hand column shows suggestions of related terms after the query has been submitted. These need not contain characters from the original query. (Reproduced with permission of Yahoo! Inc. ©2009 Yahoo! Inc. YAHOO! and the YAHOO! logo are registered trademarks of Yahoo! Inc.)

query suggestions including *baby names, barnes and nobel, barack obama*, and *bank of america*. Adding an n to make a query of ban changes the suggestions to include *banana republic, bankruptcy*, and *bangladesh*. The query suggestions are often tailored to the underlying information collection. For example, a site that shows statistics about different airports (flightstats.com) dynamically adjusts airport names as the user types in letters. Beginning with s shows hits not only on airports whose three-letter code begins with "s," but also on airports whose city name or country name begins with this letter. (These include Palma Mallorca airport in Spain, Suvarnabhumi airport in Bangkok, and SFO in San Francisco, CA.) Adding the letter f eliminates all of these except SFO, but shows less frequented airports such as Sfax El Maou airport in Tunisia. Dynamic query term suggestions are a promising intermediate solution between requiring the user to think of terms of interest (and how to spell them) and navigating a long list of term suggestions.

Returning to Figure 1.4, this search assistance tool uses a "sliding tray" that opens automatically based on heuristics corresponding to user behavior (Anick and Kantamneni 2008). For instance, if the user pauses in typing before hitting the Enter key, the tray will slide out showing dynamic query suggestions. The view shown here appears after a query has been entered, and the left hand column of suggestions in Figure 1.4 shows term suggestions that are related to the query.

A log study on 100,000 visitors to the Yahoo site over 17 weeks found that this tool was heavily used, with 30% of those exposed to it choosing to interact with it during the first exposure, increasing to 37% by the 17th week (Anick and Kantamneni 2008). There was also a high degree of iterative interaction with the tool. However, a small eye-tracking study showed that the interface includes a design error that is often seen in experimental search interfaces (Anick and Kantamneni 2008). In this error, the interface showed two kinds of hints next to each other. Users are unlikely to understand the difference in meaning between the types of suggestions in the left hand and right hand columns, because the suggestions themselves are similar and users may not know, or need to know, the difference between dynamic suggestions and after-query suggestions. (A smaller problem is that only one column has a visible label.) A better design would be to show the dynamic suggestions as the query is being typed, and then replace these with the related term suggestions after the query is entered (via hitting the return key or selecting the *Search* button). When the user resumes typing, the dynamic suggestions should replace the related terms.

It is generally not a good idea to make people remove terms to increase relevance. For instance, Ahn et al. (2007) found that keyword removal caused about four times more harm than adding keywords for building user profiles. The essence of the problem is that the space of what is not relevant is far larger than the space of what is relevant. This is not to say that adding a "NOT" operator to a query is never useful, but rather that an interface should not be founded on the idea that users will remove irrelevant terms or documents.

1.5.5. *Use Relevance Indicators Sparingly*

In the past it was common for search engines to show a numerical score or graphical bars or icons such as a row of stars alongside the document surrogate to indicate the relevance score for the documents (Shneiderman et al. 1997). However, these have fallen out of favor, most likely because the meaning of the relevance score is opaque to the users (White et al. 2007), and the vertical position on the page is a strong and effective signal of the relative relevance of the results. It should be noted that graphical indicators of other kinds of information – such as using a line of stars to indicate how favorably reviewed an item is – can be quite useful.

Innovative visualization techniques for graphically showing the distribution of the query terms within the retrieved documents have been developed (Hearst 1995; Meredith and Pieper 2006; Reiterer et al. 2005), but are used primarily in text analysis interfaces rather than in standard search.

1.5.6. *Support Rapid Response*

For search interfaces, rapid response time is critical to support effective feedback. A perceivable lag interrupts peoples' thought processes; rapid response allows searchers to work with "flow." Providing highly responsive interactive results is important for dynamic search results suggestions, and fast response time for query reformulation allows the user to try multiple queries rapidly. If the system responds with little delay, the user does not feel penalized for trying inaccurate or general queries that are "in the ballpark" but not quite right. This allows the user to rapidly move closer to their goal and learn more about their search topic with each query.

Research suggests that when rapid responses are not available, search strategies change. For instance, a search engine for users in the developing world in which the round trip for retrieval results can be a day or more requires accurate, thoughtful query formulation (Thies et al. 2002). It should also be noted that for some specialized search applications in which the results are the final desired information, users are not unduly penalized by having to wait, such as for systems that search for airline flights. These sites wisely tend to show a graphical animation while processing the user's request, to reduce feelings of impatience.

1.6. Balance User Control with Automated Actions

Greene et al. (2000) write that "Users prefer comprehensible, predictable, and controllable environments." This is a good design guideline in general. However, in the design of technology, there is often a tradeoff between the system taking control for the user versus the user being in control of details of the system's behavior. For example, millions of people enjoy the ease and convenience of taking snapshots with point-and-shoot digital cameras, where there is no need to fuss with the focus, shutter speed, or lighting because the camera automatically figures out the settings. However, on those occasions in which the user wants to override the camera's default behavior (say, in very low light), it can be difficult to quickly determine how to accomplish this. Similarly, in the design of search algorithms and interfaces, there is a delicate balance between clever but opaque operations that correctly anticipate searcher's needs most of the time and less powerful or less effective designs that are however easily understandable and give the user control over system behavior.

Below are two important types of search interface design decisions that must consider the tradeoff between opaque system control and transparent user control: results ordering and query transformations.

1.6.1. *Rank Ordering in Web Search*

The most prominent case of opacity in the operation of search interfaces is the rank ordering of retrieval results.

As discussed above, most users have little understanding of how search technology works, and the mechanisms behind search results ordering are especially mysterious. Early Web search engines used a variation of vector-based statistical ranking, which is difficult for lay users to understand, in part because the system might show a document that has many hits on a rare term higher than a document that contains a few hits on every term in the query (Lake 1998). Furthermore, Web queries usually contain only a few words, while statistical ranking was originally designed for paragraph-length queries.

Sometime in the late 1990's, the search engine Hotbot introduced conjunctive (AND-based) query analysis for Web search ranking, meaning that every word in the query must be present in the document in order for that document to be shown. Search Engines for the World Wide Web, "Alfred and Emily Glossbrenner, Peachpit Press (1999)." This behavior is more transparent than the statistical approach because the searcher knows that every page retrieved contains at least one instance of every word they typed. Behind the scenes, the system may give more weight to pages in which the terms occur more frequently, but the user does not need to know that detail in order for the retrieval strategy to be understandable. Also in the late 1990's, Google improved conjunctive ranking by assigning higher weight to documents in which query terms co-occurred in close proximity to one another, which had been shown by others to improve precision (Clarke et al. 1996; Hearst 1996), and which has the advantage of producing more useful document summaries (Tombros and Sanderson 1998). Google also incorporated a "popularity" measure, PageRank (Page et al. 1998). The fact that popular Web pages appear higher in the results is understandable for lay users even though the algorithm for computing popularity would not be widely understood.

Although AND-based ranking has been quite effective, today the pendulum is swinging the other way. Sophisticated users are issuing longer queries, and the rise of natural language search engines is encouraging longer and more complex queries. As queries get longer, it becomes necessary to relax the constraint that all words appear in the retrieved documents, or at least to downweight their importance in proximity to the content words. Today, a user can enter a query `typing while recovering from clavical surgery` into Google and it successfully finds relevant documents by ignoring the role of the syntactic structuring words `while` and `from` and returning pages in which `recovering` occurs only in hyperlinks pointing to the page. In order for this kind of sophisticated processing to avoid the confusing behavior of earlier statistical algorithms, the lack of transparency must be offset by the relevance and meaningfulness of the returned results.

Perhaps the most understandable and transparent way to order search results is according to how recently they appeared. In fact, for some information collections, such as news, chronological ordering can be preferred over rank ordering. Dumais et al. (2003) found that users preferred chronological order over rank order when searching over their personal information. Bioscience researchers often prefer to see scientific articles presented according to recency. However, for Web search, relevance ranking is a necessity because time of first appearance for a Web page is of secondary importance in most cases.

1.6.2. *Query Transformations*

Another important issue in the tradeoff between system cleverness and user control lies with query transformations. Some search engines make subtle changes to queries to improve results. For example, Microsoft's Web search automatically converts words like `vs.` to `versus`. The lack of user control in this feature is mitigated by the fact that this transformation nearly always matches the searcher's intention. As another example, Google returns pages that contain people's names for which the middle initial is missing, even if the original query specifies the middle initial. Although a useful feature, this could frustrate a searcher who is trying to distinguish between two people with similar names.

A classic case of system behavior that is opaque to system users is the elimination of *stopwords* from user queries. (Stopwords are the most common words in the language, usually what linguists call "closed-class" words in that new ones rarely enter the language. Examples from English are articles such as *a, an, the* and prepositions such as *in, on*.) In a famous example in the early days of Web search, a searcher who typed `''to be or not to be''` in a search engine would be shocked to be served empty results. In 1996, a review of eight major search engines found that only AltaVista could handle the Hamlet quote; all others ignored stopwords (Peterson 1997; Sherman 2001). (Stopword elimination is common in statistical ranking systems for which a paragraph-length query is assumed; not indexing stopwords by position results in significant savings in indexing time and disk space.) Today, this problem is solved on all the major Web search engines.

The application of morphological analysis (stemming) has long yielded mixed results in the information retrieval literature: in some cases it helps, and in others it degrades search results. From a user expectations perspective, on the one hand, searchers express surprise if the computer is not "smart" enough to do simple transformations, such as automatically converting `woman's rights` in the query to match `women's rights` in documents (Twidale and Nichols 1998). But on the other hand, if morphological analysis is done too aggressively, the meaning of the query can be distorted. For example, Google converts the word `typing` to `type` in the query `typing after clavicle surgery`, which yields some results that do not discuss the act of typing. These effects are mild so long as the stemming is applied lightly, and a mix of the word forms is allowed to contribute to the results. But if the system consistently overrules the user's intention, the user may become justifiably frustrated.

In the case of automatic spelling suggestions, the system should offer the choice to the user without forcing an acceptance of an alternative spelling, in case the system's correction does not match the user's intent. But on the other hand, if the user makes a blatantly incorrect typographical error, it can be annoying to see only irrelevant results, and the system may return low-quality Web pages. To balance this tradeoff, when encountering what the system believes is an erroneously spelled query

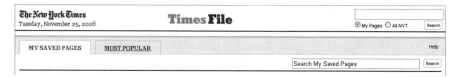

Figure 1.5. Example of a query form that provides a reminder of which set of content is being searched over, from *The New York Times*.

term, many Web search engines show some hits that contain words that they guess are the correct spelling interwoven with other hits that contain the purportedly incorrect spelling.

1.7. Reduce Short-Term Memory Load

The interface guideline "reduce the user's memory load" is very important for information-rich system interfaces. The main idea behind this heuristic is to show users relevant information rather than require them to remember or keep track of it. Several methods applicable to search interfaces are described in the subsections below.

1.7.1. *Suggest the Search Action in the Entry Form*

A useful interface trope that has arisen recently is, rather than showing a blank entry form, the designer places text within the entry form to indicate what action will result from using that form. This text is usually shown in grayed-out font to signal that it is intended to be replaced by the user's text. (The text within the form disappears when the user clicks in the form.) This is especially useful in search interfaces as a way to indicate that the user would be searching over an alternative collection, or when attempting to provide a "search within these results" feature. The lower right hand corner of Figure 1.5 shows an example from the Web site of *The New York Times*, that makes it clear that a query in that entry form searches over the user's saved pages, as opposed to searching over the site as a whole. This design works in part because the user must look at the text in the entry form in order to select the form and begin typing; it demands the user's attention, but is not distracting because it provides the information exactly at the point in the user's workflow that it is needed at.

In the upper right hand corner is shown a more standard approach to allowing users to choose between collections. It shows a search box with a radio button that selects which collection to search over. Most studies suggest that users do not notice or change the choices in this type of interface, in part because they do not notice the option while they are entering their query. A radio button or other choice selector, such as a drop-down menu, is more likely to be noticed after the query is issued when retrieval results are being viewed. Thus, selectors for sorting the search results (by date, by price, etc.) after the query are used with some frequency.

1.7.2. *Support Simple History Mechanisms*

Research shows that people are highly likely to revisit information they have viewed in the past and to re-issue queries that they have written in the past (Jones et al. 2002; Milic-Frayling et al. 2004). In one large study, 40% of people's search results clicks were on pages that they had clicked on before over the course of a year, with 71% of these using the identical query string as before (Teevan et al. 2006). In a survey associated with this study, 17% of interviewees reported "not being able to return to a page I once visited" as one of the "biggest problems in using the Web." Therefore, allowing search over recently viewed information can improve a user's productivity (Dumais et al. 2003). Web browsers, as opposed to search engines, can provide much of this functionality. For example, the Chrome Web browser supports information revisiting by showing a grid of thumbnail images representing a user's most frequently visited Web pages, and the drop-down menu from the many browser Web address bars shows recently visited pages. Search engines themselves can provide query history, as well as history of previously selected pages if the user agrees to having that information recorded. The PubMed bioscience journal service shows recently issued queries and visited documents in a simple history display (see Figure 1.6). Similarly, many shopping Web sites show recently viewed items in a graphical form. Thumbnail images have also been experimented with in search results listing, both for reminding searchers of previously visited pages and for suggesting information about the hit, such as its genre.

In Web sites that integrate category selection with search, a history mechanism called *breadcrumbs* is used for keeping track of the sequence of navigation operations that the user has taken to arrive at the current view of objects (discussed in more detail below).

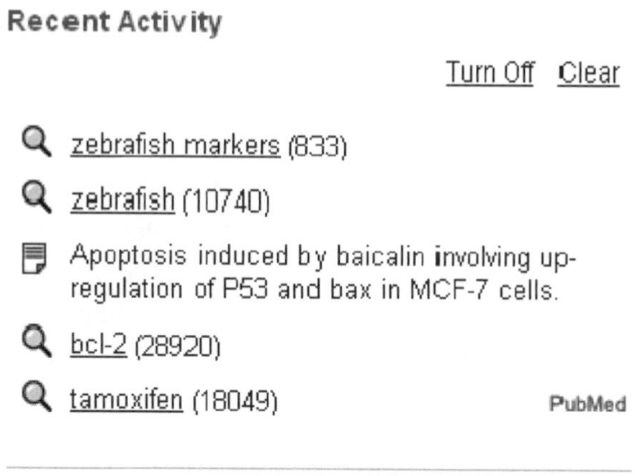

Recent Activity

Turn Off   Clear

Q   zebrafish markers (833)

Q   zebrafish (10740)

▤   Apoptosis induced by baicalin involving up-
    regulation of P53 and bax in MCF-7 cells.

Q   bcl-2 (28920)

Q   tamoxifen (18049)   PubMed

Figure 1.6. The PubMed interface, published by the U.S. National Library of Medicine, for showing recent queries and recently accessed documents in a simple history display.

1.7.3. *Integrate Navigation and Search*

A well-established principle of human memory is that it is often easier to recognize a word or name than it is to think up that word. Thus in many situations it is useful to prompt the searcher with information related to their information need. Browsable information structures, such as links on a Web site or a table of contents for a book, give an overview of the contents of a collection, allowing the searcher to navigate to the information of interest by following links or narrowing by selecting categories. Information structures can also impose an organization on the results of search. To be fully effective, navigation interfaces should allow the user to interleave keyword queries within existing information structures, smoothly integrating navigation with search. This means that after a keyword search, results should be organized into the navigation structure, and that after navigation steps, keyword search should be available over the current subset of information items.

In search interfaces, category systems are the main tool for navigating information structures and organizing search results. A category system is a set of meaningful labels organized in such a way as to reflect the concepts relevant to a domain. In search interfaces, categories are typically used either for selecting a subset of documents out from the rest, thus narrowing the results, or for grouping documents, dividing them into (potentially overlapping) subsets, but keeping the documents visible. They can also be used for ordering and sorting search results.

Category system structure in search interfaces is usually one of *flat*, *hierarchical*, or *faceted*. A flat list of categories works well for presenting a list of choices with which to narrow the contents of a collection, but needs to be limited to a small set in order to be scannable. Hierarchical (or tree-structured) category systems are useful and can be easy to understand for relatively simple information structures. However, a problem with assigning documents to single categories within a hierarchy is that many information items are best described by multiple different categories simultaneously.

This use of *hierarchical faceted metadata* provides a usable method for allowing users to browse information collections according to multiple categories simultaneously (Hearst 2000; Hearst et al. 2002). The main idea is to build a set of category hierarchies, each of which corresponds to a different facet (dimension or feature type) that is relevant to the collection to be navigated. Each facet has a set of labels associated with it, and if this set is large, it may be organized into a hierarchy. After the facet hierarchies are designed, each item in the collection can be assigned any number of labels from any number of facets. In a properly designed faceted navigation interface, the user can browse the information collection from any of the different facets as a starting point, and after starting with one facet, can then navigate using any other facet. Usability results suggest that this kind of interface is highly usable for navigation of information collections with somewhat homogeneous content (English et al. 2001; Hearst et al. 2002; Yee et al. 2003).

This kind of interface is heavily used on Web sites today, including shopping and specialized product sites, restaurant guides, and online library catalogs. Figure 1.7 shows an example in which a user interested in finding local events to attend on zvents.com can select a city in which the event is to take place (*Berkeley*) and then select a type of event (*Community*) in this case. The faceted display allows the user to select the order in which to choose the categories, and the search results are narrowed accordingly to show only those events that will take place in Berkeley and have to do with community. Beneath each facet category label are shown the subcategory labels along with *query previews* (Plaisant et al. 1999) showing how many documents are associated with each category. For instance, one can see how many of the 43 community events taking place in Berkeley take will be held each of the different neighborhoods, and one can see how many of each type of event is available (*Activism*, *Health*, *Science*, etc.). Note also the use of light-colored text within the query boxes to indicate which kind of information should be entered into each query box.

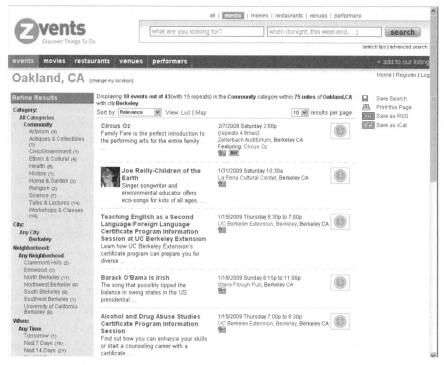

Figure 1.7. Faceted navigation interface for the zvents.com local events Web site. The user has selected the city of "Berkeley" from the *Location* facet and "Community" from the event *Category* facet, and each of these selections can be further refined (by "Neighborhood" for *Location* or by type of community activity). Beside each narrowing category is shown in parentheses how many items will result from selecting that category. Or the user can opt to narrow by another faceted entirely, such as *When*.

1.8. Provide Shortcuts

The "provide shortcuts" guideline usually refers to providing alternative interface mechanisms for practiced users of an interface. The classic example is keyboard shortcuts for menu items that otherwise require pulling down and selecting from menus. Keyboard shortcuts can save time and effort when the user is typing, as the shortcuts remove the need to move hands away from the keyboard to the mouse. But there is a barrier to using shortcuts, as they require memorization.

An alternative way to think about shortcuts, which is more applicable to search interfaces, is to provide targeted hints about where to go next. For example, certain variations on the document surrogate appear to be successful in practice. One technique that appears to be especially useful for Web search is what are known as *sitelinks* or *deep links*. In this view, in the search results, beneath the top-positioned hit, is shown an indented list of important pages from that hit on its Web site, along with a link to more pages from that Web site. Presumably the links are chosen because they represent frequently visited pages within the site, thus saving the user a step or two by allowing them to navigate directly to a page of interest from the search results page. For example, in Figure 1.4, for a query on blackberry, the top hit is the home page of a maker of mobile devices, *www.blackberry.com*. Beneath the link for this hit are shown links to important pages within the site such as *Support* and *Developers* as well as to pages for popular products such as *Blackberry Curve*. In Google's implementation of this idea, another kind of shortcut is sometimes provided: a search form is shown beneath the hit which allows the user to search within that domain directly from the search results page.

As another kind of shortcut, for certain well-defined and predictable information needs, major Web search engines today attempt to "guess" the information need from a very terse query based on what kinds of information have been found to be valuable to searchers on that type of query in the past. The relevant "answer" corresponding to that information need is shown directly in the search results page. For example, Yahoo search will display a "shortcut" showing the current local time in Kathmandu, Nepal, for any of the following queries: time kathmandu, kathmandu current time, and what time is it? katmandu. In Google, at one time a query on rentals seattle returned a special form directly in the results list that allowed the user to specify details of a housing search. All Web search engines show links to shopping sites and review sites in response to purchase-oriented queries (such as digital cameras) and images in response to queries for which images are likely to be evocative (such as sunsets). In a sense, this kind of intention prediction is a form of shortcut, eliminating the need for the user to know precisely how to specify a command, and also reducing the need to navigate to external Web pages to find the desired information.

1.9. Reduce Errors

The steps taken by interface designers to reduce the likelihood of user errors tend to overlap with other guidelines. One key example discussed above is to provide accurate suggestions for typographic and spelling errors. Some additional heuristics are described below.

1.9.1. *Avoid Empty Results Sets*

A general rule of thumb for search usability is to avoid showing the user empty results sets. Spelling correction and term expansion can help with this. Another mechanism mentioned above is to use query previews to show how many documents will result if a particular navigation step is taken. Interfaces that allow users to select many different attributes from different categories simultaneously (e.g., for a recipes interface, selecting *dessert* and *low-fat* and *cheese*) may run the risk of turning up empty results. A faceted interface with query previews would show the user that after selecting *dessert* and *low-fat*, the list of ingredients has zero hits on *cheese*, so the user would know they have to relax one of the already chosen constraints to get non-empty results.

1.9.2. *Address the Vocabulary Problem*

Another form of error can come from using wording that the user does not recognize in navigational cues or in menu items, or in the search itself. A general problem with searching via keyword matching lies with the "productivity of language" – also known as "the vocabulary problem" – that the same idea can be expressed in an astonishing variety of ways. Consider, for example, the different ways one might ask the price of a camera in English:

- *How much does that camera cost?*
- *How much for that camera?*
- *That camera. How much?*
- *What is the price of that camera?*
- *Please price that camera for me.*
- *What're you asking for that camera?*
- *How much will that camera set me back?*
- *What are these cameras going for?*
- *What's that camera worth to you?*

To prove scientifically how word choice varies among people, Furnas et al. (1987) explored the vocabulary variation phenomenon by studying spontaneous word choice for five different computer application domains. These included asking 48 typists to describe 25 text editing markup operations, and asking 337 college students to describe a set of 50 common objects. The experimenters counted how often each word or phrase was used to label each operation or object, and looked at the agreement between people.

The probability that two typists would suggest the same word to describe a markup operation was .11, and the probability that two college students would name an object with the same word was .12. Furnas et al. (1987) then measured the effect of choosing the most commonly selected word for each concept, and comparing this to the terms people originally selected. This increases the probability of agreement to .22 for the markup operations task and .28 for the common objects naming task. When they broadened the vocabulary to include the three most frequently elicited terms for each concept (simulating, in a sense, a thesaurus), they found the probability of agreement increased to .49 for the markup task and .48 for the object naming task. Further analysis indicated that even with 15 aliases per term, only 60–80% of the original terms people thought of would be matched.

The fact that different people express similar concepts in different ways has deep implications for the design of information systems. It suggests that a searcher might not use the same combinations of terms that the authors of the most relevant documents used. Term expansions have been shown to be an effective way to help with this problem. It also suggests that terminology for labeling interface elements must be chosen very carefully. In fact, terminology choice is so important that a design technique has been developed, called *card sorting*, whose goal is to attempt to converge on the most reliable, predictable categories and labels for a given information structure (Kuniavsky 2003).

1.10. Recognize the Importance of Small Details

Search interfaces must show rich and complex information, and small details can make the difference between a successful and a failed design. There is ample evidence that details in a search interface can deeply affect how the information seeker executes their search.

For example, Franzen and Karlgren (2000) found that showing study participants a wider entry form encouraged them to type longer queries. Allen (1994) showed that varying the order in which document surrogate information was shown to searchers dramatically effected how much searchers learned about the information (in this case, subject headings) available in a document collection. Russell et al. (2006) experimented with a visualization that showed documents as clusters of icons in a two-dimensional space, and concluded that this view reduced performance because the representation did not match human perceptual capabilities well. Several researchers have shown that users of Web search engines expect the first few results returned to be more relevant than those that follow, and are more likely to click on the first two hits than they should be when the results ordering is reversed (Joachims et al. 2005).

As another example of the influence of small design decisions on user experience, in an early version of the Google spelling suggestions interface, searchers generally did not notice the suggestion at the top of the page of results. In the initial design, the interface showed a suggestion sentence worded as follows: "If you didn't find what you were looking for ..." At the same time, Google was receiving feedback from searchers complaining that they were getting incorrect results for their queries. According to a product VP at Google (Hurst 2002; Sinha 2005), in many of these cases, the spelling suggestions module had suggested an appropriate correction, but searchers did not notice the information at the top of the page. Instead, they focused on the search results, scrolling down to the bottom of the page scanning for a relevant result but seeing only the very poor matches to the misspelled words. They would then give up and complain that the engine did not return relevant results. To improve the likelihood of searchers noticing the spelling suggestions, two small interface adjustments were made. The first was to repeat the spelling suggestion at the bottom of the page. The second was to test and then shorten the wording surrounding the suggestion. On the top of the page it now reads: *Did you mean: ...* and at the bottom of the results, *Did you mean to search for: ...* with an underlined hyperlink to the results for the correctly spelled words (Hurst 2002; Sinha 2005).

1.11. Recognize the Importance of Aesthetics in Design

A search interface designer must balance the choices of layout, placement and amount of blank space (often referred to as "white space"), color, contrasts among fonts' style, weight, and size. The importance of the application of graphic design principles is established in the HCI literature. For example, Parush et al. (1998) performed a study comparing 16 different versions of display layout, where they deliberately varied the quality of each design according to the graphic design principles of grouping, density, alignment, and size. In a study with 75 participants, they found that the task time for the worst layout was twice that of the best, and that over-all, the very well designed screens resulted in shorter search times and higher subjective preferences.

Aesthetic impressions also play an important role in user acceptance and have been found to correlate with perceptions of an interface's qual-ity, user satisfaction, and overall impression of a site (Hassenzahl 2004; Lindgaard and Dudek 2003). Nakarada-Kordic and Lobb (2005) report that viewers persevere longer in a search task on Web sites whose de-sign appeals to them. van der Heijden (2003) found that the visual appeal of a Web site affected participants' enjoyment and perception of ease of use, and to a small degree, the usability of the system. Norman (2004) also writes about the importance of aesthetics in perceived and real us-ability. In the study of Parush et al. (1998) mentioned above, usability and aesthetic design are often intertwined, but Ben-Bassat et al. (2006) were able to show that more aesthetic designs were perceived as more useful even when they were slightly less useful than a comparable, less attractive design.

As an example of these effects on search interfaces, in a comparative study, Hotchkiss (2007c) asked Yahoo and MSN search users to do a query using Google's Web search. They found that by almost every metric (in-cluding percentage of page scanned before choosing a link, time to choose a link, and relevance of the selected link), the participants had a better user experience on Google than using their standard search engine. Hotchkiss (2007c) attributed this difference *not* to the quality of the search results, but rather to several design choices. He noted that details in the way the information was presented made it easier to determine relevancy, and sug-gested that this might be a combination of methods of revealing informa-tion "scent" (most likely by showing more descriptive document sum-maries that are relevant to the queries), along with subtle graphic design details. In an interview (Hotchkiss 2007c), a Google VP confirmed that the Web page design is the result of careful usability testing of small design elements; for example, putting a line along the side of a textual advertise-ment within the search results page, as opposed to boxing the ad in, better integrates the ad with what people read. The Google designers pay care-ful attention to the aesthetic effects of, for example, the height and width proportions for icons. Hotchkiss (2007c) also noted that Google is careful to ensure that all information in the Web page's "sweet spot" (the up-per left hand corner that is known to be where users tend to look first for search results), including the ads, is of high relevance to the query. He sug-gested that even if the result hits for other search engines are equivalent in quality to Google's, they sometimes show ads that are not relevant at the top of the results list, thus degrading the user experience.

1.12. Conclusions

This chapter has introduced the ideas and practices surrounding user interface design in general, and search interface design in particular. It has explained some of the difficulties with search interface design and provided a set of design guidelines tailored specifically to search user interfaces. These guidelines include:

- Offer efficient and informative feedback,
- Balance user control with automated actions,
- Reduce short-term memory load,
- Provide shortcuts,
- Reduce errors,
- Recognize the importance of small details, and
- Recognize the importance of aesthetics.

This chapter has also summarized some of the most successful design ideas that are commonly in use in search interfaces today. This summary is based on generalizing over the results of years of research, experimentation, and tests in the marketplace. The coming years should reveal additional new, exciting ideas that will become reliable standards for search user interfaces.

2 The Evaluation of Search User Interfaces

Throughout this book, the merits of an interface are assessed from a usability perspective; this chapter discusses how these assessments are done. It is surprisingly difficult to design a usable new search interface, and perhaps even harder to convincingly assess its usability (Draper and Dunlop 1997). An evaluator must take into account differences in designs, tasks, participant motivation, and knowledge, all of which can vary the outcome of a study. Furthermore, as mentioned in Chapter 1, small details in the design of the interface can have a strong effect on a participant's subjective reaction to or objective success with the interface. For instance, problematic placement of controls or unintuitive text on a hyperlink can prevent a participant from succeeding in a task. Differences in font contrast and spacing can unconsciously affect a participant's subjective response to a design.

What should be measured when assessing a search interface? Traditional information retrieval research focuses on evaluating the proportion of relevant documents retrieved in response to a query. In evaluating search user interfaces, this kind of measure can also be used, but is just one component within broader usability measures. Recall from Chapter 1 that usable interfaces are defined in terms of learnability, efficiency, memorability, error reduction, and user satisfaction (Nielsen 2003b; Shneiderman and Plaisant 2004). However, search interfaces are usually *evaluated* in terms of three main aspects of usability: *effectiveness, efficiency,* and *satisfaction*, which are defined by ISO 9241-11 (1998) as:

- *Effectiveness:* Accuracy and completeness with which users achieve specified goals.

- *Efficiency:* Resources expended in relation to the accuracy and completeness with which users achieve goals.
- *Satisfaction:* Freedom from discomfort, and positive attitudes towards the use of the product.

These are the criteria that ideally should be measured when evaluating a search user interface. They can be tailored to correspond directly to search tasks; for example, the efficiency criterion can measure which positions within the search results the relevant documents appear in. Some aspects of usability may be emphasized more than others. If one is testing, for example, a new technique for suggesting alternative query terms, the focus may be more on increasing efficiency and reducing errors, but not so much on memorability of the technique. Surprisingly, many usability studies omit assessing participants' subjective reaction to the interface. In practice, this can be the most important measure of all, because an interface that is not liked is not likely to be used. It is important to measure all three aspects of usability, as a meta-analysis showed that correlation among them in usability studies tends to be low (Hornbæk and Law 2007).

This chapter summarizes some major methods for evaluating user interfaces. First, an overview is provided of traditional information retrieval evaluation. This is followed by sections discussing different major interface evaluation methods. Informal evaluation is especially useful for developing new ideas or for the early stages of development of a new design. Formal studies are useful for rigorously comparing different designs, either to help advance the field's understanding of search interfaces, or to help an organization decide which of several designs or features works best in a given context. Longitudinal studies, in which participants use the interface over time, reveal long-term usage patterns as participants become familiar with the interface and adapt it to their everyday working environment. Bucket tests, or large-scale comparison studies, allow an organization to test the effects of different designs by comparing how people use the different designs on a massive scale.

These sections are followed by a set of guidelines about special considerations to ensure successful search usability studies and avoid common pitfalls. The chapter concludes with general recommendations for search interface evaluation.

2.1. Standard Information Retrieval Evaluation

In the bulk of the information retrieval (IR) research literature, evaluation of search systems is equivalent to evaluation of ranking algorithms, and this evaluation is done in an automated fashion, without involving users. When evaluating in this paradigm, a document collection and a set of queries are defined, and then documents from the collection are identified as *relevant* for those queries (Saracevic 2007). Ranking algorithms are judged according to how high they rank the relevant documents.

This kind of evaluation has been embodied most prominently in the Text REtrieval Conference (TREC), run by the U.S. National Institute of Standards (NIST) for more than 15 years (Voorhees and Harman 2000). The goal of TREC is to advance the state of the art in IR research by coordinating tasks for different research and commercial groups to test their algorithms on. TREC tasks (also known as *tracks*) are designed by the research community in tandem with NIST, and have included question answering, video search, routing queries, gigabyte dataset search, and many other tasks. For many years, however, the marquee task of TREC was the *ad hoc retrieval* track, in which systems competed to rank documents according to relevance judgements. In the ad hoc track, the TREC coordinators supply the document collection, the queries, and the relevance judgements, which are assigned by human judges. The competing groups develop their ranking algorithms, freeze their systems, and then receive the queries. They are not allowed to change their system based on those queries – rather, they have to run their algorithms in a batch mode, on the queries as given. Thus, there are no human participants interacting with the system in the TREC ad hoc task.

The most common evaluation measures used for assessing ranking algorithms are *Precision, Recall*, the *F-measure*, and *Mean Average Precision* (MAP). Precision is defined as the number of relevant documents retrieved divided by the number of documents retrieved, and so is the percentage of retrieved documents that are relevant. Recall is the number of relevant documents retrieved divided by the number of documents that are known to be relevant, and so is the percentage of all relevant documents that are retrieved. These measures reflect tradeoffs between one another; the more documents an algorithm retrieves, the more likely it is to increase recall, but at the same time reduce precision by bringing in additional nonrelevant documents. For this reason, the F-Measure is often used to balance between precision and recall. It is defined as the weighted mean of the two measures, but is usually used with an even weighting between precision and recall, computed as $(2 * P * R)/(P + R)$. The problem with this measure is that it is taken at whatever recall level is produced by ranking k documents. Therefore, an algorithm that ranks all of its relevant documents in the first few positions is not given any more points than an algorithm that ranks the same number of relevant documents in the last positions. The measure of *average precision* addresses this deficiency by computing the precision repeatedly, at each position in the ranking for which a relevant document appears, and taking the average of these precision scores. The MAP score is the average of the average precisions, taken over a set of test queries.

The TREC evaluation method has been enormously valuable for comparison of competing ranking algorithms. There are, however, no shortage of criticisms of the approach. These include:

- In most cases "relevance" is treated as a binary "yes or no" assessment, and a system is not rewarded for returning results that are highly relevant versus those that are marginally relevant.
- A system is usually not penalized for returning many relevant documents that contain the same information, as opposed to rewarding diversity in the content of the relevant documents.
- The evaluation has a focus on retrieving as many relevant documents as possible. The TREC evaluations nearly always require systems to return 1,000 documents. This may be realistic for a legal researcher who must find every potentially relevant document, but does not reflect the goals of most searchers, especially on the Web. (To address this last concern, a variation on measuring precision has become popular, called *Precision@k*, meaning the precision for the top k documents retrieved, where k is a small number such as 10.)
- The TREC queries can be seen as unrealistic because they contain very long descriptions of the information need (see Figure 2.1) rather than the 2–3 words of a standard Web search engine query. It can be argued that creating a deep description of the information need is a large part of the problem that search systems should assist with.

More germane to the topic of this book, however, is that this evaluation does not require searchers to interact with the system, create the queries, judge the results, or reformulate their queries. The ad hoc track does not allow for any user interface whatsoever. More recently, the principles of HCI have influenced IR interface research, and the expectation has become that search user interfaces must be assessed with human participants. TREC competitions from 1997 to 2000 included an *Interactive track*, in which each group was asked to recruit about a dozen participants to tackle TREC queries, and the goal of the evaluation was to assess the process of search as well as the outcome in terms of precision and recall. This track also introduced an evaluation that judged how many different "aspects" of a topic a participant's results set contained. More recently, other

```
<num> Number:  312

<title>Title: Hydroponics

<desc>Description:
Document will discuss the science of growing plants in water
or some substance other than soil.

<narr> Narrative: A relevant document will contain specific
information on the necessary nutrients, experiments, types
of substrates, and/or any other pertinent facts related to
the science of hydroponics. Related information includes,
but is not limited to, the history of hydroponics, advantages
over standard soil agricultural practices, or the approach of
suspending roots in a humid enclosure and spraying them
periodically with a nutrient solution to promote plant
growth.
```

Figure 2.1. Sample TREC topic (number 312) from the TREC-6 ad hoc track (Voorhees and Harman 2000).

tracks have allowed for manual adjustment of queries and integration of user interaction with system evaluation.

Incorporating interfaces into evaluation of ranking algorithms can lead to richer views of evaluation methods. It can be useful to adjust the measures of precision and recall when assessing interactive systems. For instance, Pickens et al. (2008) distinguish among documents returned by the search engine, documents actually seen by the user, and documents selected by the user as relevant. There have been a number of efforts to measure the effects of graded relevance judgements, the most popular of which is called *discounted cumulative gain* (DCG) (Järvelin and Kekäläinen 2000; Kekäläinen 2005). Käki and Aula (2008) note that real users of Web search engines typically only look at one or two documents in their search results per query. Thus, they propose the measure of *immediate accuracy* to capture relevance according to this kind of behavior. It is measured as the proportion of queries for which the participant has found at least one relevant document by the time they have looked at k documents selected from the result set. For instance, immediate accuracy of 80% by second selection means that for 80% of the queries the participant has found at least one relevant document in the first two documents inspected. Käki and Aula (2008) claim this measure successfully allowed them to find meaningful differences between search interfaces, is easy to understand, and seems to reflect Web search behavior well.

2.2. Informal Usability Testing

There is no exact formula for producing a good user interface, but interface design indisputably requires the involvement of representative users. As discussed in Chapter 1, before any design starts, prospective users should be interviewed or observed in field studies doing the tasks which the interface must support (Draper and Dunlop 1997). This is followed by a repeated cycle of design, assessment with potential users, analysis of the results, and subsequent re-design and re-assessment. Involvement of members of the target user base is critical, and so this process is often referred to as *user-centered design* (Kuniavsky 2003; Mayhew 1999). Potential users who participate in the assessment of interfaces are usually referred to as *participants*.

Showing designs to participants and recording their responses – to ferret out problems as well as identify positive aspects of the design – are referred to as *informal usability testing*. Informal usability studies are typically used to test a particular instantiation of an interface design, or to compare candidate designs, for a particular domain and context. In the first rounds of evaluation, major problems can be identified quickly, often with just a few participants (Nielsen and Landauer 1993). Although participants usually do not volunteer good design alternatives, they can often accurately indicate which of several design paths is best to follow. Quick informal usability tests with a small number of participants is an example of what has been dubbed *discount usability testing* (Nielsen 1993), as opposed to full formal laboratory studies.

In the formative, early stages of design it is common to show participants rough or *low-fidelity* (low-fi) prototypes of several designs, often using paper mock-ups and sketches. Low-fi designs are also faster to produce than implemented systems, and studies suggest they can reveal similar types of usability problems as more finished designs (Virzi et al. 1996). Low-fi interfaces also allow assessors to focus on the interaction and major design elements, as opposed to more eye-catching aspects such as the graphic design, which can be easily changed. Because paper prototypes are fast to develop, designers can test a number of different options and discard the less promising ideas at little cost (Beaudouin-Lafon and Mackay 2003; Rettig 1994). Paper prototypes for information-rich interfaces (such as search interfaces) require certain special accommodations, such as pre-printed results listings and pre-determined, "canned" queries, which somewhat reduce their realism and validity, but which are nevertheless very useful in the early stages of design.

Evaluation of low-fi (paper) prototypes is not only possible, but often highly effective. The goal is that the participant should be able to move through the sequence of actions necessary for accomplishing some task and produce feedback about the interaction. Usually two or three evaluators are present while one participant examines the system. One evaluator acts as the host, and explains the goals of the design and the tasks that the user is requested to accomplish. The participant considers the tasks, and then looks at the prototype and points at buttons to click, entry forms to fill out, and so on. A second evaluator "plays computer" by moving the paper pieces around, and even improvising and devising new components to compensate for missing pieces of the design. The third evaluator sits farther away, stays silent, and records the participant's comments, impressions, confusions, and suggestions. Participants are encouraged to "think aloud" and voice what they find confusing as well as what they like (Boren and Ramey 2000; Nielsen 1993; Nielsen and Loranger 2006). As mentioned above, participants tend to be less hesistant about suggesting fundamental changes to a paper prototype than to a design that looks finished and polished.

After the low-fi design is testing well with potential users, common practice is to build more detailed or *high-fidelity* versions, with some amount of interactivity built in. These partially implemented designs are again evaluated, first with just a few participants, to help refine the design, evaluate the effectiveness of different features, assess the interaction flow, and test other holistic properties of the design. After each round of assessment, changes usually need to be made to the design, and more testing must be done until the interface is found to be working well across tasks and participants. After the more high-fidelity design is working well, it can be more fully implemented and assessed with larger numbers of participants using more formal evaluation methods.

There is an oft-debated question about how many participants are needed in informal studies in order to find the major usability problems in a design. Nielsen (2000) published results suggesting that only five participants are needed on average to find 85% of usability problems. Spool and Schroeder (2001) disputed this result, claiming that the first five participants found only 35% of the major problems. More recently, Lindgaard and Chattratichart (2007) compared the performance of several different evaluation teams who were assessing the same interface design, varying the number of participants from five to fifteen. They found no correlation between number of participants and number of problems found, but did find a correlation between the number of distinct *tasks* that participants were asked to complete and the number of problems found. This suggests that in order to assess a design thoroughly, participants must be asked to exercise its capabilities in many different ways.

Another form of discount usability testing is *heuristic evaluation* (Nielsen 1992, 1993), which is based on the assumption that a usability expert can recognize design flaws and anticipate usability problems. In the heuristic evaluation process, several usability experts study a design and critique it according to a set of usability guidelines or heuristics, which are used to assign some structure to the critique. Studies have shown that different types of assessment often reveal different, non-overlapping problems with the design (Jeffries et al. 1991; Nielsen 1994). Heuristic evaluation combined with informal usability testing works very well in the early stages of design.

Another popular form of informal usability assessment is the *field study*. In this approach, the experimenters travel to the participant and observe them using the interface in their own natural environment, be it at work or at home. The assumption is that people behave more realistically when using their own equipment and in their own settings, rather than working in someone else's unfamiliar office (Grimes et al. 2007). In a field study, experimenters can either simply observe how the interface is used, or can ask participants to do certain tasks, but it is more difficult to have participants experiment with different variations of an interface in this setting.

To help ensure a successful design process, it is important for the designers to refrain from becoming attached to any particular design. Instead, they should view a candidate design objectively, as one of many possibilities. This mental stance makes it easier for designers to accept and learn from negative responses from study participants. Often participant reactions include subtle hints about what the most promising directions for the design are, but the evaluator who is hoping for a different outcome can miss these hints. A common mistake of novice designers is to downplay or ignore the negatives and emphasize positive results.

2.3. Formal Studies and Controlled Experiments

Formal usability studies in the form of *controlled experiments* aim to advance the field's understanding of how people use interfaces, to determine which design concepts work well under what circumstances, and why. They can also be used to help decide if a new feature or a change in approach improves the performance of an existing interface, or to compare competing interfaces.

To shed light on the phenomena of interest, controlled experiments must be somewhat artificially constrained in order to identify which features, if any, make a difference in the usability of the design. Just as in a clinical trial of a pharmaceutical drug, it is important to isolate the right factors, have proper controls to compare against, and choose the study population to mirror the target population correctly. When properly designed, the results of a formal study on a particular feature or idea should be applicable to many different interface designs. This section describes some of the components of formal studies, with an emphasis of the issues specific to search interfaces, but the reader is recommended to read more extensive treatments to fully understand the details of experiment design (Keppel et al. 1992; Kohavi et al. 2007, 2008).

2.3.1. *Techniques Employed in Formal Studies*

The classic formal usability study (also known as a *lab study*) is conducted in a usability laboratory (Shneiderman and Plaisant 2004), in which observers can be hidden behind a two-way window. However, a quiet room with a desk, chairs, and computer is oftentimes sufficient. Some studies are recorded with videotape or audiotape, and the content is later transcribed. User behavior can be recorded by people taking notes, but screen-capture programs allow for higher accuracy and greater completeness, especially if paired with click-capture and logging. Some studies use eye-tracking technology (Nielsen and Pernice 2009) to determine exactly which parts of the screen people view, to better understand the mental process that participants are undergoing when assessing a search interface (see Figure 2.2).

Participants in a usability study should be asked to read and sign a consent form, indicating which modalities are being recorded (audio, video, screen capture, eye tracking) and how the participants' anonymity will be protected. Participants should be told that they are free to leave the study at any time and for any reason.

It is common to give participants warm-up or practice tasks in order to help them get familiar with the system and relax into the tasks. It is also important to pilot test usability studies before running the full study with recruited participants. Initially, pilot tests are often done using

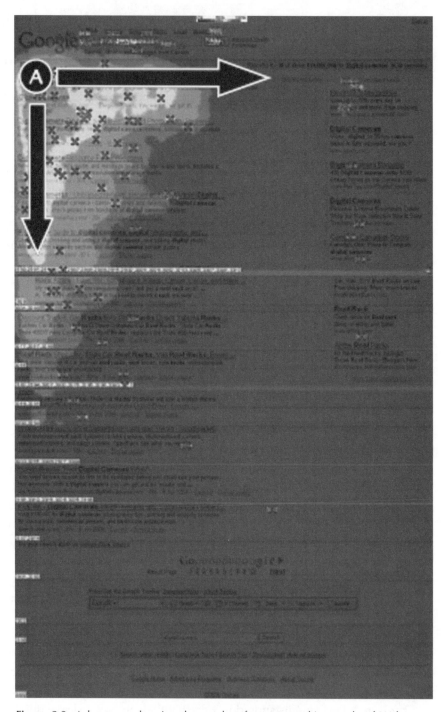

Figure 2.2. A heatmap showing the results of an eye-tracking study of Web page views, from (Hotchkiss et al. 2007). Arrows indicate dominant directions of eye movement; "hotter" colors indicate more frequent eye fixations, and X's indicate locations of clicks. From *Search Engine Results: 2010,* by Enquiro Research. (See color plate 1.)

co-workers or otherwise easy to recruit individuals, before testing on participants from the desired user base.

Formal (and informal) studies do not necessarily have to be conducted with experimenters sitting in the same room as the participant, or directly observing the participant. Several studies of *remote usability testing* find that this method yields similar results in most cases to in-person testing (Christos et al. 2007; McFadden et al. 2002; West and Lehman 2006). Remote testing has the advantage of making it easier to reach a more diverse user pool, and the study can be done in the participants' everyday work environment, and so is potentially more ecologically valid and more cost-effective than travel. Drawbacks to remote testing include difficulties in capturing facial expressions and non-verbal cues and less free-flowing communication between experimenter and participant. It might also be difficult to get experimental software working remotely, but special software has been developed to aid in remote testing that addresses this issue to some degree.

2.3.2. *Balancing Condition Ordering Effects*

A problem common to all usability studies is that order of exposure to experimental conditions can bias the results. It is common, when working with search interfaces, for participants to learn in several ways: about the tasks, the collection being searched over, and about the search interaction itself. Thus participants might get faster on a set of tasks independent of the different properties of the interfaces being compared, or they might get tired, making them slower on the later conditions. If timing data is being collected as part of a study, it is important to compute statistics that compare time taken at different phases of the study. It is also important to pilot test a study and shorten it if necessary if participants tire towards the end.

Participants learn about a topic while seeking information about it. Thus a participant should never see the same query or topic in two different conditions. The effect of prior exposure is much too great and invalidates any results seen in the second viewing. An example of this can be found in a study in which participants were asked the same question five different times, for five different visual displays. Not surprisingly, participants' performance for a given display was stronger for conditions viewed later in the study. Because the questions were repeated it is not possible to tell if this was the cause or if the task was one that got easier with practice, and any differences seen among the interfaces is called into question.

Participants can be influenced in other ways by order effects. If one interface is much better than another, then seeing the inferior interface second can cause it to have lower usability ratings than if it was viewed first. For example, in a study by the author and students comparing Flamenco, a faceted metadata interface, to a baseline standard search interface for image browsing, the order in which interfaces were viewed had a strong effect on the subjective ratings (such as "This interface is easy to use" or "This interface is flexible," etc.). When the faceted interface was viewed first, the subjective ratings for the baseline were considerably lower than when baseline was the first interface shown (thus providing additional support for the superiority of the faceted interface) (Yee et al. 2003). Because the order of the interfaces was varied for different participants in this study, it was possible to detect this effect in the data analysis. Thus, to control for order effects, the experimenter should vary the order in which participants are exposed to the key conditions.

Formal experiments must be *designed*, just as interfaces are (Keppel et al. 1992; Kohavi et al. 2007, 2008). A description of a formal study design should state the *independent (experimenter chosen) variables*, such as the different designs under study or the queries assigned, as well as the *dependent (response) variables*, such as time elapsed, number of errors made, and the participants' subjective responses. The design must also describe the *blocking* of the experiment, which refers to how the different experimental conditions are combined, that is, which tasks are assigned to which participants using which interface designs, and in which order. The research questions or hypotheses being tested can then be stated in terms of the independent and dependent variables. The experiment blocking is devised in such a way as to allow statistical tests to determine significant differences and to confirm or refute the hypotheses. A description of the participants is also important, often including demographics of the participant pool, their familiarity with relevant technology, and sometimes the results of cognitive tests.

When comparing interfaces, it is common to use a *within-participants* design, meaning each participant views each key condition (e.g., each interface, each variation of the new feature). This allows for direct comparisons of the responses of a given individual, which can be useful for comparing subjective responses, timing, and other response variables, in order to control for individual variation. On the other hand, within-participants design has its drawbacks. In some cases participants can form a bias or develop a learning effect after interacting with an interface, or the experimenter may need to have a participant spend a lot of time on one condition, thus making a session lasts too long. In these cases, it can be better to instead do a *between-participants* design, in which each participant is shown only one key interface condition. This precludes responses from being compared directly, but it eliminates any artificial effects that occur from one participant seeing multiple designs. In most cases, more participants are required in the between-participants design in order to get statistically meaningful results, but each individual session can be shorter.

Because some tasks may be harder than others, it can also be important to control for which tasks are conducted on each interface condition. In order to control for both the order of exposure of interface and for the combination of interface and task, the experimenter can employ a *Latin Square* blocking design. A Latin Square can be thought of as a matrix or table with number of rows equalling number of columns. If no row or column shares the same value, the Latin Square condition holds (thus bearing some similarity to the game of Sudoku). An easy way to build an $n \times n$ Latin Square is to lay out the first row, and then rotate the values by one position along each column, and repeating until all rows are constructed. So, if the first row of a 3×3 Latin Square is 1, 2, 3, the next would be 2, 3, 1, and the last would be 3, 1, 2. Note that this layout does not achieve all possible orderings (of which there are n factorial), but for experiment design it is usually assumed that allowing each condition to appear in each position once is sufficient to capture relevant ordering effects.

As an example, consider a usability study by Aula (2004) which had the goal of assessing the relative benefits of three methods of showing Web search results summaries (see Figure 2.3). In the *Bold* style, the summary was left unchanged from what was returned by the Google search engine, with query terms bolded, while in the *Plain* style, the summary was the same as in *Bold* but with the boldface highlighting removed. In the *List* condition, every time an ellipsis appeared in the summary, a new list item was created, preceded by a small arrow. Incomplete sentences were marked with ellipses at the start and/or end of the list item.

This study was designed so that participants always saw 10 hits for each query, and in all cases, there were 9 distractors and 1 valid answer summary for the question. The 30 test queries were divided into task sets of 10 queries each (call these A, B, and C), and one-third of the participants saw the *List* view first, one-third saw the *Bold* view first, and one-third saw the *Plain* view first. The Latin Square design might look as shown in Table 2.1. Each row represents a participant group, containing 3 out of the 27 participants. The order in which the participants see the interfaces is shown from left to right. Note that the order in which the task sets were assigned was

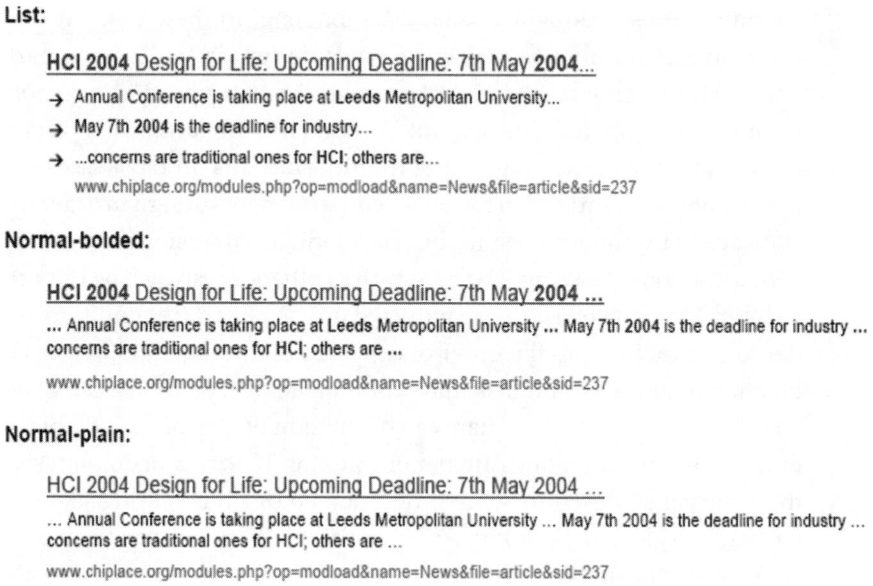

List:

HCI 2004 Design for Life: Upcoming Deadline: 7th May 2004...

→ Annual Conference is taking place at Leeds Metropolitan University...

→ May 7th 2004 is the deadline for industry...

→ ...concerns are traditional ones for HCI; others are...

    www.chiplace.org/modules.php?op=modload&name=News&file=article&sid=237

Normal-bolded:

HCI 2004 Design for Life: Upcoming Deadline: 7th May 2004 ...

... Annual Conference is taking place at Leeds Metropolitan University ... May 7th 2004 is the deadline for industry ... concerns are traditional ones for HCI; others are ...

www.chiplace.org/modules.php?op=modload&name=News&file=article&sid=237

Normal-plain:

HCI 2004 Design for Life: Upcoming Deadline: 7th May 2004 ...

... Annual Conference is taking place at Leeds Metropolitan University ... May 7th 2004 is the deadline for industry ... concerns are traditional ones for HCI; others are ...

www.chiplace.org/modules.php?op=modload&name=News&file=article&sid=237

Figure 2.3. Summary styles compared in an experiment by Aula (2004).

also varied to ensure that each query group is associated with a different interface type in each position in the test ordering.

This kind of blocking structure allows for statistical tests such as Analysis of Variance (ANOVA) (Keppel et al. 1992; Stockburger 1998) that can determine whether or not there are interaction effects among the different conditions. In the case of the Aula study (Aula 2004), ANOVAs showed

Table 2.1. Latin square design. Each participant group contains 3 participants; each task set (A, B, C) contains 10 distinct queries.

Participant group	First task set	Second task set	Third task set
1	Plain (A)	Bold (B)	List (C)
2	Plain (B)	Bold (C)	List (A)
3	Plain (C)	Bold (A)	List (B)
4	Bold (A)	List (B)	Plain (C)
5	Bold (B)	List (C)	Plain (A)
6	Bold (C)	List (A)	Plain (B)
7	List (A)	Plain (B)	Bold (C)
8	List (B)	Plain (C)	Bold (A)
9	List (C)	Plain (A)	Bold (B)

that there was a significant effect among interface types and task times meaning that there is support for the hypothesis that the variation in task completion time was caused by the differences in the interfaces. ANOVAs also showed that although participants made errors 21% of the time, there was no significant effect of error on interface type.

To account for another potential cause of variation, Aula also balanced the location in which the single relevant document would appear in each task set. She ordered the results listings in such a way as to guarantee that for each task set, a correct answer occurred in each of the 10 positions in the list one time. Thus in task set A, a relevant document would appear in position 1 for one query, in position 2 for another query, and so on. This artificial element of the design helps counteract search users' tendency to select the top-ranked hits, allowing each interface an equal chance of having the correct answer in each position in the list. On the other hand, it may introduce an artifact into the study if it is the case that, say, the bolding interface works best when the correct answer falls in the first or second hit.

2.3.3. *Obtaining Participants*

Ideally, usability study participants are drawn from a pool of potential users of the system under study; for instance, an interface for entering medical record information should be tested by nurse practitioners. Often the true users of such a system are too difficult to recruit for academic studies, and so surrogates are found, such as interns who are training for a given position or graduate students in a field.

For academic HCI research, participants are usually recruited via flyers on buildings, email solicitations, as an (optional) part of a course or by a professional recruiting firm. Often the participants are computer science graduate students, who are not representative of most user populations in terms of their approach to and understanding of computer interfaces. Participants obtained in this manner are usually not a representative sample of the population of potential users, and so the results of such studies must be regarded in this light. More recently, the field of HCI has been moving towards recruiting more realistic participants in usability studies.

The number of participants required to observe statistically significant differences depends on the study design, the variability among the tasks and participants, and the number of factors being compared (Kohavi et al. 2008). Most academic usability studies use a very small number of participants, and often these are drawn from the researchers' environment. Again, these issues suggest that results of studies should be eyed with some skepticism. This is why, throughout this book, the number of participants, as well as the pool they are drawn from, are reported when a usability study is summarized. It is also why results of multiple studies are reported whenever available.

The massive scale of deployed search engines changes the participant-recruitment situation by allowing new ideas to be tested on thousands, or even tens of thousands of users, as discussed below in the section on large-scale log-based usability testing.

Another recent approach to recruiting participants is to use a outsourcing or "crowdsourcing" service, such as Amazon's MTurk service, in which tens of thousands of people sign up online to do quick tasks for small fees. This approach to recruiting participants was found to be a fast, effective way to run studies, particularly for relevance testing (Alonso et al. 2008; Kaisser et al. 2008; Snow et al. 2008).

2.3.4. *Measuring Participants' Preferences*

As mentioned above, it is important to measure participant preferences, or subjective responses, since interfaces that are not liked will not be used, given a choice. Participant preferences are usually obtained via questionnaires using *Likert scales*. In Likert scales, participants select a point within a qualitative range, such as "difficult to easy," "strongly agree to strongly disagree," "never to always," and so on (Shneiderman and Plaisant 2004). Most Likert scales have either 5, 7, or 9 degrees to choose among; odd numbers make it clear what the central or neutral choice is. If the participants can be expected to make fine-grained distinctions in their choices, it is preferable to use a wider scale, otherwise a narrower scale should be used. For example, if comparing a new interface against one that is known already to have strong positive reactions, a wider scale allows for participants to clearly indicate a preference above and beyond what is already familiar.

The meta-analysis by Hornbæk and Law (2007) suggests ad hoc questionnaires are less reliable and have greater variability than studies that use standard questionnaires. One commonly used questionnaire for assessing subjective reactions to interactive interfaces is the *Questionnaire for User Interaction Satisfaction* (QUIS) tool (Chin et al. 1988; Shneiderman and Plaisant 2004). It assesses reactions to questions pertaining to overall reactions to the system, characteristics of the graphical view, terminology, learning difficulty, and system capabilities, on a 9-point Likert scale. A more generally applicable questionnaire consisting of 5 sets of questions was analyzed by van Schaik and Ling (2005), and was found to distinguish properties useful for measuring the quality of interaction in Web interfaces both for monitoring and improving the design of such sites. Sample questions from this questionnaire are:

- "Learning to use this site was easy."
- "I felt lost."
- "I judge the Web page to be: (very disordered 1 2 3 4 5 6 7 very ordered)"

Most of these are answered using a 7-point Likert scale ranging from "strongly agree" to "strongly disagree," but the questions on aesthetics have their own scales, as shown in the third example.

When comparing two or more designs, it can be revealing to have participants assess each interface in isolation before comparing them directly. This provides a second check on the subjectivity scores for the same questions (Hornbæk and Law 2007). For example, if in the direct comparison, interface A is rated more flexible than B, the experimenter can check the individual ratings for flexibility for the independent assessment for each interface in order to infer how strongly that difference is felt. If the participant gave a very low score for flexibility for design A and a high score for design B, then the difference can be assumed to be large, but if the scores are similar on the isolated questionnaires, the perceived differences in the comparison can be assumed to be of lesser degree. This is also useful to see if there are effects based on order of presentation. Finally, if the participant for some reason does not complete the entire session, partial subjective information will have been obtained.

Aesthetic impressions are an important form of subjective response, as they have been found to play a role in user acceptance and have been found to correlate with perceptions of an interface's quality, user satisfaction, and overall impression of a site (Hassenzahl 2004; Lindgaard and Dudek 2003). van der Heijden (2003) found that the visual appeal of a Web site affected participants' enjoyment and perception of ease of use, and to a small degree, the usability of the system. Nakarada-Kordic and Lobb (2005) report that viewers persevere longer in a search task on Web sites whose design appeals to them.

Another reason to evaluate participants' subjective responses is that objective measures and subjective preferences are sometimes only moderately correlated (Hornbæk and Law 2007). Ben-Bassat et al. (2006) hypothesized that subjective responses to a system may be only partly influenced by its usability. To prove this, they conducted a study with 150 engineering undergraduate students in which they varied the aesthetic quality of a design as well as its usability (in terms of number of keystrokes needed to get a task done). Participants were asked to complete tasks using the different interfaces and then to fill out questionnaires about the interfaces' usability and aesthetics. The experimenters found that the interfaces that required fewer keystrokes were indeed considered more usable, but they also found that the high aesthetic interfaces were seen as slightly more usable than the low-aesthetic interface, even though those were slightly faster. Ben-Bassat et al. (2006) then told participants they would be paid according to how well they did the task in a subsequent experiment. Participants were asked to make bids in an auction format on the different interfaces, to determine which they would use. In this condition, people bid higher on the more efficient designs, independent of their aesthetic scores. Thus, they found that questionnaire-based assessments were affected by aesthetics, but auction-based, financially incentivized assessments were not.

In some cases it is desirable to separate effects of usability from those of branding or of visual design. For instance, to compare the relative benefits of the ranking abilities of search engine A versus B, it is important to re-render the results in some neutral layout that uses the same visual elements for both rankings.

2.4. Longitudinal Studies

To obtain a more accurate understanding of the value and usage patterns of a search interface, (in order to obtain what is called *ecological validity* in the social sciences literature), it is important to conduct studies in which the participants use the interface in their daily environments and routines, and over a significant period of time (Shneiderman and Plaisant 2006).

A *longitudinal study* tracks participant behavior while using a system over an extended period of time, as opposed to first-time usages which are what are typically assessed in formal and informal studies. This kind of study is especially useful for evaluating search user interfaces, since it allows the evaluator to observe how usage changes as the participant learns about the system and how usage varies over a wide range of information needs (Shneiderman and Plaisant 2006). The longer time frame also allows potential users to get a more realistic subjective assessment of how valuable they find the system to be. This can be measured by question-naires as well as by how often the participant chooses to use the system versus alternatives.

Additionally, in lab studies, participants are asked to stay "on task" and so will tend to behave in a more directed manner, accomplishing tasks efficiently but not necessarily taking the time to explore and get to know new features or try new strategies. Longitudinal studies can capture more variation in usage and behavior as they occur in a more relaxed setting.

A good example of a longitudinal search study is described by Dumais et al. (2003), who assessed the usage patterns of a personal information search tool by 234 participants over a six-week period, using question-naires and log file analysis. They split the participants into two groups, giving each a different default setting for sorting results (by *Date* versus by *Ranking*). This allowed the experimenters to see if participants chose, over time, to use an ordering different than the default. They indeed found an interesting pattern: those who start with *Rank* order as the default were much more likely to use *Date* ordering than vice versa, suggesting that or-dering information by chronology is better than by a ranking metric when searching over users' personal data collections. Such an effect might not be seen in a short laboratory study.

In another example of a longitudinal study, Käki (2005b) invited par-ticipants to use a grouping search interface over a period of two months. Subjective responses were obtained both after initial usage of the system and after the completion of the trial period. The responses became more positive on most measures as time went by. Even more interestingly, the query logs showed that the average query length became shorter over time. Some participants commented on this trend, volunteering that they became "lazier" for some queries, using more general terms than they oth-erwise would, because they anticipated that the system would organize the results for them, thus allowing them to select among refining terms. Observing this kind of change in user behavior over time is a very useful benefit of a longitudinal study.

Although relatively new in their usage for search interface evaluation, and formal user interface evaluation generally, there is increasing momen-tum in support of longitudinal studies.

2.5. Analyzing Search Engine Server Logs

Most Web search engines record information about searchers' queries in their *server logs* (also called *query logs*). This information includes the query itself, the date and time it was written, and the IP address that the request came from. Some systems also record which search results were clicked on for a given query. These logs, which characterize millions of users and hundreds of millions of queries, are a valuable resource for understanding the kinds of information needs that users have, for improving ranking scores, for showing search history, and for attempts to personalize information retrieval. They are also used to evaluate search interfaces and algorithms, as discussed in the next section. In preparation, the following subsections describe some details behind the use of query logs.

2.5.1. *Identifying Session Boundaries*

Information seeking is often a complex process consisting of many steps. For this reason, many studies of query logs attempt to infer searchers' intent by observing their behavior across a sequence of steps or activities. This sequence is usually referred to as a *search session*, which can be defined as a sequence of requests made by a single user for a single navigation purpose (Huang et al. 2004).

There are several approaches for automatically distinguishing the boundaries of search sessions. The simplest method is to set a time threshold; when a user has been inactive for some amount of time, a cutoff is imposed, and all actions that happened before the cutoff are grouped into a session. He and Goker (2000) found a range of 10–15 minutes of inactivity to be optimal for creating session boundaries for Web logs. Silverstein et al. (1999) used five minutes, Anick (2003) used 60 minutes, and Catledge and Pitkow (1995) recommended 25.5 minutes.

Chen et al. (2002) recognize that timing information varies with both user and task, and so proposed an adaptive timeout method. They defined the "age" of an action to be the interval between an action and the current time. A session boundary was assigned when the age of an action was two times older than the average age of actions in the current session. Thus the time that is allowed to elapse before a session boundary is declared varies with the degree of activity the user is engaged in at different points in time.

Jansen et al. (2007a) examined 2,465,145 interactions from 534,507 users of a search engine, comparing several methods for determined session duration, finding that the best method made use of IP address, a cookie (stored client-side information), and query reformulation patterns, the latter to distinguish when a given user is searching for several different information needs in rapid succession. Using this method, they found that 93% of sessions consisted of 3 or fewer queries, with a mean of 2.31 queries per session (SD 1.5). The mean session length using this method was 5 minutes and 15 seconds (SD 39 min).

2.5.2. *Issues Surrounding Searcher Identity*

In query log analysis, an individual person is usually associated with an IP address, although there are a number of problems with this approach: some people search using multiple different IP addresses, and the same IP address can be used by multiple searchers. Nonetheless, the IP address is a useful starting point for identifying individual searchers.

Note that for typical query log analysis, no attempt is made to determine the actual identity of the users; rather, the IP address is linked to an anonymized unique ID number. Nonetheless, there are important privacy issues associated with the retention and use of query log information. Major search engine companies keep their query logs in confidence, but academic researchers are at a great disadvantage if no such logs are available to them. For this reason, in some cases, query logs have been made available to academic researchers, usually without incident, but in one case to great notoriety (Bar-Ilan 2007). Adar (2007) and Xiong and Agichtein (2007) discuss methods to anonymize the queries themselves, to balance the needs of certain types of research with user privacy, and Cooper (2008) sumarizes the issues from a policy perspective.

Despite these attempts, problems remain (Jones et al. 2007), and so query logs should be carefully handled. An alternative solution is to host a search engine and ask searchers to opt in to having their searches recorded for scientific purposes, with an option for them to remove any information they choose (Cooper 2008).

Some major Web-based companies support "toolbars" which the user must opt in to use and which provide value to the user. However, they monitor all of that user's Web-based activity – not just queries and clicks, but all navigation within the browser. This kind of information can not only lead to a much deeper understanding of peoples' information seeking processes, but can also record more potentially sensitive information. This data must be carefully anonymized and secured.

2.6. Large-Scale Log-Based Usability Testing (Bucket Testing)

An important form of usability testing that takes advantage of the huge numbers of visitors to some Web sites is *large-scale log-based usability testing*. In the days of shrink-wrapped software delivery, once an interface was coded, it was physically mailed to customers in the form of CDs or DVDs and could not be significantly changed until the next software version was released, usually multiple years later. The Web has changed this paradigm so that many companies release products in "beta," or unfinished, status, with the tacit understanding that there may be problems with the system, and the system will change before being officially released. More recently, the assumptions have changed still further. With some Web sites, especially those related to social media, the assumption is that the system is a work-in-progress, and changes will continually be made with little advance warning. The dynamic nature of Web interfaces makes it acceptable for some organizations to experiment with showing different versions of an interface to different groups of currently active users.

Large-scale studies using log analysis is also known in the industry as *bucket testing*, *A/B testing*, *split testing*, and *parallel flights* (Kohavi et al. 2007, 2008; Sinha 2005; Wroblewski 2006). The main idea is to start with an existing interface that is currently heavily used and is available over the Web, and create a variation on a design, or a new feature, to evaluate. User traffic that comes into the site is randomly split, so that one segment of the user population sees the new version or feature. The behavior of users in the experimental condition as well as the control (which is usually the standard site interface) is recorded in log files. In some cases, the study completes in a few days or even a few hours, for sites with very large customer bases.

Changes in behavior (or lack thereof) between the tested design and the standard design are ascertained from the server logs. The metrics recorded include which components are clicked on, dwell time (time elapsed between viewing and clicking), if an item is placed in a shopping cart, and so on. Feedback in the form of customer emails or online discussions can also figure into the analysis. Based on the results of these tests, a decision is made about whether to retain the feature or not. In some cases, if a new feature or design looks promising, the log studies are followed up with more standard usability evaluations, in which people are interviewed or invited into laboratory studies.

Bucket testing can be used both to test small changes in the interface, or for very large-scale innovations in the design. It is recommended that the new version first be tested with a very small percentage of the user population, and the logs and email monitored, to ensure that no errors are introduced. If the results do not appear to be problematic, then more users are included into the test condition (Kohavi et al. 2007).

This kind of study is inherently between-participants, because users see only one version of the interface and are not asked to compare different versions. But this differs from a formal study in that participants are not asked to complete certain tasks, nor is explicit feedback elicited. Therefore, in order to ensure that any differences seen in the log files are indeed significant, the study must be conducted with a very large user base, and significant-looking results need to be verified both with careful statistical significance testing and with additional studies to ensure that unforeseen causes are not at work.

Note that some of the terminology used in bucket testing is generally applicable to controlled experiments. However, bucket testing differs from standard controlled studies in several ways. As mentioned above, no tasks are assigned to the users, and no explicit feedback nor ratings are obtained, and so subjective responses can be difficult to ascertain. Bucket testing also differs from longitudinal studies, in that no explicit feedback is elicited and bucket tests last for at most a week or two. Bucket testing also differs from standard log analysis in that two or more variations of a design, presented to different sets of users, are compared.

The bucket testing approach to usability evaluation also differs from laboratory studies in that users are not asked to explicitly opt in to the study. It also differs from longitudinal studies in which participants volunteer to test out a software system over a period of time. Rather, in bucket testing, the people involved are rarely explicitly notified that they are using a non-standard version of the interface. However, the testing and logging falls within the terms of service that are listed on and standard for active Web sites.

Bucket testing has been found to be highly effective at resolving disputes about design decisions. As Kohavi et al. (2007) point out, often one's intuitions about what will work well on a large scale are simply incorrect, and numbers-based evaluation of features and designs can serve to resolve disputes when individuals from different parts of an organization are all trying to promote their own features (Kohavi et al. 2008). Kohavi et al. (2004) note that a "culture of experimentation" at Amazon.com that made running large-scale experiments easy allowed Amazon to innovate quickly; Kohavi et al. (2008) are pursuing a similar approach at Microsoft.

A major limitation of bucket testing is that the test can run effectively only over the short term because the user pool shifts over time and some users clear their cookies (which are used by the bucket tests to keep track of user IDs). Additionally, it is commonly observed that when comparing a new interface versus one that users are already familiar with, users nearly always prefer the original one at first. As Kohavi et al. (2007) note:

> If you change the navigation on a Web site, experienced users may be less efficient until they get used to the new navigation, thus giving an inherent advantage to the Control. Conversely, when a new design or feature is introduced, some users will investigate it, click everywhere, and thus introduce a 'newness' bias. . . . Both primacy and newness concerns imply that some experiments need to be run for multiple weeks.

As a corollary to this, in some cases major Web sites roll out changes only gradually. In a famous example, eBay once took 30 days to gradually change the background color of its home page from gray to white, in order to avoid offending or startling users (Helft 2008). Yahoo and Google also make changes to their most important properties gradually.

In a radical form of this approach, a Google VP claimed the use of large-scale usability testing to resolve a design dispute that engineers could not agree on (Sinha 2005). She stated that when Google first launched its News service, the designers could not decide between sorting articles by time or by location. Rather than running a formative study in-house, they decided to launch with no sorting facility whatsoever. Within a few hours, they received hundreds of emails asking for sorting by date, but only a few asking for sorting by location, and so they had their answer.

2.7. Special Concerns with Evaluating Search Interfaces

For a number of reasons, evaluating information-intensive applications such as search is somewhat different, and oftentimes more difficult, than evaluating other types of user interfaces. Some pertinent issues are discussed below, along with best practices for evaluation of search interfaces.

2.7.1. *Avoid Experimenter Bias*

A problem common to all usability studies, not just search interface studies, is that designers who evaluate their own designs often unconsciously introduce biases into the evaluation process. It is best to approach interface evaluation from a neutral scientific perspective, but this can be difficult when evaluating one's own design. One solution for getting a more objective read on the usability of an approach is to have the evaluation done by a third party, that is, different people than the designers of the new interface. It is important that the designers trust the evaluators, though, in order to have effective transfer of the results.

Unfortunately, it is often impractical to have outsiders evaluate a research design, so when evaluating one's own design, the experimenter should be aware of ways to avoid introducing bias. It is important that the experimenter does not "leak" information to the participants about which is the favored design. A common mistake is to say something like "We've developed a new interface which we'd like you to evaluate." This suggests to the participants that the experimenter may be disappointed if the interface does not perform well, and so may discourage less than fully forthcoming responses from some participants. Neutral language such as "we are evaluating several different designs" is both accurate and non-biasing. It is also good practice to assign neutral names to the different designs or conditions, for example, naming the designs after mountain ranges or colors.

2.7.2. *Encourage Participant Motivation*

Participant *motivation* or *interest* can have a significant impact on results (Buchanan et al. 2005; Spool 2002; Sutcliffe and Ennis's 1998). A highly motivated person will be inventive and try alternative avenues in a way that a bored person will not. Thus motivated participants can demonstrate how an interface will be used on the intense usage end of the spectrum. Unfortunately, many search usability studies ask people to do search on topics about which they are uninformed and/or uninterested. There is evidence that participants do not try hard when paid to participate in search studies on topics they do not care about. Rose (2004) notes that in one study conducted by AltaVista, 55% of survey results had to be discarded; in some cases participants failed a simple effort test in which they were required to distinguish actual search results from random URLs.

One way to stimulate participant motivation is to allow people to search for information that they are interested in, or perform tasks that they care about (Russell et al. 2006). However, in principle, it is preferable to require all participants to do the same task (under varying conditions), in order to facilitate comparisons within those conditions. One way to help improve motivation but still have some control over the topics tested in a study is to ask participants to select a *subset* from a pre-defined list of topics, thus allowing them to avoid subjects about which they have no knowledge or interest (Teevan et al. 2005a), but still allowing for direct comparisons of those participants who choose the same tasks to complete.

Another way to motivate participants is to match participants to the task at hand at recruiting time. An early study by the author and students on the Cha-Cha search system (Chen et al. 1999) provides a telling lesson. Undergraduate students were recruited to assess the interface whose main benefit was its ability to familiarize users with the large, diverse campus intranet, and placed search results within that context. The system ended up being popular among campus administrators, but most undergraduates care very little about campus administrative structure, and found little value in seeing this information.

Having learned from this experience, evaluations of the Flamenco system in each case matched the collection to the participant base (Hearst et al. 2002; Yee et al. 2003). For example, when evaluating on recipes, participants who like to cook were recruited; when evaluating on an architecture slide library collection, professional and student architects were recruited, and when evaluating on a fine arts collection graduate and undergraduate art history majors were chosen as participants. In each case the tasks were designed to be of inherent interest to those participant groups. Nonetheless, it is difficult to do this accurately. For the recipes study, one participant disliked the browse interface intensively; upon further questioning it turned out that despite the fact that he loved cooking, he hated recipes, and therefore had a negative reaction to any recipe interface.

Spool (2002) describes an innovative way to create a highly motivated participant – ask them to envision a product they would like to buy, show them a Web site that should contain the product, and *offer them the money* required to *buy the product*, but not for any other use. To increase the motivation still more, he suggests asking the participant to think about how they want to spend the money, and then send them away to come back a week later. When the participants return, Spool claims they are even more motivated than before, having had time to further mentally refine their desired purchase.

2.7.3. *Account for Participants' Individual Differences*

Nielsen (1993) notes that "the two most important issues for usability are the users' task and their individual characteristics and differences" (p. 43). He analyzed 30 published evaluations of hypertext systems and found that 4 of the 10 largest effects were due to individual differences between participants, and two were due to task differences (Nielsen 1989a). Nielsen contrasted users' experience with the system under study, with computers in general, and with the task domain. In some domains (such as programming skill), individual ability can vary by a factor of 20 (Nielsen 1993).

The effects of several types of individual differences on search performance have been studied in the literature: participants' knowledge of the task domain, participants' experience as searchers, and participants' cognitive differences; each of these are discussed below. The existence of these differences underscore the need to use large participant pools when conducting formal studies, in order to balance out the differences.

2.7.3.1. Participants' Domain and Task Knowledge

Many search usability studies have investigated the role of domain knowledge on search outcome, but the results are mixed (Vakkari 2000a). Hembrooke et al. (2005) found that performance on information-intensive tasks is influenced by the background knowledge and cognitive skills of the study participants. Jacobson and Fusani (1992) examined the experiences of 59 novice users with a full-text IR system, and used a regression model to assess the relative contributions of computer, system, and subject knowledge to search success. Their results indicated that all three variables played a role in the outcome. Wildemuth (2004) found that medical students' search tactics changed over time as their knowledge of the domain changed. Sihvonen and Vakkari (2004) found strong effects of domain knowledge on the use of thesaurus expansion. Vakkari (2000a) studied a set of 11 students as they formulated masters thesis topics, and observed changes in the choice of search terms and tactics as their knowledge of their topics increased. Vakkari and Hakala (2000) found that the more participants knew about the task, the fewer references they accepted as relevant. Similarly, Spink et al. (1998) found that the less knowledgable their participants were, the more items they marked as partly relevant. Kelly and Cool (2002) found, in a study of 36 participants, that efficacy of search (measured as number of relevant documents saved divided by the number of documents viewed) was significantly higher for those people who were familiar with the topic than for those who were very unfamiliar with it, meaning that the knowledgeable participants were more accurate at identifying relevant documents.

It can be stated with some assurance that when evaluating with a fixed set of tasks, it is important to ask in advance if participants already know the answer to the question or have knowledge of the topic. For example, Aula (2004) finds significant differences in the results of a summary browsing study after removing data points corresponding to questions in which participants knew the answers in advance.

2.7.3.2. Participants' Search Experience

A number of search usability studies have assessed the effects of knowledge of the search process itself, contrasting expert and novice searchers, although there is no consensus on the criteria for these classifications (Aula 2005). Some studies have observed that experts use different strategies than novices (Hölscher and Strube 2000; Lazonder et al. 2000; White et al. 2005), but perhaps more tellingly, other studies have found interaction effects between search knowledge and domain expertise (Hölscher and Strube 2000; Jenkins et al. 2003).

Tabatabai and Shore (2005), in a study of 10 novices, 9 intermediates, and 10 expert searchers, found that novices found less relevant information and were more satisfied, while experts found more relevant results, and were more nervous about having missed information. However, participants who used better strategies had better results, independent of their experience level. The two most important strategies were evaluative (assessment of relevancy of sources, search engines, and results) and metacognition (self-reflection and monitoring). Tabatabai and Shore (2005) wrote:

> Novices used backtracking to see where it would take them, hoping to get out of a labyrinth and find a comfort zone. On the contrary, intermediates and experts used it to go where they wanted to. Novices were less patient and relied more on trial-and-error. Impatience led them to navigate more, to click more, and to execute before spending enough time exploring or planning. . . . Experts were more aware of their feelings, were not surprised by them, and relied on them to modify their strategies. Their positive outlook on the search gave them patience to wait for a response from the system. Novices, on the other hand, felt lost, disoriented, and caught in a labyrinth more often than experts.

On the other hand, Zhang et al. (2005) found that, in a study including engineering students, increasing domain knowledge changed search behavior, but not search success. Lazonder et al. (2000) tested 25 Dutch students and found that training did not help much after achieving initial familiarity, and saw no effect based on domain knowledge.

2.7.3.3. Participants' Cognitive Abilities

Numerous studies show that participants who are generally more cognitively skilled perform better than other participants in information-intensive tasks, independent of the interfaces being compared. Allen (1992) assessed a range of cognitive factors using the *Kit of Factor-Referenced Cognitive Tests* (Ekstrom et al. 1976) and then assessed students searching a bibliographic database for pre-assigned topics. (It is common for evaluation of information visualization interfaces to include the paper folding test from the Kit to measure spatial ability (Chen 2000).) Allen (1992) found that perceptual speed had an effect on the quality of searches, and logical reasoning, verbal comprehension, and spatial scanning abilities influenced search tactics.

Tombros and Crestani (2000) note that fast participants remain fast and slow remain slow, independent of the interface. Pirolli et al. (2003) suggests a similar phenomenon when comparing an experimental and a standard browsing interface. When participants were ranked by their performance on an advanced file browser, and then were ranked by their performance on a standard file browser, there was a high correlation between the two rankings (high performers do well regardless of browser). They did another analysis that partitioned the sums of squares (i.e., partitioned the variance), and found that most of the performance effect in their study was due to individual differences rather than differences in the interface designs. To repeat a point made above, it is important to balance the participants in the different conditions when using a small number of participants.

2.7.4. *Account for Differences in Tasks and Queries*

Task selection in search interface evaluation can greatly affect the outcome of the study. Nielsen (1993, p. 185) notes that "the basic rule for test tasks is that they should be chosen to be as representative as possible of the uses to which the system will be eventually put in the field." He also advises that tasks be small enough to be completed within the time frame but not so small as to be trivial. The following sections describe the effects of task variations, query descriptions, and bias in task selection when evaluating search interfaces.

2.7.4.1. Account for The Effects of Task Variability

In fully automated IR system evaluations, such as those performed for the TREC ad hoc track, it is well-established that differences in the queries can overwhelm the outcome of a comparison between systems. It has been shown that in a typical TREC task, variation *within* a system across queries is usually higher than variation *among* top-scoring systems (Buckley and Walz 2000). Usually no system is the best for all topics in the task, and in fact it is rare for any system to be above average for all topics (Buckley and Walz 2000). The track administrators typically use 50 different queries in order to control for effects of the task, but even this is insufficient (Voorhees and Harman 2000).

Adding human participants to the evaluation most likely increases the sensitivity to task variation. A person might respond emotionally to a query, or may have expert knowledge in a topic, or may find a topic excruciatingly boring. Individualized reactions such as these can influence the results of a search usability study. To compound the problem, human participants can tire, and so can only be expected to do a limited number of queries within a test session, thus reducing the number of queries that can be run and increasing the likelihood of irrelevant artifacts having an effect on the outcome.

As mentioned above, Lindgaard and Chattratichart (2007) found no correlation between number of participants and number of problems found for usability testing of entire interfaces, but did find a correlation between the number of distinct *tasks* that participants are asked to complete and the number of problems found. This suggests that differences in tasks uncover different problems with the interface. For these reasons, search usability studies are increasingly differentiating query types, and assuming different interfaces will work better or worse when attempting different query types. Examples of varying the information need in this way is given by Woodruff et al. (2001) and Baudisch et al. (2004).

One way to reduce the variability somewhat is to pre-test the queries to determine if they are of similar difficulty, along either subjective or objective measures. It is common practice when conducting a formal study to show queries to one set of participants and have them rate them according to difficulty, interestingness, requiring external knowledge, and so on, and then select a subset with equivalent properties to show to a distinct set of participants in a usability study.

Although post-hoc analyses have found a lack of correlation between human estimates of difficulty and system performance on the TREC ad hoc task (Voorhees and Harman 2000), and between system estimates of difficulty and system performance (Voorhees 2004), there is some work suggesting that the weakest-performing queries can be predicted with some accuracy (Kwok 2005). A recent large-scale analysis of query-system failures suggests that systems often fail for the same reasons on the same queries: the systems emphasize some aspects of a topic while ignoring others, do not handle general concepts well, and lack sufficient natural language understanding (Buckley 2004). This analysis may prove useful in future for manual identification of query difficulty.

In addition, it does seem that people are good at estimating difficulty for other people (as opposed to for automated ranking evaluations), especially if the pre-testers use the search system that the study participants will be using (Bell and Ruthven 2004).

2.7.4.2. Control for Variation in Expression of the Query

As noted above, people find many different ways to express the same concept. Different query terms submitted to the same system can produce radically different results (Buckley and Walz 2000), thus leading to significant differences in outcome that have little to do with the interface.

To control for this variability, many usability studies pre-assign the query terms that the participant enters. Pre-writing the queries of course greatly reduces the realism of the assessment. Martzoukou (2004) argues against the artificiality of using pre-chosen queries for evaluation of information seeking studies, and Bilal (2002) found children were more successful with self-generated queries than with assigned topics and terms.

However, depending on what is being evaluated, pre-assigned query terms can be acceptable. For example, for the search results summary display experiment described above, the query formulation process is far less important than the results assessment process, and so the artificiality of the pre-written queries is less questionable. But for a study of relevance feedback term suggestions, pre-entering the query terms may be quite unrealistic.

2.7.4.3. Avoid Bias in Query and Task Selection

A common way to introduce experimenter bias is in the selection of tasks or queries (Käki and Aula 2008). For example, in numerous studies of information visualization of search results, the tasks chosen are along the lines of "Which interface allows the user to say how many documents have K instances of term A?" or "Which directory has the largest number of documents?" Although visualization can help with tasks of this sort, counting questions like these are not particularly common search tasks for most users, and so violates Nielsen's (Nielsen 1993) call to evaluate using realistic tasks. This kind of evaluation is quite common because it is often difficult to show that a visualization improves search results in a meaningful way. Separating out different components in order to isolate which makes a difference is good experimental practice, but the components tested must be meaningful or realistic in some way in order to truly inform the field.

As another example, it can be quite difficult to show significant timing differences in Web search evaluations. In one study, the queries were pre-determined and the terms used for the queries were pre-written. The evaluators were successful at showing timing improvements for a category-based view. However, the queries were designed to be maximally ambiguous so that any kind of grouping information would be helpful. For example, a query for the home page of the alternative rock band *They Might Be Giants* was written as *giants*, which is unrealistic from a query generation point of view (people searching for music and movie titles use most of the title words in their queries (Rose and Levinson 2004)) and is guaranteed to return a wide array of irrelevant results. A much better approach that showed more realistically that participants used grouping to help disambiguate queries was to use a longitudinal study as done by Käki (2005b) and discussed above.

Biasing can of course result from other considerations discussed above; by not varying the order of presentation properly, by asking participants to repeat tasks, and by polluting timing data by having documents pre-loaded for some conditions but not for others.

2.7.5. *Control Test Collection Characteristics*

When doing a formal usability test, it is important to evaluate the system on a large underlying collection (Willett 1988). In the early days of experimental IR, much of the testing was done on the tiny Cranfield collection, which consisted of just 1,398 abstracts. In 1985, a revolutionary paper by Blair and Maron (1985) investigated search over an important legal case consisting of 40,000 documents, showing that high recall remained distressingly elusive with modern systems. The TREC experiments expanded test domains to another order of magnitude in size, starting with about 1 GB of text for training and another gigabyte for testing in 1992 (Harman 1993).

Unfortunately, the problem of testing IR systems on small collections still occurs today. In one study comparing search information visualization techniques, a collection of only 651 documents was used and another used only 163 documents. Testing a search visualization on such a small collection can yield misleading results, since it is much easier to show a graphic display with 10 or 100 hits than with 1,000 or 10,000; the results on such a small study are unlikely to scale well to a realistic collection.

It is also important to compare two interfaces which index the same underlying collection. Experimenters who wish to compare a new design against a commercial system, or against a research system whose software is unavailable, are tempted to do a study with systems indexing different documents. Unfortunately, the results of a comparison over different collections is rarely valid, as the behavior of search systems is very sensitive both to the queries issued and the underlying collection. If one collection contains a great deal of information that is of interest to a participant and the other does not, the interface is likely to be blamed for the difference. Similarly, if the format of the contents of the two collections is quite different – for example, one containing full text and the other containing abstracts, or one containing poor content and the other containing high-quality content – the participants are likely to conflate the differences in the collections with the differences in the interfaces.

2.7.6. *Account for Differences in the Timing Response Variable*

Some of the most important metrics for evaluation of interfaces include time required to complete tasks, effort level required, and number and severity of errors made. However, comparing search interfaces based on time required to complete tasks can be fraught with problems. As mentioned above, task difficulty and participant differences and query knowledge can have effects that must be factored into the study design. In addition, any search system that allows participants to follow hyperlinks and move away from the search results page is likely to find widely varying timing data. Thus, most timing-based Web search studies require the users to look at a page of results listings, or at most view documents one link away from the results page (Käki and Aula 2008). Timing data can also be misleading as sometimes the value of a new information access interface is in that it allows users to browse and get to know a collection of information, and thus longer usage times can signal a more successful design. In some cases, a deeper search session, in which the user can comfortably explore, iterate, and refine their search, may take more time than an unsatisfying interface that makes the user want to get in and get out as quickly as possible (Rose 2004).

Käki and Aula (2008) point out that there is no standard timing measure for search speed, and suggest a proportional measure called *qualified search speed* that measures answer per minute, in terms of quality of answers. Using this measure, the experimenter can compare system A with B in terms of relevant answers per minute and irrelevant answers per minute. They found in several studies that the differentiating measure between interfaces was the increase in relevant speed, with irrelevant speed remaining nearly constant.

On a more practical note, timing data can be affected by variable network delays or contrasts between pages that have already been visited, either by the participant or by a preceding participant, and so are in the cache and fast to access. (A related mistake is to allow a participant to see a previous' participants query history in the Web browser drop-down menu.) Best practice suggests downloading all pages that will be seen in advance, and having the participants access them locally, if the study allows for that, and clearing out the cache of all prior history when running multiple participants in the same environment.

As another way around the timing quandary, longitudinal studies can show changes in use over time, and can be used to differentiate which types of queries induce different types of response times.

2.7.7. Compare Against a Strong Baseline

Yet another way to bias the outcome of a usability study is to compare a new design against an unrealistic baseline system. For example, one study compared a visualization of search results against a Web search interface that hid the summaries, even though this kind of view is standard for Web search engines and is the one to beat.

All designs should be equally aesthetically pleasing; as discussed in Chapter 1, unattractive designs de-motivate participants, and vice versa. And as mentioned above, all designs being compared should index the same underlying collection.

2.8. Conclusions

This chapter has described a wide range of methods for evaluating search user interfaces, and interfaces more generally. First was a discussion of standard information retrieval evaluation, which focuses on the performance of the ranking algorithms but not on user interaction. Next was a description of informal and formal methods for evaluating search interfaces, longitudinal studies which allow the participant to experience the interface over long periods of time, and large-scale evaluation that makes use of an existing user population to compare different variants of an interface. The chapter then provided extensive advice on how to avoid the many potential pitfalls that await those who evaluate search interfaces.

Given all this information, how should one design an evaluation? One strategy is, when designing the new search interface initially, begin by thinking about the evaluation, and then work backwards from this to the new design concept. Ensure that there is a way to measure the new design against a strong baseline that is representative of the state of the art.

It is also important to define realistic tasks that reflect what the user base will actually want to do with the system, and test on this kind of task, and to test against a wide range of tasks in order to tease out which aspects of the system succeed and which do not. The study participants should feel motivated to complete the tasks and their characteristics should match that of the true user base to the degree possible. Informal evaluations should be used to quickly determine what works and what does not. More formal studies should be used after the new design is being received well in informal studies, in order to pinpoint detailed problems, and to gather preference data to determine if the new design is better received than the state-of-the art. Longitudinal studies are a useful mechanism for determining the long-term likelihood of the success of the design. Finally, a good resource for ideas about how to evaluate an interface is to study research papers that evaluated similar interfaces in the past.

3 Models of the Information Seeking Process

In order to design successful search user interfaces, it is necessary to understand the human information seeking process, including the strategies people employ when engaged in search. Numerous theoretical treatments have been proposed to characterize this complex cognitive process (Belkin et al. 1982; Jarvelin and Ingwersen 2004; Kuhlthau 1991; Marchionini 1995; Saracevic 1997; Sutcliffe and Ennis's 1998). This chapter presents the most commonly discussed theoretical models of the search process: the standard model, the cognitive model, the dynamic model, search as a sequence of stages, search as a strategic process, and sensemaking. The chapter concludes with a discussion of information needs, including methods for inferring information needs from their expression as queries.

3.1. The Standard Model of Information Seeking

Many accounts of the information seeking process assume an interaction cycle consisting of identifying an information need, followed by the activities of query specification, examination of retrieval results, and if needed, reformulation of the query, repeating the cycle until a satisfactory result set is found (Salton 1989; Shneiderman et al. 1998). As Marchionini (1989) puts it:

> "Information-seeking is a special case of problem solving. It includes recognizing and interpreting the information problem, establishing a plan of search, conducting the search, evaluating the results, and if necessary, iterating through the process again."

This model is elaborated by Sutcliffe and Ennis's (1998) oft-cited information seeking process model, which they formulate as a cycle consisting of four main activities:

- Problem identification,
- Articulation of information need(s),
- Query formulation, and
- Results evaluation.

Sutcliffe and Ennis's (1998) associate different types of search strategies with each of these activities (for instance, scanning titles is associated with results evaluation). Their model also accounts for the role of the searcher's knowledge, the system, the information collections, and of searching in general.

A similar four-phase framework is described by Shneiderman et al. (1997), who outline the main steps as:

- Query Formulation,
- Action (running the query),
- Review of Results,
- Refinement.

Marchionini and White's (2008) description of the information-seeking process consists of:

- Recognizing a need for information,
- Accepting the challenge to take action to fulfill the need,
- Formulating the problem,
- Expressing the information need in a search system,
- Examination of the results,
- Reformulation of the problem and its expression, and
- Use of the results.

These represent the core actions within general information seeking tasks. Figure 3.1 (from Broder 2002) illustrates the process, in tandem with a sketch of the information access system that is used within the process. Standard Web search engines support query specification, examination of retrieval results, and to some degree, query reformulation. The other steps are not supported well in today's Web search interfaces, but systems that support *sensemaking* (see below) do attempt to help with problem formulation, information re-organization, and creation of new representations

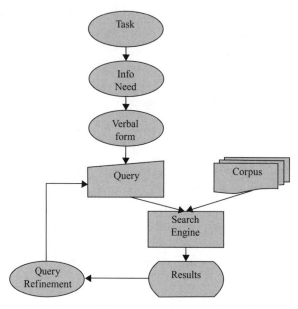

Figure 3.1. The standard model of the search process, adapted from Broder (2002).

from gathered information. These models are based primarily on observations of people engaged in information seeking processes.

3.2. Cognitive Models of Information Seeking

A cognitive account of the standard model can be derived from Norman's influential model of general task performance (Norman 1988), which presents a broad perspective on how people operate in the world. According to this model, a person must first have a basic idea of what they want – the goal to be achieved. Then they use their mental model of the situation to decide on some kind of action in the world that affects themselves, other people, or objects, with the aim of achieving their goal. The notion of a *mental model* is often invoked in the field of HCI as a mechanism for explaining one's understanding of a system or interface. A person's mental model is a dynamic, internal representation of a problem situation or a system which can take inputs from the external world and return predictions of effects for those inputs (Marchionini 1989).

Norman divides actions into the doing (*execution*) and the checking (*evaluation*) of the result. After taking an action, a person must assess what kind of change occurred, if any, and whether or not the action achieved the intended goal (see Figure 3.2). Norman describes the gap between what

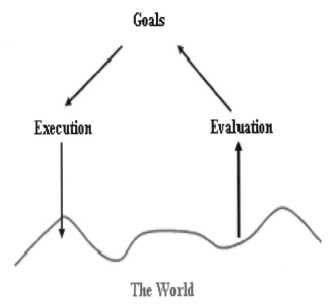

Figure 3.2. A sketch of Norman's cognitive execution-evaluation model, adapted from Norman (1988).

was intended and what was achieved as the *gulf of execution*, and the challenge of determining whether or not one's goals have been met as the *gulf of evaluation*. In the case of user interface design, the smaller these gulfs, the more usable the system. This also suggests that the less knowledge a person has about their task, the less they will be able to successfully formulate goals and assess results.

Norman's model can be seen as providing cognitive underpinnings for the standard model as described in the previous section. Recognizing a need for information is akin to formulating and becoming conscious of a goal. Formulating the problem and expressing the information need via queries or navigation in a search system corresponds to executing actions, and examination of the results to determine if the information need is satisfied corresponds to the evaluation part of the model. Query reformulation is needed if the gulf between the goal and the state of the world is too large.

3.3. The Dynamic (Berry-Picking) Model

The standard model of the information seeking process contains an underlying assumption that the user's information need is static and the information seeking process is one of successively refining a query until all

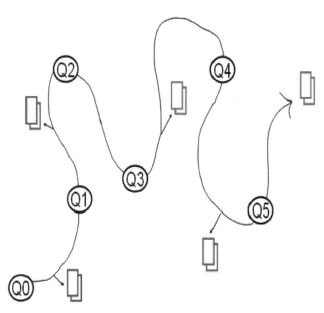

Figure 3.3. A sketch of an information seeker engaged in "berry-picking" style information seeking process, in which the query shifts as relevant information and documents are found along the way.

and only those documents relevant to the original information need have been retrieved. However, observational studies of the information seeking process find that searchers' information needs change as they interact with the search system. Searchers learn about the topic as they scan retrieval results and term suggestions, and formulate new subquestions as previously posed subquestions are answered. Thus while useful for describing the basics of information access systems, the standard interaction model has been challenged on many fronts (Bates 1989; Borgman 1996; Cousins 1997; Hendry and Harper 1997; O'Day and Jeffries 1993).

Bates (1989) proposed the *berry-picking* model of information seeking, which has two main points. The first is that, in the process of reading and learning from the information encountered throughout the search process, the searchers' information needs, and consequently their queries, continually shift (see Figure 3.3). Information encountered at one point in a search may lead in a new, unanticipated direction. The original goal may become partly fulfilled, thus lowering the priority of one goal in favor of another. The second point is that searchers' information needs are not satisfied by a single, final retrieved set of documents, but rather by a series of selections and bits of information found along the way. This is in contrast to the assumption that the main goal of the search process is to hone down the set of retrieved documents into a perfect match of the original information need.

The berry-picking model is supported by a number of observational studies (Borgman 1996; Ellis 1989), including that of O'Day and Jeffries (1993), who interviewed 15 business analysts about their typical search tasks. They found that the information seeking process consisted of a series of interconnected but diverse searches. They also found that search results for a goal tended to trigger new goals, and hence search in new directions, but that the context of the problem and the previous searches was carried from one stage of search to the next. Finally, the main value of the search was found to reside in the accumulated learning and acquisition of information that occurred during the search process, rather than in the final results set.

3.4. Information Seeking in Stages

Some researchers have examined how the information seeking process develops over extended periods of time. Kuhlthau (1991) conducted studies that showed that, for complex information seeking tasks, searchers go through different stages, both in terms of their knowledge of and their attitude towards the task. To develop her model of the information seeking process, Kuhlthau (1991) conducted numerous field studies as well as focused case studies. The final field study was very large (compared to most such studies), involving 385 academic, public, and school library users at 21 sites. Participants were primarily students in high school or college whose task was to write a term paper or research paper. In these studies, the information seeking task took place over several months, and in most cases the students were assigned the topic rather than choosing it themselves. Kuhlthau's (1991) method was also unusual in that in addition to asking participants about their search process, she also asked questions about their emotional state.

Kuhlthau's (1991) findings revealed both a common information access process and common emotional patterns. She divides the process of information seeking into six stages:

- *Initiation:* The task is to recognize a need for information. Searches relate to general background knowledge. As the participant becomes aware of their lack of understanding, feelings of uncertainty and apprehension are common. Thoughts center on comprehending the task and relating the problem to prior experience.

- *Selection:* The task is to select the general topic or the approach to pursue. Thoughts are general and undifferentiated, and center on requirements, time constraints, and which topic or approach will yield the best outcome. Feelings of uncertainty often give way to optimism after the selection is made.
- *Exploration:* The task is to investigate information on the general topic in order to extend understanding. At this stage, an inability to express what information is needed degrades the participant's ability to formulate queries and judge relevance of retrieval results. Information encountered at this stage often conflicts with pre-existing knowledge and information from different sources can seem contradictory and incompatible. This phase is characterized by feelings of confusion, uncertainty, and doubt, and participants may feel discouraged or inadequate, or may feel frustrated with the information access system itself.
- *Formulation:* This phase marks the turning point in the process, in which a focused perspective on the topic emerges, resolving some of the conflicting information. Searches may be conducted to verify the working hypotheses. A change in feelings is experienced, with uncertainty reducing and confidence growing. Unfortunately, half of the study participants did not show evidence of successfully reaching a focused perspective at any time during their search process.
- *Collection:* At this stage the search system is most productively useful for the participant, since the task is to gather information related to a focused topic. Searches are used to find information to define, extend, and support the focus. Relevance judgements become more accurate and feelings of confidence continue to increase.
- *Presentation:* In this phase, the final searches are done; searches should be returning information that is either redundant with what has been seen before or of diminishing relevance. The participants commonly experience feelings of relief, and satisfaction if the search went well, or disappointment if not.

Similar results were found by Vakkari (2000b), who studied 11 students doing research for a masters project over 4 months. Vakkari (2000b) writes:

> In general, all the participants proceeded in their task according to Kuhlthau's (1991) model at varying paces. In the first search session, the students were moving from topic selection to exploration of the topic. In the middle of their task they were typically exploring the topic and trying to formulate a research problem. By the end of the project most of the students had been able to construct a focus and they were at the collection or presentation stage.

Note that these stages characterize changes in searches over time for a deep and complex information need, and are not necessarily representative for more light-weight tasks. Note also that these studies reflect the experiences of students doing required, challenging tasks; it is likely that the feelings of apprehension reported might not be observed in other information-intensive task environments. Additionally, the tools used by Kuhlthau's students were probably less familiar and usable than search tools available today.

3.5. Information Seeking as a Strategic Process

Some information seeking models cast the process in terms of *strategies* and how choices for next steps are made. As Marchionini et al. (2000) note, "search is an interplay of analytical and interactive problem solving strategies." In some cases, the strategy-oriented models are meant to reflect conscious planning behavior by expert searchers. In others, the models are meant to capture the less planned, potentially more reactive behavior of a typical information seeker. The next subsections discuss the theoretical characterizations of information seeking strategies.

3.5.1. *Strategies as Sequences of Tactics*

Bates (1979) suggests that a searcher's behavior can be characterized by search strategies which in turn are made up of sequences of search *tactics*. Tactics are the immediate choices or actions taken in the light of the current focus of attention and state of the search. Strategies refer to combinations of tactics used in order to accomplish information access tasks. Thus strategies are sequences of tactics which, viewed together, help achieve some aspect or subgoal of the user's main goals. Bates enumerates a set of search tactics which she groups into four categories, which are paraphrased slightly below.

Term tactics: refer to tactics for adjusting words and phrases within the current query. These include making use of term suggestions provided by the search system and selecting terms from an online thesaurus.

Information structure tactics: are techniques for moving through information or link structures to find sources or information within sources. An example of an information structure tactic for an academic researcher is looking at the research articles that cite a given paper, and following the citation chain. Another example is, when searching within an online collection or Web site, following promising hyperlinks or searching within a category of information, for example, searching only within the technology section of a news Web site.

Query reformulation tactics: examples include narrowing a given query specification by using more specific terms or gaining more control over the structure of the query by using Boolean operators.

Monitoring tactics: monitoring refers to keeping track of a situation as it unfolds. Bates discusses several high-level monitoring tactics, including making a cost–benefit analysis of current or anticipated actions (weighing), continuously comparing the current state with the original goal (checking; note the similarity to Norman's (1988) gulf of evaluation), recognizing patterns across common strategies, and recording incomplete paths to enable returning at a later time. Bates also notes that one of the fundamental issues in search strategies is determining when to stop; monitoring tactics can help with this determination.

A question arises as to how a searcher who is monitoring their search knows to stop following one strategy and take up another. O'Day and Jeffries (1993) defined a number of *triggers* that motivate a seeker to switch from one search strategy to another. These triggers include:

- The completion of one step and beginning of the next logical step in a plan,
- Encountering something interesting that provides a new way of thinking about a topic of interest, or a new, interesting angle to explain a topic or problem,
- Encountering a change or violation of previous expectations that requires further investigation, and
- Encountering inconsistencies with or gaps in previous understanding that requires further investigation.

O'Day and Jeffries also attempted to identify stop conditions – circumstances under which people decided to stop searching. These were fuzzier than the triggers for changing strategies, but they did find that people stopped searching when:

- There were no more compelling triggers,
- An "appropriate" amount of material had been found, or
- There was a specific inhibiting factor (such as discovering a market was too small to be worth researching).

These stop conditions can be cast in terms of a cost–benefit analysis (see discussion below); for example, the second point might be interpreted as a drop below a threshold for continuing the current line of inquiry.

Bates (1979) notes that some search tasks are straightforward enough that a strategy per se is not required. Simple fact-searching on the Web is an example of this; the searcher opens a Web browser, navigates to a search engine entry form, types in their information need, and scans the retrieval results to find the answer or a link to a page that contains the answer.

3.5.2. *Cost Structure Analyses and Information Foraging Theory*

As mentioned above, Bates (1979) discusses the importance of monitoring the progress of the current search and weighing the costs and benefits of continuing with the current strategy or trying something else. Russell et al. (1993) also cast the activity of monitoring the progress of a search strategy relative to a goal or subgoal in terms of a *cost structure analysis*, or an analysis of diminishing returns. This account assumes that at any point in the search process, the user is pursuing the strategy that has the highest expected utility. If, as a consequence of some local tactical choices, another strategy presents itself as being of higher utility than the current one, the current one is (temporarily or permanently) abandoned in favor of the new strategy.

This cost structure analysis method was subsequently expanded into *information foraging theory* by Pirolli and Card (1999). This theoretical framework contains several ideas relevant to understanding the search process. It takes an evolutionary stance, noting that humans' ancestors evolved perceptual and cognitive structures that were well-adapted for exploring the environment in the task of finding food. The theory assumes that, in the modern world, awash with information of our own creation, humans transfer food-finding cognitive mechanisms over to the task of exploring, finding, and ultimately "consuming" information (Pirolli 2007).

Information foraging theory attempts to model and make predictions about peoples' strategies for navigating within information structures. One important concept is a cost–benefit analysis for navigation, in which searchers make tradeoffs between two questions. Nielsen (2003a) formulates this as:

(i) What gain can I expect from a specific information nugget (such as a Web page)?

(ii) What is the likely cost in terms of time and effort of discovering and consuming that information?

Thus, an information consumer compares the cost of evaluation and immediate "consumption" of information with the cost of additional search. This model can account for the decreasing returns on, say, reading information from a search results list: after some number of documents on a topic have been read, the tradeoff between finding new information versus reading information already seen or of lower quality begins to tip in favor of ending the information consumption session. That is, the theory assumes that search strategies evolve toward those that maximize the ratio of valuable information gained to unit of cost for searching and reading.

When foraging, information can appear in "patches"; it might make sense to read a few pieces of information from one Web site, and then move to another Web site to get more variety in the "diet"; however, one must consider the payoff in finding new kinds of information versus the cost of getting to a new good patch of information. Nielsen (2003a) points out that in the early days of the Web, search quality was poor and there was not very much content available, so it made more sense to focus all one's attention on an information-rich Web site once it was found. But as the content increased and search results improved in the late 1990s, the cost of finding high-quality additional sources of information fell, and so it often became more cost-effective and advantageous to forage briefly on each of a variety of different sites.

3.5.3. Browsing vs. Search as an Information Seeking Strategy

A bedrock psychological result from cognitive science is *recognition over recall*; that is, it is usually easier for a person to recognize something by looking for it than it is to think up how to describe that thing. A familiar example is experienced by learners of a foreign language; it is usually easier to read a sentence in that language than to generate a sentence oneself. This principle applies to information seeking as well. Rather than requiring the searcher to issue keyword queries and scan retrieval results, the system can provide the searcher with structure that characterizes the available information.

There are a number of theories and frameworks that contrast *querying/searching* and *browsing/navigating*, along several dimensions (Belkin et al. 1993; Chang and Rice 1993; Marchionini 1995; Waterworth and Chignell 1991). One way to distinguish searching versus browsing is to note that search queries tend to produce new, ad hoc collections of information that have not been gathered together before, whereas navigation/browsing refers to selecting links or categories that produce pre-defined groups of information items. Browsing also involves following a chain of links, switching from one view to another, in a sequence of scan and select operations. Browsing can also refer to the casual, mainly undirected exploration of navigation structures. Hertzum and Frokjaer (1996) word the contrast as follows:

> Browsing is a retrieval process where the users navigate through the text database by following links from one piece of text to the next, aiming to utilize two human capabilities ... the greater ability to recognize what is wanted over being able to describe it and ... the ability to skim or perceive at a glance. This allows users to evaluate rapidly rather large amounts of text and determine what is useful.

Aula (2005) writes:

> Considered in cognitive terms, searching is a more analytical and demanding method for locating information than browsing, as it involves several phases, such as planning and executing queries, evaluating the results, and refining the queries, whereas browsing only requires the user to recognize promising-looking links.

Thus, in principle, in many situations it is less mental work to scan a list of hyperlinks and choose the one that is of interest than it is to think up the appropriate query terms to describe the information need. But there are diminishing returns to scanning links if it takes too long to find the label of interest, and there is always the possibility that the desired information is not visible. That is, browsing works only so long as appropriate links are available, and they have meaningful cues about the underlying information.

In a comparative study with 96 student participants finding information in online software manuals, Hertzum and Frokjaer (1996) found that browsing a hierarchical table of contents produced the best mean performance (compared to Boolean queries) but did not provide *stable* good performance, presumably because for some tasks the information structure used for the browsing was not suitable for the information need. They concluded that browsing is well-suited for some tasks, but unsuited for others. A study of the SuperBook system (Landauer et al. 1993) found similar results: when the queries were well-represented by hits on a table-of-contents representation, browsing worked better than keyword search, but did not improve results when the information structure did not match the information need.

The field of information architecture makes a distinction between *information structure* and *navigation structure*. Information structure defines the organization, textual labels, and controlled vocabulary terms for the content items of the site (Morville and Rosenfeld 2006). Navigation structure determines the paths that can be taken through the information structure, via the hyperlinked user interface (Newman and Landay 2000). Thus the success of a browsing interface depends in part on how well the presented information matches searchers' information needs and expectations. Another important property of browsing interfaces is that they should seamlessly integrate keyword querying with navigation of the underlying information structure. Many Web sites use dynamically generated metadata to provide a flexible, browsable information structure. Chapter 8 discusses information and navigation structures that aid in navigation and discovery within information collections.

3.5.4. *Information Scent for Navigating Information Structures*

When navigating within information structures, in order to make decisions about which information "patches" are promising to pursue, searchers must examine clues about where to find useful information. One part of Card's (2005) information foraging theory discusses the notion of information *scent*: cues that provide searchers with concise information about content that is not immediately perceptible. Pirolli (2007) notes that small pertubations in the accuracy of information scent can cause qualitative shifts in the cost of browsing; improvements in information scent are related to more efficient foraging. The detection of diminishing information scent is involved in decisions to leave an information patch.

Furnas (1997) also discusses the idea of information scent, stating that a target has scent at a link if the associated outlink information would lead an information navigator to take that link in pursuit of the given target. Furnas puts forward the *navigability proposition* that states that in order for a target to be findable by navigation from anywhere in the information structure, the path to that target must have good scent at every link.

Search results listings must provide the user with clues about which results to click; the notion of information scent can be applied to this problem. Spool (2007) suggests operationalizing the idea of information scent in Web site design by showing users informative hints about what kind of information will be found one hop away from the current Web page. One example suggestion is to augment links to product categories with a short list of the types of items to be found in that category. Nielsen (2003a) suggests, for the design of Web site home pages, showcasing sample content and prominently displaying navigation and search features, so searchers have the "scent" for what can be found by exploring further on the Web site. Nielsen (2004a) also points out that misleadingly strong scent can cause information browsers to overlook the best location to find their object of interest. Figure 3.4b shows the home page of the U.S. government's Bureau of Labor Statistics Web site, which has been carefully designed to have good information scent. Its design was refined via several iterations of evaluation and redesign, progressively adding more information as the information needs of the users of the site became clear (Marchionini and Levi 2003). An early version of the interface is shown in Figure 3.4a. In the earlier design, a graphical display of the main categories provided few cues about the rich information sources that lay behind them.

3.5.5. *Orienteering and Other Incremental Strategies*

A commonly observed search strategy is one in which the information seeker issues a quick, imprecise query in the hopes of getting into approximately the right part of the information space, and then doing a series of local navigation operations to get closer to the information of interest (Bates 1990; Marchionini 1995). O'Day and Jeffries (1993) use the term *orienteering* to describe search strategies in which searchers use information from their current situation to help determine where to go next, as opposed to trying to find the answer in one jump by writing a long complex query indicating the full information need.

A number of studies have shown that searchers tend to start out with short or general queries, inspect the results, and then modify those queries in an incremental feedback cycle (Anick 1994; Bates 1989; Eysenbach and Kohler 2002; Teevan et al. 2004; Waterworth and Chignell 1991). Bates (1979) also notes that a good tactic is to "break complex search queries down into subproblems and work on one problem at a time. This tactic is a well-established and productive technique in general problem solving."

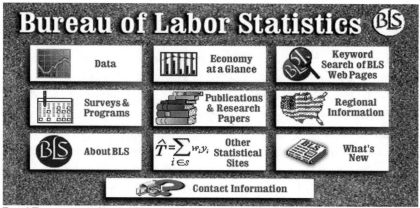

Data | Economy at a Glance | Keyword Search of BLS Web Pages
Surveys & Programs | Publications & Research Papers | Regional Information
About BLS | Other Statistical Sites | What's New | Contact Information

The Bureau of Labor Statistics is an agency within the U.S. Department of Labor.

(a)

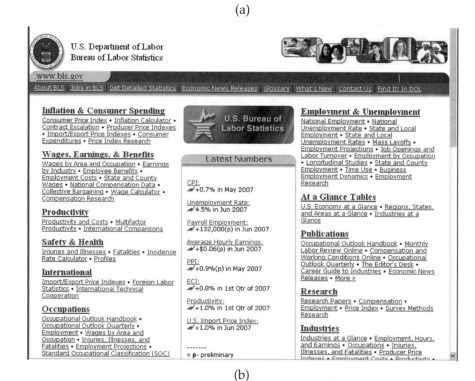

(b)

Figure 3.4. (a) [Before] An early version of the home page for the U.S. Bureau of Labor Statistics, which hid most of the content behind graphics, requiring users to make guesses as to what kind of information is available, and where on the site it might reside, from Marchionini and Levi (2003). (b) [After] The same home page redesigned to have high-quality information scent; intended for heavy users of government statistics.

Hertzum and Frokjaer (1996) noted this kind of behavior in a search interface usability study, finding that participants issue a sequence of queries rather than one all-inclusive query, enabling them to exploit information obtained earlier in the query sequence. This strategy is not without its drawbacks, as people can become too fixed on the their starting strategy. Hertzum and Frokjaer (1996) write:

> When a subject starts on a task, the first query expresses his initial, incomplete attempt to reach a solution. If this query does not provide the subject with the information needed, another must be formulated. At this point the user is subject to what psychologists call anchoring, i.e., the tendency to make insufficient adjustments to initial values when judging under uncertainty... Thus, the subjects may tend to refrain from abandoning the initial query terms or from adjusting them very far, making the subsequent queries biased toward the initial one.

Russell (2006) also observed this kind of "thrashing" behavior in Google search engine logs.

Teevan et al. (2004) studied the information seeking behavior of 15 computer science graduate students over a period of one week. They observed extensive use of orienteering behavior, even when a more direct search might be more efficient. In most of these cases, participants began with an information resource that they were already familiar with, and followed links from that resource. For example, one student wanted to find the office number for a particular professor. As he had seen that professor's Web page previously, rather than search for it via a query on a search engine, he first navigated to the mathematics department Web page for the university, and from there to a link for faculty Web pages, and from there to the desired page. It might have required fewer steps to simply type in a query containing the professor's name and the phrase "office number" to find the same result, but this approach requires the searcher to spell the professor's name correctly, rely on the word "office" appearing on her Web page, and make other guesses about the behavior of the search engine that may not hold true. In other examples, searchers took conceptually large steps followed by smaller ones. Teevan et al. use the term *teleporting* to distinguish orienteering from a more directed behavior in which a long, precise query is typed. In a large study with 714 participants, Bergman et al. (2008) found that, when looking for files on their desktop computer, desktop search was used only 10–15% of the time, with navigation of file structure strongly preferred.

Thus, in many cases, searchers followed known paths that require small steps that move them closer to their goal, potentially reducing the likelihood of error. Teevan et al. (2004) speculated that this approach is cognitively less taxing than fully specifying a query, as searchers do not have to articulate exactly what they are looking for precisely. Teevan et al. also noted that this kind of behavior allows the searcher to retain information about the context in which the information occurs.

The typical use of a Web search engine is often incremental in the fashion described above. This may be in part because today Web search engines are very fast; a typical query returns results within a fraction of a second. This makes natural a strategy that relies on "testing the water" with general queries followed by rapidly narrowing the results with reformulation. It is well-known from search engine query logs that a large proportion of search sessions contain query reformulations (Jansen et al. 2005, 2007a). It is furthermore known that searchers tend to look at only the top-ranked retrieved results (Granka et al. 2004; Joachims et al. 2005). This suggests that the orienteering strategy is a common one for Web search: users issue general queries, get information about the results, reformulate based on information seen in the results, and then navigate to promising-looking links or else give up.

Some of today's Web search engines support longer queries well, and there is evidence that expert searchers tend to issue longer queries. If this trend continues, and/or if Web search engines begin to support full natural language queries reliably, searchers may begin to use more teleporting in their queries.

3.6. Sensemaking: Search as Part of a Larger Process

It is convenient to divide the entire information access process into two main components: information retrieval through searching and browsing, and analysis and synthesis of results. This broader process is often referred to in the literature as *sensemaking* (Pirolli and Card 2005; Russell et al. 1993, 2006). Sensemaking refers to an iterative process of formulating a conceptual representation of a large volume of information. Search plays only one part in this process; some sensemaking activities involve search throughout, while others consist of doing a batch of search followed by a batch of analysis and synthesis. Sensemaking is most often applied to information-intensive tasks such as intelligence analysis, scientific research, and the legal discovery process.

Several studies have elucidated the different components of sensemaking. A study by Cowley et al. (2005) of nine intelligence analysts working in a simulated task environment found that they spent on average an equal amount of time in a Web browser (searching and reading results listings and documents themselves), in a word processor (saving references and analyzing them), and in the file system (organizing files and directories and using the desktop) (Wright et al. 2006).

Patterson et al. (2001), in a study of intelligence analysts, noted that a tool is needed that "would allow the easy manipulation, viewing, and tagging of small text bundles, as well as aids for identifying, tracking, and revising judgments about relationships between data." Their study also suggested that analysts need tools to help to corroborate data and rule out competing hypotheses, and they need to recognize the absence of or gaps in information.

After interviewing intelligence analysts about how they do their work, Pirolli and Card (2005) described the process as consisting of an information foraging loop consisting of seeking, filtering, reading, and extracting information, and a sensemaking loop consisting of iterative development of a mental model that best fits the information seen as well as what was known beforehand.

O'Day and Jeffries (1993) studied business analysts working with search intermediaries. They observed three main kinds of information seeking tasks: monitoring a well-known topic over time (such as researching competitors' activities each quarter), following a plan or stereotyped series of searches to achieve a particular goal (such as keeping up to date on good business practices), and exploring a topic in an undirected fashion (as when getting to know an unfamiliar industry). Information seeking was only one part of the full work process their subjects were engaged in. In between searching sessions many different kinds of work was done with the retrieved information, including reading and annotating (O'Hara and Sellen 1997) and analysis. O'Day and Jeffries (1993) examined the analysis steps in more detail, finding that 80% of this work fell into six main types: finding trends, making comparisons, aggregation, identifying a critical subset, assessing, and interpreting. The remainder consisted of cross-referencing, summarizing, finding evocative visualizations for reports, and miscellaneous activities.

The standard Web search interface does not do a good job of supporting the sensemaking process. Patterson et al. (2001) also reported on a controlled observational study in which 10 professional intelligence analysts performed an information gathering and analysis task. (The analysts were asked to determine the causes and impacts of the failure of the first flight of the Ariane 501 rocket launcher in 1996.) They were given 3–4 hours to complete the task, a collection of 2,000 documents, 9 of which had been pre-determined to be "high-profit" (of high topical relevancy and high utility for analyzing the event), and a "baseline" toolset that supported keyword queries, browsing articles by dates and titles sorted by relevance or date, and cutting and pasting of selected portions of documents to a text editor.

The resulting reports were judged in terms of quality and accuracy; the better reports were defined as those whose authors found high-profit documents. The overall characteristic that distinguished analysts who discovered high-profit documents from those who did not was the persistence of the analysts; those who read more documents and spent more time on the task did better than those who did not. A similar result was found in another intelligence analysis study by Jonker et al. (2005).

In the same vein, Tabatabai and Shore (2005) found that expert searchers were more patient than novices, and this, along with a positive attitude, led to better search outcomes. Factors that did *not* predict success included the kinds of queries issued, the percentage of retrieved documents that were of high-profit in the results, and the number of years of experience of the analysts (which ranged from 7 to 14 years). Nevertheless, it is likely that interfaces designed to support the sensemaking task directly could lead to improvements for users of all backgrounds. Chapter 7 discusses user interfaces to support the sensemaking process explicitly.

3.7. Information Needs and Query Intent

Information seeking encompasses a broad range of information needs, from focused fact finding to exploratory browsing (Sutcliffe and Ennis's 1998). People have different search needs at different times and in different contexts. Search problems span the spectrum from looking up a fact such as "What is the typical height of an adult male giraffe?" to building up knowledge about a topic, such as "What shall we do during our vacation in Barcelona?" to browsing collections, such as art museum images, to supporting ground-breaking scientific research, such as synthesizing the literature to help determine the cause of Raynaud's disease. Shneiderman (2008) makes a distinction between "1-minute" search and "1-week to 1-month search," reflecting the difference between a fast, passing question and a longer-term information need.

The term *information need* is used throughout the search interface literature. Wilson (1981) points out the problematic nature of attempting to define it, but does propose the following:

> [W]hen we talk of users' "information needs" we should not have in mind some conception of a fundamental, innate, cognitive or emotional "need" for information, but a conception of in-formation (facts, data, opinion, advice) as one means towards the end of satisfying such fundamental needs.

Others have defined information need in terms of the search system. Shneiderman et al. (1997) define it as:

> [T]he perceived need for information that leads to someone using an information retrieval system in the first place.

In response to this, Dearman et al. (2008) define information need as:

> [W]hen an individual requires any information to complete a task, or to satisfy the curiosity of the mind, independent of the method used to address the need, and regardless of whether the need is satisfied or not.

A number of researchers have attempted to taxonomize and tally the types of information needs that searchers have, and to categorize and characterize individual queries. Some of these efforts made use of surveys and questionnaires, others used in-person observation, and still others used query log analysis as a way to acquire a large-scale, representative understanding of the user population. The resulting query classifications are not necessarily ideal, but because they are often referred to, and because the authors of the studies computed relative frequency of occurrence of the entries in the taxonomies, it is useful to look at their findings in detail. There have also been attempts to automatically classify queries according to the underlying intent, also discussed below. Today, Web search engines are incorporating query classification into their ranking analysis.

3.7.1. *Web Log-Based Query Taxonomies*

Prior to the Web, search engine designers could safely assume that searchers had an informational goal in mind (Broder 2002; Rose and Levinson 2004). This was due in part to the limited population of searchers (primarily students, legal analysts, scientific researchers, business analysts) and to the kind of data that could be searched (newswire, legal cases, journal article abstracts). The queries to these systems were often long, or contained Boolean operators. Users had to carefully craft their queries, because they often paid by the minute, and careless query formulation was expensive.

As the Web developed, it became the case that not only were queries shorter and simpler, but the types of information available were quite different. As opposed to legal cases or academic papers, the Web included information about organizations (where they are located, what their phone numbers are, what their business is), products, and individuals. Correspondingly, the underlying goals of user queries were often quite different than in the older systems. In an attempt to demonstrate how information needs for Web search differ from the assumptions of pre-Web information retrieval systems, Broder (2002) created a taxonomy of Web search goals. He then estimated the frequency of such goals by a combination of an online survey (3,200 responses, 10% response rate) and a manual analysis of 1,000 query from the AltaVista query logs. The three types of "need behind the query" that he identified were:

- *Navigational*: The immediate intent is to reach a particular site (24.5% survey, 20% query log).
- *Informational*: The intent is to acquire some information assumed to be present on one or more Web pages (39% survey, 48% query log).
- *Transactional*: The intent is to perform some Web-mediated activity (36% survey, 30% query log).

This taxonomy has been heavily influential in discussions of query types on the Web.

Rose and Levinson (2004) followed up on Broder's (2002) work, again using Web query logs, but developing a taxonomy that differed somewhat from Broder's (2002). They retained the navigational and informational categories, but noted that much of what happens on the Web is the acquisition and consumption of online resources, such as song lyrics, knitting patterns, and software downloads. Thus they replace Broder's (2002) transactions category with a broader category of *resources*, meaning information artifacts that users consume in some manner other than simply reading for information (although they somewhat confusingly categorize shopping queries under the informational category). They also introduced subcategories for the three main categories, including the interesting subcategory of *advice seeking* (which has become popular on human question answering sites; see Chapter 12).

Rose and Levinson (2004) manually classified a set of 1,500 AltaVista search engine log queries. For two sets of 500 queries, the labeler saw just the query and the retrieved documents; for the third set the labeler also saw which item(s) the searcher clicked on. They found that the classifications that used the extra information about clickthrough did not significantly change the proportions of assignments to each category. However, because they did not directly compare judgements with and without click information on the same queries, this is only weak evidence that query plus retrieved documents is sufficient to classify query intent. (To bolster their claim, a similar result was found by Shen et al. (2005a), who developed an algorithm to effectively classify queries into subject-matter topics without using clickthrough data.)

Rose and Levinson (2004) found a smaller proportion of navigational queries than did Broder's (2002) (an average of 13% compared to his average of 22%), but this difference may have to do with differences in sampling and search engine user bases for the two studies. They also found that informational queries were about 61% of the information needs, a much higher proportion than Broder's (2002) average of 45%.

3.7.2. *Web Log-Based Query Topic Classification*

Queries from Web query logs can be classified according to the *topic* of the query, independent of the type of information need. For example, a search involving the topic of weather can consist of the simple information need of looking at today's forecast, or the rich and complex information need of studying meteorology.

Over many years, Spink and Jansen et al. (Jansen and Spink 2006; Jansen et al. 2005, 2007a; Spink et al. 2002) have manually analyzed samples of query logs to track a number of different trends. One of the most notable is the change in topic mix. In one article, they compared a manual analysis on AltaVista logs from 1997 with queries from the Dogpile metasearch engine in 2005 (Jansen et al. 2007b). They found that queries relating to sex and pornography declined from 16.8% in 1997 to just 3.6% in 2005. Commerce-related queries now dominate the query logs, claiming 30.4% in this study, up from 13.3% in 1997 (Spink et al. 2002) (see Table 3.1.).

As an alternative to manual classification of query topics, Shen et al. (2005a) described an algorithm for automatically classifying Web queries into a set of pre-defined topics. The main idea is to use a Web search engine to retrieve the top *n* results for a query, and then look at the categories that have been manually associated with those results in the past (using the Open Directory Project, ODP). They used a voting method to combine

Table 3.1. Topics manually assigned to 2,500 queries against the Dogpile metasearch engine in 2005 (Jansen et al. 2007b).

Rank	Topic	Number	Percent
1	Commerce, travel, employment, or economy	761	30.4
2	People, places, or things	402	16.0
3	Unknown or other	331	13.2
4	Health or sciences	224	8.9
5	Entertainment or recreation	177	7.0
6	Computers or Internet	144	5.7
7	Education or humanities	141	5.6
8	Society, culture, ethnicity, or religion	119	4.7
9	Sex or pornography	97	3.8
10	Government or legal	90	3.6
11	Arts	14	0.5

evidence from several measures, and returned the top scoring categories (up to five per query). Their results were quite strong, (an F-score of about 0.45 on 63 categories). Table 3.2. shows the results for five arbitrarily chosen queries. Another approach to this problem is described by Pu et al. (2002).

More recently, Broder et al. (2007) presented a highly accurate method (around 0.7 F-score) for classifying short, rare queries into a taxonomy of 6,000 categories. Because rare or infrequent queries are approximately half of all queries, this is an important advance. Using a commercial taxonomy which contained many documents assigned to each category, they trained a set of text classifiers. Given a query, they retrieved the top k documents using a search engine, classified documents according to the text classifier, and then used a voting algorithm to determine which class(es) best categorize the query. Gauch (2003) found that a similar approach worked well for creating profiles of user interests based on which documents they visited (see Chapter 9).

Table 3.2. Top two categories returned for five arbitrarily chosen queries submitted to the system of Q2C@UST (Shen et al. 2005a).

Query	Top category	Second category
chat rooms	Computers/Internet	Online Community/Chat
lake michigan lodges	Info/Local & Regional	Living/Travel & Vacation
stephen hawking	Info/Science & Tech	Info/Arts & Humanities
dog shampoo	Shopping/Buying Guides	Living/Pets & Animals
text mining	Computers/Software	Information/Companies

3.7.3. *Web Log-Based Analysis of Query Ambiguity*

Ambiguous queries are those queries that can be understood as corresponding to two or more distinct meanings: a query on `apple` may refer to the fruit or the computer manufacturer or the record label. A number of search interface ideas that are discussed in this book, although intended to be useful in a general way, turn out to be effective mainly for ambiguous queries (see Chapters 8 and 9). For this reason, some researchers have tried to estimate what proportion of queries truly are ambiguous.

One way to predict query ambiguity is to see what the diversity of clicks is for a given query. The thinking is that if users tend to click on the same set of links for a given query, that query indicates a single set of intentions, but if there is great diversity in the links clicked on, then the query is likely to be ambiguous either in meaning or in what user intentions it reflects.

Wen et al. (2002) did a clickthrough analysis of queries to an online encyclopedia, and found that identical query terms produced nearly identical clicks. They speculated that users were self-disambiguating by their choice of terms. Song et al. (2007) described an algorithm for estimating how many queries in a query log are ambiguous. They had 5 judges label 60 queries as either ambiguous or not, achieving 90% agreement. They then used a search engine to retrieve the top *n* documents for each query, and categorized those documents into a pre-defined ontology using the technique of Shen et al. (2005a). If the documents returned for a query fell into multiple categories, they considered that query to be ambiguous. Using this approach, they achieved 87% accuracy on a test set of 253 queries (using cross-validation). Applying this algorithm to a larger sample, they estimated that that sample contained only 16% ambiguous queries.

3.7.4. *Web Log-Based Analysis of Re-access Patterns*

Many searches are characterized by people re-accessing information that they have seen in the past (Aula et al. 2005a; Jones et al. 2001, 2002). This can be accomplished by saving previously visited information via Web browser bookmarks or using bookmarking Web sites such as delicious.com. The observations of Teevan et al. (2004) suggested that searchers often navigate to Web pages they have visited in the past rather than issuing a search engine query. However, there is also ample evidence that people use search engines as re-finding instruments. In another study,

Teevan et al. (2007) examined 13,000 queries and 22,000 search result clicks from a query log, and found that 40% of the queries led to a click on a result that the same user had clicked on in a past search session.

As is discussed in Chapter 9, researchers have made use of query log behavior to try to improve ranking algorithms, as well as to attempt to predict individual user's behavior and preferences based on past actions.

3.7.5. *Classifying Observed Search Behavior*

The previous section describes the classification of information needs based on query log analysis. Another approach is to observe people more directly and classify their search activities more broadly.

Kellar et al. (2006) collected statistics for self-reported task type frequency for Web browser users. Twenty-one university student participants used an instrumented Web browser that recorded their actions for one week, resulting in 1,192 task sessions (13,500 web pages). Participants were asked to label every Web page access with a task type from the taxonomy. The authors carefully developed a task type taxonomy to remove confusion about their meaning and ensured that the study participants would be able to consistently assign labels. The five main categories were:

- *Fact Finding:* Looking for specific facts or pieces of information; usually short lived tasks, completed over a single session. Examples were looking, searching or checking for tomorrow's weather, a recipe, a file (for download), a research paper, definitions, help with a game, java documentation, song lyrics, the average mass of a bullet.
- *Information Gathering:* A task that involves the collection of information, often from multiple sources. Can take place over multiple days. It is not always clear when the task is completed and there is not always one specific answer. Examples were looking for or researching information on a new laptop, conferences, new wireless card, making a resume, papers on policy-based network, renting a car, risk analysis, summer school courses.
- *Browsing:* A serendipitous task where Web pages are visited with no particular goal other than entertainment or to "see what's new." Sometimes this is done as part of a daily routine. Examples were looking for or reading blogs, browsing a Web site, the news, listening to music, movie trailers, updates on movie Web site, comics, wasting time.

Table 3.3. Web page task usage statistics from a study by (Kellar et al. 2006).

Task	% of total Web use	% that were repeats
Fact Finding	18.3	55.5
Information Gathering	13.5	58.5
Browsing	19.9	84.4
Transactions	46.7	95.2
Other	1.7	–

- *Transactions:* Online actions. Examples were checking or acting on email, banking, applying for a credit card, blogging, logging diet and exercise information, online shopping, sending a greeting, taking part in a survey.
- *Other:* Other activities, such as Web page maintenance.

Table 3.3. shows the frequency of activities according to the taxonomy. Nearly half the Web usages were attributable to online transactions, primarily email usage. Fact finding constituted about 18% of the tasks, and more than 55% of these were repeat activities. Repeated fact finding often had a monitoring aspect, such as checking the weather forecast daily. Information gathering was about 13% of the activities; many stretched over several days including one that lasted six days (researching graduate schools to apply to). Browsing constituted 19% of the tasks and included news reading, reading blogs, visiting gaming-related sites, and reading entertainment-related Web pages. There was evidence that monitoring occurs with different frequencies across different tasks.

Unfortunately, there are problems with attempting to compare these results to the query log studies described above. These are broader task classifications, so a subgoal like find the home page of an e-commerce site would be subsumed into online shopping. Thus, statistics of the more fine-grained activities seen at the query level (e.g., navigational queries) are not categorized as such. The tasks described correspond to all Web pages viewed, as opposed to only those examined in response to a search. And finally, many of the categorizations differ from both Broder's (2002) and Rose and Levinson's (2004). For example, in Kellar et al. (2006) accessing information about iPod prices is classified as information gathering, while the online shopping part of the process (potentially including the price comparison component) is categorized as transactional. Rose and

Levinson (2004) would list the search for the shopping information under informational and Broder (2002) would classify it as transactional.

3.8. Conclusions

This chapter has summarized the major theoretical models of information seeking, including:

- The Standard model,
- The Cognitive model,
- The Dynamic (Berry-picking) model,
- Information seeking in stages,
- Information seeking as a strategic process, including
  - Strategies as sequences of tactics,
  - Cost structure analysis and foraging theory,
  - Browsing versus search,
  - Orienteering and other incremental strategies, and
- Sensemaking.

The chapter also defined the notion of information need and summarized research on inferring the user's information need from records of their queries, and presented the major query intent taxonomies that are in common use today. These taxomonies are not comprehensive; they do not, for example, distinguish between ad hoc queries (spur of the moment, or one-time) and standing queries (an information need that a user is continually interested in), but they are referred to heavily in the literature and have helped shape thinking about query intent.

In the chapters that follow, an attempt is made to link the various interfaces designs and issues to aspects of these theoretical models. A potentially fruitful strategy for designing new search interfaces is to notice the gaps in support of these models, or the aspects that are not well-served in current designs. Additionally, many types of information needs are not currently supported well in search algorithms and interfaces. The next breakthrough in search interface design could arise from finding new techniques that better support how people are naturally inclined to conduct their searches.

4 Query Specification

In the query specification part of the information access process, the searcher expresses an information need by converting their internalized, abstract concepts into language, and then converting that expression of language into a query format that the search system can make use of. This chapter discusses the mechanisms by which information needs are expressed. The two main dimensions for the query specification process are:

(1) The kind of information the searcher supplies. Query specification input spans a spectrum from full natural language sentences, to keywords and key phrases, to syntax-heavy command language-based queries.

(2) The interface mechanism the user interacts with to supply this information. These include command line interfaces, graphical entry form-based interfaces, and interfaces for navigating links.

Each is discussed in the sections below.

4.1. Textual Query Specification

Queries over collections of textual information usually take on a textual form (querying against multimedia is discussed in Chapter 12). The next subsections discuss different kinds of textual input for query specification.

4.1.1. Search Over Surrogates vs. Full Text

In older bibliographic search systems, users could only search over metadata that hinted at the underlying contents. To look for a book on a topic in an online library catalog, the searcher was restricted to the text in the title or the few subject labels that the librarian who had catalogued the book had used to describe it (Borgman 1996). A book that mentions an interesting idea, but only in a secondary manner, would most likely not be indexed with that term (Cousins 1992). Using a standard library catalog, a searcher who was interested in discussions of narwhales in literature would not have been able to discover that *Moby Dick* contains several discussions of these unicorn-like fish. Search over full text gives users direct access to the words used by the author, rather than being restricted to matching against a document surrogate. Full-text search has become the norm for most kinds of search over textual content.

4.1.2. *Keyword Queries*

With the rise of the Web came the dominance of keywords as the primary query input type. Keyword queries consist of a list of one or more words or phrases – rather than full natural language statements – whose intention is to find documents containing those words that are likely to be relevant to the user's information need. Example English keyword queries (from Google Trends and Dogpile SearchSpy, November 1, 2008) include flip cam, fresh chilli paste recipes, and video game addiction. Some keyword queries consist of lists of different words and phrases, which together suggest a topic (e.g., early voting florida). Many others are noun compounds and proper nouns (thanksgiving wallpaper, jedi mind tricks, sherlock holmes, and daylight savings time change). Less frequently, keyword queries contain syntactic fragments including prepositions (tots to teens, matron of honor speech) and verbs (watch pokeman), and in some cases, full syntactic phrases (history of fish farming in nigeria, construction plans for a trebuchet).

4.1.2.1. Keyword Query Statistics

Statistics on query length and composition have been recorded since early in the Web's existence. These measures have shown that the average query length has grown over time, and the percentage of one-word queries has shrunk. Average query lengths were approximately 2.4 in 1997 and 1998 (Jansen et al. 1998; Silverstein et al. 1999). One-word queries occupied 31%

Table 4.1. Frequencies of query lengths (in words), rounded to the nearest thousand. The longest query was of length 25. Data from Jansen et al. (2007b), based on query logs from Dogpile.com on May 6, 2005.

Length	Occurrences	Percent
1	281,000	18.5
2	491,000	32.3
3	373,000	24.5
4	194,000	12.7
5	95,000	6.3
6	45,000	3.0
7	22,000	1.5
8	12,000	0.8
9	6,000	0.4

of the queries in a study using data from 1997 (Jansen et al. 1998) and 26% from a study using data from 1998 (Silverstein et al. 1999). Jansen and Spink (2006) found inconclusive evidence for a slight trend toward the shrinking of the percentage of one-word queries. By contrast, another study by Jansen et al. (2005) found the percentage of three-word queries increasing from nearly 28% in 1998 to 49% in 2002. More recently, Jansen et al. (2007b) conducted a study using 1.5M queries gathered in May 2005, from the Dogpile.com search engine. This study found that the mean length of the queries was 2.8 terms, with only 18.5% as one-word queries. Table 4.1. shows the distribution of query lengths for this dataset.

4.1.2.2. Keyword Queries: Statistical Ranking vs. Conjunctions

In the early days of the Web, search engines used statistical ranking functions, but these did not work well with the short keyword queries that Web searchers were writing. Furthermore, searchers were not usually interested in high recall for the kinds of information available on the Web. Searchers also found statistical ranking on short queries to be confusing, not understanding why, say, the highest ranked documents might contain only one query term out of three (Lake 1998).

The meaning of search term conjunction is more easily understood than statistical ranking (Muramatsu and Pratt 2001). However, when only a small collection of documents is available, a ranking algorithm that automatically requires all terms in a query to be present in the retrieved documents will end up with empty results sets (and very frustrated users) much of the time. With a larger document pool, a query on any combination of three or fewer terms is likely to return a result, even if all the terms are conjoined. Because the number of (English) pages on the Web is so enormous, conjoining query terms is likely to return many results, and because they are more transparent to the user than a weighted term score, conjunction-based queries became the default for Web search.

Conjunction-based queries, combined with giving higher priority to results in which keywords occur close together, displaying of query keywords in context in the document summary (Clarke et al. 2007), and giving higher ranking to pages from higher-quality Web sites, combined to make search engine ranking of keyword queries more successful and more understandable than in its early days.

4.1.2.3. Keyword Queries vs. Natural Language Queries

As discussed above, in Web search engines, keyword specification and matching has become the norm. An alternative to keyword queries is to allow users to enter full sentence questions or search statements, and have the system attempt to find relevant information and/or supply answers to questions. Evidence from the literature suggests that asking questions using natural language is a more intuitive input method, and that people who are new to using search engines tend to assume that asking a question is the right way to start. This is not surprising, since asking questions is how we seek information from other people.

In an early study from 1997, Pollock and Hockley (1997) found that some novices try to enter natural language queries to Web search engines. Studies of the behavior of children who have not yet learned the limitations of search engines show that for many their natural inclination is to simply ask the search system a question. Bilal (2000) found, in a study of 22 seventh-grade children searching for factual information, 35% attempted to begin with a natural language question. The search engine under study produced empty results sets with this kind of query, and so the children had to unlearn the question-asking approach. In another study by Schacter et al. (1998), 63% of 32 fifth- and sixth-grade children used full-sentence queries on Web search engines. In a pre-Web study using an electronic encyclopedia, Marchionini (1989) found that many younger searchers entered full sentence questions into the system. Finally, in the early days of the Web, the search engine AskJeeves (now Ask) purported to allow people to ask natural language questions. Although it never really supported this functionality in a robust and scalable way, many people were attracted to the engine because they thought it would be able to answer questions.

Pollock and Hockley (1997) also found that, for novice searchers, the notion of iterative searching was unfamiliar. They assumed that if their first attempt failed then either they were incapable of searching or the system did not contain information relevant to their interest. Thus, novice searchers must learn to expect that they must scan a search results list, navigate through Web sites, and read through Web pages to try to find the information they seek. A novice searcher who starts with a question like "For NFL players who have suffered depression after sustaining multiple concussions, which positions did they play?" quickly learns that the search engine does not respond by answering this question. Searchers must learn that search engines work by finding articles that match the words that they typed in, and that they must guess which combinations of words are likely to be found in documents that contain relevant information, for example, `NFL depression concussions`.

Aula et al. (2005a) note one expert explicitly articulating a strategy to reflect the unnatural nature of keyword querying, stating "I choose search terms based not specifically on the information I want, but rather on how I could imagine someone wording a site that contains that information." Reflecting on the disconnect between keyword search and what might be a more natural search strategy, a lead engineer for ranking at Google was recently quoted as saying "Search over the last few years has moved from 'Give me what I typed' to 'Give me what I want.' " (Hansell 2007).

4.1.3. *Automated Question Answering*

The most natural use of natural language queries is in the asking of questions. The main reason search engines did not originally support automated question answering is that the technology did not exist to do so in a robust, scalable manner. (There were also early efforts to supply natural language interfaces to database systems, which did not catch on for similar reasons (Androutsopoulos et al. 1995).)

There has recently been an upsurge of research in full-sentence question answering, propelled in large part by an increase in government funding and by a TREC-based question answering task and competition (Voorhees 1999, 2003). For several years starting in 1999, the track focused on *factoid* questions: fact-based short-answer questions such as What Spanish explorer discovered the Mississippi? and When did World War I end? Subsequent competitions added the tasks of finding a list of answers to the question, for example, Who were the members of the Oakland A's starting lineup in 1976?, definition questions such as What is a golden parachute?, and general biographical questions such as Who is Marilyn Monroe? that require systems to combine information from multiple documents, and to synthesize a more general answer. In 2005 the task was made still harder, requiring systems to provide answers for a series of cascading questions. For example, When was Amway founded?, Where is it headquartered?, Name the officials of the company., and What is the name 'AMWAY' short for? The corresponding research has resulted in systems that, for factoid-type questions especially, can enjoy great success.

4.1.3.1. Techniques for Automated Question Answering

Rather than generating an answer from scratch, question answering systems attempt to link a natural language query to the most pertinent sentence, paragraph, or page of information that has already been written. They differ from standard search engines in that they make use of the structure of the question and of the text from which the answers are drawn. An early example of an automated general-topic question answering system was the Murax system (Kupiec 1993), which determined from the syntax of a question if the user was asking for a person, place, or date. It then attempted to find sentences within encyclopedia articles that contain noun phrases that appear in the question, since these sentences are likely to contain the answer to the question. For example, given the question "Who was the Pulitzer Prize-winning novelist that ran for mayor of New York City?" the system extracted the noun phrases "Pulitzer Prize," "winning novelist," "mayor," and "New York City." It then looked for proper nouns representing people's names (since this is a "who" question) and found, among others, the following sentences:

> The Armies of the Night (1968), a personal narrative of the 1967 peace march on the Pentagon, won *Mailer* the *Pulitzer Prize* and the National Book Award.

> In 1969 *Mailer* ran unsuccessfully as an independent candidate for *mayor* of *New York City*.

Thus the two sentences link together the relevant noun phrases and the system hypothesized (correctly) from the title of the article in which the sentences appear that Norman Mailer was the answer.

Another early approach to automated question-answering was the FAQ Finder system (Burke et al. 1997) which matched question-style queries against question–answer pairs on various topics. The system used a standard IR search to find the most likely FAQ (frequently asked questions) files for the question and then matched the terms in the question against the question portion of the question–answer pairs.

Numerous more recent approaches use variations of the Murax approach, adding statistics that utilize the vast collection of the Web to successfully answer many kinds of questions (Dumais et al. 2002; Harabagiu et al. 2000; Ittycheriah et al. 2001; Ramakrishnan and Paranjpe 2004; Ravichandran and Hovy 2001). There are a number of startup companies that build on this research and attempt to support natural language querying and question answering using scalable natural parsing and other computional linguistics technologies. For example, the startup Powerset (recently acquired by Microsoft) successfully responds to questions like `What did Steve Jobs say about the iPod?` with sentences like *Steve Jobs has stated that Apple makes little profit from song sales, although Apple uses the store to promote iPod sales.* and *Steve Jobs has argued that the iPod nano was a necessary risk*...and questions such as `origins of the word Halloween?` with sentences like *The term Halloween is shortened from All Hallows' Even.* This works in part by expanding words like "say" to "has argued" and "word" to "term."

Major Web search engines currently do not support full-sentence queries or question answering, most likely because the technology still is not reliable enough to present in mature products. However, as discussed in Chapter 1, some are becoming more adept at responding to long queries. Natural language queries are also likely to become an important supplement for organizations' Web sites and for software products, to more effectively handle customer questions.

4.1.3.2. Answer Types for Question-Like Queries

An interesting aspect of question answering that differentiates it from standard information retrieval is that the answer of interest contains words that are *not* in the query. Thus boldfacing the query terms in answer to a question is not the right thing to do – rather, it is the answer that should be highlighted. A question also arises as to what kind of and how much context to show surrounding the answer. An advantage of question answering is that the user can receive a simple, terse answer, such as *30 feet* to the question How deep is it safe to dive without worrying about getting the bends? But a contextless answer from a machine-based source is not necessarily the best interface, as a reasonable user would want the system to justify, explain, or at least show the context supporting the answer. Lin et al. (2003) conducted a usability study with 32 computer science graduate students comparing four types of answer context: exact answer, answer-in-sentence, answer-in-paragraph, and answer-in-document. To remove effects of incorrect answers, they used a system that produced only correct answers, drawn from an online encyclopedia. They found that most participants (53%) preferred paragraph-sized chunks, noting that a sentence did not supply much more information beyond the exact answer, and a full document was oftentimes too long. That said, 23% preferred full documents, 20% preferred sentences, and one participant preferred exact answer. Kaisser et al. (2008) performed a followup-study which showed that for many queries, the ideal answer length and type can be predicted by a person by seeing only the query. They also found that people judging relevance prefer results of different lengths, depending on the type of query. For a fact-based query, phrase or sentence-length results were preferred. For queries seeking advice or general information about a topic, longer answers were preferred.

4.1.4. *Paragraph-Length Textual Queries*

Another form of text-based querying is one in which the user requests that the system find documents that are substantially similar to a very long query or a user-supplied document. This kind of query was much studied in the information retrieval research literature in the 1980s–1990s. The emphasis was on producing retrieval results with high recall, since finding all relevant documents can be quite useful for scholars trying to do thorough literature reviews, legal professionals trying to find all information about a case (Blair and Maron 1985), and intelligence analysts trying to assess a situation.

This desiderata of high recall was embodied in the TREC competition *ad hoc* ranking task (TREC is discussed in Chapter 2), where the goal was to retrieve 1000 relevant documents for every query. In the TREC scoring, what mattered was whether or not a document had been judged relevant,

not how relevant it was, nor how much new information it brought beyond what had already been seen. (A system would not be penalized if
the first *k* retrieved documents all contained redundant information.) It
was found that long (paragraph-length) queries produced higher recall
than short queries.

For long queries, it is unlikely that every term will be found in one document within a collection, and so are best served by statistical ranking algorithms which apply empirically determined weights to each query term,
and combine them statistically to provide a ranking.

It is unclear how realistic it is to expect people to search for documents
that are similar to other documents. (A startup company named Deep-
Dyve is currently promoting search using large paragraphs of text as the
query, and research documents as the collection, to improve search as a research tool.) However, text similarity measures are very useful for specialized tasks, such as automatic text categorization (Sebastiani 2002), matching reviewers to submitted manuscripts (Dumais and Nielsen 1992), and
clustering similar news articles for news aggregation services (Das et al.
2007).

4.1.5. *Automated Transformations of Textual Queries*

Search engines may manipulate or transform textual queries in several
ways. Some systems automatically normalize morphological variants of
words, that is, convert a query on `dogs` to one on `(dog OR dogs)` or convert `building` to `(build OR building)` (the latter may lead to poor
results, because the noun form of `build` is conflated with the verb form
derived from `building`). This practice is sometimes known as *stemming*.
Other transformations include ignoring common function words (*stopwords*), and expanding terms with synonyms or related forms (e.g., converting `mold` to `mould`).

Search engine ranking algorithms must walk a fine line between making transformations that are hidden but helpful and making the user feel
that the system is inscrutable. As mentioned in Chapter 1, Muramatsu
and Pratt (2001) studied users' understanding of the transformations that
search engines apply to query terms. Fourteen participants were asked
to issue one pre-specified query across two search engines for each of four
transformation types: Boolean operators, stopword removal, suffix expansion, and term order variation. Queries and search engines were carefully
chosen to exaggerate and highlight the effect of the query transformation,

and participants were asked to first state what they thought would happen before seeing the results. In detail, the transformations investigated and the participants' responses to them were:

- Application of Boolean operators, comparing a search engine that automatically OR'd all terms versus one that AND'd terms. The query was `scuba snorkel arooba`; the misspelling of "aruba" was used to force the AND'ed engine to produce an empty results listing. Eight out of 14 participants expected the system to return many results related to both scuba and snorkeling but few if any mentions of Aruba. After seeing the results, 5 participants could not come up with a meaningful explanation of the results; 6 were close to accurately describing the difference, but 3 required the side-by-side comparison to do so. The last 3 participants could explain the behavior for the AND query but not the OR. (For more on Boolean usability, see Section 4.4.)
- Stopword removal, comparing a system that removed stopwords versus one that did not, on the query `to be or not to be` (all stopwords). Before the query was issued, 10 out of 14 expected to see results related to Shakespeare and/or Hamlet. After seeing the empty results for one engine, 3 participants assumed the search engine did not contain literature in its collection or had a different collection, 6 expressed low expectations for good results because of the commonality of the words, but only 3 expressed the notion of the search engine dropping the results. 9 out of 14 were unable to explain the results in a way that remotely resembled removal of stopwords.
- Suffix term expansion, comparing a search engine that does the expansion versus one that does not (in this case the query was `run` which would be expanded to `running` and `runner`). Participants were surprised at the lack of results pertaining to athletics for the engine that did not do term expansion, and only 3 participants were able to explain the results in a manner related to suffix expansion.
- Term order sensitivity, comparing a search engine that changes results based on term order and proximity versus one that does not consider either property. In this case, two queries were compared: `fire boat` and `boat fire`. Only 5 out of 14 participants expected the results for the two queries to differ, and only 5 participants had a vaguely accurate explanation for the difference, with one person stating that one engine "separates the two words and searches for the meaning" while the other "understands the meaning of the phrase." In scanning the

bolded query term hits in the document surrogates, some participants noticed the difference in proximity for ranking.

These results suggest that stemming is useful, but removing stopwords can be hazardous from a usability perspective. It also suggests that certain features, such as taking order and proximity into account, can be used to improve the results without confusing users despite the fact that they may not be aware of or understand those transformations. Other studies suggest that it is better to show potential transformations to users and let them decide whether or not to use them than to do them explicitly; however, if automatic transformations are unlikely to lead to misconceptions, they can be beneficial.

Another way search systems use query transformations is to show them as suggestions for revising the query. This topic is discussed extensively in Chapter 6.

4.2. Query Specification via Entry Form Interfaces

Today, the standard interface for query specification is an entry form and an activation button. The label on the button ranges from *Go* to *Search* to *Fetch*, and Microsoft's search engine dispenses with the textual label entirely, instead showing only a magnifying glass icon (see Figure 4.1a). (Just prior to completion of this book, Microsoft renamed their search engine Bing and made major changes to its interface.) Execution of the search action usually can also be triggered by striking the keyboard Return key when the entry form is selected. Today, search forms often include dropdown menus that show previously issued queries whose prefix matches what has been typed so far (see an example from Microsoft's search in Figure 4.1b). On Web sites whose content is divided into different categories, some search engines use a combination of a drop-down menu to select a category of content to search within, alongside the entry form. This is sometimes called *scoped search*, and an example from eBay is shown in Figure 4.2. The default is usually set to search across the entire site or collection.

Some interfaces allow the searcher to cut-and-paste long swaths of text into the search box, whereas others present short entry forms and limit the number of terms that the system will accept for processing. Researchers have speculated that short query forms lead to short queries. To test this hypothesis, Franzen and Karlgren (2000) designed two different query

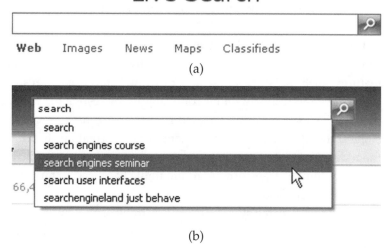

(a)

(b)

Figure 4.1. Standard query specification forms. (a) Microsoft's Live search does not include a textual label on the activation button. (b) An illustration of the increasingly common interaction mechanism in which a search engine query form provides a drop-down list showing queries that the user has issued in the past that matches the prefix typed so far. From live.search.com. (Microsoft product screen shot reprinted with permission from Microsoft Corporation.)

entry form boxes. The first showed one empty line and only 18 visible characters (but would accept up to 200 characters) and the second showed 6 lines of 80 characters each, which allowed arbitrarily long queries to be entered. The authors asked 19 linguistics students to use one of the two interfaces and to find relevant documents for three queries. There was a statistically significant difference between the two conditions, with those using the short box using 2.81 words on average, versus 3.43 for those using the larger box.

The wording above the text box can influence the kind of information that searchers type in. Belkin et al. (2003) presented 32 participants with

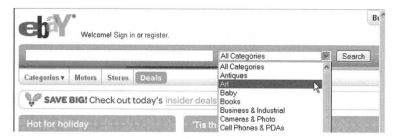

Figure 4.2. eBay.com's search form with subject-oriented drop-downs for "scoped" search.

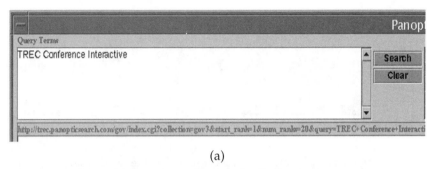

(a)

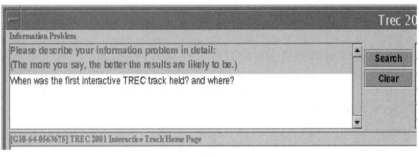

(b)

Figure 4.3. Interfaces used in an experiment in which the message for query specification was varied. (a) The sparse version and (b) the more verbose version, from
Belkin et al. (2003).

a large query box (5 lines of 40 characters each) and varied the message
shown (see Figure 4.3). In one case searchers saw a heading of "Query
Terms" above the search box, and in another they saw "Information Problem" above the box, and within the box, the message: "Please describe
your information problem in detail: (The more you say, the better the results are likely to be.)." They found on average that participants entered
longer queries with the more verbose interface (6.02 words versus 4.19)
and performed significantly fewer iterations (2.09 versus 2.64). However,
they did not find a relationship between correctness of results and query
length.

After many years of small search forms, it has recently become fashion-
able on many Web sites to make the font in the search box entry form very
large and colorful, thus drawing attention to the search facility. It has also
become common to put a hint into the search box to indicate what kind of
search the user should do (see Figure 4.4 and Figure 1.6).

Studies and query logs show that people often confuse the web
browser's address bar with a search entry form (Hargittai 2002). In recent
years, Web browsers have implemented support for Web search directly

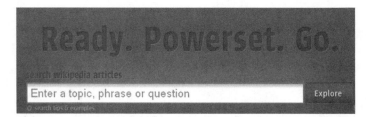

Figure 4.4. An example of a modern style entry form, with a large font size for the text of the query and a grayed-out hint indicating what kind of information to enter. From powerset.com. (Microsoft product screen shot reprinted with permission from Microsoft Corporation.)

into the address bar, and the Chrome browser has gone so far as to elimi-nate the distinction between an address bar and the query form altogether. In that browser, everything is assumed to be a query to a Web search en-gine unless URL syntax is used explicitly.

When presenting a query interface, it is important not to force the user to make selections before offering a search box. For instance, the search dialogue box for Microsoft Windows XP forces the user to decide which type of information, in terms of file format, they want to search over before seeing a search box (see Figure 4.5). An entry form should immediately be offered that defaults to searching all file types, with an option to refine. Alternatively, refinement can be offered after the initial query, as shown in Microsoft Researcher's Phlat interface (Cutrell et al. 2006b) (see Figure 8.3 in Chapter 8).

Figure 4.5. Microsoft desktop search start dialogue box, which requires the user to select a type of infor-mation to search over before making a search entry form available. (From Microsoft Windows XP Profes-sional Version 2002. Microsoft product screen shot reprinted with permission from Microsoft Corpora-tion.)

Figure 4.6. One view of dynamic query term suggestions. An example from Microsoft in which only the first word in the query is matched against past queries.

4.3. Dynamic Term Suggestions During Query Specification

Chapter 6 discusses interfaces for suggesting terms to augment the user's query after they have received results. More recently, interfaces have appeared that suggest query terms dynamically, *as the user enters them*. In some cases, these *dynamic term suggestions* appear before the searcher has seen any retrieval results, and in others, the system dynamically shows documents that match the characters typed so far, adjusting the results list as more characters are typed. Dynamic query term suggestions (sometimes referred to as *auto-suggest, autosuggest,* or *search-as-you-type*) are a promising intermediate solution between requiring the user to think of terms of interest (and how to spell them) and navigating a long list of term suggestions.

Some dynamic term suggestion systems show only query suggestions whose prefix matches what has been typed so far. Figure 4.6 shows an example from Microsoft's dynamic query suggestions interface, which shows frequent queries whose first words contain the prefix that has been typed so far, canc, including cancer, cancun weather, and cancel. Dynamic query suggestions are not restricted to matching the prefix of the query alone. For instance, at eBay, typing in the letter d in the query form shows suggestions such as holiday doorbusters, digital cameras, and nintendo ds lite. Continuing to do shows suggestions like holiday doorbusters, dooney & bourke, and american girl doll. Web search engines today provide similar functionality in their toolbars.

The dynamic query suggestion approach falls within guidelines for dynamic queries by Shneiderman (1994). Although no usability studies have been done for this kind of interface, a large log study by Anick and Kantamneni (2008) found that, when measuring on four distinct days over a period of 17 weeks and 100,000 users, users clicked on the dynamic suggestions in the Yahoo Search Assist tool in 30–37% of the sessions (see Figure 1.4 in Chapter 1). The rapid spread of this facility suggests that dynamic real-time term suggestions are becoming the norm.

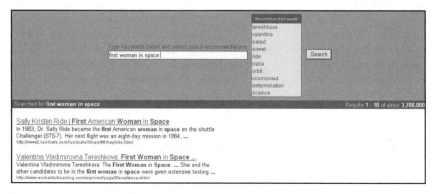

Figure 4.7. Experimental dynamic query suggestion form, from White and Marchionini (2007). New terms are suggested only after the space key is pressed.

White and Marchionini (2007) performed a study on a similar interaction method, on what they call *real time query expansion* (see Figure 4.7). After the user types a word and presses the keyboard space bar, the system queries a Web search engine and extracts terms from the surrogates for the 10 top-ranked documents. The top 10 term suggestions are shown after the first term is typed. The user can select one or more of the suggested terms by double-clicking it, or ignore the suggestions. This process continues with the system suggesting additional terms after each word is entered, until the query is completed (by pressing the Return key). Thus, the idea is similar to dynamic term suggestions, but less interactive, and responsive at the word level only, as opposed to at the character prefix level.

White and Marchionini (2007) compared this approach to a baseline system with no feedback (using Google Web search with identifying information removed) and another version of their system in which term suggestions are shown alongside the search results, after the query is entered (standard term suggestions). The study consisted of 36 students who compared the interfaces in a within-participants design. Using pre-defined queries, the study distinguished between known-item searches and open-ended exploratory searches, hypothesizing that term expansion would be more effective for the latter. When comparing time taken and quality of results, there were no significant differences among the systems, although the numbers trended towards the real time query expansion being more effective. The quality of search results were assessed by two judges, and the precision was found to be higher in the exploratory task for the dynamic term suggestions than for the post-retrieval suggestions, and both were higher than for the baseline. No quality differences were found for the known-item tasks.

Satisfaction scores revealed that participants found the baseline to be more effective and more usable, but found the dynamic suggestions to be more engaging and more enjoyable. Post-study questionnaires suggested that if the response time for the query suggestions had been faster, participants would have found them more useful. Many commented negatively on the delay (1.8 seconds average) between hitting the space bar and seeing the suggestions. Since modern term suggestion interfaces are much more reactive, this suggests that they are most likely found useful. Participants also made positive comments about the post-query suggestions, indicating that they were often helpful when the first query was unsuccessful.

White and Marchionini (2007) point out the potential danger in showing query term suggestions before retrieval results are seen, as the suggestions can lead the searcher down an erroneous path. They cite as an example the high prevalence of the suggested term `ride` for the query `Who was the first female astronaut in space?`. The correct answer is Soviet cosmonaut Valentina Tereshkova, but mention of Sally Ride, the first American woman in space, is frequent in the retrieved document summaries. This, compounded with the fact that the verb *ride* is a meaningfully related term to space travel, caused some participants to erroneously augment their query with this term. White and Marchionini (2007) note that if users see search results first, they are less likely to make this kind of mistake.

4.4. Query Specification Using Boolean and Other Operators

Before the rise of the Web, most commercial full-text systems and most bibliographic systems supported only Boolean and command-based queries. In many systems, users could query only over document surrogates, and not the text of the documents themselves as they were not available in electronic format (Cousins 1992). When full text was available, as seen in newswire and case law, Boolean queries were used as well, in part because they are more efficient to compute than statistical ranking (Rose 2006). A typical example drawn from commands from the Dialog Pocket Guide 2006 (Dialog, Inc 2006) is shown here:

```
(PCR OR POLYMERASE(W)CHAIN(W)REACTION? OR DNA(W)SEQUENC?)
AND (CANCER? OR PRECANCER? OR NEOPLASM? OR CARCINO?)
```

The question mark indicates a request for stemming match and the (W) notation requests that the terms be located adjacent to each other and in the order specified. The sequence of terms separated by OR's are to be treated as a disjunction; two long disjunctions are connected by an AND, or conjunction operator. Thus, this is a complex query requesting documents that discuss cancer and DNA sequencing. It is richer than a standard keyword query in that it suggests alternative wordings for each key concept.

Most people who used Boolean command-line systems had extensive training on their use, and often were willing to spend time carefully formulating their queries, especially if they were charged by the query or by the minute. Thus, the users of these systems may not have had problems with the complexity of this syntax. Unfortunately, however, studies have shown time and again that most users have difficulty specifying queries in Boolean format and often misjudge what the results will be (Boyle et al. 1984; Dinet et al. 2004; Greene et al. 1990; Hertzum and Frokjaer 1996; Hildreth 1989; Michard 1982; Young and Shneiderman 1993).

One problem with Boolean queries is that their strict interpretation tends to yield result sets that are either too large, because the user includes many terms in a disjunct, or are empty, because the user conjoins terms in an effort to reduce the result set. This problem occurs in large part because the user does not know the contents of the collection or the role of terms within the collection.

Boolean queries are also problematic because most people find the basic semantics counter-intuitive. Many English-speaking users assume everyday meanings are associated with Boolean operators when expressed using the English words AND and OR, rather than their logical equivalents. To inexperienced users, using AND implies the widening of the scope of the query, because more kinds of information are requested in such a query. For instance, in English, the phrase "dogs and cats" may imply a request for documents about dogs and documents about cats, rather than documents about both topics at once. Similarly, "tea or coffee" usually implies a mutually exclusive choice in everyday language, as opposed to the union of the concepts as dictated by Boolean semantics. In addition, most query languages that incorporate Boolean operators also require the user to specify rigid syntax for other kinds of connectors and for descriptive metadata. Most users are not familiar with the use of parentheses for nested evaluation, nor with the notions associated with operator precedence.

Another problem with pure Boolean systems is they do not rank the retrieved documents according to similarity to the query. In the pure

Boolean framework a document either satisfies the query or it does not. Commercial systems with Boolean queries usually order documents according to some kind of descriptive metadata, usually reverse chronological order. (Since these systems usually index time-sensitive data such as newswires, date of publication is often one of the most salient features of the document. To some degree, this is still true for specialized search, such as blog search, where ordering by currency or by popularity is a common ranking mechanism.)

Despite the generally poor usability of Boolean operators, most search engines support notation using AND, OR, and NOT, as well as characters for wildcarding, stemming, and range specification for dates. For example, in the Dialog system (Dialog, Inc. 2006) the operator *?* appended to a sequence of characters allows for matching of all words that begin with those characters, for example, *biome?* would match *biometric, biometrics, biomedical*, etc. In the AOL Web search engine, *?* is a wildcard for one character only. The Google search engine allows a wildcard character operator *, which allows for one or more unspecified words to appear between the two specified words; multiple stars allow for multiple unspecified words. For example, *"president * lincoln"* will match pages that contain the former president's full name. Google also supports number ranges; the query `abraham lincoln 1860..1863` brings up hits that mention the former president along with one or more years in that range.

4.4.1. *Term Proximity in Boolean Queries*

In general, proximity information can be quite effective at improving precision of searches (Clarke et al. 1996; Hearst 1996; Tao and Zhai 2007). The most commonly used operator on the Web is the double-quote operator `""`, used to surround adjacent words, as in `"San Francisco"`, which signifies that the enclosed terms must be found directly adjacent in the retrieved text. The disadvantage of exact match of phrases is that it is often the case (in English) that one or a few words fall between the terms of interest (as in `big black dog` when searching on `big dog`). Another consideration is whether or not stemming is performed on the terms included in the phrase. The AOL adjacency operator is similar to double quotes except that it allows for morphological variants, and can be combined with other operators, for example, *(abraham OR abe) ADJ lincoln* will find matches for both *abe lincoln* and *abraham lincoln*. The AOL search engine also supports proximity queries in the form of a NEAR operator, for example, *dogs NEAR/3 cats* means find the word *dogs* within 3 words of

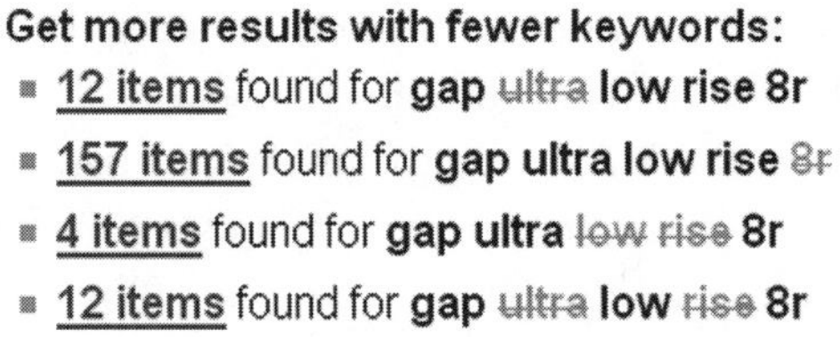

Get more results with fewer keywords:
- **12 items** found for **gap ~~ultra~~ low rise 8r**
- **157 items** found for **gap ultra low rise ~~8r~~**
- **4 items** found for **gap ultra ~~low rise~~ 8r**
- **12 items** found for **gap ~~ultra~~ low ~~rise~~ 8r**

Figure 4.8. eBay quorum ranking suggestions, indicating the number of hits that would be returned if each of the terms shown in strikeout font were removed from the query.

cats, in either order. In some cases the best solution is to allow users to specify exact phrases but treat them as if they indicated small proximity ranges, with perhaps an exponential fall-off in weight according to the distance between the terms. This has been shown to be a successful strategy in non-interactive ranking algorithms (Clarke et al. 1996). Some Web search engines provide behavior related to this in select circumstances. For example, Google often ignores middle initials when doing matches against people's names, even when those names are enclosed in double quotes.

4.4.2. *Post-Coordinate and Faceted Boolean Queries*

One technique for imposing an ordering on the results of Boolean queries is *post-coordinate* or *quorum-level* ranking (Salton 1989, Ch. 8). In this approach, documents are ranked according to the size of the subset of the query terms they contain. So given a query consisting of cats dogs fish mice, the system would rank a document with at least one instance of cats, dogs, or fish higher than a document containing 30 occurrences of cats but no occurrences of the other terms. eBay introduced an interesting way of expressing search results according to coordinate or quorum-level ranking. When no results are found for a query such as gap ultra low rise 8r, the searcher is shown a view indicating how many results would be brought back if only *k* out of *n* terms were included in the query, as illustrated in Figure 4.8.

Another approach to improving results with Boolean queries is to have the searcher break their query up into different *facets*, that is, different topics, and specify each facet with a set of terms combined into a disjunction. The entire query is then combined into one conjunction, in effect indicating that at least one term from each concept should be present in the retrieved documents (Meadow et al. 1989). Combining faceted queries with quorum ranking yields a situation intermediate between full Boolean syntax and free-form natural language queries.

An interface for specifying this kind of interaction can consist of a list of entry lines. The user enters one topic per entry line, where each topic consists of a list of semantically related terms that are combined in a disjunct. (This sort of query works naturally with the interface shown in Figure 4.9.) Documents that contain at least one term from each facet are ranked higher than documents containing terms only from one or a few facets. Hearst (1996) showed that when at least one representative term from each facet is required to be in close proximity with one another, the resulting precision is very high. However, this kind of querying specification is not commonly used in practice. Instead, facets are now widely used in *navigation* interfaces for collections (see Chapter 8).

4.4.3. Web-Based Improvements to Boolean Query Specification

In command-line based interfaces, Boolean operators and their operands are typically typed on one line, and combined using parentheses (see Figure 4.10a). Although Web search engines support use of operators directly in the query box, they usually also supply a graphical form-based method for using filters and restrictions. Figure 4.9 from the Education Resources Information Center (ERIC) shows an example.

By serving a massive audience possessing little query-specification experience, the designers of Web search engines devised what were intended to be more intuitive approaches to Boolean query specification. Early versions of Web search interfaces used drop-down menus and Web forms that allowed users to choose from a selection of simple ways of combining query terms, including "all the words" (place all terms in a conjunction) and "any of the words" (place all terms in a disjunction). These kinds of options are still available in the "Advanced Search" option of many Web search engines (see Figure 4.11).

Another early Web-based solution was to allow syntactically based query specification, but to provide a simpler or more intuitive syntax. In the mid-1990s, the AltaVista Web search engine introduced the *mandatory* operator, meaning that the results retrieved must include the query term, indicated with a + as a prefix before the required word. At that time, Web search results were ranked using statistical algorithms, and so the top results for a three-keyword query might not contain all of the query terms

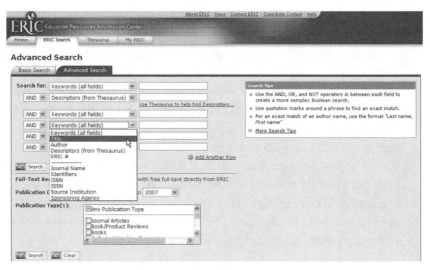

Figure 4.9. An example of a Web forms-based interface from the Education Resources Information Center (ERIC) search system for specifying complex combinations of Boolean operators over keywords and other fields.

(if, for example, the algorithm chose to rank a document with 100 occurrences of the first keyword ahead of a document with one occurrence of all three keywords). The mandatory operator gave users more control over how the search engine treated their keywords. Unfortunately, users sometimes mistakenly thought the + acted as an infix AND rather than a prefix mandatory operator, thus assuming that `cat + dog` will only retrieve articles containing both terms (where in fact this query requires dog but allows cat to be optional). The need for this operator became obviated after search engines began returning only those documents that contain every keyword.

Researchers have developed many clever interface designs to improve Boolean query specification via visual interfaces. These attempts at visualizing Boolean queries are discussed in Chapter 10, but have not been widely adopted in practice. The one exception is for *database* query specification, an area in which graphical command building applications have become popular. However, searching over structured information is inherently different than searching over unstructured text.

4.4.4. *Query Operator Usage Statistics*

As discussed above, the major search engines offer a number of operators that can be applied to queries to make them more focused and exact.

However, Web log statistics show that only a small fraction of queries take advantage of these operators. It is difficult to obtain accurate statistics from current Web search engines, so below are reported a set of statistics that have been gleaned by researchers using the few available open Web log resources. The actual numbers most likely fall somewhere in the middle of the reported ranges.

A meta-analysis by Jansen and Spink (2006), which analyzed seven query log studies between 1997 and 2002, found that the percentage of search operator use has remained steady over time. Spink et al. (2002) showed a Boolean usage rate of about 10% for Excite users. Jansen et al. (2005) reported a Boolean usage of about 6% and a usage of other query operators at approximately 15%. The most recent study by Jansen et al. (2007b), conducted over 1.5M queries, found that 2.1% contained Boolean operators and 7.6% contained other query syntax, primarily double-quotation marks for phrases. White and Morris (2007) studied interaction logs of nearly 600,000 users issuing millions of queries over a period of 13 weeks in 2006. They found that 1.1% of the queries contained at least one of the four main Web operators (double quotes, +, -, and `site:`) and 8.7% of the users used an operator at least one time.

Hargittai's (2004) study showed that even among the small fraction of users who did attempt to use operators, several completely misunderstood their meaning. None of the participants used the negation operator -, although at least one put a space before the hyphen in what was intended to be a hyphenated term: `lactose intolerant -recipes`, thus ensuring that no relevant results were returned. 16% of the participants used double quotation marks, but a few of them used them incorrectly or superfluously. One participant put quotation marks around almost every individual word, and another, apparently having misunderstood some advice from a friend on how to improve her results, put them around all terms in her query, thus often yielding empty result sets.

It may be the case that operators are only used by advanced searchers. For the White and Morris (2007) study described above, they partitioned users into experts and non-experts based on whether or not they had used operators in their queries. They found significant differences in search behaviors between these two groups; the experts had different behavior when navigating search results, and they were more successful at eliciting and clicking on relevant documents. Aula and Siirtola (2005) also found evidence that expert searchers were those more likely to use operators, based on questionnaire data filled out by 236 experienced Web users.

Those with information seeking professions were more likely to say they use Boolean and other operators.

There is evidence that Web search engine ranking algorithms have been successful at compensating for the fact that their users do not use query operators. Eastman and Jansen (2003) studied the effects of removing search operators from 100 queries selected from query logs and compared the resulting documents to those retrieved by the advanced query. They found the use of most query operators had no significant effect on coverage, relative precision, or ranking, although the impact did vary depending on the search engine.

4.5. Query Specification Using Command Languages

Most systems that support Boolean logic allow it to be embedded within a command language, meaning a syntax that usually includes commands (sometimes referred to as "verbs") followed by arguments. For instance, in the old University of California Melvyl system (Lynch 1992), the syntax would look like:

COMMAND ATTRIBUTE value {BOOLEAN-OPERATOR ATTRIBUTE value}*

e.g.,

FIND PA darwin AND TW species OR TW descent

or

FIND TW Mt St. Helens AND DATE 1981

The user must remember the commands and attribute names, which are easily forgotten between usages of the system (Meadow et al. 1989). Compounding this problem, despite the fact that the command languages for the two main online bibliographic systems at UC Berkeley had different but very similar syntaxes, after more than 10 years one of the systems still reported an error if the author field was specified as PA instead of PN, as is done in the other system. This lack of flexibility in the syntax was characteristic of older interfaces designed to suit the system rather than its users.

The functionality of command languages allows selection of collections to search over, resources to use (including thesauri), fields to search over, and format of results display. Some of these languages rival database query languages in their expressiveness. However, they are also complex and difficult to use, requiring the user to remember and accurately type cryptic commands. Most older search systems required special training and expertise, and many users relied on skilled intermediaries such as corporate or university librarians to issue queries.

A common strategy for dealing with this problem, employed in early systems with command-line based interfaces, and in Web-based library catalogs, was for the system to encourage the user to create a series of short queries, show the number of documents returned for each, and allow the user to combine those queries that produce a reasonable number of results (Dialog, Inc. 2002a; Dialog, Inc. 2002b). For example, in the early Dialog system, each query produced a resulting set of documents that was assigned an identifying name. Rather than returning a list of titles themselves, Dialog showed the result set number with a listing of the number of matched documents. Titles could be shown by specifying the set number and issuing a command to show the titles. Document sets that were not empty could be referred to by a set name and combined with AND operations to produce new sets. If this set in turn was too small, the user could back up and try a different combination of sets, and this process was repeated in pursuit of producing a reasonably sized document set.

To use these older systems to their fullest, users also needed to know the names of the different fields to query against, and the names of the sources they wanted to search over. The following more complex example, also derived from the Dialog Pocket Guide 2006 (Dialog, Inc. 2006), illustrates this:

```
?s (biometric? and security)/TI,LP
        1621 BIOMETRIC?/TI,LP
       40268 SECURITY/TI,LP
S1       678 S (biometric? and security)/TI,LP
?s S1 and CS=(HARVARD AND MEDIC?)
S2        52 S1 and CS=(HARVARD AND MEDIC?)
?T S2/3/1-10
```

The first line begins with s, a shorthand for the command *select*. The question mark indicates a request for stemming match and the /TI,LP notation indicates that the search should be done over titles and lead paragraph fields only. The number of results found for each part of the query are shown on the following three lines, along with an automatically named results set S1. The next command restricts the results to only those whose corporate source contains the terms HARVARD and a name that

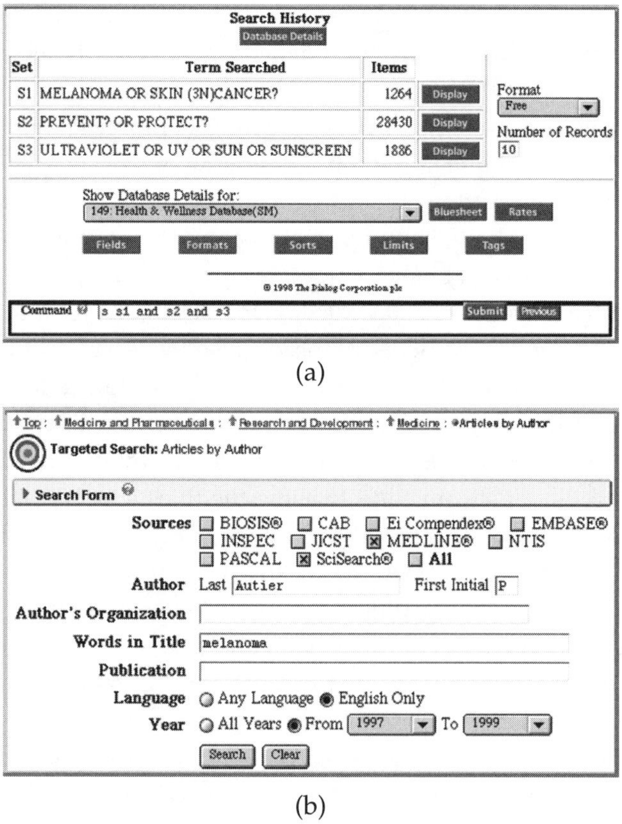

(a)

(b)

Figure 4.10. Web-based interfaces for the Dialog command-based search system, originating in 1998. (a) Query specification form, including search history, from Dialog, Inc. (2002a). (b) Source and field selection form, from Dialog, Inc. (2002b). Images published with permission of Dialog LLC. Further reproduction prohibited without permission.

begins with MEDIC. The next command requests the system to show the first 10 results from the preceding results set, in format number 3.

Needless to say, non-specialist users are not able to specify queries of this complexity. In the late 1990s, systems like Dialog and online library catalogs upgraded to Web-based forms interfaces, thus lessening the memory burden. Figure 4.10 shows versions of the query specification form and results modification forms, which still bear a great deal of resemblance to their TTY-based counterparts.

Search engines typically supply a forms-based interface to aid with command specification, in addition to supporting free typing of the commands within the main entry form. Figure 4.11 shows an example of such a form.

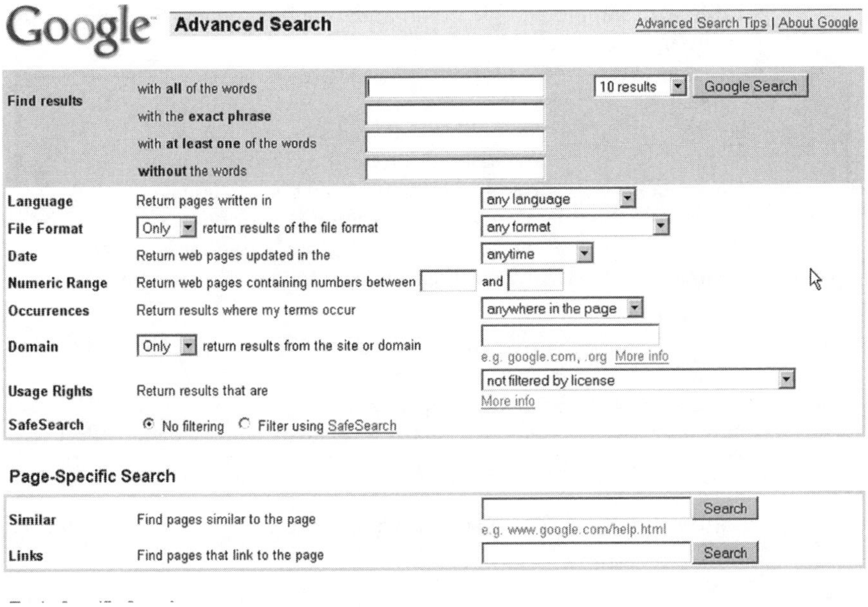

Figure 4.11. Google Web search engine advanced search form that supports search commands, from July 2007.

Interestingly, Web search engines have recently been building command languages into their query specification abilities. These are not required for use but can provide a savvy searcher with considerable power. These allow both for traditional uses of search commands, such as restricting the query to search over a particular field, as well as for more innovative commands that map to very specific information needs. The Google search engine has a wide range of these (see Table 4.2.), including commands such as *SWA 49* (what is the status of Southwest Airlines flight 49?) and *stocks:NOK* (what is the current stock performance of Nokia?).

These commands are associated with what is known as search *shortcuts*: specialized searches for commonly sought types of information such as weather, stock quotes, and airplane flight status information. The results of these shortcuts are also shown, when appropriate, in some search results listings. For example, maps and weather may be shown in response to a search on a city's name. Google also allows users to enter calculations (e.g., *298 * 23.4/23*) and unit conversions (e.g., *30 dollars in euros*) directly into the search box.

Google's mobile search takes the command language notion still farther (see Chapter 12). The problem with command languages like these, of course, is that the user must remember a command correctly in order to

Table 4.2. Sample Google commands. Each is meant to be followed by an argument.

Collections	
book	Search full text of books
define:	Show a definition for the given word
phonebook:	Show (residential) phone book listings
movie:	Find reviews and showtimes for films
stocks:	Show stock information for a given ticker symbol
weather	Show weather forecasts for a given location
Web search:	
site:	Search within the specified Web site or domain
allinachor:	Search within anchor text of links to page
intitle:	Search within page titles
source:	Search within the given source in the news collection

use it, although a current research trend is to support ever-more flexible variations on command languages.

4.6. Conclusions

The query is the bridge between the user's current understanding of their information need and the information access system. Query specification today is primarily accomplished by the user typing keyword queries into an entry form or following hyperlinks at a known Web site (the use of links as a form of query specification is discussed in detail in Chapter 8).

This chapter discussed two main aspects of query specification: the kind of information supplied by the searcher and the style of interface used for expressing that information. Query specification was described as an activity in which the user specifies:

- Keyword queries,
- Natural language queries, including queries as questions,
- Paragraphs of text,
- Queries containing Boolean operators, and
- Queries with command-based syntax.

The chapter discussed how textual queries are modified by the underlying search system, including stemming and stopword removal. The chapter also described graphical entry forms for query specification, and discussed the increasing importance and popularity of dynamic term suggestions that appear as the user types their query. Other query modifications such as spelling suggestions and term expansions are discussed in detail in Chapter 6.

The decline of syntax-driven command languages (except for use by specialists) provides an instructive example of how interfaces that were originally designed to be easy to implement in a computer are being replaced by interfaces that are intuitive for users. It is impressive that today people respond in surveys saying that Web search engines are easy to use; for the first few years of their existence, people complained that their behavior was confusing. Not only did the algorithms change, but also the assumptions behind them changed to have a focus on intuitiveness for the everyday user.

In future it is likely that query specification by spoken language will become increasingly popular; this is discussed in the section on mobile search in Chapter 12. It is also likely that long queries, including queries structured as questions, will continue to increase in usage as the algorithms responding to them improve.

5 Presentation of Search Results

This chapter describes interfaces for the search results presentation portion of the information seeking process, focusing for the most part on ideas that are currently in use.

5.1. Document Surrogates

The most common way that search results are displayed is as a vertical list of information summarizing the retrieved documents. (These search results listings are often known as "search engine results pages," or *SERPs*, in industry.) Typically, an item in the results list consists of the document's title and a set of important metadata, such as date, author, source (URL), and length of the article, along with a brief summary of a relevant portion of the document (see Figure 5.1). The representation for a document within a results listing is often called a search *hit*. This collection of information is sometimes referred to as the *document surrogate*. Marchionini and White (2008) note that document surrogates are summary information intended to help the user understand the primary object, as opposed to metadata more broadly construed, which can also serve this purpose but is often more tailored towards use by computer programs.

The quality of the document surrogate has a strong effect on the ability of the searcher to judge the relevance of the document. Even the most relevant document is unlikely to be selected if the title is uninformative or misleading. (Some Web search algorithms try to capture the quality of the title description as part of the ranking score.) The descriptiveness of the summary is also very important and is discussed in detail below.

120

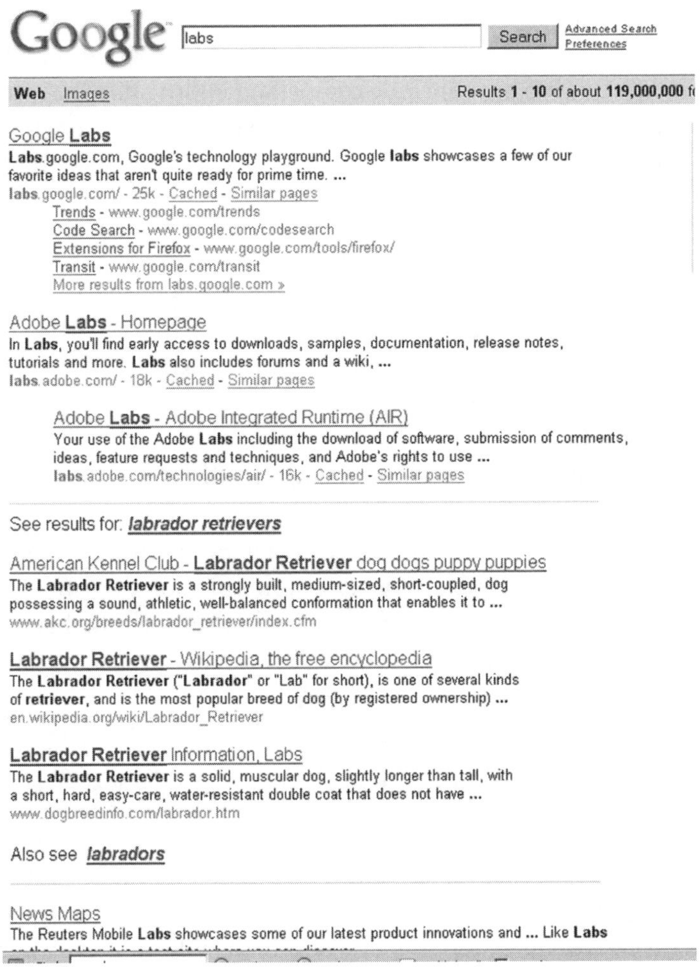

Figure 5.1. Results shown for the ambiguous query labs at google.com. This results listing shows sitelinks – a list of links to important pages within the site – beneath *Google Labs*, an indented link showing an additional hit at the *Adobe Labs* site, and horizontal rule lines to separate hits for different senses of the query labs, which is an ambiguous term.

To determine which of the many aspects of a document surrogate lead to the best usability for Web search engine results, Clarke et al. (2007) tested which features of surrogates (consisting of query-biased summaries along with a title and URL) were associated with receiving significantly more clicks in a query log. They used the evaluation trick of *clickthrough inversion*, in which the features of the clicked-on surrogate are compared to those of the surrogate directly above it in the search results listings. The motivation is that because users are known to be biased towards clicking

documents higher up in the rankings (Joachims et al. 2005), if they buck
the trend and click on a lower-ranked document, the features of that document's surrogate must include compelling information that prompted the
click. Evaluating on 10,000 pairs of summaries, where hit A appears above
B, but B receives more clicks, Clarke et al. (2007) found significant effects
for the following features:

- Summary is present in hit B but is missing in A.
- Summary is long in hit B (>100 characters) but short (<25 characters)
  in hit A.
- Title of hit B contains more query term matches than A's title.
- Title of hit B starts with a phrase contained in the query, but A's title
  does not.
- Title, summary, and URL together for hit B contain the query as a
  phrase match, but do not for A.
- Summary for hit B contains one match for every query term; for hit A
  there are more matches for some terms but some are missing.
- URL for B is of the form www.*query*.com but is not in this format for A.
- URL for B is shorter, in terms of slashes, than A's.
- URL for B is shorter, in characters, than A's.
- Summary B, but not A, passes a simple readability test.

Clarke et al. (2007) concluded that these and other results supported the
following heuristics:

(i) Where possible, all the query terms should appear in the surrogate,
    reflecting their relationship to the corresponding Web page.
(ii) When the query terms are present in the title for the hit, they need not
     appear in the summary.
(iii) Length and complexity of URLs should be reduced, and URLs should
      be selected and displayed in a manner that emphasizes their relation-
      ship to the query.

They also found effects for the appearance of particular words. Among
others, *official, and, tourism, attractions, sexy,* and *information* had positive
influence on clickthrough, whereas *encyclopedia, wikipedia,* and *free* had
negative influence.

5.2. KWIC, or Query-Oriented Summaries

As mentioned above, most search results listings today show an extract
from a retrieved document that summarizes its contents. This extract is

referred to with several different names, including *summary*, *snippet*, and *abstract*.

An important property of modern Web search surrogates is the display of a summary that takes the searcher's query terms into account. This is referred to as *keyword-in-context* (KWIC) extractions for use in display of retrieval results. In KWIC views (also referred to as *query-biased, query-dependent, query-oriented*, or *user-directed summaries* (Tombros and Sanderson 1998)), sentence fragments, full sentences, or groups of sentences that contain query terms are extracted from the full text and presented for viewing along with other kinds of surrogate information (such as document title and abstract). Early versions of this idea were developed in the Snippet Search tool by Pedersen et al. (Pedersen et al. 1991; Rao et al. 1994) and the SuperBook tool (Landauer et al. 1993) (see Figure 8.4 in Chapter 8).

A KWIC, or query-oriented extract, is different than a standard abstract, whose goal is to summarize the main topics of the document but might not contain references to the terms within the query. A query-oriented extract shows sentences that summarize the ways the query terms are used within the document. In addition to showing which subsets of query terms occur in retrieved documents, this display also exposes the context in which the query terms appear with respect to one another.

Research on document summarization indicates that the most generally applicable heuristic for making a good short summary is to show the first few sentences of a document (Kupiec et al. 1995). By contrast, research suggests that query-biased summaries are superior to showing the first few sentences in retrieval results. Tombros and Sanderson (1998), in a study with 20 participants using TREC *ad hoc* data, found higher precision and recall and higher subjective preferences for query-biased summaries over summaries showing the first few sentences of retrieval results. Those using query-biased summaries also invoked significantly fewer views of the full text articles, effectively avoiding many of the non-relevant documents. Similar results for timing and subjective measurements were found by White et al. (2003a) in a study with 24 participants.

With a query-biased summary, in many cases, an information need can be satisfied by viewing the document surrogate alone. For example, for a search on `how to prevent cheese from molding` on Google, some of the query extracts contain answer suggestions alongside the query terms themselves, while others are cut off and require a visit to the full page (see Figure 5.2).

Figure 5.2. The role of keywords in context for showing relevance of retrieved documents at google.com.

Although KWIC and query term highlighting has been thought to be an effective technique for decades (Luhn 1959), the prevalence of query-biased summaries is relatively recent. Hearst (1999b) wrote:

> The KWIC facility is usually not shown in Web search result display, most likely because the system must have a copy of the original document available from which to extract the sentences containing the search terms.

At that time, costs of storage and concerns about intellectual property rights prevented search engines from storing entire copies of the crawled data. Instead, they stored and displayed only the first few sentences of text from each document. Subsequent to that writing, Google began storing full text of documents, making them visible in their cache and using their content for query-biased summaries. Keyword-in-context summaries have become the de facto standard for Web search engine result displays.

5.2.1. *Sentence Selection for Query-Oriented Summaries*

There are significant design questions about how best to formulate and display query-biased summaries. As with standard document summarization and extraction, tradeoff decisions must be made between how many lines of text to show and which lines to display.

Several researchers have experimented with models in which sentences are scored according to attributes such as position in the document, the words they contain, and the proportion of query terms they contain. The highest scoring sentences are then included in the summary. White et al. (2003a) experimented with different sentence selection mechanisms, including giving more weight to sentences that contained query words along with text formatting (e.g., boldface or italics). Goldstein et al. (1999) augmented this kind of model with linguistic cues, finding that summary sentences tended to begin with articles more than non-summary sentences, and included indefinite articles more frequently than definite articles (e.g., a versus the). Proper nouns and other named entities tended to appear at a higher percentage in summary vs. non-summary sentences. Goldstein et al. (1999) found negative evidence for inclusion of anaphoric references (e.g., this, these) negations (e.g., not, no), evaluative or vague words (e.g., often, about, several), along with a number of other features.

Those approaches ignore relationships between sentences. Varadarajan and Hristidis (2006) presented a method to create query specific summaries by identifying the most query-relevant fragments and then combining them using graphs representing the document structure. In a small comparison study, 15 participants assigned higher ratings to the resulting summaries than to those produced by two commercial desktop search systems.

5.2.2. *Summary Length for Query-Oriented Summaries*

For determining how many words or sentences to show, there is an inherent tradeoff between showing long, informative summaries and minimizing the screen space required by each search hit. There is also a tension between showing short snippets that contain all or most of the query terms and showing coherent stretches of text. If the query terms do not co-occur near one another in the same sentences, then the extract has to become very long if full sentences are to be shown. Some Web search engine snippets compromise by showing fragments of sentences instead.

Paek et al. (2004) experimented with showing differing amounts of summary information in results listings, where only one result in each list of 10 was relevant. For half of the test questions, the results were visible in the original snippet, and for the other half, the participant needed to view more information from the relevant search result. They compared three interface conditions:

(i) A standard search results listing, in which a mouse click on the title brings up the full text of the Web page,

(ii) "Instant" view, which upon a mouseclick, expanded the document summary to show additional sentences from the document, where those sentences contained query terms and the answer to the search task, and

(iii) A "dynamic" view that responded to a mouse hover, and dynamically expanded the summary with a few words at a time.

Eleven out of 18 participants preferred the instant view over the other two views, and on average all participants produced faster and more accurate results with this view. Seven participants preferred dynamic view over the others, but many participants found it disruptive. The dynamic view suffered from the problem that, as the text expanded, the mouse no longer covered the selected results, and so an unintended, different search result sometimes started to expand. Notably, none of the participants preferred the standard results listing view.

Cutrell and Guan (2007) compared search summaries of varying length: short (1 line of text), medium (2–3 lines), and long (6–7 lines), using search engine-produced snippets (it is unclear if the summary text was contiguous or included ellipses). In a study with 22 participants, they found that adding more information to the summary significantly improved performance for information tasks (e.g., "find when the Titanic set sail for its only voyage and what port it left from") but degraded performance for navigational tasks (e.g., "find the home page of World Cup 2006 soccer games"). They postulated that this effect resulted from the extra text distracting searchers from the URL. Using eye tracking, they found that participants spent a larger proportion of time looking at information other than the URL for the navigational queries with long contexts, thus suggesting that the less relevant information was distracting them. They did not report on subjective responses to the different summary lengths.

Lin et al. (2003) found that a short paragraph was preferred over a single sentence and an entire document for a question-answering system. Kaisser et al. (2008) asked judges to categorize a large set of long (question-like) queries according to the expected answer type (person, place, product, advice, general information, etc.) and preferred response length (word or phrase, sentence, one or more paragraphs, full document). They then developed high-quality answer passages of different lengths for a subset of these queries, and asked judges to rate the quality of these answers. They found that different query types are best served with different response lengths, and that for a subset of especially clear queries, human judges can predict the preferred result length. Their results furthermore suggest that standard summaries are too short in many cases, assuming that a longer summary shows information that is relevant for the query.

Thus, the evidence suggests that for queries that are more exploratory in nature, a paragraph-length excerpt may be preferable to a short, elided snippet, despite the extra scrolling it requires to see more results, so long as that paragraph is not too long.

5.2.3. *Sentence Fragments vs. Full Sentences for Query-Biased Summaries*

It is unclear if sentence fragments are preferable to full sentences, despite the fact that sentences take up more space on the page. Aula (2004) performed a controlled experiment comparing three different layouts for query-biased summaries, as shown in Figure 2.3 in Chapter 2, with the aim of determining if showing a series of sentence fragments separated by ellipses is desirable. In the "Bold" case, the summary was left unchanged from what was returned by the Google search engine, with query terms bolded and fragments separated by ellipses, while in the "Plain" style, the summary was the same as in "Bold" but with the boldface weighting removed. In the "List" condition, the fragmented paragraph was replaced with a bulleted list; every time an ellipsis appeared in the summary, a new list item was created, preceded by a small arrow. Incomplete sentences were marked with ellipses at the start and/or end of the list item. The 27 participants each performed 30 tasks, doing 10 tasks in each display condition. They were asked to find the right answer for a query from the results list as quickly as possible. The list style view produced significantly better results than the standard bolded style or the standard style without bolding. In fact, in the bolded view, participants were significantly slower than with the standard view without boldface. However, the task of finding the one answer out of a list of 10 incorrect answers is different than that of determining if a document is relevant to a query or not, and the author cautions against drawing conclusions against this kind of highlighting based on this study alone.

Rose et al. (2007) varied search results summaries along several dimensions, finding that text choppiness and sentence truncation had negative effects, and genre cues had positive effects. They did not find effects for varying summary length, but they only compared relatively similar summary lengths (2 vs. 3 vs. 4 lines long). White et al. (2003b) performed an experiment with 18 participants that found that showing high-ranking sentences alone might be better than showing snippets.

Kanungo and Orr (2009) obtained hand-labeled readability scores and then used a machine learning algorithm to determine which of a small set of features predicted readability. They found that the following features negatively influenced readability scores: a large percentage of capital letters, a large percentage of punctuation, a large percentage of stopwords (as it can signal spam), and a large number of characters per word.

5.3. Highlighting Query Terms

Highlighting of query terms has been found time and again to be a useful feature for information access interfaces (Landauer et al. 1993; Lesk 1997; Marchionini 1995). Term highlighting refers to altering the appearance of portions of text in order to make them more visually salient, or "eye-catching." Highlighting can be done in boldface, reverse video, or more commonly today, by displaying a colored background behind each occurrence of a query term, assigning a different color to each term. This display helps draw the searcher's attention to the parts of the document most likely to be relevant to the query, and to show how closely the query terms appear to one another in the text. As discussed in Chapter 4, query term proximity is a strong indicator of relevance.

Highlighting can occur both in retrieval results listings and in the retrieved documents themselves. In systems in which the user can view the full text of a retrieved document, it is often useful to highlight the occurrences of the terms or descriptors that match those of the user's query. The Firefox Web browser and Google toolbar allow users to search for words within the currently viewed document, and then display the hits with color highlighting. Color highlighting has also been found to be useful for scanning lists of citation records (Baldonado and Winograd 1998).

Figure 5.3. Query term highlighting in the scrollbar of the Chrome browser. (See color plate 2.)

If the text is long, then showing an overview of where the highlighted terms occur throughout the document can be useful. This can be done in several ways. One way is to use the document scrollbar to show the location of term hits. The Read Wear/Edit Wear system (Hill et al. 1992) used the scrollbar to indicate information such as the amount of time a reader has spent looking at a particular location in the document, or locations of query term hits. Byrd (1999) suggested applying a different color to each query term, and showing the corresponding colors to the appropriate locations within a scrollbar-like widget (see Figure 10.13). The Thumbar system (Graham 1999) used a similar scrollbar widget on the left hand side and a visualization of hits for the important terms of the document on the right hand side. This idea has been applied in the Chrome Web browser, which uses such a visualization to show where search hits occur within a searched Web page (see Figure 5.3).

Another way to highlight query term hits in a long document is to use an overview display. Baudisch et al. (2004) asked 13 participants to

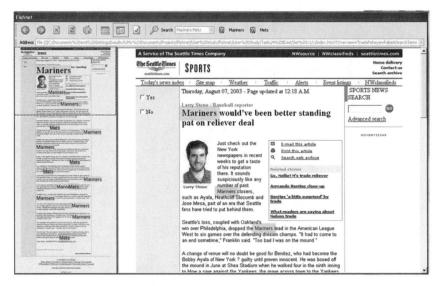

Figure 5.4. Query term highlighting with overview on a Web page, from Baudisch et al. (2004). (See color plate 2.)

compare three different methods of viewing long Web pages retrieved for pre-defined queries. In the first case, the Web page was shown as usual, but each query term was highlighted with a different color. In the second (see Figure 5.4), an overview screen on the side showed a miniature version of the entire document with query terms highlighted, as well as providing highlighting on the main page as in the first case. The third design was similar to the first but also showed a fisheye view with term highlighting at the bottom of the page. The participants were asked to perform 4 tasks. The time taken depended on the task and the interface, but 10 out of 13 participants preferred the highlighted overview version over the other two. Chapter 10 discusses other variations on these ideas.

5.4. Addition Features of Results Listings

In addition to the standard metadata of title, author, date, etc., and search result summaries, this section discusses several other features that have been found useful (or not) for search results listings.

Number of Hits per Page: Web search engines typically show 10 results, or "hits," per page, with hyperlinks to additional pages of results. In the earlier days of the Web, this was not standardized and as many as 30 hits per page were often shown (Reiterer et al. 2005). A Google VP reported that despite the fact that users said they wanted more hits per page, an experiment in which the number of hits was increased to 30 hits per page showed a 20% reduction in traffic (Linden 2006). The reason turned out to be that while the page with 10 results took 0.4 seconds to generate, the page with 30 results took 0.9 seconds on average. Linden (2006) found similar user sensitively to half-second delays at Amazon.com.

Graphical Displays of Relevance Score: For many years, systems that use statistical ranking showed a numerical score or an icon alongside the title, indicating the computed degree of match or probability of relevance to the query. Icons included partially filled horizontal bars or a line of graphical stars, as in movie ratings, indicating degree of match or relevance.

Thus graphical or numerical displays of relevance scores have fallen out of favor and are now rarely shown; there are several possible explanations for this. First, in order to understand the score one must have some knowledge of the complex underlying ranking algorithm, which is of course not to be expected for general users. Second, often the top scores are close together numerically, and so showing the score does not add information beyond the rank ordering provided by the vertical results list. Third, other surrogates such as query terms in context are often more informative than a general relevance score. Fourth, showing the score gives information to a search engine's competitors and spammers who might try to reverse-engineer the ranking algorithm. And finally, usability studies that compare interfaces with and without graphical bars tend to find that users do not prefer them, nor do they affect the timing scores (Tanin et al. 2007; White et al. 2007) (although these studies did not use standard search results listings). More elaborate graphical representations of search results matches are discussed in Chapter 10.

Previews of Document Content: In most graphical search interfaces, clicking on the document's title or an iconic representation of the document shown beside the title will bring up a view of the document itself, either in another window, or replacing the listing of search results. Some systems have experimented with making the document content more immediately available without the need to leave the Web page; Figure 5.5 shows content prefetching when viewing a hyperlink using Snap's Snap Shot system.

Figure 5.5. Showing a preview of content available from a link, from Snap.com.

Indicators of Search Result Diversity: Some Web search engines attempt to support a notion of "diversity" in the first few results displayed. This is especially important for ambiguous queries for which there are several common interpretations or meanings for a given word. For example, a search on the term labs at Google at the time of writing shows three sets of results on the first page, separated by horizontal rules (see Figure 5.1). The first set shows hits on two research laboratories, the second shows the message *See results for labrador retrievers* along with hits on this topic, and the third section is general search results ordering.

Indicators of Additional/Related Hits: Some Web search engines group related hits from one Web site using an indented link, along with a link to more hits from that site; an example can be seen under the link *Adobe Labs - Homepage* in Figure 5.1.

Sitelinks: More recently, Web search engines have adopted a feature that shows an indented list of important pages from the top-scoring Web site

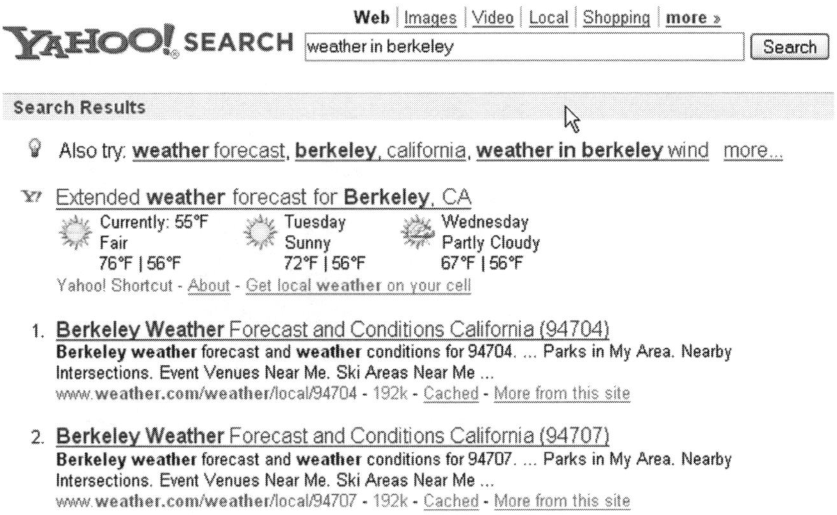

Figure 5.6. "Short cut" information provided by Yahoo in response to the query `weather in Berkeley`. (Reproduced with permission of Yahoo! Inc. ©2009 Yahoo! Inc. YAHOO! and the YAHOO! logo are registered trademarks of Yahoo! Inc.)

for a query, along with a link to more pages from that Web site. This feature is referred to in the industry as *sitelinks* or *deep links*, and informal reports suggest they are frequently clicked on. Presumably, these links are chosen based on clickthrough popularity for other queries as well as descriptive titles on the links. This feature exposes some of the content that is buried one or more levels within the Web site, thus potentially saving the user time and effort in scanning the site's home page to find the next link, and also eliminating the need to load the home page. (This interface is a simpler version of the idea of exposing the structure of a site's hits espoused by the Cha-Cha (Chen et al. 1999) and AMIT (Wittenburg and Sigman 1997) projects.) In Figure 5.1, sitelinks for the Google Labs site point to Trends, Code Search, and other pages on the site.

Shortcuts: Search engines are also attempting to provide "shortcuts" for directed or focused information needs directly on the search results page, becoming in effect "answer engines" for certain queries (Nielsen 2004b). Figure 5.6 shows the extensive, contextually relevant information provided by Yahoo in response to the query `weather in Berkeley`.

Blended Results and Media Types: Web search engines are increasingly blending search results from multiple information sources, not just Web pages (iProspect 2008). Figure 5.7 shows results for a very general query

Figure 5.7. Gallery view for results for the general query `cats` at hakia.com.

on `kittens` at Hakia, which the search engine converts into a query on `Cats`. Recognizing that this is a very general query, the system provides general resources about the topic, separated by tabs, including news headlines, general pet care sites, general sites for finding a pet, and a table of contents for these different types of information.

Figure 5.8 shows results for the general query `jets` at Microsoft's search engine, which blends sports scores, news, and Web search results. Note also the diversity of topics in the first few results, including a link to the New York Jets football team site, a link to a site selling private jets, and a link to an engineering society.

Informal reports suggest that in most cases, these kinds of multimedia results best placed a few positions down in the search results list; when they replace the first hit they can cause people to leave the site. When placed just above the "fold" (above where scrolling is needed) they can increase clickthrough. Eye-tracking studies suggest that even when placed lower down, an image often attracts the eye first (Hotchkiss et al. 2007).

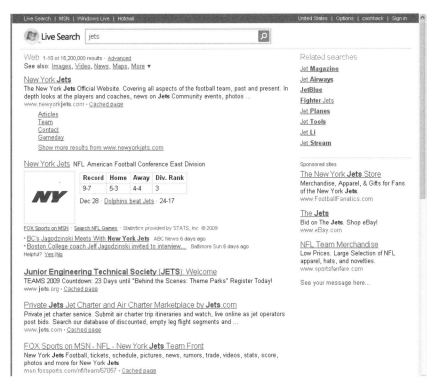

Figure 5.8. View combining results from several different resources for the general (ambiguous) query `jets` at Microsoft search.

It is unclear if information-rich layouts such as those used by Ask.com and Hakia galleries are desirable or if this much information is too overwhelming for users on a daily basis. It may be best to show this richness only for certain types of queries, such as the general ones shown here.

Organic Results vs. Advertisements: In most Web search engines, the search hits are shown in order of computed relevance to the query. In some cases, however, paid advertisements are shown at the top and/or to the side of search results. These are usually visually distinguished to differentiate the ads from the "organic" results, as those hits based solely on relevance as called. The discussion of search ads is outside the scope of this book.

5.5. The Effects of Search Results Ordering

Search results are often listed in an order specified by a relevance metric. Alternatively, results are ordered according to a metadata attribute, such as reverse chronological order for news search and email search, or number of citing papers for journal article search. It is also common to group results by well-defined metadata fields, such as grouping email by sender name or journal article by author name.

Studies and query logs show that searchers rarely look beyond the first page of search results. If the searcher does not find what they want in the first page, they usually either give up or reformulate their query (Chapter 6 discusses query reformulation in detail). Furthermore, several studies suggest that Web searchers expect the best answer to be among the top one or two hits in the results listing, and this expectation influences whether or not they will click on a result. Several of these studies are discussed below.

An eye-tracking study by Granka et al. (2004) on 26 participants and 397 queries found that on average, participants took 7.78 seconds to select a document, but the time varied significantly among the 10 pre-defined search tasks, from 5–6 seconds up to 11 seconds for the most difficult questions. The first result was selected approximately 85% of the time, and the second link about 10% of the time. Furthermore, the first and second results were by far the most viewed, with a sharp dropoff starting with the third result.

A followup eye-tracking study by Joachims et al. (2005) with 29 participants showed that the percentage of times a search result in the top ten listings was looked at dropped off sharply from first search result to sixth, and then flattened at around 5% of the time for results 7–10. Likelihood of clicking on the result, however, dropped much more dramatically, falling from 43% of the time for the first hit to 15% of the time for the second hit, 10% of the time for the third hit, and 5% or less for the rest. This result held despite the fact that 5 of the 22 participants were shown the results in *reverse* order of their original ranking, and another 5 of the participants were shown the top two hits in swapped position.

Joachims et al. (2005) also found that participants tended to view the first- and second-ranked results right away, with a large gap before viewing the third-ranked abstract. They also found that while participants did not necessarily view all abstracts above a click, they view substantially more abstracts above than below the click. More surprisingly, they also found that the abstract right below a click is viewed roughly 50% of the time.

Joachims et al. (2005) also found bias in relevance judgements based on placement location. They did a followup experiment focusing on the top two results, since these are scanned equally frequently. They compared how often a participant clicked on either result 1 or result 2 depending on the manually judged relevance of the abstract. They found that participants were influenced in their relevance assessment by the order of presentation, since the number of clicks on link 1 was significantly higher than its relevance would merit.

Despite these results, Joachims et al. (2005) found that participants were not blindly following link order. In a condition in which they complete reversed the rank order of the top 10 results, they found that in the reversed condition, participants viewed lower-ranked links more frequently, scanning significantly more results than in the normal condition. Those who saw the reversed condition were also much less likely to click on the first link and were more likely to click on a lower-ranked link. The average rank of a click in the normal condition was 2.66 and 4.03 in the reversed condition. However, the average *relevance* of the selected documents in the reversed condition was lower than in the normal condition.

Guan and Cutrell (2007) performed an eye-tracking study in which they pre-determined the queries and results, and controlled which of the top 10 positions the one relevant result appeared in. They also contrasted navigational and informational query types. In a study with 18 participants, they found a significant main effect of target position on total task time and on query type. Participants spent more time when the target was farther down the result list, but this extra time did not result in more success at making the correct choice. The click accuracy rates dropped from about 84% when the target result was in position 1 or 2, to about 11% when the correct response was in position 8. For navigational queries, when participants did not find the result below position 3, they either selected the first hit (40% of the time) or reformulated their query. For informational search, participants rarely reformulated the query without first trying to click on the first hit (about 50% of the time) or clicking on the other links at random. One might infer from this that participants are more confident in the search engine ranking for the relatively easier navigational queries than for the more general informational ones. Guan and Cutrell (2007) examined the results of the eye-tracking data and found that participants did look at the lower-ranked results. They concluded that the participants' behavior was caused by their expectation that the relevant results would be at or near the top.

A somewhat different kind of behavior was seen in an eye-tracking study by Aula et al. (2005b). They analyzed the eye movements of 42 students on 10 pre-defined queries, and found two distinct styles of scanning results list: 46% of the participants were "economic," scanning at most

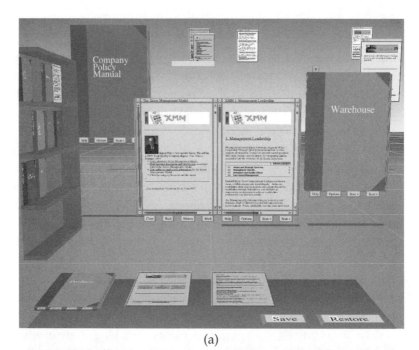

(a)

(b)

Figure 5.9. (a) The WebForager search system placed search results into virtual "books" that could be "flipped through" using animation in a 2.5D rendering. (Courtesy Stuart Card.) (b) The search results interface from Searchme.com shows a small set of retrieval results for the query Obama as rendered Web pages that are "flipped through" using the CoverFlow animation.

138

half of the 6–7 visible search results in 50% of the tasks. The remaining 54% were "exhaustive" evaluators, who for most queries viewed more than half of the visible results, and in some cases scrolled down to see the full list of 10 hits. The difference in time before first action was significantly shorter for the economic searchers, especially when good results were available. The authors find a marginal difference between the evaluation style and computer experience, with more experienced searchers tending to use the economic style, and speculate that the Granka et al. (2004) study may have employed only expert searchers, thus explaining the different results.

5.6. Visualization of Search Results

The bulk of the information visualization ideas that are tried for search apply to the display of retrieval results. Most of these ideas do not survive in mainstream search interfaces, but some ideas are currently getting some play. One frequently suggested idea is to show search results as thumbnail images rather than as textual surrogates (Czerwinski et al. 1999; Dziadosz and Chandrasekar 2002; Woodruff et al. 2001), but none have shown a proven advantage for search results viewing. Nonetheless, a startup company called SearchMe presents a search engine using a "cover flow" interface, which seems to be influenced by the Web Forager/Web Book interface of Card et al. (1996), as shown in Figure 5.9. It remains to be seen if people will use this kind of interface on a regular basis. The extreme sensitivity of searchers to delays of even 0.5 seconds suggests that such highly interactive and visual displays need to have a clear use-case advantage over simple text results before they will succeed. Other approaches to using information visualization for search results display are described in detail in Chapter 10.

5.7. Conclusions

Search results presentation is a critical component of the search cycle. This chapter has summarized empirical research showing which aspects of a document are best shown in retrieval results, along with the characteristics of the results listing itself. Although the basic look of Web search results listings is similar to what was seen ten years ago, a number of subtle innovations have been introduced and found useful for helping searchers make decisions about which links to select for further investigation. These include showing query terms in the search results surrogate, striving for proximity of the query terms to one another where possible, balancing a tradeoff between length and informativeness in document summaries, providing information "scent" about the top-ranked Web site, where appropriate, and differentiating the presentation for ambiguous queries.

Additional important aspects in the design of search results listings that were not covered in this chapter but were discussed in Chapter 1 include providing highly responsive (fast) results, paying attention to small details in the layout, font, color and spacing of the results, and being attuned to aesthetic issues in design. In addition, presentation of search results has been a major focus of the work on employing visualization techniques to search interfaces; these efforts are discussed in detail elsewhere.

6 Query Reformulation

And as noted in Chapter 3, a common search strategy is for the user to first issue a general query, then look at a few results, and if the desired information is not found, to make changes to the query in an attempt to improve the results. This cycle is repeated until the user is satisfied or gives up. The previous two chapters discussed interfaces for query specification and presentation of search results. This chapter discusses the query reformulation step.

6.1. The Need for Reformulation

Examination of search engine query logs suggests a high frequency of query reformulation. One study by Jansen et al. (2005) analyzed 3 million records from a 24 hour snapshot of Web logs taken in 2002 from the AltaVista search engine. (The search activity was partitioned into sessions separated by periods of inactivity, and no effort was made to determine if users searched for more than one topic during a session. 72% of the sessions were less than five minutes long, and so one-topic-per-session is a reasonable, if noisy, estimate.) The analysis found that the proportion of users who modified queries was 52%, with 32% issuing 3 or more queries within the session. Other studies show similar proportions of refinements, thus supporting the assertion that query reformulation is a common part of the search process.

Good tools are needed to aid in the query formulation process. At times, when a searcher chooses a way to express an information need that does not successfully match relevant documents, the searcher becomes reluctant to radically modify their original query and stays stuck on the original formulation. Hertzum and Frokjaer (1996) note that at this point "the user is subject to what psychologists call anchoring, that is, the tendency to make insufficient adjustments to initial values when judging under uncertainty." This can lead to "thrashing" on small variations of the same query. Russell (2006) remarks on this kind of behavior in Google query logs. For example, for a task of "Find out how many people have bought the new Harry Potter book so far," he observes the following sequence of queries for one user session:

- `Harry Potter and the Half-Blood Prince sales`
- `Harry Potter and the Half-Blood Prince amount sales`
- `Harry Potter and the Half-Blood Prince quantity sales`
- `Harry Potter and the Half-Blood Prince actual quantity sales`
- `Harry Potter and the Half-Blood Prince sales actual quantity`
- `Harry Potter and the Half-Blood Prince all sales actual quantity`
- `all sales Harry Potter and the Half-Blood Prince`
- `worldwide sales Harry Potter and the Half-Blood Prince`

In order to show users helpful alternatives, researchers have developed several techniques to try to aid in the query reformulation process (although existing tools may not be sophisticated enough to aid the user with the information need shown above.) This chapter describes interface technologies to support query reformulation, and the ways in which users interact with them.

6.2. Spelling Suggestions and Corrections

Search logs suggest that from 10 to 15% of queries contain spelling or typographical errors (Cucerzan and Brill 2004). Fittingly, one important query reformulation tool is spelling suggestions or corrections. Web search engines have developed highly effective algorithms for detecting potential spelling errors (Cucerzan and Brill 2004; Li et al. 2006).

Before the Web, spelling correction software was seen mainly in word processing programs. Most spelling correction software compared the author's words to those found in a pre-defined dictionary (Kukich 1992), and did not allow for word substitution. With the enormous usage of Web search engines, it became clear that query spelling correction was a harder problem than traditional spelling correction, because of the prevalence of proper names, company names, neologisms, multi-word phrases, and very short contexts (some spelling correction algorithms make use of the sentential structure of text). Most dictionaries do not contain words like `blog`, `shrek`, and `nsync`.

But with the greater difficulty also came the benefit of huge amounts of user behavior data. Web spelling suggestions are produced with the realization that, queries should be compared to other queries, because queries tend to have certain special characteristics, and there is a lot of commonality in the kinds of spelling errors that searchers make. A key insight for improving spelling suggestions on the Web was that query logs often show not only the misspelling, but also the corrections that users make in subsequent queries. For example, if a searcher first types `schwartze-neger` and then corrects this to `schwartzenegger`, if the latter spelling is correct, an algorithm can make use of this pair for guessing the intended word. Experiments on algorithms that derive spelling corrections from query logs achieve results in the range of 88–90% accuracy for coverage of about 50% of misspellings (Cucerzan and Brill 2004; Li et al. 2006).

For Web search engine interfaces, one alternative spelling is typically shown beneath the original query but above the retrieval results. The suggestion is also repeated at the bottom of the results page in case the user does not notice the error until they have scrolled through all of the suggested hits. As noted in Chapter 1, in most cases the interface offers the choice to the user without forcing an acceptance of an alternative spelling, in case the system's correction does not match the user's intent. But in the case of a blatantly incorrect typographical error, a user may prefer the correction to be made automatically to avoid the need for an extra click. To balance this tradeoff, some search engines show some hits with their guess of the correct spelling interwoven with others that contain the original, most likely incorrect spelling.

There are no published large-scale statistics on user uptake of spelling correction, but a presentation by Russell (2006) shows that, for those queries that are reformulations, and for which the original query consisted of two words, 33% of the users making reformulations used the spelling correction facility. For three-word query reformulations, 5% of these users used the spelling suggestion.

In an in-person study conducted with a statistically representative subject pool of 100 people, Hargittai (2006) studied the effects of typographical and spelling errors. (Here *typographical* means that the participant knows the correct spelling but made a typing mistake, whereas *spelling* error means the participant does not know the correct spelling.) Hargittai (2006) found that 63% of the participants made a mistake of some kind, and among these, 35% made only one mistake, but 17% made four or more errors during their entire session. As might be predicted, lower education predicted higher number of spelling errors, but an interesting finding was that the higher the participant's income, the more likely they were to make a typographical error. Older participants were more also likely to make spelling errors. The most surprising result, however, was that of the 37 participants who made an error while using Google search, none of them clicked on the spelling correction link. This would seem to contradict the statistics from Russell (2006). It may be the case that in Hargittai's data, participants made errors on longer queries exclusively, or that those from a broader demographic do not regularly make use of this kind of search aid, or that the pool was too small to observe the full range of user behavior.

6.3. Automated Term Suggestions

The second important class of query reformulation aids are automatically suggested term refinements and expansions. Spelling correction suggestions are also query reformulation aids, but the phrase *term expansion* is usually applied to tools that suggest alternative words and phrases. In this usage, the suggested terms are used to either replace or augment the current query. Term suggestions that require no user input can be generated from characteristics of the collection itself (Schütze and Pedersen 1994), from terms derived from the top-ranked results (Anick 2003; Bruza and Dennis 1997), a combination of both (Xu and Croft 1996), from a hand-built thesaurus (Sihvonen and Vakkari 2004; Voorhees 1994), or from query logs (Cucerzan and Brill 2005; Cui et al. 2003; Jones et al. 2006) or by combining query logs with navigation or other online behavior (Parikh and Sundaresan 2008).

Usability studies are generally positive as to the efficacy of term suggestions when users are not required to make relevance judgements and do not have to choose among too many terms. Some studies have produced negative results, but they seem to stem from problems with the presentation interface. Generally it seems users do not wish to reformulate their queries by selecting multiple terms, but many researchers have presented study participants with multiple-term selection interfaces.

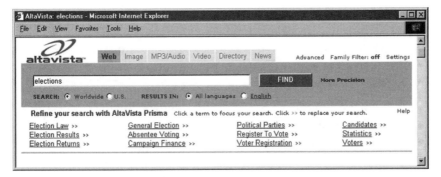

Figure 6.1. Illustration of Prisma term suggestions from Anick (2003).

For example, in one study by Bruza et al. (2000), 54 participants were exposed to a standard Web search engine, a directory browser, and an experimental interface with query suggestions. This interface showed upwards of 40 suggested terms and hid results listing until after the participant selected terms. (The selected terms were conjoined to those in the original query.) The study found that automatically generated term suggestions resulted in higher average precision than using the Web search engine, but with a slower response time and the penalty of a higher cognitive load (as measured by performance on a distractor task). No subjective responses were recorded. Another study using a similar interface and technology found that users preferred not to use the refinements in favor of going straight to the search results (Dennis et al. 1998), underscoring the search interface design principle that search results should be shown immediately after the initial query, alongside additional search aids.

6.3.1. *Prisma*

Interfaces that allow users to reformulate their query by selecting a single term (usually via a hyperlink) seem to fare better. Anick (2003) describes the results of a large-scale investigation of the effects of incorporating related term suggestions into a major Web search engine. The term suggestion tool, called Prisma, was placed within the AltaVista search engine's results page (see Figure 6.1). The number of feedback terms was limited to 12 to conserve space in the display and minimize cognitive load. Clicking on a hyperlink for a feedback term *conjoined* the term to the current query and immediately ran a new query. (The chevron (>>) to the right of the term *replaced* the query with the term, but its graphic design did not make it clearly clickable, and few searchers used it.) Term suggestions were derived dynamically from an analysis of the top-ranked search results.

The study created two test groups by serving different Web pages to different IP addresses (using bucket testing, see Chapter 2). One randomly selected set of users was shown the Prisma terms, and a second randomly selected set of users was shown the standard interface, to act as a control group. Analysis was performed on anonymized search logs, and user sessions were estimated to be bursts of activity separated by 60 minutes of no recorded activity. The Prisma group was shown query term refinements over a period of five days, yielding 15,133 sessions representing 8,006 users. The control group included 7,857 users and 14,595 sessions. Effectiveness of the query suggestions was measured in terms of whether or not a search result was clicked after the use of the mechanism, as well as whether or not the session ended with a result click.

In the Prisma group, 56% of sessions involved some form of refinement (which includes manual changes to the query without using the Prisma suggestions), compared to 53% of the control group's sessions, which was a significant difference. In the Prisma condition, of those sessions containing refinements:

- 25% of the sessions made use of the Prisma suggestions,
- 16% of the users applied the Prisma feedback mechanism at least once on any given day,
- When studied over another two weeks, 47% of those users used Prisma again within the two-week window, and
- over that period, the percentage of refinement sessions using the suggestions increased from 25 to 38%.

Despite the large degree of uptake, effectiveness when measured in the occurrence of search results clicks did not differ between the baseline group and the Prisma group. However, the percentage of clicks on Prisma suggestions that were followed immediately by results clicks was slightly higher than the percentage of manual query refinements followed immediately by results clicks.

This study also examined the frequency of different refinement types. Most common refinements were:

- Adding or changing a modifier (e.g., changing *buckets wholesale* to *plastic buckets*): 25%
- Elaborating with further information (e.g., *jackson pollock* replaced by *museum of modern art*): 24%

- Adding a linguistic head term (e.g., converting *triassic* to *triassic period*): 15%
- Expressing the same concept in a different way (e.g., converting *job listings* to *job openings*): 12%
- Other modifications (e.g., replacing with hyponyms, morphological variants, syntactic variants, and acronyms): 24%.

6.3.2. *Other Studies of Term Suggestions*

In a more recent study, White et al. (2007) compared a system that makes term suggestions against a standard search engine baseline and two other experimental systems (one of which is discussed in the subsection below on suggesting popular destinations). Query term suggestions were computed using a query log. For each query, queries from the log that contained the query terms were retrieved. These were divided into two sets: the 100 most frequent queries containing some of the original terms, and the 100 most frequent of queries that *followed* the target query in query logs – that is, user-generated refinements. These candidates were weighted by their frequency in each of the two sets, and the top-scoring six candidates were shown to the user after they issued the target query. Suggestions were shown in a box on the top right hand side of the search results page.

White et al. (2007) conducted a usability study with 36 participants, each doing two known-item tasks and two exploratory tasks, and each using the baseline system, the query suggestions, and two other experimental interfaces. For the known-item tasks, the query suggestions scored better than the baseline on all measures (easy, restful, interesting, etc). Participants were also faster using the query suggestions over the baseline on known item tasks (although tied with one experimental system), and made use of the query suggestions 35.7% of the time. For those who preferred this query suggestion interface, they said it was useful for saving typing effort and for coming up with new suggestions. (The experimental system for suggesting destinations was more effective and preferred for exploratory tasks.)

In the BioText project, Divoli et al. (2008) experimented with alternative interfaces for terms suggestions in the specialized technical domain of searching over genomics literature. They focused specifically on queries that include gene names, which are commonly used in bioscience searches, and which have many different synonyms and forms of

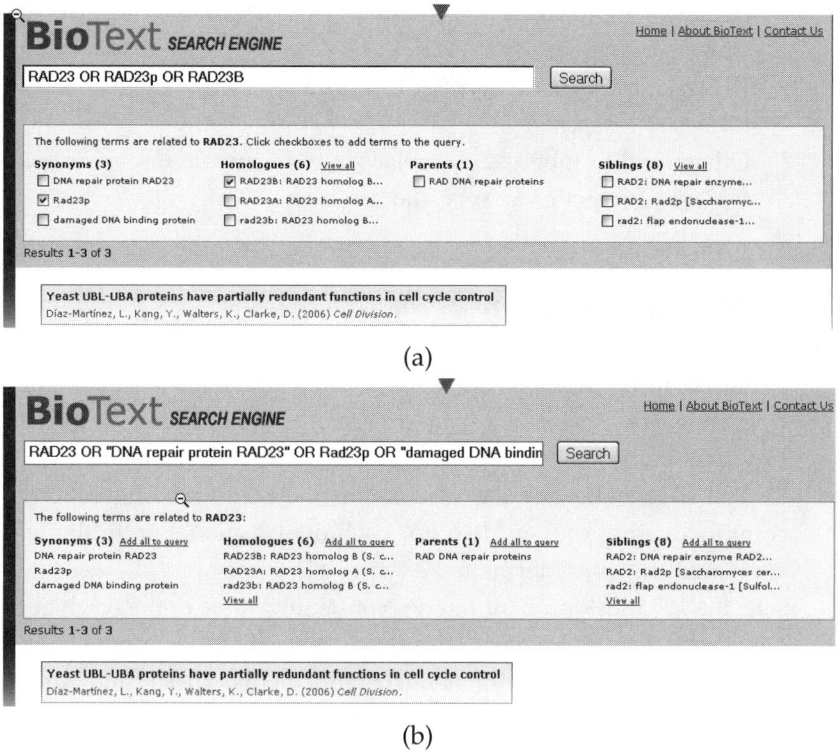

(a)

(b)

Figure 6.2. Term suggestion interface mock-ups from (Divoli et al. 2008). (a) Design 3 and (b) Design 4 (see text for details).

expression. Divoli et al. (2008) first issued a questionnaire in which they asked 38 biologists what kind of information they would like to see in query term suggestions, finding strong support for gene synonyms and homologues. Participants were also interested in seeing information about genes associated with the target gene, and localization information for genes (where they occurs in organisms). It should be noted that a minority of participants were strongly opposed to showing additional information, unless it was shown as an optional link, in order to retain an uncluttered look to the interface.

A followup survey was conducted in which 19 participants from biology professions were shown four different interface mock-ups (see Figure 6.2). The first had no term suggestions, while the other three showed term suggestions for gene names, organized into columns labeled by similarity type (synonyms, homologues, parents, and siblings of the gene). Because participants had expressed a desire for reduced clutter, at most three suggestions per columns were shown, with a link to view all choices.

Figure 6.3. Illustration of term suggestions from Dogpile.com, ©2008 InfoSpace, Inc. All rights reserved.

Design 2 required selection of the choices by individual hyperlink, with an option to add all terms. Design 3 allowed the user to select individual choices via checkboxes, and Design 4 allowed selecting of all terms within a column with a single hyperlink. Design 3 was most preferred, with one participant suggesting that the checkbox design also include a select all link within each column. Designs 4 and 2 were closely rated with one another, and all were strongly preferred over no synonym suggestions. These results suggest that for specialized and technical situations and users, term suggestions can be even more favored than in general Web search.

6.3.3. Query Refinement Suggestions in Web Search Interfaces

The results of the Anick (2003) and the White et al. (2007) studies are generally positive, and currently many Web search engines offer term refinement. For example, the Dogpile.com metasearch engine shows suggested additional terms in a box on the right hand side under the heading "Are you looking for?" (see Figure 6.3). A search on *apple* yields term suggestions of *Apple the Fruit* (to distinguish it from the computer company and the recording company), *Banana, Facts about Apples, Apple Computers, Red*

Apple, and others. Selecting *Apple the Fruit* retrieves Web pages that are about that topic, and the refinements change to *Apple Varieties, Apple Nutrition, History Fruit Apple, Research on Fruit, Facts about the Fruit Apple*, and others. Clicking on *Facts about the Fruit Apple* retrieves Web pages containing lists of facts.

The Microsoft search site also shows extensive term suggestions for some queries. For instance, a query on the ambiguous term `jets` yields related query suggestions including *Jet Magazine, Jet Airways, JetBlue, Fighter Jets, Jet Li*, and *Jet Stream* (see Figure 5.8 in Chapter 5).

Jansen et al. (2007b) studied 2.5M interactions (1.5M of which were queries) from a log taken in 2005 from the Dogpile.com search engine. Using their computed session boundaries (mean length of 2.31 queries per session), they found that more than 46% of users modified their queries, 37% of all queries were parts of reformulations, and 29.4% of sessions contained three or more queries. Within the sessions that contained reformulated queries, they found the following percentage of actions for query modifications (omitting statistics for starting a new topic):

- Assistance (clicked on a link offered by the question *Are you Looking For?*, which are term refinements): 22.2%
- Reformulation (the current query is on the same topic as the searcher's previous query, and shares one or more common terms with it): 22.7%
- Generalization (same topic, but seeking more general information): 7.2%
- Specialization (same topic, but seeking more specific information): 16.3%
- Content change (identical query, but run on a different collection): 11.8%
- Specialization with reformulation: 9.9%
- Generalization with reformulation: 9.8%

(Here, collections refer to Web pages versus searching images, videos, or audio data.) Thus, they found that 8.4% of all queries were generated by the reformulation assistant provided by Dogpile (see Figure 6.3), although they do not report on what proportion of queries were offered refinements. This is additional evidence that query term refinement suggestions are a useful reformulation feature. A recent study on Yahoo's search assist feature (Anick and Kantamneni 2008) found similar results; the feature was used about 6% of the time.

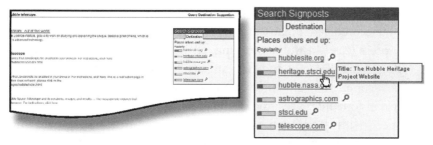

Figure 6.4. Query trail destination suggestions, from White et al. (2007).

6.4. Suggesting Popular Destinations

White et al. (2007) suggested another kind of reformulation information: showing popular destination Web sites. They recorded search activity logs for hundreds of thousands of users over a period of five months in 2005–2006. These logs allowed them to reconstruct the series of actions that users made from going to a search engine page, entering a query, seeing results, following links, and reading Web pages. They determined when such a session *trail* ended by looking for a stoppage, such as staying on a page for more than 30 minutes, or a change in activity, such as switching to email, or going to a bookmarked page. They distinguished session trails from query trails; the latter had the same stopping conditions as the former, but could also be ended by a return to a search engine page. Thus they were able to "follow" users along as they performed their information seeking tasks.

White et al. (2007) found that users generally browsed far from the search results page (around 5 steps), and that on average, users visited 2 unique domains during the course of a query trail, and just over 4 domains during a session trail. They decided to use the information about which page the users ended up at as a suggestion for a shortcut for a given query. Given a new query, its statistical similarity to previously seen query–destination pairs was computed, and popular final destinations for that query were then shown as a suggested choice (see Figure 6.4). They experimented with suggestions from both query trails and sessions trails.

In the same study of 36 participants, they compared these two experimental approaches against a standard search engine baseline and a query suggestions interface, testing on both known-item tasks and exploratory tasks. For exploratory tasks, the destination suggestions from the query trails scored better than the other four systems on perceptions of the search process (easy, restful, interesting, etc.) and usefulness (perceived as producing more useful and relevant results) for the exploratory tasks. The task completion time on exploratory tasks was approximately the same for all four interfaces; the destination suggestions were tied in terms of speed with query term suggestions in known-item tasks. In exploratory tasks, query trail destination suggestions were used more often (35.2% of the time) than query term suggestions and session trail destination suggestions.

Participants who preferred the destination suggestions commented that they provided potentially helpful new areas to look at and allowed them to bypass the need to navigate to pages. They suggested that destinations were selected because they "grabbed their attention," "represented new ideas," or users "couldn't find what they were looking for." Those who did not like the suggestions stated as a reason the vagueness of showing only a Web site; presumably augmenting the destination views with query-biased summaries would make them more useful. The destination suggestions produced from session trails were sometimes very good, but were inconsistent in their relevance, a characteristic which is usually perceived negatively by users. The participants did not find the graphical bars indicating site popularity to be useful, mirroring other results of this kind.

6.5. Relevance Feedback

Another major technique to support query reformulation is *relevance feedback*. In its original form, relevance feedback refers to an interaction cycle in which the user reads retrieved documents and marks those that appear to be relevant, and the system then uses features derived from these selected relevant documents to revise the original query (Ruthven and Lalmas 2003). In one variation, the system uses information from the marked documents to recalculate the weights for the original query terms, and to introduce new terms. In another variation, the system suggests a list of new terms to the user, who then selects a subset of these to augment the query (Koenemann and Belkin 1996). The revised query is then executed and a new set of documents is returned. Documents from the original set can appear in the new results list, although they are likely to appear in a different rank order. In some cases the relevance feedback interface displays an indicator such as a marked checkbox beside the documents that the user has already judged. For most relevance feedback techniques, a larger number of marked relevant documents yields a better result.

In a method known as *pseudo-relevance feedback* (also known as *blind relevance feedback*), rather than relying on the user to choose the top *k* relevant documents, the system simply assumes that its top-ranked documents are relevant, and uses these documents to augment the query with a relevance feedback ranking algorithm. This procedure has been found to be highly effective in some settings (Allan 1995; Kwok et al. 1995; Thompson et al. 1995). However, it does not perform reliably when the top-ranked documents are not relevant (Mitra et al. 1998).

Relevance feedback in its original form has been shown – in artificial settings – to be an effective mechanism for improving retrieval results (Buckley et al. 1994; Harman 1992; Mitra et al. 1998; Salton and Buckley 1990). For instance, a study by Kelly et al. (2005) compared carefully elicited user-generated term expansion with relevance feedback based on documents that were pre-determined by an expert to be the most relevant. The results of relevance feedback using the top-ranked documents far outstripped user-generated term expansion. Kelly et al. (2005) used the highly relevant documents as an upper bound on performance, as it could not be expected that ordinary users would identify such documents.

This finding is echoed by another study for the TREC HARD track in which an expert was shown the documents pre-determined to be most relevant and spent three minutes per query choosing documents for relevance feedback purposes. The resulting improvements over the baseline run was 60% over the metric used to assess improvements from clarification dialogues (Allan 2005). The results of using user-generated additional terms were that queries that were already performing well improved more than queries that were not performing well originally. This study also found that spending more time in the clarification dialogue did not correlate with improved final results.

Despite its strong showing in artificial or non-interactive search studies, the use of classic relevance feedback in search engine interfaces is still very rare (Croft et al. 2001; Ruthven and Lalmas 2003), suggesting that in practice it is not a successful technique. There are several possible explanations for this. First, most of the earlier evaluations assumed that recall was important, and relevance feedback's strength mainly comes from its ability to improve recall. High recall is no longer the standard assumption when designing and assessing search results; in more recent studies, the ranking is often assessed on the first 10 search results. Second, relevance feedback results are not consistently beneficial; these techniques help in many cases but hurt results in other cases (Cronen-Townsend et al. 2004; Marchionini and Shneiderman 1988; Mitra et al. 1998). Users often respond negatively to techniques that do not produce results of consistent quality. Third, many of the early studies were conducted on small text collections. The enormous size of the Web makes it more likely that the user will find relevant results with fewer terms than is the case with small collections. And in fact there is evidence that relevance feedback results do not significantly improve over web search engine results (Teevan et al. 2005b).

But probably the most important reason for the lack of uptake of relevance feedback is that the method requires users to make relevance judgements, which is an effortful task (Croft et al. 2001; Ruthven and Lalmas 2003). Evidence suggests that users often struggle to make relevance judgements (White et al. 2005), especially when they are unfamiliar with the domain (Vakkari 2000b; Vakkari and Hakala 2000; Spink et al. 1998). In addition, when many of the earlier studies were done, system response time was slow and the user was charged a fee for every query, so correct query formulation was much more important than for the rapid response cycle of today's search engines. (By contrast, a search engine designed for users in the developing world in which the round trip for retrieval results can be a day or more has renewed interest in accurate query formulation (Thies et al. 2002).) The evidence suggests it is more cognitively taxing to mark a series of relevance judgements than to scan a results listing and type in a reformulated query.

6.6. Showing Related Articles (More Like This)

To circumvent the need for multiple relevant document selection, Aalbersberg (1992) introduced an incremental relevance feedback that requires the user to judge only one document at a time. Similarly, some Web-based search engines have adopted a "one-click" interaction method. In the early days of the Web, the link was usually labeled as "More like this," but other terms have been used, such as "Similar pages" or "Related articles" at the biomedical search engine Pubmed. (This is not to be confused with "Show more results at this site" which typically re-issues the query within a subdomain.)

Figure 6.5. View similar articles function, from PubMed, published by the U.S. National Library of Medicine.

More recently in PubMed, after a user chooses to view an article, the titles of some related articles are shown along the right hand side (see Figure 6.5). Related articles are computed in terms of a probabilistic model of how well they match topics (Lin and Wilbur 2007). These related articles are relatively heavily used by searchers. Lin et al. (2008) studied a week's worth of query logs from PubMed in June 2007, observing about 2M sessions that included at least one PubMed query and abstract view. Of these, 360,000 sessions (18.5%) included a click on a suggested related article, representing about one fifth of non-trivial search sessions. They also found that as session lengths increased, the likelihood of selecting a related article link grew, and once users started selecting related articles, they were likely to continue doing so, more than 40% of the time.

Thus, the evidence suggests that showing similar articles can be useful in literature search, but it is unclear what its utility is for other kinds of search. Related article links act as a "black box" to users, meaning they cannot see why it is that one set of articles is considered related and others are not. Furthermore, they do not have control over in what ways other articles are related. Interfaces which allow users to select a set of categories or dimensions along which documents are similar may be more effective for this, as discussed in Chapter 8 on integrating navigation and search.

6.7. Conclusions

When an initial query is unsuccessful, a searcher can have trouble thinking
of alternative ways to formulate it. Query reformulation tools can be a
highly effective part of the search user interface. Query reformulation is
in fact a common search strategy, as evidenced by the statistics presented
throughout this chapter – roughly 50% of search sessions involve some
kind of query reformulation.

Both spelling suggestions and term expansions are effective reformulation tools – term suggestion tools are used roughly 35% of the time that
they are offered to users. Additionally, showing popular destinations for
common queries, and showing related articles for research-style queries
have both been shown to be effective. However, relevance feedback as
traditionally construed has not been proven successful in an interactive
context.

7 Supporting the Search Process

Chapter 3 discussed the various theories associated with the information seeking process, and the subsequent chapters described interfaces for supporting query specification, results presentation, and query reformulation – the standard stages of the search process. This chapter describes interface ideas for other aspects of the search process: search starting points, search history, and interfaces that support the process as a whole. The final section discusses attempts to integrate search into the sensemaking process.

7.1. Starting Points for Search

The first step in addressing an information need is deciding which tools to use and which collections to search over, a process which is sometimes referred to as *source selection*. Today there are many choices, including phoning, emailing, or texting a friend, reaching for a physical book, going to a physical library, or sitting down at a networked computer and starting up a Web browser.

7.1.1. *Starting Points in Web Search*

For those who go online, today the most common starting point is to open a Web browser and start with a Web search engine. Today, Web browsers make that choice even easier by including an always-visible entry form in the browser's "chrome" or by supporting search directly in what used to be the address entry form. But people also commonly start searches

157

from favorite information resources, such as bookmarked Web sites (Teevan et al. 2004). Web browsers have always allowed users to retain bookmarks, but today are making site revisitation even easier by showing usage history as a drop-down menu within the address bar, and matching that history as the user types. The Chrome Web browser shows a grid of thumbnail images of the user's commonly visited sites directly on the browser's home page.

In the early days of the Web, hyperlinked directories of Web sites were quite popular as search starting points, in part because the set of interesting sites was smaller, and because for many years search engines were perceived as inaccurate and slow (Piontek and Garlock 1996). Hyperlinked directories like Yahoo's remained popular until the Web became too large both for the editors manually editing the sites, and for users navigating through the hierarchies. (In May of 1996, Yahoo had 200,000 Web sites in its directory, out of what was estimated to be half a million sites and 21 million pages (Steinberg 1996).) Web directory sites also became crowded with advertising and other material in the quest to build lucrative "portals," which led to a backlash against the "clutter." The use of Web directories has declined markedly, replaced by search engines as starting points.

Traditionally, librarians have prided themselves on acting as information curators, selecting information collections and ensuring the authenticity and reliability of information presented within those collections. There is a general concern that Web search obliterates the distinction among sources, and provides searchers with few cues about the quality or reliability of retrieved information sources (Rieh 2002). Web search engines do employ internal quality metrics, in part to eliminate spam, and in part to improve ranking, but they are influenced by popularity of Web sites as well as by a computed measure of "authority" for those sites. These measures in some cases correspond to what information scientists deem to be quality measures (Amento et al. 2000), but do not use their notions of quality explicitly. (For instance, a few years back, the top results for Web search on the query `Joe McCarthy` were primarily sites that praised this political figure and claimed he had gotten an unfair treatment by historians, a view significantly outside the mainstream.) What is not in dispute is that Web search result surrogates do not provide adequate information to allow users to judge the underlying quality of the information sources (Rieh 2002), and those credibility cues that do appear on Web sites can be easily mimicked (Fogg et al. 2001).

To address these concerns, the Google Co-op project provides vetted sites for certain types of queries. For instance, for health-related queries

such as `tamoxifen`, some of the search results after selecting a Co-op refinement link indicate which trusted Web site they have been endorsed by
(see Figure 8.1 in Chapter 8). More ambitiously, the Mahalo.com Web site
is a relatively new portal that provides a curated set of Web sites and news
sources.

Nonetheless, source selection interfaces are still lacking in Web search.
Even the relatively easy task of providing search results limited to Web site
sources with educational as opposed to commercial or political sources is
not supported. This may reflect a lack of demand for such kinds of results, or it may be that automatically classifying sources in this manner is
not yet possible with sufficient accuracy. Furthermore, most Web users are
not accustomed to searching for sources explicitly (although navigational
queries are in fact queries for already known sources). Good interface design could overcome this particular barrier.

7.1.2. *Starting Points in Online Library Catalogs*

For many years, online library catalogs required users to begin by looking through a list of names of sources and choosing which collection to
search on (Dempsey 2006). Often the user had to repeat the same search
across different collections within an online library catalog, in part due to
technology limitations, and in part due to ownership restrictions over the
different collections. More recently, library catalog interfaces have become
integrated, allowing the user to issue their query once and see the results
for multiple resources in one place. But this produces another problem, as
search engine interfaces tend to remove distinctions between sources and
place the user into the middle of a Web site or other resource with little
information about context. To counter this, library catalog interfaces have
recently begun adopting faceted navigation interfaces (Hearst et al. 2002)
that will eventually allow the user to group and select search results according to source, along with other attributes (see Figure 7.1). Faceted navigation interfaces have been shown to exhibit good usability results in online library catalogs (Olson 2007), and are discussed in detail in Chapter 8.

An even more recent innovation can be seen in the Lexis-Nexis interface for statistical databases. This system provides a standard form-based
starting-points interface, but unlike systems of old, allows for searching
over a huge collection of tables of data, including allowing search over
specific fields such as table titles and table text (Figure 7.2 shows the query
forms and search results). This is a powerful interface, but because it uses

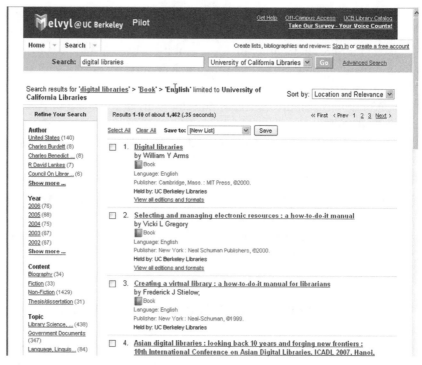

Figure 7.1. An experimental digital library interface with faceted navigation grouping capabilities, from the University of California at melvyl.worldcat.org. The screenshot is taken from OCLC's WorldCat® database; the screenshot is used with OCLC's permission; WorldCat® is a registered trademark of OCLC Online Computer Lbrary Center, Inc.

a parametric design (where users have to select all the fields up front) the user often ends up with empty results sets (as opposed to a faceted inter-face with query previews, which prevents the user from selecting fields that would yield empty results sets). For instance, if the query shown in Figure 7.2 is modified to select annual data with hits in table titles, no re-sults are returned. An even more radical interface is shown in Figure 7.3 in which the data from the datasets is exposed directly in the search start-ing point. The user can select alternative views within datasets and can do comparisons, on the datasets directly. This is a strikingly different form of search starting point.

7.1.3. Interactive Dialogues as Search Starting Points

Another approach for getting started with search is the interactive dia-logue, which provides support for a series of question–answer interactions

(a)

(b)

Figure 7.2. LexisNexis search over collections of statistical databases. (a) This is a conventional form-based interface, but it allows the user to search for words within the text and titles of the statistical tables in the collection. (b) The search results show links to pages that include the matching tables extracted. Copyright 2009 LexisNexis, a division of Reed Elsevier Inc. All Rights Reserved. LexisNexis and the Knowledge Burst logo are registered trademarks of Reed Elsevier Properties Inc. and are used with the permission of LexisNexis.

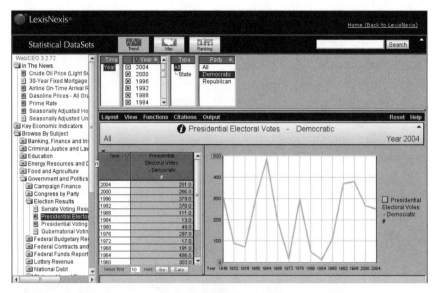

Figure 7.3. LexisNexis interface for collections of statistics data, but in this case the starting point is a browsable visualization of the contents of the datasets themselves. Copyright 2009 LexisNexis, a division of Reed Elsevier Inc. All Rights Reserved. LexisNexis and the Knowledge Burst logo are registered trademarks of Reed Elsevier Properties Inc. and are used with the permission of LexisNexis.

between the user and the system. Dialogue-based interfaces have been explored since the early days of information retrieval research, in an attempt to mimic the interaction provided by a human search intermediary (e.g., a reference librarian). Early work in the THOMAS system provided a question and answer session within a command-line based interface (Oddy 1977). Others have defined quite elaborate dialogue interaction models (Belkin et al. 1993). More recently, interactive question-and-answer interfaces have been developed for specialized information seeking tasks, such as choosing a laptop computer (McSherry 2003). Dialogue-style interactions have not yet become widely used, most likely because they are still difficult to develop for robust performance.

7.2. Supporting Search History

Another way to support the search process is to help users retain the context of their queries, sources, and results sets. The most straightforward way to do this is to record queries and search history and allow users to re-access these records. As seen in Chapter 4, even the primitive

TTY-style interfaces of early search systems like Dialog allowed users to name queries and results sets and use those to build up complex Boolean queries. In Web-based search systems, query history is sometimes shown as a chronologically ordered list of most-recently issues queries (as is done in the PubMed interface, as shown in Chapter 1). And as discussed above, Web browser address forms now show previously visited Web pages in a drop-down history list. Search engine toolbars, such as those supplied by Yahoo, Google, and Microsoft search, also support a facility to record and view search history.

Many researchers have experimented with incorporating thumbnails as memory aids in browser and search history. Chapter 10 discusses the use of thumbnail images in search results (suggesting that at best they do not improve upon textual search results displays, but using them in page history seems to be useful).

A particular kind of history mechanism used primarily in vertical web sites, is the *breadcrumb*. These are especially common on e-commerce sites and sites that use faceted navigation. A distinction is often made between *path* breadcrumbs that reflect the sequence of links that a user has clicked on since beginning a navigation session (hence earning their name, after the Grimm's fairy tale of *Hansel and Gretel*), and *location* – or *information structure-based* breadcrumbs that reflect the site structure, indicating where in the Web site's information architecture the current page is situated. (An example of the path version is shown in Figure 7.1 below the search entry form.) Nielsen (2007) argues in favor of structural breadcrumbs, noting that showing the site structure is useful for when users arrive at a page directly from a search engine, rather than when navigating to it, and because the Web browser back button works very well for allowing searchers to retrace their actions. Nielsen (2007) states:

> Despite their secondary status, I've recommended breadcrumbs since 1995 for a few simple reasons: Breadcrumbs show people their current location relative to higher-level concepts, helping them understand where they are in relation to the rest of the site. Breadcrumbs afford one-click access to higher site levels and thus rescue users who parachute into very specific but inappropriate destinations through search or deep links. Breadcrumbs never cause problems in user testing: people might overlook this small design element, but they never misinterpret breadcrumb trails or have trouble operating them. Breadcrumbs take up very little space on the page.

Rogers and Chapparo (2003) found in a controlled study with 45 participants that the structure-based breadcrumbs led to a better understanding of site structure than no breadcrumbs. Hearst (2006b) also supports structure-based breadcrumbs, noting that in faceted navigation, the path within each facet should be shown in a separate visual element, to both reinforce the understanding of the facet structure, and to allow for more flexible expansion or retraction of the query.

7.3. Supporting the Search Process as a Whole

Much less well-understood is how to devise interfaces to support the search process as a whole. Marchionini et al. (2000) describe a framework they call *agileviews* which consists of six kinds of views: *primary views, overviews, previews, reviews, peripheral views,* and *shared views*. The primary view is represented by the documents that have been accessed, and the results listing. Overviews show starting points and orient the user to the choices that are available. Previews show the user what will happen if a certain choice is made, allowing for informed decisions of what to do next (these include document surrogates, as discussed in Chapter 4 and query previews as discussed in Chapter 8). Reviews allow for revisiting past choices, essentially providing search history as described above, and peripheral views show information "in the background" that may become of interest but are not the current focus of attention, such as minimized windows of previously viewed information. Shared views show the state of search actions performed by other people. The agileviews framework underscores the need to support fluid interaction among the different views to support the search process.

Not many interfaces support all of this functionality. Most attempts show query history, organized results, and suggested terms in a window or set of views. The Protofoil/Infogrid interface (Rao et al. 1992; Rao et al. 1994; Rao et al. 1995) was an early example of a visually oriented interface to support the search process that displayed a number of the views described by Marchionini et al. (2000) (see Figure 7.4). The layout of this interface was a grid divided into fixed areas used for different purposes: showing the query, showing retrieval results, viewing the current document, a side panel for storing selected documents, and a lower gutter viewing a history of retrieved documents. The results viewing section of the interface allowed for flexibly moving between different views of retrieval results. There is some evidence that allowing flexible switching between different views of retrieval results is useful (Hearst et al. 1998; Reiterer et al. 2000).

Several of the digital library research systems developed in the 1990s experimented with more elaborate ways to support the search process

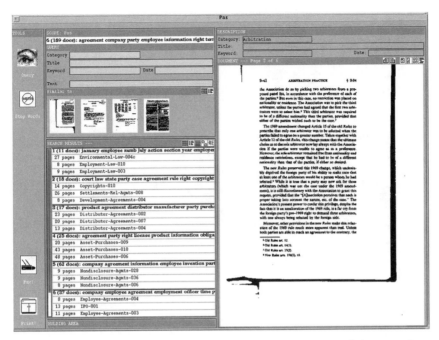

Figure 7.4. The Protofoil interface for supporting the entire search process, from Rao et al. (1995). The query appears in the upper left, retrieval result with multiple different views in the lower left, and the document under view on the right. In this image, Scatter/Gather-style clusters (Cutting et al. 1992) are used to group the search results.

(Baldonado and Winograd 1997). For example, in the Ariadne system (Twidale and Nichols 1998), queries were run against a library catalog system, which produced textual output. The designers converted this text-heavy view into a visualization of a sequence of cards containing thumbnail outlines of the query and result screens. The cards were arranged on three horizontal tiers, where the top row's cards indicated a meta-activity (selecting a command from the system's menu), the middle row represented queries and results, and the bottom row contained documents viewed or saved. This view allowed the user to review and re-visit their sequence of actions (see Figure 7.5).

The DLITE system (Cousins 1997; Cousins et al. 1997) presented a creative extension on these ideas (see Figure 7.6). It split functionality into two parts: control of the search process and display of results. The control portion was a graphical direct-manipulation display with animation. Queries, sources, documents, and groups of retrieved documents were represented as graphical objects. The user created a query by filling out the editable fields within a query constructor object. The system

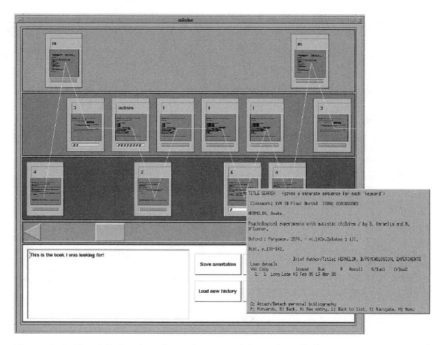

Figure 7.5. The Ariadne interface, from Twidale and Nichols (1998). Queries and results are represented visually as cards, although their underlying content is shown as text screens. Each row signals a different search activity, and time is indicated by position from left to right.

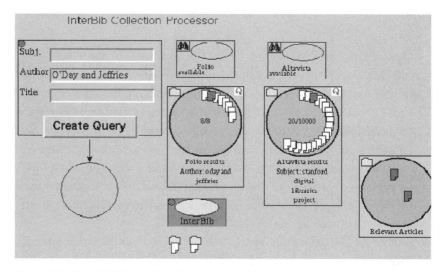

Figure 7.6. The DLITE interface for supporting the process of search, from Cousins et al. (1997). The rectangular query constructor object is shown at left. Two service objects are shown in the upper center and right. Three circular results sets are shown below and to the right of these and a summarizer service object is shown in the lower center region, with two icons representing document summaries below it.

manufactured a query object, which was represented by a small icon which could be dragged and dropped onto iconic representations of collections or search services. If a service was active, it responded by creating an empty results set object and attaching the query to it. A set of retrieval results was represented as a circular pool, and documents within the result set were represented as icons distributed along the perimeter of the pool. Documents could be dragged out of the results set pool and dropped into other services, such as a document summarizer or a language translator. The user could also make a copy of the query icon and drop it onto another search service. Placing the mouse over the iconic representation of the query caused a "tool-tips" window to pop up to show the contents of the underlying query. Queries could be stored and reused at a later time, thus facilitating retention of previously successful search strategies.

A flexible interface architecture freed the user from the restriction of a rigid order of commands. However, such an architecture must provide guidelines to help get the user started, give hints about valid ways to proceed, and prevent the user from making errors. The graphical portion of the DLITE interface made liberal use of animation to help guide the user. For example, if the user attempted to drop a query in the document summarizer icon – an operation that is not permitted – rather than failing and giving the user an accusatory error message (Cooper 1995), the system took control of the object being dropped, refusing to let it be placed on the representation for the target application, and moved the object left, right, and left again, mimicking a "shake-the-head-no" gesture. Animation was also used to help the user understand the state of the system, for example, in showing the progress of the retrieval of search results by moving the result set object away from the service from which it was invoked.

DLITE used a separate Web browser window for the display of detailed information about the retrieved documents, such as their bibliographic citations and their full text. The browser window was also used to show Scatter/Gather-style cluster results (see Chapter 8) and to allow users to select documents for relevance feedback. Earlier designs of the system attempted to incorporate text display into the direct manipulation portion, but this was found to be infeasible because of the space required (Cousins 1997). Thus DLITE separated the control portion of the information access process from the scanning and reading portion. This separation allowed for reusable query construction and service selection, while at the same time allowing for a legible view of documents and relationships among retrieved documents. The selection in the display view is linked to the graphical control portion, so a document viewed in the display could be used as part of a query in a query constructor.

DLITE also incorporated the notion of a workspace, or "workcenter," as it was known in this system. Different workspaces are created for different kinds of tasks. For example, a workspace for buying computer software could be equipped with source icons representing good sources of reviews of computer software and good Web sites to search for price information and links to the user's online credit service.

7.4. Integrating Search with Sensemaking

As discussed in Chapter 3, the term *sensemaking* refers to the process of interweaving the seeking of information with the interpretation of information. Russell et al. (1993) observe that most of the effort in sensemaking goes towards the synthesis of a good representation, or way of thinking about, the problem at hand. They also describe the process of formulating and crystallizing the important concepts for a given task. Search plays only one part in this process; some sensemaking activities involve search throughout, while others consist of doing a batch of search followed by a batch of analysis and synthesis. Sensemaking is most often used to refer to information-intensive tasks like intelligence analysis, scientific research, and the legal discovery process. But even more mundane tasks like researching information and making reservations for travel could benefit from more helpful interfaces than are available today.

How should sensemaking interfaces differ from search interfaces? Patterson et al.'s (2001) analysis highlights the many ways in which search tools are lacking for deep analytical tasks. A more supportive search tool would give an overview of the contents of the collection, would help the analysts keep track of what they had already viewed, would suggest what to look for next, would encourage analysts to try new queries, and would find additional documents similar to those already found, but would distinguish duplicates. Studies also suggest that analytical search tools should allow for aliasing of terms and concepts.

In these studies, one source of error resulted from analysts reading documents that occurred early in the sequence of events, when information is less well-established, rather than later reports that explained the phenomena more fully. This suggests that an interface that shows temporal relationships among related documents could improve performance. Another source of error occurred when analysts incorporated inaccurate information into their analysis. Some of the more successful analysts used judgements of source quality in their assessment of the selected documents. Thus, a facility to aid with various forms of quality assessment would also be useful. No current interfaces support all of these goals, but progress is being made especially in the context of supporting intelligence analysts.

As noted above, a sensemaking interface should support the ability to flexibly arrange, re-arrange, group, and name and re-name groups of information. It has often been observed that users use the physical layout of information within a spreadsheet to organize information (Malone 1983; Nardi 1993; Shipman et al. 1995). People tend to arrange physical papers in piles around them as an organizational and memory device (Fass et al. 2002; Robertson et al. 1998; Rose et al. 1993; Russell et al. 1993; Whittaker and Hirschberg 2001), and as Malone (1983) notes, a function of information organization is to help remind people of things to do, not just help them find information. Studies have found that tools for organizing partially formed ideas must support informal interaction, in order to avoid interrupting peoples' train of thought (Marshall et al. 1991).

Thus, a number of research and commercial tools have been developed that attempt to mimic physical arrangement of information items in a virtual representation. The Aquanet and VIKI projects (Marshall et al. 1991, 1994) designed and evaluated tools to help people organize their thoughts as they process information. These interfaces made use of a canvas or workspace, upon which a user could flexibly arrange snippets of retrieved and processed information. The goal was to allow the user to just point and type, without having to stop to categorize or label the information. These interfaces also allowed users to represent relational information, both according to spatial layout and using visual cues, such as using boxes of different shapes for different idea types. Marshall et al. (1994) found that once the user is ready to apply labels, the labeling mechanism should be flexible, and it should be very easy to group different items together into more structured units. It should also be easy to incorporate additional structure when needed. They also developed spatial layout templates that allowed for representations of argument structure and discussion.

Some of these ideas for storing, organizing, and arranging information have appeared in commercial tools like Microsoft's OneNote. In the Web space, a number of tools have been developed to help users keep track of and organize "clippings" of information extracted from Web sites, as seen in the Internet Scrapbook (Sugiura and Koseki 1998) and the Hunter Gatherer interface (Zhu et al. 2002). More recently, Doncheva et al. (2006)

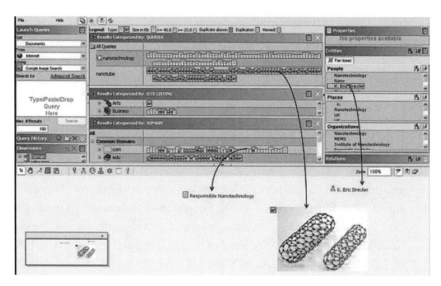

Figure 7.7. Moving information of different granularities from TRIST to the Sandbox workspace, from Wright et al. (2006).

describe a system which allows users to select and store elements from Web pages and arrange them on an information canvas, and visually lay out the components using a combination of user labels and pre-determined templates (such as a map or a grid).

The flexible analysis tools of Marshall et al. (1994) did not focus on how to integrate information search within the sensemaking process. An early system to address the two together was the SketchTrieve interface (Hendry and Harper 1997). The guiding principle behind SketchTrieve was to support information access as an informal process, in which half-finished ideas and partly explored paths can be retained for later use, and the results combined via operations on graphical objects and connectors between them. SketchTrieve showed sets of related retrieval results as a stack of cards within a folder and allowed the user to extract subsets of the cards and view them side by side. The Data Mountain 3D desktop interface by (Robertson et al. 1998) extended this idea by showing retrieved documents as physical-looking cards in 3D virtual space, allowing the user to group and re-arrange the cards by "pushing" them around the space. (This work was in turn an extension of the Information Visualizer Workspace and Web Forager work (Card et al. 1991, 1996); see Figure 5.9 in Chapter 5).

The Sandbox system by Wright et al. (2006) takes these ideas even farther (see Figures 7.7–7.9). This and companion tools were demonstrated

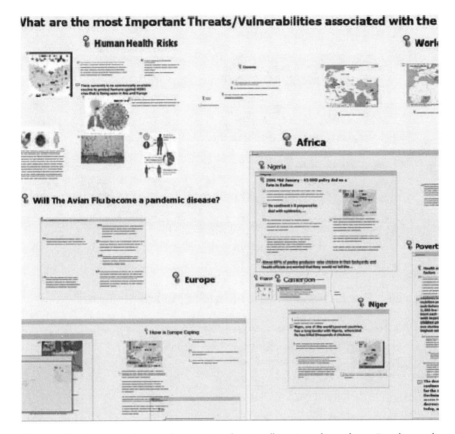

Figure 7.8. An emerging analysis using the Sandbox interface, from Proulx et al. (2006).

in detail on a complex epidemiological investigation of Avian Flu (Proulx et al. 2006). Sandbox allows for free-form organization of retrieved results, and automatically retains links to the original sources, which can be dragged and dropped to the workspace from its companion retrieval system, TRIST (Jonker et al. 2005) (see Figure 7.7). The tool allows information to exist in the workspace at different levels of representation, from a simple word or phrase, to a set of retrieved documents, to the results of a simulation derived from a different tool (see Figure 7.8). Users can draw arbitrary-shaped lassos to gather scraps of information into a new group. A simple up-line gesture allows for temporary zooming in for detail, or to zoom in or out of the entire view.

Sandbox has a simple mechanism for making room at any point on the workspace. In response to a simple up-arrow gesture at the desired spot on the workspace, the system automatically clears an open space, moving

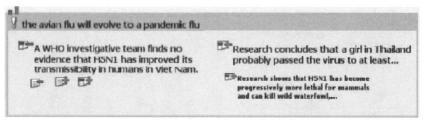

Step 1. Exploration workspace, in this case an assertion.

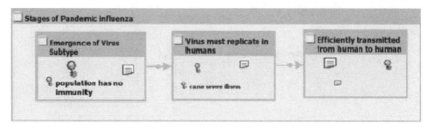

Step 2. Process Template on the Stages of Pandemic Influenza.

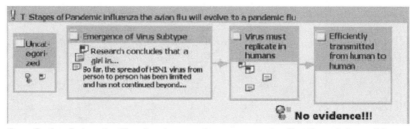

Step 3. Applying the Pandemic template automatically placed the evidence from the exploration workspace in this new perspective.

Figure 7.9. Hypothesis formulation in Sandbox, aided by predefined templates, from Proulx et al. (2006).

the existing pieces of information out of the way, but retaining the relative orientation and layout of the pre-existing items. The amount of room cleared is a function of the size of the gesture. The system also allows the user to "grasp" one item and use it to "knock away" other items (Hutchings and Stasko 2002).

Sandbox offers a structured template showing how a given problem has been reasoned about in the past (e.g., known paths for transmission of infectious disease, see Figure 7.9). The analyst is instructed to find supporting information for each part of the process, thus drawing attention to information that should be available but currently is missing. The system also allows the analyst to represent structured arguments, in the form of hypotheses, and support for and against. Transparency is used to indicate the degree of confidence in the various statements, to remind the user that not all information can be relied upon. The system displays a glyph in the corner of the window that shows a running total of supporting and refuting evidence. The visualization of retrieval results for the TRIST search system that underlies Sandbox is discussed in Chapter 11.

7.5. Conclusions

This chapter has described interfaces for search starting points, for retaining search history, for supporting the entire process, and for making sense of retrieved information as it is gathered. This technology is not as mature as the components discussed in the preceeding three chapters. Most pressing is the need for better interfaces to support complex information seeking tasks. By way of illustration, it is still a complex and time-consuming task to plan a trip to a new location, even with the bountiful information available online. This difficulty lies in part with the fact that this task requires an understanding of the needs and preferences of the individual or group who is doing the search, and because the results of such a search have interlocking parts and dependencies. Better supporting these aspects of search are active areas of research, and new ideas should be expected to appear in future.

8 Integrating Navigation with Search

This chapter describes interfaces to support navigation (or browsing) as part of the search process. Chapter 3 discusses theoretical models of browsing versus search as information seeking strategies, as well as the notion of information scent and information architecture. As mentioned there, one way to distinguish searching versus browsing is to note that search queries tend to produce new, ad hoc collections of information that have not been gathered together before, whereas navigation/browsing refers to selecting links or categories that produce pre-defined groups of information items. Browsing activities can also include following a chain of links, switching from one view to another, in a sequence of scan and select operations. Browsing can also refer to the casual, mainly undirected exploration of navigation structures.

Navigation structures lend themselves more successfully to books, information collections, personal information, Web sites, and retrieval results than to vast collections such as the Web. Nonetheless, there have also been attempts to organize very large information collections such as the Web.

Category systems are the main tool for navigating information structures and organizing search results. A category system is a set of meaningful labels organized in such a way as to reflect the concepts relevant to a domain. A fixed category structure helps define the information space, organizing information into a familiar structure for those who know the field, and providing a novice with scaffolding to help begin to understand the domain. Category system structure in search interfaces is usually either *flat*, *hierarchical*, or *faceted* (this is discussed in detail below).

In search interfaces, categories are typically used either for selecting a subset of documents out from the rest, thus narrowing the results, or for grouping documents, dividing them into (potentially overlapping) subsets, but keeping the documents visible. They can also be used for ordering and sorting search results. Faceted category navigation integrated with keyword search has become especially successful for search over information collections.

In most browsing structures, a set of category labels is manually defined and documents are assigned to those categories, either by hand or automatically. However, in an attempt to avoid the need for manual category creation and assignment, *clustering* algorithms have often been explored to aid in the exploration of collections and retrieval results. The advantage of clustering is that the groups and labels are automatically derived from the document collection, but the disadvantage is that the outcome is usually less predictable and less understandable than that of category systems.

The following sections discuss interfaces for grouping search results and collections by flat categories, hierarchical categories (including table-of-contents structures), and faceted categories. Then the use of clustering for creating flat and hierarchical organizations is discussed. Finally, the relative merits of categories versus clusters are discussed.

8.1. Categories for Navigating and Narrowing

Many of today's Web sites have sophisticated, well-designed information structures that use categories to help the user navigate the site and narrow down the content to what is of most interest. In some specialized content domains (sometimes known as *verticals*), the top-level categories tend to become standardized across Web sites over time. (How this happens has not been studied; presumably the designers of major Web sites examine other sites' categories, as well as study their navigation and search logs to see what people are looking for. For some commercial sites, sellable products presumably help determine the categories.) For example, the top-level categories for U.S. sports Web sites are usually named after sports organizations, including NFL, MLB, NBA, NHL, etc. Table 8.1. shows the top-level categories for three major sports Web sites, used in the main navigation menu.

Not only are the top-level categories nearly the same, but the submenus for the different sports (*Teams, Statistics,* etc.) are nearly identical as

Table 8.1. Categories as navigation aids for three major sports Web sites (espn.go.com, www.usatoday.com/sports, and msn.foxsports.com) as of Summer 2007. Numbers indicate the position, from left to right, across the navigation bar. Note the uniformity both in the names of the top-level categories and their positioning. The naming exceptions are that only ESPN distinguish Men's and Women's basketball (the other two names are *College basketball* and *NCAA BK*), and a distinction between *College Football, NCAA FB,* and *College FB*).

	ESPN	USA today	MSN/Foxsports
Fantasy	1	1	12
NFL	2	3	1
MLB	3	2	2
NBA	4	4	3
NHL	5	5	4
ESPNU	6	–	–
College FB	7	6	6
Men's BB	8	8	7
Women's BB	9	8	7
NASCAR	10	–	5
Auto	11	9	–
Golf	12	10	9
Soccer	13	–	–
Tennis	14	–	10
Boxing	15	–	–
AFL	16	–	–

well. The categories serve a narrowing function; first navigating to *MLB* (Major League Baseball) and then to *Teams* shows information about baseball teams. Consequently, the categories keep similar types of information across different sports separated from one another; there is no way on these sites to see, say, statistics across all sports simultaneously. For the purposes of the users of most of these sites, that kind of comparison is not important, and so the restricted category structure works well.

As another example of category systems used for narrowing information content, Google has recently developed a system called Co-op in which experts manually assign category labels to Web pages for a limited set of topic areas (Health, Travel, Computers, etc.). Each topic, has a predefined set of categories associated with it, organized into facets. Facets in the Health topic include *Drug Information* (*drug uses, side effects,* etc), *For doctors* (*research overview, practice guidelines,* etc.), and *Information type* (*from medical authorities, alternative medicine, for patients, support groups,* etc.). Figure 8.1 shows the results of a search on the query *tamoxifen*, after selecting the category *Treatment* within the facet *Condition Information*. These labels are currently only used for refining search results – that is, they

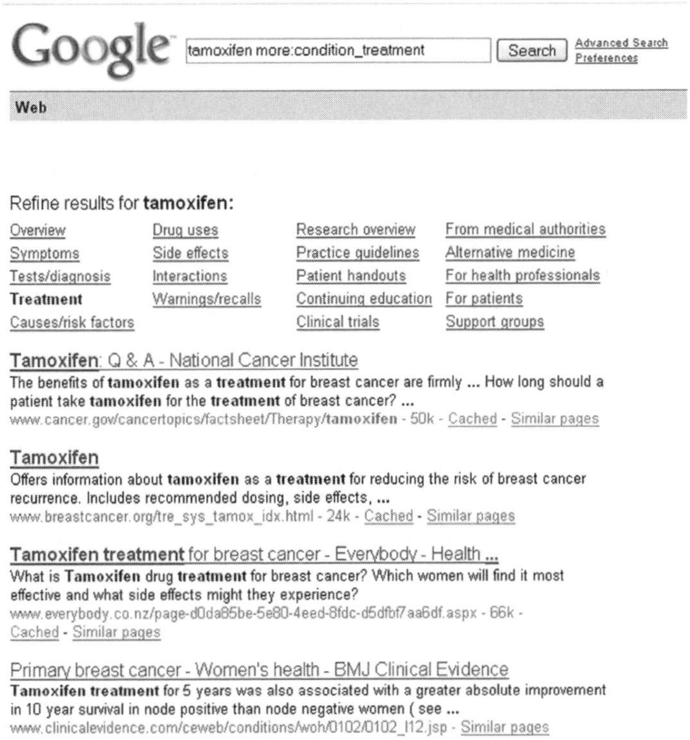

Figure 8.1. Search result refinement with faceted categories in the Health topic in Google Co-op. Refinement may be done with only one facet label at a time.

narrow the set of retrieved documents; they are not used to group the results, and currently the results may be refined with only one label at a time. Thus selecting *Interactions* within the *Drug Information* facet after selecting *Side Effects* replaces the latter query with the former.

Although this looks like the query term suggestions of Chapter 6, there are important differences. Rather than replacing the original query with a different term that may help refine the sense of the word (as in substituting `Apple computer` for the query `apple`), the Co-op method uses category metadata (manually) assigned to documents to determine whether to retrieve the documents in the selected subset (as opposed to running a keyword match).

8.2. Categories for Grouping Search Results

A weakness of many Web sites' navigation structure is that the Web sites do not integrate their browsing with their searching functions. For example, the Google Co-op system described above uses faceted categories only for narrowing search results; only one category's information can be seen at any time. The sports sites described above do not use their category systems to organize the results of keyword search. A search on Bonds mixes articles about the baseball player Barry Bonds with writings about the football player Mark Bonds. (However, these sites do sometimes group search hits by genres: breaking news versus older news versus blog posts and columnist's essays.)

For Web search, Chapter 5 shows some simple approaches to grouping retrieval results for highly ambiguous queries (see Figures 5.1 and 5.7), but much more power is needed for collection or site search, as there is ample evidence that it can be useful to organize search results by grouping hits according to the categories that the documents fall into.

Dumais et al. (2001) use a text categorization algorithm to classify Web pages into one of ten top-level general categories (e.g., *Automotive, Computers & Internet, Entertainment & Media, Travel & Vacations, Shopping & Services, Society & Politics,* and *Not Categorized*). They experimented with seven different ways of showing the search results, varying whether category groupings, category names, document titles, and document summaries were shown (see Figure 8.2). They evaluated the results by timing how long participants took to find the first relevant document for each of several pre-determined queries. The most significant result was that the category *groups* were responsible for the biggest time savings. Results listings that grouped categories together but did not label the categories performed nearly as well as results that showed groups with labels, and far better than linear results listings that contained category names beneath each search result. In fact, no significant difference was seen between a linear listing of search results and the same listing with category names alongside each search hit. (For many years, major Web search engines showed category labels drawn from manual directories alongside search results. That is no longer common practice, and the results of this study support this omission.) Subjective results indicated a strong preference for the category grouping interfaces, although the interface that showed groups but no group labels was disliked, despite the fact that it helped achieve higher scores in the study.

Further analysis revealed that most of the timing gain came from those queries for which the relevant results were not in the top 20 search results in the linear listings. This means that, in these cases, a category selection operation moved relevant documents up from farther down in the results listing, showing them alongside similar documents.

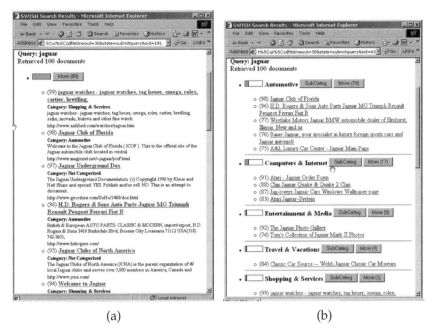

(a)   (b)

Figure 8.2. Two of the experimental conditions from Dumais et al. (2001). (a) Results shown in a linear view with category labels shown, but results not grouped by the categories. (b) Results grouped by categories, with category labels.

It is important to note, however, that the queries for the Dumais et al. (2001) study were in fact carefully designed to maximize the disambiguation effects of category usage. For example, one task was to *Find the home page for the band called "They Might be Giants."* The query in this case was giants, which is a rather unrealistic formulation for a query on a band of this name (titles of books, movies, musical groups, etc., are common Web queries). Another task was to *Find the Giants Ridge Ski Resort*, and again the query that was input for the participants was giants, which is also an unlikely query for this information need. Thus the large timing differences are most likely artificial and would probably become much smaller or could even disappear with a more realistic set of queries. Studies of clustering (see below) suggest that grouping is less effective for unambiguous queries.

A more recent study by Kules and Shneiderman (2008) exposed participants to two versions of an interface: the baseline with standard search results listings and the experimental design that used the same results listings but categorized hits in a list of categories with query previews on the left hand side. Participants were 24 journalism students who were asked to conduct Web searchers to find ideas for articles to write on four different topics. The top 100 pages of a search engine's results were classified automatically into top-level categories drawn from the Open Directory Project (ODP), as well as into government and geographic categories.

The experimenters found no significant differences in the quality of the ideas generated, but on subjective scales participants found the categorized interface more appealing and the results felt more organized than the baseline. Participants also viewed a broader portion of the results listings in the category interface, an effect which is echoed in other studies discussed below (Käki 2005c; Zamir and Etzioni 1999). Several participants commented that they changed their search tactics by looking at the category listings before looking at the results listings, or using it as a backup when they felt stuck. However, participants voiced discontent with category labels that were not representative of the expected meaning of the underlying documents, for example, categorizing a news story about human smuggling under *TV* because the Web page was from the BBC. Additionally, many of the categories were vague or general (e.g., *Reference, Society*), which lessened the usefulness of the category system. The participants did not find the category interface more difficult to use, but two participants commented on the complexity of the categories and one asked for a method to hide them.

More evidence for the value of grouping search results by categories is provided in the section on faceted navigation.

8.3. Categories for Sorting and Filtering Search Results

In addition to being used for navigating content within Web sites and grouping search results, categories can be used for *sorting* search results, that is, for reordering results according to one or more attributes' values.

Some sorting interfaces allow for ordering along only one dimension at a time, as seen in the lower region of the eBay Express example in Figure 8.12. The user has the option of sorting the search results by *Best Selling, Best Match,* or *Price*. Other sorting interfaces present results in a *sortable-column* format in which results can sorted by one dimension after another, usually by clicking on the label of the column, as seen in Figure 8.3 and in Figure 10.17(a) of Chapter 10. Figure 8.3 shows the Phlat interface (Cutrell et al. 2006b) for navigating and searching personal information, including email, calendar events, locally stored documents, and recently visited Web pages. The results section on the right hand side allows the user to sort search results according to the title (by alphabetical order), by date, by

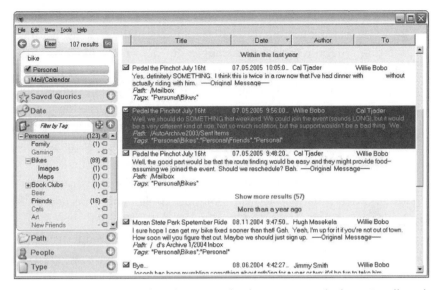

Figure 8.3. The Phlat interface for personal information search, from Cutrell et al. (2006b).

author/sender, by recipient name, and by a number of other attributes not shown in the figure. As is common in file browser interfaces, a click on the title of the column sorts the contents by the corresponding attribute, toggling between ascending and descending sort order. An advantage of the sortable-column format is that after sorting along one dimension, such as date, the user can sort along another, such as author, while retaining the date sort order from the prior sorting action within each author's message list (this is referred to as *stable sorting*).

Sorting is especially useful for attributes which have a naturally understandable sequential order (attributes with real, integer, or ordinal values); for instance, it makes sense to see products ordered by increasing price or email ordered by decreasing recency. Sorting does not work well if the attribute of interest does not have an inherently meaningful ordering. For example, people's names are often listed alphabetically, and it is easy to select or look up a name within alphabetical order, but scanning people's names according to alphabetical order is not meaningful in the same way as scanning products by increasing price. That is, there is usually no *meaning* inherent in showing messages from Charles Adams immediately adjacent to messages from Douglas Adams. (These ideas are discussed in more detail in Chapter 10.)

For nominal attributes which do not have a meaningful order, it can be more useful to provide users with a *filtering* function, to be used in conjunction with sorting. Filtering is the application of a category or attribute to select out from the search results only those items that meet the filtering criterion. (Sorting rearranges but does not remove any results.) Filtering is thus used to eliminate some records to help focus on categories of interest. In the Phlat example of Figure 8.3, after doing an initial query on the keyword bike, the user chose a filter that selects only messages labeled as *Personal*. In this example, the user also chose a file type filter, restricting results to only email and calendar hits. Finally, the results were sorted according to date, showing the most recent items first.

Activating a filter is functionally similar to navigating via a category, but differs conceptually in terms of interface design and expectations. While both perform narrowing functions, a filter is intended to be toggled on and off, to manipulate the subset of search results without disturbing the other constraints on the results, while selecting a topic category is meant to hide the other category choices and reduce the set in view.

In a longitudinal study of the use of the Phlat system by more than 200 people over an 8-month period, Cutrell et al. (2006b) found that 47% of all queries used some kind of filter. Of these, the most common were people followed by file type and then date (note however that the default sort order was date; an earlier study (Dumais et al. 2003) showed that date/time was the preferred organization for personal information collections). One-third of all searches that used filters used more than one filter, and 17% of searches used *only* filters, with no query term at all.

8.4. Organizing Search Results via Table-of-Contents Views

The sections above have described the use of flat, or linear, categories for navigating, sorting, filtering, and grouping of search results. Another common information organization structure is that of the hierarchy or tree structure. One simple version of the hierarchy is the table-of-contents (TOC) view used in books and other information systems. A number of research systems have put forward the idea of supporting search results organization by making use of a TOC structure.

The SuperBook system (Egan et al. 1989a,b; Landauer et al. 1993) pioneered a number of search user interface ideas, but its major emphasis was to make use of the structure of a large document to display query term hits in context. The TOC for a book or manual were shown in a hierarchy on the left hand side of the display, and full text of a page or section was shown on the right hand side. The user manipulated the TOC to expand or contract the view of sections and chapters. A focus-plus-context mechanism (see Chapter 10) was used to expand the viewing area of the sections currently being looked at and compress the remaining sections. When the user moved the cursor to another part of the TOC, the display changed dynamically, making the new focus larger and shrinking down the previously observed sections.

After the user specified a query on the book, the search results were shown in the context of the TOC hierarchy (see Figure 8.4). Those sections that contain search hits were made larger and the others were compressed. The query terms that appeared in chapter or section names were highlighted in reverse video. When the user selected a page from the TOC view, the page itself was displayed in the right hand side and the query terms within the page were highlighted in reverse video.

To evaluate the interface, the SuperBook system was compared against using paper documentation and against a more standard online information access system (Landauer et al. 1993). Participants were asked to complete several kinds of carefully selected tasks: browsing topics of interest, citation searching, searching to answer questions, and searching and browsing to write summary essays. For most of the tasks participants were faster and more accurate or equivalent in speed and accuracy using Super-Book over a standard system. The investigators examined the logs carefully and hypothesized plausible explanations for differences between the systems.

After the initial studies, they modified SuperBook according to these hypotheses and usually saw improvements as a result (Landauer et al. 1993). The usability studies on the improved system showed that participants were faster and more accurate at answering questions in which some of the relevant terms were within the section titles themselves, but they were also faster and more accurate at answering questions in which the query terms fell within the full text of the document only, as compared both to a paper manual and to an interface that did not provide such contextualizing information. SuperBook was not faster than paper when the query terms did not appear in the document text or the TOC. This and other evidence from the SuperBook studies suggest that query term highlighting is at least partially responsible for improvements seen in the system (see the related discussion in Chapter 5).

Several researchers have experimented with placing Web search results into a TOC-like format, using the structure of web sites' hyperlinks. Figure 8.5 shows an example from the Cha-Cha system (Chen et al. 1999; Chen and Hearst 1998). This system differs from SuperBook in several ways.

The SuperBook Document Browser Features

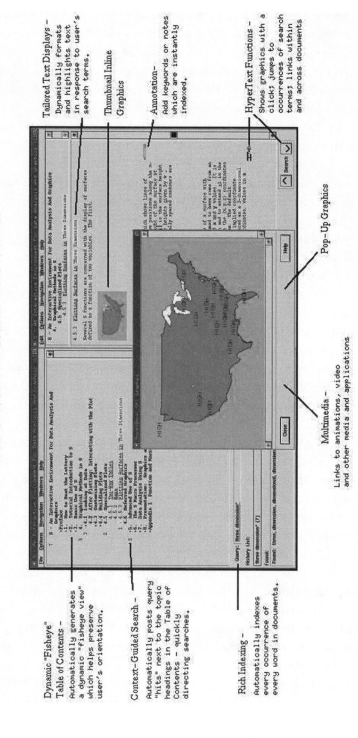

Tailored Text Displays – Dynamically formats and highlights text in response to user's search terms.

Thumbnail Inline Graphics

Annotation– Add keywords or notes which are instantly indexed.

HyperText Functions – Shows graphics with a click; jumps to occurrences of search terms; links within and across documents

Pop-Up Graphics

Multimedia – Links to animations, video and other media and applications.

Rich Indexing – Automatically indexes every occurrence of every word in documents.

Context–Guided Search – Automatically posts query "hits" next to the topic headings in the Table of Contents – quickly directing searches.

Dynamic "Fisheye" Table of Contents – Automatically generates a dynamic "fisheye view" which helps preserve user's orientation.

Figure 8.4. The SuperBook interface for showing retrieval results in context, using the table of contents from a large manual, from Landauer et al. (1993).

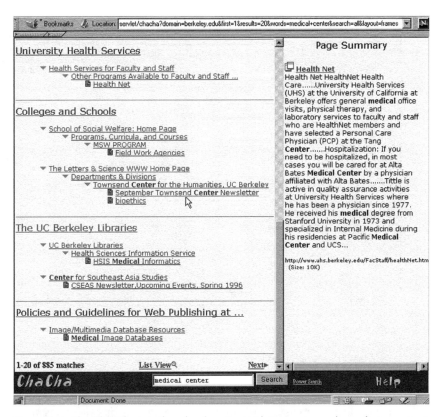

Figure 8.5. The Cha-Cha interface for showing Web intranet search results in context, from Chen and Hearst (1998).

On most Web sites there is no existing real TOC or category structure, and an intranet like those found at large universities or large corporations is usually not organized by one central unit. Cha-Cha uses link structure present within the site to create what is intended to be a meaningful organization on top of the underlying chaos. After the user issues a query, the shortest paths from the root page to each of the search hits are recorded and a subset of these are selected to be shown as a hierarchy, so that each hit is shown only once. The AMIT system (Wittenburg and Sigman 1997) also applied the basic ideas behind SuperBook to the Web, but focused on a single-topic Web site, which is more likely to have a reasonable topic structure than a complex intranet. The WebTOC system (Nation 1997) was similar to AMIT, but focused on showing the structure and number of documents within each Web subhierarchy, and was not tightly coupled with search.

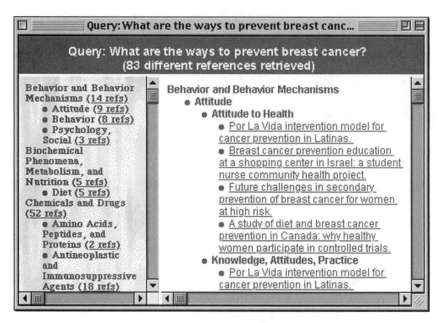

Figure 8.6. The DynaCat interface for viewing retrieval results organized according to a set of pre-defined categories selected to correspond to pre-determined query types, from Pratt et al. (1999).

In the Dynacat system (Pratt et al. 1999), a set of categories was pre-selected from a large taxonomy, in a particular domain. A set of query types was also pre-determined. In this particular case, the domain studied was cancer, so sample query types are "What are the potential complications of Procedure X?" or "What are the ways to prevent Condition Y?". The retrieved documents were organized according to which types of categories were known in advance to be important for a given query type. Results were grouped into relevant category hierarchies such as Behavior, Nutrition, Chemicals and Drugs, etc. (see Figure 8.6). The left window showed the categories in the first two levels of the hierarchy, providing a TOC view of the organization of search results. The right pane displayed all the categories in the hierarchy and the titles of the documents that belong in those categories. A 15-person between-participants usability study comparing this tailored category-based interface to a linear list and a polythetic clustering interface (see below) found a strong subjective preference for category organization over both of the other search results interfaces.

Despite the experimental evidence in favor of TOC structures, they are still not widely used to organize search results or online book search Web sites.

Figure 8.7. Yahoo directory in April 1997 (courtesy www.waybackmachine.org). (Reproduced with permission of Yahoo! Inc. ©2009 Yahoo! Inc. YAHOO! and the YAHOO! logo are registered trademarks of Yahoo! Inc.)

8.5. The Decline of Hierarchical Navigation of Web Content

In the early days of the Web, hand-built category hierarchies (Web directories) such as those supplied by Yahoo and LookSmart and more recently the open-source directory ODP were very popular ways to navigate the Web (Pollock and Hockley 1997). Figure 8.7 shows the Yahoo directory circa 1997, when it was heavily used.

As the growth in the number of Web sites accelerated and the accuracy of search engines improved, the importance of such general directories declined markedly. In addition to the improvement in Web search ranking, this decline is probably linked to the poor navigability of the directory Web sites. Such hierarchies are difficult to navigate in large part because to accurately describe information, different categories often need to be mixed together. In particular, for the Yahoo directory, content categories are often intermixed with categories describing location and categories describing commercial concerns. This mixing of category types would lead to complex navigation paths for finding information. Consider the following sequence of links that must be traversed to find a kayaking Web site called *Outdoor Adventures* (www.kayaking.com) from dir.yahoo.com:

> Directory > Regional > U.S. States > California > Cities > Lotus > Business and Shopping > Paddling

The Yahoo directory does have more direct paths to other kayaking web sites, for example,

> Directory > Recreation > Outdoors > Paddling > Canoeing and Kayaking

but following this path will not lead the user to the Outdoor Adventures Web site. The user can take a different path:

> Shopping and Services > Outdoors > Paddling

but this yields yet a different set of Web sites. These convolutions arise because of the difficulty of modifying hierarchy and retaining semantically consistent labels within hierarchy. It appears that, although hierarchical structures are commonly used and are useful when applied to smaller collections, as a navigation structure, they become unwieldy when applied to very large collections. Classification of information items more naturally requires access via multiple category starting points; this alternative is discussed below.

8.6. Faceted Navigation

A problem with assigning documents to single categories within a hierarchy is that most documents discuss several different topics simultaneously. Text consists of abstract discussions of ideas and their interrelationships. It is a rare document that is only about trucks; instead, a document might discuss recreational vehicles, or the manufacturing of recreational vehicles, or for that matter the trends in manufacturing of American recreational vehicles in Mexico before vs. after the NAFTA agreement. The tendency in building taxonomic hierarchies is to create ever-more-specific categories to handle cases like these. A better solution is to describe documents by a *set* of categories, as well as attributes (such as source, date, genre, and author), and provide good interfaces for manipulating these labels.

This use of what is known as *faceted metadata* provides a usable solution to the problems with navigation of strict hierarchies. The main idea is to build a set of category hierarchies each of which corresponds to a different facet (dimension or feature type) that is relevant to the collection to be navigated. Each facet has a hierarchy of terms associated with it. After the facet hierarchies are designed, each item in the collection can be assigned any number of labels from the facet hierarchies. The resulting interface is known as *faceted navigation*, or sometimes as *guided navigation*. An alternative design, usually known as *parametric search*, requires the user to select a number of attributes from drop-down menus all at once, thus often leading to empty results sets. (For instance, at a Web site selling shoes, selecting women's shoes of size 4.5, width M, color black, and price $39.99 to $69.99 yields no results and provides no suggestions as to which attributes to remove.) For this reason, parametric search has largely fallen out of favor and been replaced by faceted navigation.

8.6.1. *The Flamenco Faceted Navigation Interface*

Faceted classification and faceted navigation are now widely used in Web site search and navigation. In research on the Flamenco project, Hearst et al. (Hearst 2000, 2006b; Hearst et al. 2002; Yee et al. 2003) described the importance of faceted classification systems for Web site navigation, and designed and studied a series of user interfaces to support faceted navigation for everyday users. The overarching design goals of the Flamenco project were to support flexible navigation, seamless integration of browsing with directed (keyword) search, fluid alternation between refining and expanding, avoidance of empty results sets, and at all times allowing the user to retain a feeling of control and understanding.

Another of the Flamenco project's goals was to promote the idea of faceted navigation in online systems, as an alternative to the hierarchical focus of Web site structure, and in response to the failure of subject searching in online catalogs (Hert et al. 2000; Larson 1991). The term "faceted" was chosen by this project to reflect the underlying spirit of the idea from library science. Ranganathan (1933) is often credited with introducing the idea with his colon classification system, which suggested describing information items by multiple classes, and Bates (1988) advocated for faceted library catalog representations in the 1980s. (Of course, how to use such systems in user interface was not addressed by Ranganathan (1933) and Bates's (1988) view was restricted to that of TTY-based interfaces.) It should be noted that the Dewey Decimal system, often used in local libraries, has aspects of facet analysis because it combines multiple categories into one description string (Maple 1995), but it does not allow for the flexible application of ordering and combination of categories that online faceted navigation affords.

Hearst et al. (2002) describe faceted metadata as being composed of "orthogonal" sets of categories, meaning each category describes a different, usually independent aspect of the information items. For example, in the domain of fine arts images, possible facets might be *Media* (etching, woodblock, ceramic, etc.), *Locations* (Asia, North America, Europe, etc.), *Animals & Plants, Earth & Sky* (mountains, rivers, clouds, etc), as well as information about the art, including artist names, time of creation, etc. A facet may be *flat* ("by Pablo Picasso") or *hierarchical* ("located in Vienna > Austria > Europe"). A facet may be *single-valued* or *multi-valued*. That is, the data may allow at most one value to be assigned to an item ("measures 36 cm tall") or it may allow multiple values to be assigned to an item ("uses oil paint, ink, and watercolor"). Portions of the hierarchies within a facet are sometimes referred to as the facet's *subcategory* or *subhierarchy*.

In a faceted search interface, labels are assigned to items from the collection. Figure 8.8 shows the faceted metadata associated with a woodcut by the Japanese artist Inoue Yasuji entitled "Toshagu Shrine, Ueno." Within the *Media* facet, it has been assigned the category label *Print > woodcut*, within the *Location* facet it is assigned *Asia > Japan*. The painting contains a depiction of a snowy scene at night, with a Torii gate in the foreground through which runs a road leading to a red shrine in the background. Categories have also been assigned from the facet *Heaven and Earth* and *Built Places* as well as *Shapes and Colors > Color > Red* and *Objects: Lighting > lantern*. Because this object is indexed under these different, separate categories, a user can navigate to this image in a number of different ways.

For example, the user might start by selecting the *Location* facet, and within this, select *Asia*, and then the subcategory *Japan*. Figure 8.9 shows the results of this navigation. There are 538 pieces of art in this subcollection. The facets are shown on the left hand side, indicating with *query previews* (Plaisant et al. 1997a) how many of each kind of media

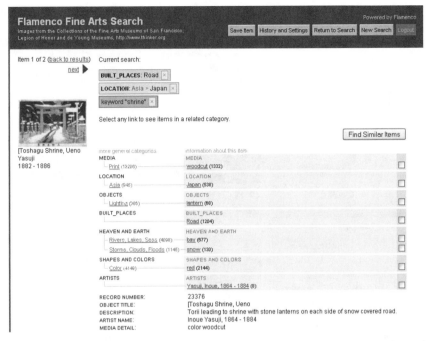

Figure 8.8. Flamenco interface for browsing and search using hierarchical faceted metadata. Item view showing the leaf-level metadata, placed in the context of their facets. Image credits shown in the Appendix.

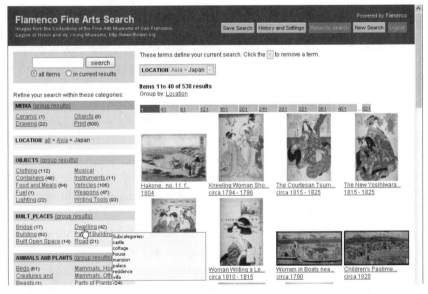

Figure 8.9. Flamenco interface for browsing and search using hierarchical faceted metadata. Shown are the results after first selecting *Location: Asia* and then selecting *Japan* within *Location: Asia*. A tooltip shows the categories that appear beneath *Built Places: > Dwelling*, but without the preview counts. Image credits shown in the Appendix.

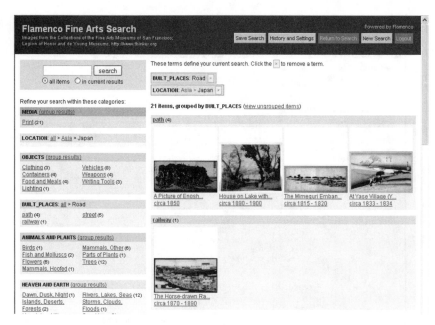

Figure 8.10. Flamenco interface for browsing and search using hierarchical faceted metadata, continued from Figure 8.9. Shown are the results after selecting *Location > Asia > Japan* and *Built Places > Road* and grouping by the subcategories of *Road*. Image credits shown in the Appendix. (See color plate 3.)

(Drawing, Print, etc.) are in the collection, as well as the proportion of images from each media type, the number of prints whose images contain different object types and different building types. The documents that match the query are shown in the right hand pane. The user may now choose to navigate via a different facet, such as *Built Places*, and select *Road* (see Figure 8.10), and then grouping by the subcategories of *Road*, showing images containing *Paths, Railways*, etc.

A key component to successful faceted search interfaces is the seamless integration of keyword search. In this example, if the user now chooses to issue a keyword query, such as shrine, the category structure is retained; the keyword search is done over the metadata and text associated with the current result set; the resulting narrowed result set is again grouped by the facet categories (see Figure 8.11). These results include the image of the Toshagu Shrine (see Figure 8.8). Looking again at the metadata assigned to that artwork, the user may choose to make a lateral move within the collection, by clicking on *lantern* to see all artworks assigned this term.

This example is intended to illustrate the ease with which the user can navigate through the collection, with keyword search tightly integrated

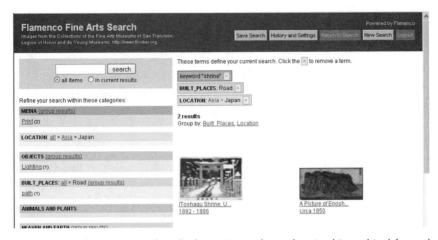

Figure 8.11. Flamenco interface for browsing and search using hierarchical faceted metadata, continued from Figure 8.10. Shown are the results after adding the keyword shrine to the query. Image credits shown in the Appendix.

with the category system, and both narrowing and expanding of choices part of a smooth interaction flow.

Many important design details must be done well in order to ensure that a content-rich navigation system like Flamenco is easy to use. The graphical depiction of a users' navigation history or trail is often referred to as a *breadcrumb*. In standard Web site usage, breadcrumbs simply record the sequence of actions that the user has taken within the query session, and thus mix and match fields of various types (see Chapter 7). Faceted systems should instead keep the path within each facet in a separate visual component. This both reinforces the notion of the query consisting of a conjunction of different categories at different levels of hierarchy, and allows for flexible expansion of the query, since the user can eliminate an entire facet by clicking on the iconic x or "delete" link, or expand up within a category by clicking on a parent term. In Figure 8.9 this would mean generalizing from *Japan* to *Asia* by clicking on the latter link in the breadcrumb.

There is a question of how to expose the hierarchical categories without crowding the display or confusing the user. Flamenco adopted a step-by-step drill-down approach in which the level just below the currently selected level is visible, along with a trail indicating the higher-level concepts positioned just above the labels. In addition, when the mouse hovers over a label, its immediate children are displayed in a tooltip, so the user can in fact see three levels simultaneously (see Figure 8.9).

Hearst et al. (English et al. 2001; Hearst et al. 2002; Yee et al. 2003) conducted a series of usability studies that found that participants like and are successful using hierarchical faceted metadata for navigating information collections, especially for browsing tasks. In one study (Yee et al. 2003), 32 art history students evaluated the Flamenco design in comparison with a baseline Google images-type interface for navigating a fine arts museum image collection containing about 35,000 items. The tasks were designed to reflect the contents of the collection and the art history background of the students. Participants completed four tasks on each interface, two structured and two unstructured. One of the structured tasks used metadata categories clearly visible in the start page and facet labels, but the other was carefully worded so as not to correspond to the wording of any facet.

Each participant used both interfaces (order was balanced), and filled out a questionnaire immediately after finishing each interface individually. Participants were significantly in favor of the faceted interface for the measures of "easy to use," "easy to browse," "flexible," "interesting," and "enjoyable." For "simple" and "overwhelming," there was no significant difference between the two designs, which is surprising given how much more information is shown in the Flamenco interface. The order in which interfaces were viewed had a strong effect on these ratings. When the faceted design was viewed first, the interface ratings for the baseline were considerably lower than when the baseline was the first interface shown.

At the end of the study, participants were asked to compare the two interfaces directly. For finding images of roses (a simple, single-facet task), about 50% preferred the baseline. However, for every other type of searching, the Flamenco interface was preferred: 88% said that Flamenco was more useful for the types of searching they usually do and 91% said they preferred Flamenco to the baseline overall. Those who preferred the baseline commented on its simplicity and stated that the categories felt too restrictive. These results were especially notable given that the faceted interface was an order of magnitude slower than the baseline (although participants did remark negatively about the slowness).

Some participants at the start of the study said they considered themselves the type of information seeker who like to use keyword search rather than select links. These participants did indeed start out with keywords, but as they became more familiar with the system, started initiating their tasks using links rather than keyword queries.

There are some deficiencies with the faceted paradigm. If the facets do not reflect a user's mental model of the space, or if items are not assigned

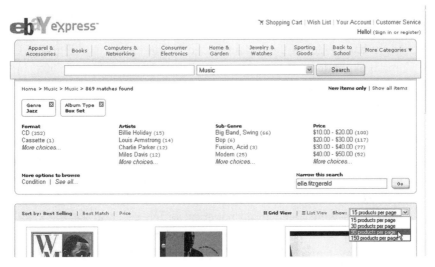

Figure 8.12. eBay Express faceted navigation interface.

facet labels appropriately, the interface will suffer some of the same problems as directory structures. The facets should not be too wide nor too deep (with exceptions for long lists such as author names that cannot be organized meaningfully) and the interface must be designed very carefully to avoid clutter, dead ends, and confusion.

8.6.2. *Faceted Navigation at eBay Express*

Faceted navigation has become the de facto standard way to support the integration of browsing and search on information-rich Web sites, ranging across collections as diverse as the WebMD health care Web site, the Dell Web site for purchasing computers, and the online catalog at Michigan State university (see Figure 8.15).

One site that had some particularly interesting design choices is the eBay Express online shopping interface (although eBay Express is no longer supported, a similar interface has since been adopted by the Yelp local reviews Web site, and the example is instructive). The designers determined in advance which subset of facets were of most interest to most users for each product type (shoes, art, etc.), and initially exposed only four of these fully, listing additional choices on one compact line below (see Figure 8.12). This interface positions the expanded facets across the top of the screen, in the "sweet spot" (the region of a Web page that users tend to look at first since it usually contains the most important content on the page). After the user selected a facet, one of the compressed facets from the list below was expanded and moved up to the end of the line (right hand side) of the expanded facets. For instance, in Figure 8.12, the initial expanded facets were *Artist, Genre, Album Type*, and *Price*, but the list was adjusted to account for the fact that two of these have been selected. The ordering of the facets in the query breadcrumbs reflected their order of selection by the user.

This interface also limited the number of labels shown for each facet, and customized which facets were shown on the basis of the type of information. In Figure 8.12, the labels beneath the *Genre* facet listed the four most common genres of music in the *Boxed Set* albums. Within these four, the genres were listed in alphabetical order. By contrast, the *Price* facet showed price ranges in ascending numerical order.

In this system, if a label within a hierarchical facet was chosen, the next level was shown as a *separate* facet. For example, in Figure 8.12, the user chose two labels: the first as *Album Type > Box Set* and the second was *Genre > Jazz*. Below the query were shown the available subcategories for the selected genre, Jazz. The facet name was *Sub-Genre* and the relevant labels included *Big Band, Swing, Bop, Latin Jazz*, and so on.

eBay Express had a particularly interesting approach to handling keyword queries. The system attempted to map the user-entered keywords into the corresponding facet label, and simply added that label to the query breadcrumb. For example, a search on "Ella Fitzgerald" created a query consisting of the *Artists* facet selected with the *Ella Fitzgerald* label. Search within results was accomplished by nesting an entry form within the query region. The eBay Express team commissioned third-party usability assessments that found that users understood these innovative aspects of the faceted interface design (Hearst et al. 2006).

8.7. Navigating via Social Tagging and Social Bookmarking

Another likely reason for the decline in popularity of hand-built classifications of Web content is that they cannot keep up with the contents of the Web. The early directories such as Yahoo and LookSmart were closed systems that only allowed employees of their respective companies to determine which categories Web pages fell into. The ODP system is open and allows contributors from all over the Internet to donate content. However, annotation is time-consuming as users must navigate a complex hierarchy and carefully consider which category to place a Web page into.

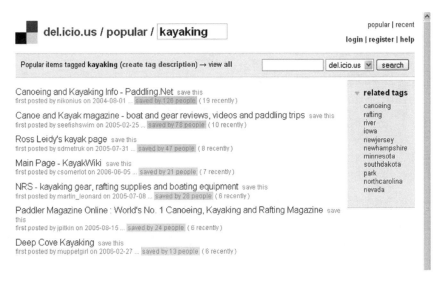

Figure 8.13. del.icio.us output on the tag *kayaking*, sorted by most frequently tagged. (Reproduced with permission of Yahoo! Inc. ©2009 Yahoo! Inc. YAHOO! and the YAHOO! logo are registered trademarks of Yahoo! Inc.)

An important and growing alternative to Web directories are social bookmarking sites which allow any user to assign any category label to web pages. These category labels are usually referred to as *tags*. A user may assign any number of tags to an item, and can use any label that they think of, as opposed to having to determine the one "proper" category from within a hierarchy to assign. The popularity of tagging (or *folksonomies*, as user-generated tag systems are also known) is largely attributable to the relatively low cognitive overhead required in assigning tags without the need to refer to a controlled vocabulary, and to the ease with which multiple labels may be assigned. When a user tags a Web page, they simultaneously save the page to their own personal collection. Social bookmarking Web sites have search engines built in and are easily accessible from any networked computer, unlike bookmarking facilities provided by Web browser software. Thus, social bookmarking sites have distinct advantages over Web browser bookmarks for the individual assigning the labels, and so tagging is an activity that helps the labeller directly, and as a side-benefit, produces content that is useful for other people.

Figure 8.13 shows the results of a search on the tag *kayaking* on the social bookmarking site delicious.com. In this view the seven most popular sites are shown. Unfortunately, the search interfaces for social tagging sites tend to be lacking; on delicious.com, the site is rather limited in its search options, allowing the user to view only the few most popular sites or else

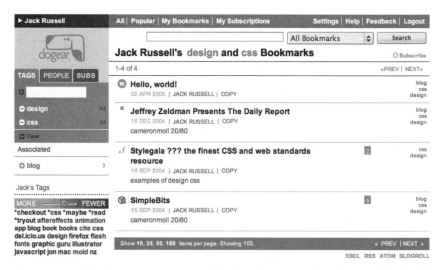

Figure 8.14. The dogear intranet social bookmarking interface, from Millen et al. (2006).

view all sites labeled with a tag in terms of recency of labeling by any user. The site also does not allow users to see all tags associated with a given site. It does however provide a list of related tags; most likely these are tags that are co-assigned to the same items as the target tag.

The dogear system (Millen et al. 2006) provides more powerful navigation of tag structures within a social bookmarking site that is meant to be used within an organization's intranet. Figure 8.14 shows the bookmarks corresponding to first selecting the user named Jack Russell's tags, and then selecting both the *design* and the *css* tags within this set. Other tags associated with Jack Russell's bookmarks, but which are not applicable to the currently selected subset are shown under the "Jack's Tags" heading. The "People" tab in the upper left hand side of the interface shows bookmarks associated with the currently selected tags, but assigned by other people within the organization. Thus tags in this design act as faceted categories; the user can remove the tag *css* from the breadcrumb to expand the set of selected bookmarks to all those about *design* and then select another associated tag to narrow the set along another dimension.

Some interfaces are experimenting with a blend of structured facets and user-generated tags. Figure 8.15 shows a university library catalog which allows navigation according to traditional structured metadata such as publication year and collection, as well as narrowing by user-generated tags.

Figure 8.15. The online catalog at Michigan State University which shows structured metadata such as publication year and collection in a faceted format, in combination with narrowing by user-generated tags. (Software by Innovative Interfaces, Inc. Used with permission. Screen image courtesy of Michigan State University.)

8.8. Clustering in Search Interfaces

A disadvantage of category systems is that they require the categories to be assigned by hand or by an algorithm. Automated methods exist for created faceted hierarchies (Stoica et al. 2007; Dakka and Ipeirotis 2008) and assignment of documents to categories works reasonably well for limited category sets (Sebastiani 2002), but fully automated information organizations remain appealing to system developers.

Many attempts to display overview or grouping information have focused on automatically extracting the most common general themes that occur within the collection. These themes are derived via the use of unsupervised analysis methods, usually variants of document clustering. Clustering refers to the automated grouping of items according to some measure of similarity. In document clustering, similarity is typically computed using associations and commonalities among features, where features are usually words and phrases (Cutting et al. 1992); the centroids of the clusters determine the themes in the collections. The greatest advantage of clustering is that it is fully automatable and can be applied to any text collection without manual labeling.

Kummamuru et al. (2004) make a distinction between *monothetic* and *polythetic* clustering, where monothetic clusters are based on a single shared feature, while polythetic clusters determine membership based on multiple shared features, thus grouping documents by overall similarity (this includes K-means and agglomerative clustering algorithms (Willett 1988)). Early work in document clustering for search results interfaces was done with polythetic clusters, as seen in the Scatter/Gather system (described below), but more recent work suggests that monothetic clusters may be easier for users to understand, since the criterion for cluster membership is relatively transparent. The choice of clustering algorithm influences which clusters are produced, although there is little agreement about which algorithms work best (Willett 1988), particularly for presentation in search interfaces.

8.8.1. *Clustering via Inter-Document Similarity*

The best-known and earliest research on document clustering for search user interfaces is the Scatter/Gather project (Cutting et al. 1992, 1993). The goal was to automatically and dynamically create a TOC-type structure for navigating the contents of a text collection, by clustering documents into topically coherent groups, and presenting descriptive textual summaries to the user.

Document terms were weighted and represented as vectors, and clustering was done via hierarchical agglomerative clustering, which is a polythetic approach. The summaries consisted of topical terms that characterized each cluster generally, and a set of typical titles that hinted at the contents of the cluster. Informed by the summaries, the user could select a subset of clusters (gather) that seem to be of most interest, and re-cluster their contents (scatter). Thus the user could examine the contents of each subcollection at progressively finer granularity of detail. The reclustering was computed on-the-fly; different themes are produced depending on the documents contained in the subcollection to which clustering was applied.

A usability study by Pirolli et al. (1996) showed that the use of Scatter/Gather on a large text collection successfully conveyed some of the content and structure of the corpus. However, that study also showed that Scatter/Gather without a search facility was less effective than a

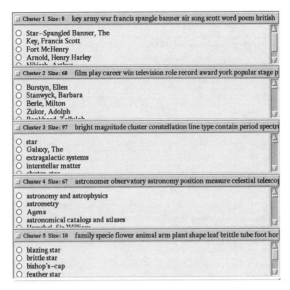

Figure 8.16. Display of Scatter/Gather clustering on retrieval results, showing clustering the top 250 results of a query on the ambiguous term *star* in well-behaved encyclopedia text.

standard similarity search for finding relevant documents for a query. That is, participants allowed only to navigate, not to search over, a hierarchical structure of clusters covering the entire collection were less able to find documents relevant to the supplied query than subjects allowed to write queries and scan through retrieval results.

It seems to be more useful to integrate a document clustering method like Scatter/Gather with conventional search technology by applying clustering to the results of a query to organize the retrieved documents (see Figures 8.16 and 8.17). An off-line experiment by Hearst and Pedersen (1996) suggested that clustering may be more effective if used in this manner. The study found that documents relevant to the query tended to fall mainly into one or two out of five clusters, if the clusters were generated from the top-ranked documents retrieved in response to the query. The study also showed that precision and recall were higher within the best cluster than within the retrieval results as a whole. The implication was that a user might save time by looking at the contents of the cluster with the highest proportion of relevant documents and at the same time avoiding those clusters with mainly non-relevant documents. Thus clustering of retrieval results might be useful for helping direct users to a subset of the retrieval results that contain a large proportion of the relevant documents.

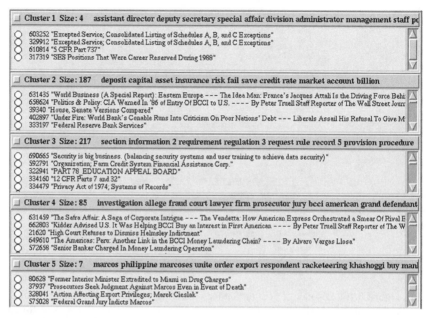

Figure 8.17. Display of Scatter/Gather clustering on retrieval results, showing clusters on the top 500 results of the query *bank financial institution failed criminal officer indictment* applied to newswire, magazine, and government documents.

General themes do seem to arise from document clustering, but the themes are highly dependent on the makeup of the documents within the clusters (Hearst 1998; Hearst and Pedersen 1996). The unsupervised nature of clustering can result in a display of topics at varying levels of description. For example, clustering a collection of documents about computer science can result in clusters containing documents about artificial intelligence, computer theory, computer graphics, government, and legal issues. The latter two themes are more general than the others, because they are about topics outside the general scope of computer science. Thus clustering can result in the juxtaposition of very different levels of description within a single display. Usability study results suggest that users dislike organizations that show inconsistent levels of description (Chen et al. 1998).

Another problem with clustering by overall document similarity is that documents are similar to (and different from) one another in many different ways simultaneously. Consider articles about the auto industry. Should an article about cars that use alternative energy be placed in an energy cluster if it is about meeting the legal requirements for emissions standards, or in a legal category? What if there are articles about Japanese versus German cars' emissions? Should these be grouped by geolocation

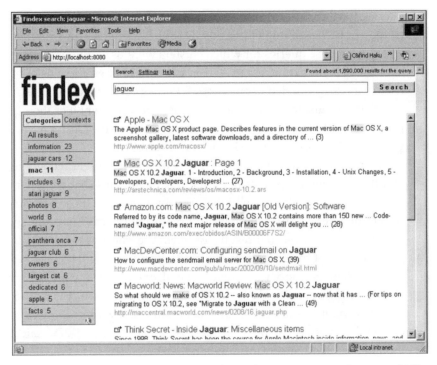

Figure 8.18. Output of Findex (Käki 2005b) on the query *jaguar*. (Courtesy of Mika Käki.)

or into the alternative energy group, or somewhere else? As discussed below, usability studies suggest that polythetic clustering is dispreferred compared to organizing results by hand-built category labels which allow mixing and combining of topics.

Scatter/Gather shows a textual representation of document clusters. Numerous researchers attempted to show document clusters graphically; these are discussed in Chapter 10.

8.8.2. *Clustering According to a Shared Common Term*

Monothetic clustering algorithms (Käki 2005b; Kummamuru et al. 2004) build clusters around dominant phrases, which give rise to more understandable labels. Käki (2005b) performed several usability studies using a monothetic clustering algorithm interface called Findex (see Figure 8.18). These included a longitudinal study in which 16 participants used the interface for two months each. Log analysis on this system revealed that on average the participants chose to click on the clusters for 26% of their queries. Furthermore, the proportion of cluster use increased over the time of the study, becoming as high as 39% of the queries towards the last weeks. For those queries for which clusters were used, the participant selected 2.3 clusters on average. When asked how often the clusters were useful, most responded "sometimes." Participants' comments also suggest that the clusters helped them quickly determine whether their query produced useful results or not, presumably because the cluster terms provide a quick summary of the kinds of results returned.

An analysis of the queries for which clusters were selected suggested that they are helpful primarily for moving documents that are low in the standard search rankings up higher. This happened on those occasions in which the query was ambiguous and the primary sense was not shown near the top of the search results, or when the query was specified very generally. Six of the participants explicitly commented that clusters were helpful when the query was vague, general, or contained words with multiple meanings. A particularly interesting result of this study is that 45% of the participants reported that they began to use less precise query terms as they became accustomed to the cluster interface, and 27% said they thought less about query formulation than before.

The Findex clusters seemed beneficial for exploratory tasks in which more than one result was desired, because participants selected multiple documents more often after clicking on a cluster than when selecting from the straight results listing. Participants also spent almost twice as long selecting the first search result when they used clusters versus when using the results listing. This may be due to the cognitive overhead of interpreting the clusters, but may also suggest that clusters were used in those cases when finding the desired result is more difficult. The latter explanation is supported by some of the participants' comments about how and when they used the clusters.

An important question for interfaces that group search results is: how many groups should be shown? The answer probably differs for faceted navigation interfaces that allow selection of multiple categories as opposed to clustering or categorization interfaces that only permit drilling down into one group at a time.

Käki (2005c) performed a controlled experiment which compared presenting 10, 20, or 40 groups using monothetic clusters. The 27 participants were asked to find as many relevant documents as possible for a set of pre-written queries, within a one-minute time limit. When 40 groups were presented, participants took longer to select the first relevant document, took longer to finish the tasks, and selected fewer relevant documents than with 10 and 20 groups, although the differences were not statistically significant. Participants' subjective scores stated that 20, and especially 40, groups were perceived as too many. This echos results seen with automated term suggestion interfaces (see Chapter 6). These and other results can be summarized as fewer is better from the perspective of general users.

The Findex longitudinal results echo some results found by Dumais et al. (2001) described above, in the role of grouping results by a small set of categories. These results also echo what was found by Zamir and Etzioni (1999) when studying logs of their Grouper system. Grouper used a hybrid of polythetic and monothetic clustering. Documents were grouped according to sets of shared phrases, and those phrases they shared, along with the percentage of document in the group that contained those phrases, were displayed to the user as the cluster description. As is standard in polythetic clustering, two documents could be in the same cluster even if they did not share a common phrase, but did share phrases with other documents in the cluster. In this algorithm, documents frequently fell into multiple clusters, which is not standard for polythetic document clustering.

In a log analysis, Zamir and Etzioni (1999) found that multiple search results were clicked on more often when one or more clusters were selected. They also found that more time elapsed before the first document was selected when using the clusters than when selecting from the straight search results. These two points together were also seen in the Findex study, suggest that finding the first relevant document requires more effort with the grouping interface, but finding additional interesting documents requires less effort than with the ranked results listing.

In another study Wu et al. (2003) selected terms from document snippets and organized these terms into a subsumption hierarchy, highlighting the query terms in the retrieved summaries. Nineteen undergraduate participants used the system for their own queries and had a significant preference for the system with the grouping interface compared to its linear interface (although it may be the case that the linear interface was inferior to that of standard search engines; it was not described in detail). In a second followup study, 6 participants' queries were logged and studied in detail. As seen in the studies discussed above (Dumais et al. 2001; Käki 2005c; Kules and Shneiderman 2008; Zamir and Etzioni 1999), participants delved deeper into the results list (with reference to the original ranking) when they used the grouping interface, and they saved more documents per query when using the grouping mechanism.

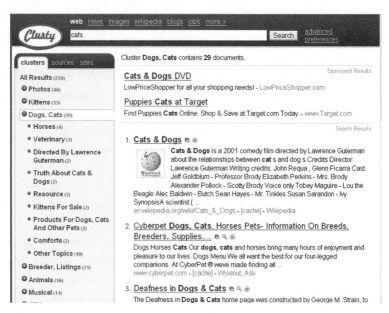

Figure 8.19. Output of Clusty.com on the query *cats*.

Most clustering algorithms end up with at least one "miscellaneous" cluster where documents that do not fit well into the remaining clusters end up. Zamir and Etzioni (1999) refer to these less coherent clusters as index clusters, and found in their logs that users clicked on these less-coherent groups about 21% of the time (although they could not discern if users benefited from following these links or not).

8.8.3. *Clustering on the Web*

Over the years, a number of Web sites have supported cluster-based search results. Although these algorithms are not published, they appear to be a variation of monothetic clustering.

Figure 8.19 shows results for the query `cats` using the Clusty.com search engine (from Vivisimo.com), with the cluster named *Dogs, Cats* expanded. The topmost clusters are labeled *Photos, Kittens, Dogs/Cats, Breeder Listings, Animals, and Musical*. Note that, although one can infer the meaning of these labels, they are somewhat disorganized and vary widely in level of description (kitten is a kind of cat, and cat is a kind of animal, and all three levels are seen as cluster labels). The subclusters within *Dog, Cat* include horses, names of films with animals in them, general terms

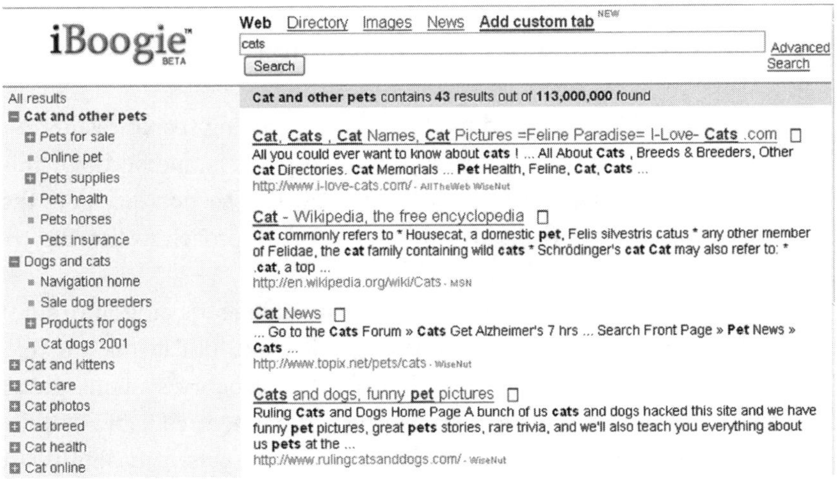

Figure 8.20. Output of iBoogie.com on the query *cats*.

like *Resource*, and kittens for sale, despite the fact that the cluster above this one is named *Kittens*. Thus, the list of topics is not particularly coherent, and the subclusters often confusingly repeat topics from the clusters above. The example results for the iBoogie clustering engine shown in Figure 8.20, when run on the same query, appear to have more coherent labels. These systems tend to produce better results when focused within a topic domain. Figure 8.21 shows the results of the technology behind Clusty applied to a biomedical collection, on the query `tinnitus`.

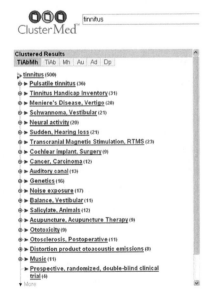

Figure 8.21. Output of Clusty applied to a biomedical text collection on the query *tinnitis*.

8.9. Clusters vs. Categories in Search Interfaces

This chapter has discussed methods for organizing search results and integrating navigation and search. The two primary methods for this are category systems and document clustering. This section discusses the relative advantages and disadvantages of each approach (following the arguments of Hearst (2006a)).

Clustering methods have the notable advantage of being fully automatable, and thus applicable to any text collection, but at the cost of consistency, coherence, and comprehensibility. Category systems provide a logical and consistent organization on a document collection, and have been shown to be superior to clusters and flat lists in usability studies (Dempsey 2006; Dumais et al. 2001; Kules and Shneiderman 2008; Pratt et al. 1999; Yee et al. 2003). However, categories require manual curation, may not fully reflect the topics within the collection, and documents need to be manually assigned to categories (and automated methods are about 75% correct on average) (Sebastiani 2002). The disadvantages of polythetic clusters for user interfaces include their lack of predictability, their conflation of many dimensions simultaneously, the difficulty of labeling the groups, and the counter-intuitiveness of cluster subhierarchies.

Clustering algorithms can be more responsive to the idiosyncrasies of a given query's retrieval results. For example, in September 2005, shortly after the devastation wreaked by Hurricane Katrina, a query on `New Orleans` at Clusty.com produced a top-ranked cluster labeled *Hurricane*, followed by the more standard clusters labeled *Hotels, Louisiana, University*, etc.

By contrast, categories present well-understood and predictable meaning units. For example, in Google Co-op, a query on the name of a travel destination such as `New Orleans` produces a standard list of categories such as *Dining, Lodging, Attractions, Shopping, Transportation*, and so on.

Clustering can be useful for clarifying and sharpening a vague query, by showing users the dominant themes of the returned results. Clustering also works well for disambiguating ambiguous queries, particularly acronyms. For example, ACL can stand for Anterior Cruciate Ligament, Association for Computational Linguistics, Atlantic Coast Line Railroad, etc. A clustering algorithm will group together those documents that contain the same long form of the acronym. However, because not every document will use the long form of the acronym, and because clustering algorithms are imperfect, they do not neatly group all occurrences of each acronym into one cluster, nor do they allow users to issue followup queries that only return documents from the intended sense (e.g., "ACL meeting" will return meetings for multiple senses of the term).

By contrast, a category system will neatly and consistently place the anatomical sense of ACL within a medical category, and the computational linguistics sense within a technical category. However, if the automated category assignment algorithm has not been exposed to training data containing acronyms, it may not be able to properly assign documents that do not contain the long form.

Clusters are also useful for *eliminating* groups of documents from consideration. This result is supported by participants' comments found in several studies (Käki 2005b; Kleiboemer et al. 1996; Hearst and Pedersen 1996). For example, if most documents in a set are written in one language, clustering will very quickly reveal if a subset of the documents is written in another language. Categories can of course be used to eliminate or ignore irrelevant topics as well.

A primary problem with clusters, especially polythetic clusters, is that their contents can be difficult to understand. One study found that for non-expert users the results of clustering were difficult to use, and that graphical depictions (for example, representing clusters with circles and lines connecting documents) were much harder to use than textual representations (for example, showing titles and topical words, as in Scatter/Gather), because documents' contents are difficult to discern without actually reading some text (Kleiboemer et al. 1996).

Another major problem with polythetic clustering systems is that the subdivision produced by hard clustering (where documents appear in only one cluster) forces choices about where to place documents: should the article on government controls on RU486 be placed in a cluster on pharmaceuticals, or one on women's rights, religion, or politics? Documents are simultaneously about many concepts.

Faceted category systems allow the user to easily navigate according to several different topics; clustering is usually limited to just one topic. Category systems also lend themselves well to navigation within is-a hierarchies. Most clustering interface studies do not assess usability of the hierarchical aspect of the clusters, but the available online systems do not produce readily understandable results, as seen in the Clusty.com discussed earlier.

In fact, those studies that do compare categories to clusters find that categories prevail. In a study examining image collection presentation, Rodden et al. (2001) found that participants preferred images organized by meaningful categories over images clustered by visual similarity. As mentioned above, a usability study comparing the Dynacat system, which organizes results into a pre-determined category hierarchy, was preferred by participants over a linear list and a polythetic clustering interface (Pratt et al. 1999). Chapter 10 reports on the results of additional usability studies on visualization of document clusters. In all cases, the results are negative.

8.10. Conclusions

As seen in several discussions throughout this book, an oft-preferred method of search makes use of small steps that allow users to retain the context of their activities. Navigation structures are useful both for imposing an organization on retrieval results, and for re-ordering, narrowing, and filtering those results. An information structure can also provide a useful starting point for getting to know a collection of information.

This chapter has discussed an extensive range of approaches to providing navigation structure and integrating it with keyword search. Methods covered include category systems (flat, hierarchical, and faceted), TOC views, and automated clustering techniques. It was seen that although hierarchical organization can work for some smaller collections, faceted navigation with query previews has been found to be highly successful for searching within a wide range of information collections. It was also seen that although clustering has the advantage of being fully automatable, the results tend to be difficult for users to understand, although the more recent focus on monothetic clusters is more promising than the earlier predominant polythetic clusters. Faceted navigation has the drawback of requiring the category structure to be designed and assigned to items, although automated methods are under development. Most likely in future, hybrids with somewhat more flexible information structures will be explored.

9 Personalization in Search

Currently most Web search engines produce the same results independently of who the user is; search engines are in fact designed to do well at meeting the average goals of the group over the specific goals of the individual (Teevan et al. 2005a). Nonetheless, researchers, marketers, and search pundits alike often state that search results should reflect the fact that people differ in their needs, goals, and preferences (Pitkow et al. 2002). As a typical example, an avionics expert should see a different results ranking for a query on jets than a football fan from New York.

Tailoring search results to an individual's interests is just one form of information *personalization*. The term is currently applied to a diverse array of information applications. Given a profile of a user's interests, information content can be personalized by: re-ranking search results listings to better reflect the user's preferences, automatically notifying a user when new articles of interest appear or important changes are made to existing documents, recommending items that are related in some way to an item currently being viewed, and customizing the look and content of a Web site or other information artifact.

Information personalization approaches vary along several dimensions. Some make use of information that users *explicitly* specify about themselves and their interests, while others attempt to infer users' preferences *implicitly* from their actions. Some approaches note that individuals tend to have both *long-term*, stable interests, and *short-term* temporary interests, and that these can come into conflict when proposing recommendations based on past actions. Some approaches make use of an *individual's* actions alone, while others attempt to improve results for an individual by harnessing the actions of the many users of the system, using what can be referred to as *social* or *collective* information. When determining how

211

Table 9.1. A classification of approaches to information personalization. "Individual" refers to preference information obtained from just one person; "Collective" refers to information gathered from the behavior of a number of people.

	Using explicit preferences
Individual	User-created customization of Web sites (9.1.1) User-created alerts and interest profiles (9.1.2) User-specified relevance judgements for creating alerts (also called Routing, Filtering, and Standing Queries) (9.1.3) Combining user-created and machine-augmented alerts (9.1.4)
Collective	Content determined by explicitly selected user groups (9.1.5) Collaborative Filtering, based on similarity to other users' explicit relevance judgements (9.1.6.1) Collaborative Filtering, based on similarity of content to explicitly selected content (9.1.6.2) Item-based collective recommendations (9.1.7)
	Using implicit preferences
Individual	Information alerts and profiles built from the user's search history (9.2.1) The same, combined with document viewing history (9.2.2) The same, combined with mapping viewed pages into categories (9.2.3)
Collective	Re-ranking of search results based on collective clickthrough (9.2.4) Collaborative filtering based on similarity to other users' implicit document viewing behavior (9.2.5)
	Explicit + implicit
Individual	Modifying implicit alerts with explicit relevance judgements (9.3.1) Personal information assistants or agents (9.3.2)

to make recommendations, some systems make *content-based* suggestions, based on similarity of keywords and text, whereas others make *user-based* recommendations, in which the searcher is grouped with other individuals who have expressed similar preferences in the past.

This chapter discusses information personalization applications along the dimensions described above. The combinations are summarized in Table 9.1. Section 9.1 discusses personalization based on information explicitly specified by users, including customization of Web sites, manual profile creation, creation of profiles via explicit relevance judgements, and collaborative filtering. Section 9.2 discusses personalization methods that make use of the information implicit in users' actions as they go about their information seeking tasks. Topics include: building profiles based on observing which documents a user looks at while doing their information seeking, organizing this implicit information into pre-defined category structures, using the information about the behavior of large numbers of people clicking on information items, and using implicit information as data for collaborative filtering. Section 9.3 describes personal information assistants (also known as agents), which engage the user more interactively, and combine explicit and implicit relevance information. Section 9.4 discusses the related area of search over users' personal information. Finally, Section 9.5 summarizes the current status of the use of personalization in information delivery systems.

9.1. Personalization Based on Explicit Preferences

9.1.1. *User-Driven Customization*

Web portals allow users to customize the kinds of information they see on their home page, including which news feeds to receive, which cities to show the current weather for, and which sports teams to track (Manber et al. 2000; Pierrakos et al. 2003). These portals provide users with an enormous breadth of choices over content. However, it is often reported that users tend to be reluctant to change default settings and use customization features; a study of MyYahoo users found that "a majority of active users" did not customize their pages (Manber et al. 2000). To encourage customization, some sites require users to customize their preferences when they register. At one time in the past, the sports Web site ESPN.com required users to indicate their favorite sports and teams directly on the new user registration page. (However, this information was not used to customize the appearance of the user's pages on the site.)

Semi-automated customization is in wide use on the Web; mapping sites and portals keep track of a registered user's zip code and use this information to geographically customize content such as weather and local shopping search results. Airline sites retain information about a user's favorite travel destinations, seating, and meal preferences. E-commerce sites retain payment information to accelerate the purchasing process. By contrast, customization for search results is not widely used.

An early version of Google search results personalization asked users to specify their interests (Teevan et al. 2005a). More recently, Google introduced a personalization interface that the user sees only when logged into their Google account. The interface allows the user to explicitly move

Personalization - Wikipedia, the free encyclopedia 🔼❌
Personalization involves using technology to accommodate the differences between
individuals. Once confined mainly to the Web, it is increasingly becoming a ...
en.wikipedia.org/wiki/**Personalized** - 42k - Cached - Similar pages - 💬

Personalized Gifts from **Personalization** Mall 🔼❌
It shows you went out of your way to find the perfect gift a̶ to **personalize** it to make it
theirs alone! At PersonalizationMall.com, we design most of our ...
www.**personalization**mall.com/Default.aspx?&did=111028 - 47k -
Cached - Similar pages - 💬

What is **personalization**? - a definition from Whatis.com 🔼❌
Mar 6, 2007 ... On a Web site, **personalization** is the process of tailoring pages to individual
users' characteristics or preferences.
searchcrm.techtarget.com/sDefinition/0,,sid11_gci532341,00.html - 72k -
Cached - Similar pages - 💬

Figure 9.1. Google explicit personalization of search results listings.

search hits up in the rankings or by clicking on a button labeled with an
arrow, or hide the hits in a menu at the bottom of the page by clicking on
an "x" icon (see Figure 9.1). The changes in rank ordering are preserved
for the next time the user issues the same query; it is unclear if the user
operations are used for reweighting hits for other queries. No usability
results have yet been reported on this feature.

9.1.2. *User-Created Alerts and Interest Profiles*

A commonly used form of explicitly personalized information is customized alerting services, which are commonly offered by Web-based content brokers. Examples are services that send a subscriber news of standing interest (e.g., "send me all articles that mention my company's name"),
or alert a researcher to late-breaking journal articles on a particular topic.
Information filtering via explicit user profiles has been studied for many
years, and goes by many names, including *alerts, routing, filtering, content-
based recommendations, standing queries,* and *user modeling* (Adomavicius
and Tuzhilin 2005; Croft et al. 2001; Fischer 2001; Hanani et al. 2001; Stadnyk and Kass 1992).

To set up an alert, the user typically builds a *profile* for a topic of interest. In some cases, construction of a user profile requires the user to
specify a list of required, optional, and banned terms that characterize
which documents to retain and which to exclude (Kamba et al. 1995; Yan
and Garcia-Molina 1995); this is the most common approach in commercial systems today (Wærn 2004). After the profile is created, the system

continually retrieves documents that match the profile as new information becomes available. Google Alerts and Yahoo Alerts allow users to specify a set of search terms for monitoring news and Web sites; as new articles arrive they are compared to the user-specified profile, and those articles that match the profile are presented to the user. Profiles can also be used to block out information; when used this way they are usually referred to as *filters*, as is seen with spam filters for email.

The evidence suggests that manual creation of alert profiles does not work very well. Yang and Jeh (2006) interviewed 18 Google engineers, finding that only 3 participants used the Google Web Alerts system. Two participants who had used the alert service in the past said that the quality of the recommendations was too low to justify creating more alerts. Those who did not use alerts said that setting up the profiles for a query of interest required too much effort. These results led Yang and Jeh (2006) to assert that alert systems will only be useful if they can automatically recognize which queries represent information needs that users really care about seeing again, and if the alerts can be automatically configured. As a step towards automating alert creation, Yang and Jeh (2006) identified several criteria for good recommendations from alert systems, including: the information should be new for that user, or should be newly modified information where the modifications make it "interesting;" information should not be too similar to already viewed information; and the retrieved information should be of high quality. Section 9.2 discusses their attempts to use implicit information to build alert profiles.

9.1.3. *Creating Profiles from Explicit Relevance Judgements*

As an alternative to specifying keywords manually to produce a query, a user can be asked to rate a set of documents as interesting or not, and from these ratings a profile can be created using machine learning techniques. Thus, this approach is a combination of relevance feedback and text categorization (Sebastiani 2002).

In support of this kind of profile generation, from 1993 to 2002 the TREC competition included a routing and filtering track. In TREC-9 (Robertson and Hull 2001), a three-way distinction was made among *adaptive filtering*, *batch filtering*, and *routing*. In adaptive filtering the system started with a user profile (represented in this case as a set of relevant documents) and was then fed a stream of documents, each of which had been manually assigned a relevance judgement. The system was expected to adaptively update the filtering profile. Batch filtering was identical to adaptive filtering, except that the system also started with a large sample of evaluated training documents, which made it similar to a text categorization problem. Routing was similar to batch filtering, but the system was expected to return a ranked list of documents, as opposed to a binary relevant-or-not decision. Most participating systems in the TREC task used machine learning techniques.

Despite the TREC research efforts, explicit relevance-judgement based approaches are not widely used. This may be because, as seen in the discussion of relevance feedback (see Chapter 6), making relevance judgements is an effortful and error-prone task (Croft et al. 2001; Ruthven and Lalmas 2003; White et al. 2005). Another problem with this approach is the profiles become out-of-date as the vocabulary of the relevant documents changes over time, so users must continually make relevance judgements in order to keep the profiles up to date.

9.1.4. *Modifying Machine-Built Profiles*

Several researchers have studied the effects of allowing users to modify their explicitly created profiles, after they are created by or augmented by machine learning algorithms. Unfortunately, the outcome of these studies tends to be negative. For example, a study by Wærn (2004) showed that allowing users to set up the initial profile made the subsequent training algorithms perform better than those that used relevance judgements but no initial user setup. However, they also found that allowing users to explicitly modify the trained profile did not result in improvements.

Another more recent study by Ahn et al. (2007) examined whether allowing users to modify a machine-generated profile for news recommendations could improve the results. In this case they represented user profiles as weighted term vectors, and they showed this information in the form of lists of words whose varying font size reflected the weight of the term in the profile (see Figure 9.2). Participants could click on words to remove them from the profile; the words were subsequently shown in a strike-through font; clicking on the word a second time would add it back into the profile. Participants could also type in new words. Changes provided immediate feedback; after a change was made, the user would see which documents were promoted or demoted. Hovering the mouse over an article would also show the weighted keywords that caused it to be retrieved.

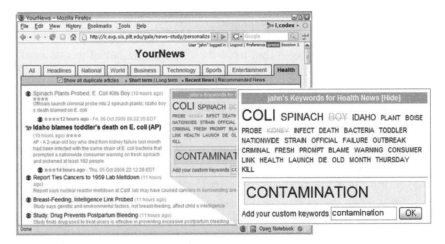

Figure 9.2. Interface allowing users to modify terms in a machine-built user profile, from Ahn et al. (2007).

Ahn et al. (2007) conducted a study with 10 information science graduate students, and found that allowing them to adjust the profiles significantly worsened the results. Keyword removal caused about 4 times more harm than adding keywords. There were no significant differences in participants' subjective responses to the interactive versus the automated system. In exit interviews, participants noted that although they liked the idea of having more control, they were frustrated by the resulting system performance (in part because redundant articles were shown at the top of the results, a flaw in the study design). It may be the case that if a more transparent model had been used, the participants would have been more successful at adjusting their profiles; these results suggest that the results of vector space ranking and statistical weighting are unintuitive. This finding echoes results found for relevance feedback term suggestions by Koenemann and Belkin (1996); participants wanted the system to suggest relevant terms, but also wanted to have control over which terms were used to augment the query.

9.1.5. *Explicit Group Recommendations*

As user participation on Web sites has expanded, many tools have arisen that make use of the "wisdom of crowds," or massive user behavior, to recommend information. In its simplest form, collective behavior can be used to show information that is currently popular. News sites show the most viewed or most emailed articles, which is an implicit form of recommendation information. Web sites like Digg.com allow users to explicitly mark news articles, images, or Web pages as being of special interest, and those pages that have the highest number of recent marks are shown prominently on that Web site.

Recently, social bookmarking sites such as delicious.com and furl.com have become popular. In these sites, users mark Web pages as being of high quality or interest. A user can specify a network of people whose bookmarks and recommendations they want to see in their search results. For example, on Yahoo's MyWeb, an information retrieval researcher can indicate that their personal network consists of colleagues in their field. Then when that person issues a query, say visualization, the search results will show those Web pages that contain the term and that have been marked by the members of their network as being interesting (see Figure 9.3). This kind of personalization uses explicitly indicated relevance information, based on annotations made by people other than the searcher, but personalized by the knowledge of that searcher's explicitly indicated social group.

9.1.6. *Collaborative Filtering (Social Recommender Systems)*

9.1.6.1. User Similarity-Based Collaborative Filtering

An important kind of socially determined explicit recommendation is seen in the area of collaborative filtering, also known as social recommender systems. This is well-established technology that uses ratings from a large number of different users to assign scores to information objects, such as movies. An individual indicates their own preferences, and is matched with other people who indicated similar scores for the same information items (Resnick and Varian 1997). The explicit recommendations discussed above are essentially "most popular" lists; those that are most often viewed, voted on, or bought. By contrast, collaborative filtering tries to match an individual with a subset of like-minded people, so that those people whose interests do not coincide with mainstream interests can still get useful recommendations. For example, a movie recommender system like MovieLens (Herlocker et al. 2004) asks users to explicitly rate (both positively and negatively) a set of movies they have seen in the past. It then tries to recommend movies the user hasn't seen based on ratings that other people have made who have seen those films. The special twist is

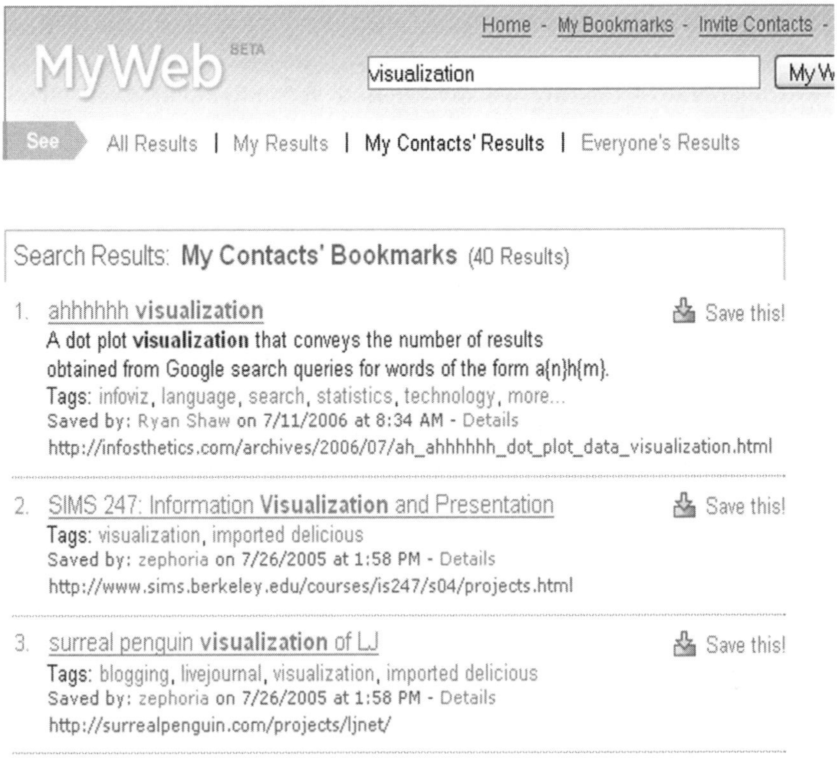

Figure 9.3. Socially labeled search results on Yahoo's MyWeb. The user sees hits for the query `visualization` that have been tagged as relevant for this query by other people in the user's social network. The user can also choose to see only those Web pages they themselves have tagged, or Web pages that have been tagged by everyone in the system. (Reproduced with permission of Yahoo! Inc. ©2009 Yahoo! Inc. YAHOO! and the YAHOO! logo are registered trademarks of Yahoo! Inc.)

that the system first attempts to match a given user to other users, based on which movies they have all rated similarly in the past. Then it shows the user additional items that have been highly rated by like-minded filmwatchers.

Collaborative filtering that matches a user with like-minded users seems to work well for information items that have an aspect of *taste* to them, for example, movies and music (Sharanand and Maes 1995), and recommender tools have become important parts of many online systems. The results of collaborative filtering when applied to information needs do not seem to be as successful. This makes sense intuitively, as it is usually easier to predict if a friend will like an arbitrarily chosen piece of music than to predict whether or not they will find a particular Web page interesting.

9.1.6.2. Content Similarity-Based Collaborative Filtering

Collaborative filtering usually refers to recommendations in which the user is shown items that people with similar preferences have seen and rated in the past. A related but different technology is content-based recommendations, in which the user is recommended items similar in content to those already seen by that user and judged relevant, similar to routing queries discussed above.

There have been a number of attempts to combine content-based and collaborative-filtering based methods (Balabanović and Shoham 1997; Basu et al. 1998; Claypool et al. 1999; Sarwar et al. 1998), but they are not clearly successful. Content-based similarity works better at, for example, recommending related research papers to a given paper, for citation purposes (McNee et al. 2006). It does not work so well at suggesting content of general interest, although it is sometimes better at suggesting novel or unexpected recommendations (McNee et al. 2002).

9.1.7. *Item-Based Collective Recommendations*

A different collective-based recommendation technique is well-known from the Amazon.com Web site. When looking at an item, a user is shown other items purchased by people who purchased the target item, or rated both the target and the suggested items highly (Linden et al. 2003). In other words, if both item A (say, the film *Being John Malkovich*) and item B (say, *Adaptation*) are judged to be high-quality by many different people, when a new user comes along and chooses for some reason to view item A, then that user will also be shown item B as a recommendation. This differs from collaborative filtering, in that people are not matched to other people based on shared judgements. Rather, an item is matched to another item based on the fact that individuals have indicated they like both items.

This technique can be implemented in either an explicit or implicit manner, depending on whether recommendation of the items comes from explicit ratings or implicit approval signalled by a purchasing or viewing action. (It should be noted that Amazon.com's recommendations are especially accurate because they are based on purchase history – paying money for something is a strong endorsement – and because their recommendations are conservative; they present only a very limited number of related books for any given book.) If an individual has unusual tastes, then this kind of recommendation may not work well for them, since it is absent the personalization that comes from being matched to other people with similar taste. But choosing to view a particular item gives a strong signal as to the user's current interests.

9.2. Personalization Based on Implicit Relevance Cues

As mentioned above, because most people find it difficult or undesirable to provide explicit relevance judgements (Wærn 2004), today most personalization efforts make use of preference information that is implicit in user actions. The subsections below discuss profiles based on monitoring user activity as they search for and view information item.

9.2.1. *Alerts Based on a User's Search History*

As discussed in Chapter 2, search engine logs can record queries issued by users over time. Often the same user's queries can be tracked via information from a cookie or a session variable, yielding what is sometimes referred to as a *search history*.

As discussed above, Yang and Jeh (2006) attempted to build alerts for users without requiring the users to indicate explicitly what their interests were. Based on users' search histories, they first developed an algorithm to predict user's ideal standing queries. After predicting these topics, a second algorithm attempted to automatically classify new documents as to whether or not they fit the standing queries. The goal was to alert users to the appearance of new documents that might be of interest based on what they had viewed in the past.

Yang and Jeh (2006) first evaluated implicit features derived from 159 users' search history logs to determine which would be useful for automatically identifying what the topics are that the user is interested in. The best features were: a large number of clicks in the search session (>8), a large number of refinements in the search session (>3), and a strong history match score, meaning that terms from a query within a session matched queries from other sessions in the user's search history. The resulting precision/recall tradeoffs varied from 90/11 to 57/55, so the results were promising if not steller.

Yang and Jeh (2006) next assessed features for determining which documents should be recommended for the user's topics as standing queries. They found that a combination of a statistical ranking score combined with in-link information multiplied by the inverse of the search engine ranking produced good results – precision/recall tradeoffs in the 70/88 range. Thus, this approach which uses searchers' prior behavior to implicitly come up with articles to recommend, is a promising way to improve alert systems.

9.2.2. *Profiles Based on Information Viewed During a Search Session*

Going beyond query logs, another method of gathering implicit preference information that seems especially potent is recording which documents the user examines while trying to complete an extended search task. In this framework, users examine documents for their own understanding, and do not have to make explicit relevance judgements about those documents. They may in fact view irrelevant documents as they browse and navigate, but the idea is that these "noisy" views do not significantly hurt the overall results. This approach can thus be thought of as occupying a middle ground between pseudo-relevance feedback and traditional relevance feedback. The information "trails" that users leave behind them as a side-effect of doing their tasks have been used to suggest term expansions (White et al. 2005, 2007), automatically re-rank search results (Teevan et al. 2005b), predict next moves (Pitkow and Pirolli 1999), make recommendations of related pages (Lieberman 1995), and determine user satisfaction (Fox et al. 2005).

Several studies have found a correlation between reading time and relevance of documents, despite the fact that this data is often noisy (Agichtein et al. 2006a; Claypool et al. 1999; Kim et al. 2001; Morita and Shinoda 1994). A study by Fox et al. (2005) found an association between explicit ratings of user satisfaction and implicit measures that are commonly used to infer this. The strongest indicator for individual Web page satisfaction was a combination of click history, time spent on search result page, and how the user ended the search session (e.g., killing the browser window, navigating to bookmarks, printing the document). These implicit measures also predict satisfaction across a user session, although less strongly.

Markov models of navigation path accesses (Deshpande and Karypis 2004) and longest substring grouping computed over large numbers of user sessions (Pitkow and Pirolli 1999) have been used for making predictions about which pages a user will view next. Heer and Chi (2002) tracked the clicks of participants who were asked to complete certain tasks on a Web site. The resulting analysis found that the time spent reading each page in combination with information about similarity among the contents of the pages accessed could be used to categorize the clicks according to activity types.

Shen et al. (2005b) asked participants to find documents relevant to particularly difficult TREC queries and kept track of which documents the participants clicked on while completing the task. They found that immediate query history did not improve a search results re-ranking algorithm. They also investigated incorporating terms from search results summaries that participants clicked on while performing the given search task, in effect doing implicit relevance feedback. Using the summary information from clicked on documents from the first four queries in the session achieved significant improvements in rank ordering for what would have been the fifth round of querying, and these improvements were robust even though only one third of the clicked-on documents were relevant. However, since they used the 30 most difficult TREC queries, these results may not be representative for more typical queries.

In a followup study, Tan et al. (2006) gathered query history for four users for one month. After their time was up, the participants were asked to select 15 queries from their usage history (these queries had to match their general interests or belong to a long chain of queries). They were then asked to rank the top 20 search results produced by a standard search engine for each of these 15 queries. Tan et al. (2006) then tried to predict these relevance judgments, based on prior search activity. They found mild improvements in rank order for first-time queries and significant improvements for repeated queries.

Teevan et al. (2005b) developed a user profile by making use of a large number of implicit features gathered over time. These features included all documents that the individual had looked at in the past, whether or not this information was accessed in the last month, and the participants' query history. The profile was then used to re-rank search results, using a relevance feedback algorithm (see Chapter 6). They found that the richer the previously visited information, the better the relevance feedback results. However, the personalized ranking performed significantly worse than a Web-based ranking baseline. Combining the personalized results with the Web-based ranking yielded a slight improvement over Web-based ranking alone.

The use of implicit information from viewing of documents described in this section makes use of a user's interaction history over many query sessions. An alternative is to automatically adjust the rankings in real time, during a single search session. Singh et al. (2008) use a version of the clickthrough inversion idea described in Chapter 5 to re-rank the hits returned for a single query and the user views those results. The terms associated with the links that have been clicked on so far are weighted positively, while those not clicked on are weighted negatively, to provide a real-time re-ranking. A similar idea is being promoted by the startup company SurfCanyon. This can be seen as an implicit version of the explicit re-rankings used in the Google search results personalization interface described above.

9.2.3. *Profiles Based on Implicit Behavior Assigned to Categories*

Because it is difficult to differentiate one click from another, click history has sometimes been used in combination with an ontology or category structure to improve results.

Qiu and Cho (2006) combined topic-based PageRank (Haveliwala 2003) with user click history to reorder search results. (Topic-based PageRank is computed similarly to standard PageRank except that inlinks must originate from pages about a given topic.) The algorithm estimated which topics a user was most interested in by examining the user's click history and mapping pages clicked on to the top levels of the ODP (an open source category system in which volunteers classify Web pages manually). This algorithm obtained an improvement over both standard PageRank and topic-based PageRank, but they found that the improvement derived primarily from highly ambiguous queries.

Chen et al. (2002) used an individual's long-term access history on a hierarchical category structure to predict which categories would be accessed next, thus in effect creating a topic-based prediction model. (Here, access means provide a rating on an item in the Epinions Web site.) They found that an individual's category re-access patterns were better predictors than path-based models using combined history of many users without category classification. They also found improvements when taking recency into account, reflecting the fact that users' interests shift over time. Liu et al. (2002) and Gauch (2003) also found evidence that mapping click history to category structure can successfully determine categories of interest for users. By contrast, Dou et al. (2007) implemented simplified versions of algorithms in which user profiles were based on category information, and found this performed less well than standard search results.

Topic-based personalization seems especially suited for topic-specific information collections. For example, a sports site could track which sports a user read about in the past and automatically promote prominence to these sports when the user views the site in future. However, automatic inference of preference does not seem have caught on for vertical sites other than news; instead, explicit customization is the norm for domain-specific Web sites.

9.2.4. *Socially Determined Relevance Using ClickThrough*

An alternative to personalizing an individual's search results based on that person's actions is to use many different peoples' actions to determine which results are generally relevant for the population as a whole. Recent work has explored how to use implicit relevance judgements from multiple users to improve search results rankings. This section discusses the use of user clicks on search results document summaries, or *clickthrough* data.

One version of this idea used the clicks observed for a small group of users. Joachims (2002) presented the merged results of a metasearch engine to a group of 20 AI researchers, and recorded which search result links they clicked on in response to 260 queries. He built a machine learning model from the attributes of the clicked-on search results and used this model to re-rank the output of the metasearch engine. When evaluated on 180 user-generated queries, he found that users clicked on more links from the improved ranking on average than on the individual and combined search engines' rankings.

Joachims (2002) analyzed which features most influenced the successful re-ranking and found that the best features were those that can be incorporated into a standard (unpersonalized) ranking algorithm, such as cosine similarity between abstract and query. Only a few highly weighted features reflected the particular properties of the user group, such as whether the domain name was "nec" (because the user pool often obtained references from the citeseer citation system hosted at this domain). It is unclear though if the results of this limited study would generalize over longer use, since interests shift over time, or if it would work for large groups whose interests are more heterogeneous. However, similar results were found in another small study (Mislove et al. 2006).

In later work, Joachims et al. (2005) conducted experiments to assess the reliability of clickthrough data when compared against explicit relevance judgements. They found a significant bias based on the rank order of the results presented, showing that users select higher-ranked links even if the original output from the search engine is presented in reverse order (see Chapter 5). They concluded that this bias makes it difficult to use clickthrough as *absolute* feedback, but introduced several new effective ways for generating *relative* signals from this implicit information. They showed, for example, that assigning negative weight to an unclicked link that immediately follows a clicked on search result link can improve estimation of implicit relevance.

Agichtein et al. (2006b) built upon this work and showed even more convincingly that clickthrough and other forms of implicit feedback are useful when gathered across large numbers of users. They randomly chose 3,500 queries from a search log and recorded clickthrough data for more than 120,000 searches over instances of these queries. Their approach made use of information about which links had been clicked on for the *identical* query in the past by other users, thus essentially gathering human rankings on search results for a given query (the work of Joachims (2002) learns features *across* queries). Not surprisingly, the more click data available for a given query, the more reliable the predictions, but even with just 10 prior clicks, results can be improved over a state-of-the-art ranking function.

Agichtein et al. (2006b) found especially effective a clickthrough model which compared the actual clicks on a given link to its expected clickthrough given its position in the results listing. The algorithm downweights unclicked links that precede and follow a clicked link in the original results order, with the assumption that the user looked at and rejected those other links. Agichtein et al. (2006b) then discovered that a machine learning model trained on user browsing features worked even better than clickthrough data. These features included time spent viewing a page, time spent viewing pages from the search result's domain, and distance in clicks of the viewed page from the original search results. They showed that this community-generated implicit information can improve rank order over that of a state-of-the-art ranking algorithm that uses hundreds of other features – the best results occur when combining the implicit information with those other features. They noted, however, that this approach does not work well on low-frequency queries and may perform poorly on ambiguous queries in which there is more than one common interpretation of relevance.

Work by Dou et al. (2007) sheds even more light on the advantages and disadvantages of different kinds of implicit personalization algorithms for re-ranking search results. They gathered a large collection of queries and clickthroughs, examining data for 10,000 users, 56,000 queries, and 94,000 clicks over 12 days. They used the first 11 days' worth of data to form user profiles and to gather information about which links were clicked for each query. They then simulated the application of five different personalization algorithms on the remaining 4,600 queries from the last day of the log. They retrieved the top 50 results for each query from the comparison search engine and assumed that clicking a link indicated a relevance judgement for the query, acknowledging but ignoring the known problem of search-result position bias.

Dou et al. (2007) used one individual-level reranking strategy that assumed for a query q submitted by user u, pages frequently clicked on by u in the past for q are more relevant than those seldom clicked on. (Thus, this measure will not work for a new query that the user has never run.) They also tested a very simple version of socially determined relevance, computing pairwise similarity between users based on past clicks, and used historical clicks by similar users to re-rank search results. They also tried three profile-based methods, using 67 pre-defined topic categories. They contrasted profiles based on short-term history (the current session), long term history (the entire 11-day history) and a linear combination of the two.

For the test queries, they isolated out those queries that could not be improved on by re-ranking, because the search engine's top result was the one chosen by users. They called the remaining set of queries non-optimal. They also defined an entropy measure, because it has been suggested that queries which show less variation among click choices are less likely to be improved by personalization (Teevan et al. 2005a). The entropy measure is higher for ambiguous queries, for which different users click on different results.

Dou et al. (2007) found that for queries with low click entropy, the personalization methods had similar or even worse performance than the comparison search engine's rankings. However, on higher-entropy queries, the click-based personalization strategies worked well. The individual-level strategy improved results 1.4% over the default rankings on all queries, and 3.6% on the non-optimal queries. On those queries whose click entropy was ≥ 2.5, individual-level clicks improved results by an impressive 23.7%.

These results suggests that a good search history interface should substantially improve the search experience for users. They also suggest that personalization should be used with caution for queries with low click variation. These results do *not* suggest that this kind of clickthrough information improves results for ambiguous queries without other context. The clickthrough algorithms were designed to work only for queries already clicked on in the past by the user, and in this study 33% of the queries in the log were repeated by the same user. The authors did not examine in isolation how well the clickthrough results worked on never-seen queries with high entropy, which include the truly ambiguous queries.

In the Dou et al. (2007) study, the profile-based methods that try to suggest hits based on estimated similarity to other queries did not perform as well. As Tan et al. (2006) note, search history contains noise that can be irrelevant to the current query, and this may be part of the reason for the degraded results. Dou et al. (2007) did find that the combined long-term and short-term history information was more stable than either alone.

In summary, search results re-ranking based on implicit clickthrough data by many people, for queries that have already been seen, can be more accurate than a search engine algorithm alone. But the clickthrough-based techniques do not work well for queries that have not been seen before, which means they are applicable for only about 50% of queries. Socially-based clickthrough-based techniques also do not work well when there is more than one common interpretation for a given query, which is where an individual's general preferences and current context determines relevance. Individual-based personalized rankings seem to work best on highly ambiguous queries, so the two solutions appear to be complementary.

9.2.5. *Implicit Social Recommendations*

Das et al. (2007) made an ambitious attempt to improve Google's personalized News service. Their approach was to use collaborative filtering on content data using implicit relevance information. They report on experiments in which they compared several different algorithms for making recommendations based only on user similarity, not taking content into account. As their source of implicit relevance information, they used clicks on articles in the Google News service as a proxy for interest in those articles (as opposed to ratings or relevance judgements which are typically used for collaborative filtering). An unusual aspect of this problem is that the pool of news items is constantly changing, unlike most collaborative filtering applications which capitalize on having a large number of ratings over a stable, slowly growing set of items.

Das et al. (2007) tried two model-based algorithms and one memory-based algorithm, but the latter did not scale to the entire problem (much of the Das et al. (2007) work is concerned with scalability, as the system must handle millions of users and produce new results within milliseconds). The two model-based algorithms were indistinguishable in performance. Bearing in mind the difficulty of the problem due to the rapid turnover of news items, and reflecting other attempts to apply collaborative filtering to content rather than taste-based information (e.g., Sarwar et al. 1998), the precision/recall graphs for the news data were not particularly strong. The highest precision achieved on a large sample of users is 17% with a recall of 10%. However, when evaluated on millions of users over a 5–6-month period, the clicks on the suggested items were 38% better on average than a baseline of showing the most popular news items.

In another twist on this idea, Sugiyama et al. (2004) combined implicit information from user browsing history with collaborative filtering to achieve mild improvements in rank ordering.

9.3. Combining Implicit and Explicit Information

9.3.1. *Modifying Implicit Recommendations with Explicit Information*

Sakagami and Kamba (1997) did a small study on recommending news articles, comparing an individual's explicit ratings to implicit information based on time spent reading articles. They found that explicit rating information on every item read produced better results than implicit alone. However, they also found that results were nearly as good when most information was gathered implicitly, with the caveat that users could indicate explicit information on occasion, when they were especially interested in an article.

9.3.2. *Personal Information Assistants: Interactively Combining Explicit and Implicit Relevance Information*

In the field of artificial intelligence, researchers have attempted to develop systems that monitor users' progress and behavior over long interaction periods in an attempt to make intelligent recommendations of information the user may want to see in the future, as well as take actions on behalf of the user (Jameson 2003). These systems are called semi-automated *assistants* or recommender *agents*, and often make use of machine learning techniques. Some of these systems required explicit user input in the form of a goal statement (Joachims et al. 1997) or relevance judgements (Pazzani et al. 1996), while others quietly recorded users' actions and tried to make inferences based on these actions (Horvitz et al. 1998). These systems are related to the recommender systems described earlier in this section, but were intended to act more explicitly as agents working on behalf of the user, and are more interactive in nature.

Many attempts have been made to automatically classify email (Kushmerick and Lau 2005; Sahami et al. 1998). Early work by Kozierok and Maes (1993) used both explicit and implicit information to make predictions about how users would handle e-mail messages (what order to read them in, where to file them) and how users would schedule meetings in a calendar manager application by "looking over the shoulder" of the users, recording every relevant action into a database. After enough data had been accumulated, the system used a nearest-neighbors method (Stanfill and Kahle 1986) to predict a user's action based on the similarity of the current situation to situations already encountered. This system integrated learning from both implicit and explicit user feedback. If a user ignored the system's suggestion, the system treated this as negative feedback, and accordingly added the overriding action to the action database. After certain types of incorrect predictions, the system asked the user questions that allowed it to adjust the weight of the feature that caused the error. Finally, the user could explicitly train the system by presenting it with hypothetical examples of input–action pairs.

The goal of another early system, Letizia (Lieberman 1995), was to bring to the user's attention a percentage of the available next moves that are most likely to be of interest, given the user's earlier actions. Upon request, Letizia provided recommendations for further action on the user's part, usually in the form of suggestions of links to follow when the user was unsure what to do next. Using only implicit information, the system monitored the user's behavior while navigating and reading Web pages, and concurrently evaluated the links reachable from the current page. Saving a page as a bookmark was taken as strong positive evidence for the terms in the corresponding Web page while links skipped are taken as negative support for the information reachable from the link. Selected links could indicate positive or negative evidence, depending on how much time the user spent on the resulting page and whether or not the decision to leave a page quickly was later reversed. Additionally, the evidence for user interest remained persistent across browsing sessions. Thus a user who often read kayaking pages and who was at another time reading the home page of a professional contact may be alerted to the fact that the colleague's personal interests page contains a link to a shared hobby. The system used a best-first search strategy and heuristics to determine which pages to recommend most strongly.

More recently, a large multi-team research project called CALO investigated how to build an intelligent personal agent, using information extracted by analyzing a user's email, contact information, calendar information and other documents (Chaudhri et al. 2006; Mitchell et al. 2006). These ideas are being incorporated into a product by the startup company Siri.com.

9.4. Searching over Personal Information

An important distinction exists between personalizing search engine behavior based on an individual's (or group's) past behavior and preferences, and searching over an individual's personal materials and information. This is sometimes referred to as *desktop search*, but since personal information is distributed across many machines and services, the term *personal information management* is more commonly used today (Teevan et al. 2006) for this wider scope of application.

The definition of personal information is often stretched to mean not only those documents that an individual has produced or been given, but anything that person has viewed in the past. Research shows that people are highly likely to revisit information (Jones et al. 2002; Milic-Frayling et al. 2004), so allowing search over recently viewed information can improve a user's productivity (Dumais et al. 2003). Research also suggests that users' search strategies differ when searching over previously seen materials (Barreau and Nardi 1995; Jones et al. 2002). Bergman et al. (2008) found that, when searching for files on their own computers, participants strongly preferred navigating their file system over using desktop search.

Certain organizational features are more salient for information that a person has already seen, or which pertains to an individual's life, so search over personal information can use memory cues that are not salient for information artifacts that the user has not seen in the past. The Stuff I've Seen project (Cutrell et al. 2006a; Dumais et al. 2003) built a search index over all materials that a user had stored in their personal directories along with all external Web pages they accessed, their email messages, their calendar appointments, and so on. They evaluated this system with a longitudinal study across several months and hundreds of users. Users reported that the system was especially helpful when they could remember contextual cues surrounding the previous use of the information, but not more detailed information. For example, a user looking for an address of a restaurant whose name he could not remember might search on `restaurant`, filter the results to see emails from his daughter, sort the narrowed results by date, and then scan for an email from the last week that contains the restaurant address. This study also finds that organizing by time is often important, but only in certain contexts – for when an email was sent, for example, but not for when a Web page was created. The study also finds that sorting by time was preferred over ranked sorting, and that sorting by people's names was also quite important.

9.5. Conclusions

Although there is a great deal of research in this area, to date automated personalization has yet to have a major impact (Fischer 2001; Jameson 2003). The main reason seems to be that it is difficult to make predictions accurately. Additional problems relate to user privacy and the need for user control coupled with the desire by users for the system to be unobtrusive.

Some results indicated that re-ranking can *reduce* search efficiency. Teevan et al. (2007) found that searchers tended to look for information they had found in a previous search session 40% of the time, and that changing ranking order increased the time it took for users to find a link they'd clicked on for a similar search in the past. For automated re-ranking based on a user's actions, most controlled experiments results suggest that when it works at all, it works best for very ambiguous queries (Croft and Wei 2005; Qiu and Cho 2006; Teevan et al. 2005a). (This is also true for some other interface techniques like clustering, see Chapter 8.) However, disambiguation of general words is easily solved by simple query reformulation (e.g., adding the word `engines` to the ambiguous query `jets`), and represents only a small fraction of queries (see Chapter 3). Thus, if disambiguation of ambiguous queries is the primary benefit of personalized results rankings, it may not make a noticable difference for most users. As noted above, the best application of personalized ranking seems to be for repeated queries that are naturally ambiguous. To address these issues, Teevan et al. (2008) report on an algorithm for predicting which queries can most benefit from personalization.

Several major search engines currently offer a personalization feature that attempts to rank search results based on what the user has searched for in the past, but no details beyond anecdote are available as to their efficacy. When asked to comment on the behavior of Google's personalization system, a Google VP stated that it is used cautiously, adjusting results only in about one out of five queries, and changing at most two hits in the first page of ten (Hotchkiss 2007b).

The appropriateness of automatically taking "intelligent" action on behalf of users has been called into question (Nielsen 1998; Norman 2007a; Shneiderman and Maes 1997). Systems that use implicit information to try to infer what the user wants to do are often poorly received. The widespread and virulent dislike of animated agents such as "Clippy" introduced into the Microsoft Windows 97 operating system is a famous example of the failure of automated agents in a user interface (Whitworth 2005). In the case of term suggestions for query reformulation, White et al. (2005) found that participants wanted the system to quietly track the information they accessed and use it for suggesting additional terms, but wanted to have control over which terms were automatically added.

Another example can be seen in interfaces for automated spelling correction. Google's initial spelling suggestion system did not work well and was not well-received. After the algorithm was improved and became highly accurate, the reception became positive when the interaction allowed just one spelling suggestion below the original query (Hurst 2002). At one point Google automatically replaced the original spelling with a correction when few results were found, but this feature was discontinued, presumably because of negative user reaction. However, Google does automatically massage some queries behind the scenes, for example, by removing middle initials in the retrieval results when matching against queries consisting of people's names with no middle initial.

10 Information Visualization for Search Interfaces

The preceding chapters have discussed user interfaces to support search, with a focus on what is known to be successful (from a usability perspective) for the vast majority of searchers. This and the following chapter describe efforts to improve search interfaces by incorporating *visual* information into the display using techniques from the field of *information visualization*.

The human perceptual system is highly attuned to images, and visual representations can communicate some kinds of information more rapidly and effectively than text. For example, the familiar bar chart or line graph can be much more evocative of the underlying data than the corresponding table of numbers (Larkin and Simon 1987). The goal of information visualization is to translate abstract information into a visual form that provides new insight about that information. Visualization has been shown to be successful at providing insight about data for a wide range of tasks.

The field of information visualization is a vibrant one, with hundreds of innovative ideas burgeoning on the Web. However, applying visualization to textual information is quite challenging, especially when the goal is to improve search over text collections. As discussed in earlier chapters, search is a means towards some other end, rather than a goal in itself. When reading text, one is focused on that task; it is not possible to read and visually perceive something else at the same time. Furthermore, the nature of text makes it difficult to convert it to a visual analog.

Most likely for these reasons, applications of visualization to general search have not been widely accepted to date, and few usability results are positive. For example, Chen and Yu (2000) conducted a meta-analysis of information visualization usability studies, with a focus on information retrieval problems. The purpose of a meta-analysis is to combine many

234

different points in the evaluation space in order to come up with more robust and general results. Chen and Yu (2000) focused on six visualization interface studies from five papers (Allen 2000; Combs and Bederson 1999; Robertson et al. 1998; Sebrechts et al. 1999; Swan and Allan 1998). The conclusions of the meta-analysis were:

- Individual cognitive differences among participants, as opposed to differences among the interfaces, had the largest effect, especially on accuracy, and to some degree on efficiency,
- Holding cognitive abilities constant, participants performed better with simpler visual-spatial interfaces than with complex ones, and
- The combined effect of visualization in the studies was not statistically significant.

Thus, this meta-analysis found no evidence that visualization improved search performance. This is not to say that advanced visual representations cannot help improve search; rather that there are few proven successful ideas today.

On the other hand, for analytical tasks, visualization of textual information appears more promising. A visualization that is not appropriate for a general search audience might instead be quite valuable for someone with expertise and deep interest in understanding data. Thus it is useful to make a distinction between visualization of text for the purposes of text analysis versus visualization for search.

This and the following chapter are intended to be read together. This chapter provides a brief a summary of the core principles and standard tools of information visualization, followed by a discussion of how different data types are best visualized. This chapter also describes why visualizing nominal data, which includes textual data, is difficult. It then describes how researchers have attempted to improve search using visualization techniques. Chapter 11 discusses the vibrant area of visualization for text analysis tasks.

10.1. Principles of Information Visualization

Guidelines for designing information visualizations are available from writers such as Few (Few 2009) and Tufte (Tufte 1983, 1990). Some of these guidelines overlap with guidelines from graphic design, including the need to present information clearly, precisely, and without extraneous or distracting clutter. Other guidelines relate to the special purposes of

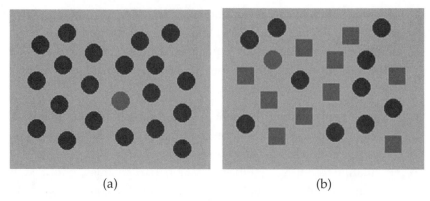

(a)   (b)

Figure 10.1. (a) Viewers can preattentively recognize differences in color. (b) Viewers cannot preattentively recognize simultaneously variation of color plus shape. From Healy (1993).

visualization. Good visualizations use graphics to organize information, highlight important information, allow for visual comparisons, and reveal patterns, trends, and outliers in the data. Visualization guidelines are also derived from principles of human perception, and urge the designer to be aware of the perceptual properties which can affect the design. Few (2009) provides a good overview of these principles, which are described briefly below.

One important perceptual property is that of *preattentiveness* (Triesman 1985). This term refers to visual properties that a person can perceive in fewer than 250 milliseconds, without having to scan the visual field serially (since eye movement and focus take about 200 ms) (Ware 2004). Preattentive observations take the same amount of time regardless of the number of objects being viewed. For example, people can accurately determine whether or not one red circle is presented among a field of blue circles in fewer than 200 ms (see Figure 10.1a). However, determining the *number* of items with the alternative color is *not* preattentive; it requires a serial scan of all the objects to do the counting (Healy 1993). *Combinations* of properties are also usually not preattentive. Although people can detect one square among many circles of the same color (because the angular corners of the square are preattentively differentiated from the curves of the circles), the eye cannot detect the combination of the color distinction and the shape distinction simultaneously; this requires serial scanning. Figure 10.1b shows an example; viewers cannot preattentively detect that there is a red, circular-shaped object among a field of blue and red circles and squares.

Preattentiveness explains why a small amount of color highlighting against a white page is so effective at drawing the attention. As discussed in earlier chapters, a notable successful use of visual cues in search interfaces is color highlighting of query terms in documents, and bolding of query terms in document summaries in retrieval results. (However, if there are many colors in a display, color highlighting does not work well at drawing attention.) Note that not all cues in a visualization need to be preattentive to be useful; rather, it is important to know which visual components cause a preattentive reaction in order to know what will stand out in a display.

Another important set of perceptual principles pertains to the visual components that are useful for making quantitative comparisons (Mackinlay 1986). Bertin (1983) defines a *graphical vocabulary* consisting of *marks* (points, lines, areas), *retinal variables* (color, size, shape, orientation, scale), and *position* (relative locations of marks within a spatial field). Cleveland (1985) and Cleveland and McGill (1984) discuss the proper ways to combine these variables. For example, relative length can be assessed precisely, and so the relative positions of the tops of a row of bars in a bar chart can be used to accurately compare quantitative values. The perceptual system naturally associates a larger value to a larger size mark. The shape of lines are also evocative; a line graph can be used to indicate changes over time and other trends, and line cross-overs and relative positions are perceptually salient (see Figure 10.3).

Gestalt principles are also important for visualization (Few 2009). Among the most important of these is the principle of *proximity*, meaning that objects that are located spatially near one another are perceived as belonging to the same group. This principle is used extensively in interface design; for example, text labels are perceived to label those lines or entry forms that are nearest. Blank areas surrounding proximally close objects help contribute to the perception of grouping. Another gestalt principle, that of *similarity*, reflects the tendency to see objects that share the same visual attributes as being part of the same group.

10.2. Techniques for Interactive Visualization

Several interactive techniques are important to information visualization. In the technique known as *brushing and linking*, highlighting objects in one part of a visualization causes those same objects to be highlighted in a different view. For example, selecting points at the uppermost corner of a scatter plot would show the positions of those same points in a bar graph plotting other attributes of the same dataset. User interaction of this nature can improve comprehension and can help find interesting associations within the data. The brushing-and-linking technique is heavily used in text analysis interfaces.

For large or densely packed visualizations, movie camera-style interaction techniques include providing an *overview* of the data, *zooming* in to see details or zooming out to see the bigger picture, and *panning* laterally across a view of the data. These kinds of interaction are used heavily in online map applications. Zooming has been found in several studies to be less optimal than showing multiple views of the same information when complex visual comparisons must be made (Plumlee and Ware 2006).

The judicious use of *animation* is important in interactive visualization, to draw attention, retain context, and help make occluded information visible (Card et al. 1991; Robertson et al. 1993). A recent study found evidence that, with careful design, animated transitions can improve perception of changes between different graphical representations of information (Heer and Robertson 2007).

Distortion-based techniques are often proposed as a way to draw the viewer's attention to the most important part of the display, while shrinking down the less important information. The idea is to keep the information that is not in focus available to retain the context of that which is in focus. The distortion-based technique that has been experimented with most often is the *fisheye view*, where the focus is of normal size but the information around it is miniaturized and distorted, usually with a gaussian function. However, most studies show that users do not find these kinds of views helpful (Baudisch et al. 2004; Hornbæk and Frøkjær 2001; Hornbæk and Hertzum 2007).

A recent innovation is Tufte's (2006) *sparklines*, which are "small, high-resolution graphics embedded in a context of words, numbers, images." A typical data graphic like a line graph or a bar is shrunk down, and most details removed, to show a general trend with perhaps just the endpoints labeled. Sparklines can be inserted directly into running text, to illustrate a trend, or as part of a more complex interface (see the bar charts in Figure 10.17).

10.3. The Effects of Data Types on Information Visualization

For the purposes of visualization, it is useful to classify data as either *quantitative* or *categorical*. Quantitative data is defined as data upon which arithmetic operations can be made (integers, real numbers). Categorical data can be further subdivided into *interval*, *ordinal*, *nominal*, and

Auto Fuel Efficiency (Average MPG), by Year and Country of Origin									
				Year					
Origin	70	71	72	73	74	75	76	77	78	79
Europe	25.20	28.75	22.00	24.00	27.00	24.50	24.25	29.25	24.95	30.45
Japan	25.50	29.50	24.20	20.00	29.33	27.50	28.00	27.42	29.69	32.95
US	15.27	17.74	16.28	15.03	18.14	17.55	19.43	20.72	21.77	23.48

Figure 10.2. A table of statistics about several brands of automobiles from the U.S., Europe, and Japan, from 1970 to 1979.

hierarchical. Interval data is essentially quantitative data that has been discretized and made into ordered data (e.g., time is converted into months, quarters, and years). Ordinal data is data that can be placed in an order, but the differences among the values cannot be directly measured (e.g., hot, warm, cold, or first, second, third). Nominal data includes names of people and locations, and text. Finally, hierarchical data is nominal data arranged into subsuming groups.

Quantitative, interval, and ordered data are easier to convey visually than nominal data such as text. To understand why, consider an example dataset consisting of statistics about various brands of automobile. Quantitative data includes miles per gallon (MPG), weight, number of cylinders, and horsepower. Ordinal data consists of model year. Nominal data includes country of origin, brand name, and model name. In Figure 10.2, a table shows average MPG values for the years 1970–1979 for autos made in three geographic regions. This view does not aid the eye in discerning patterns or trends. By contrast, Figure 10.3 shows this same data plotted as a line graph, with year on the x-axis and average MPG on the y-axis. The general upward slope of the lines indicates a general increasing trend in average MPG over time for all regions and models. The relative positions of the lines in this graph clearly show that on average, U.S. fuel efficiency lagged that of Japanese and European cars. The cross-over points of the top two lines visually indicate that in some years Japan's average MPG was higher than Europe's, and in other years lower.

Visualization is at its most powerful when combining visual features in a meaningful way. Figure 10.4 uses several visual components at once. Spatial positions indicate the relationship between fuel efficiency values for models of cars and their respective weights. A mark distinguished by shape is used to indicate the region of origin, and the color shading gradient distinguishes later model years from earlier. From this graph one can see at a glance the inverse relationship between higher fuel efficiency and higher weight of the car. The grouping pattern of the cross-marked shapes clearly shows the concentration of U.S. models in the lower right

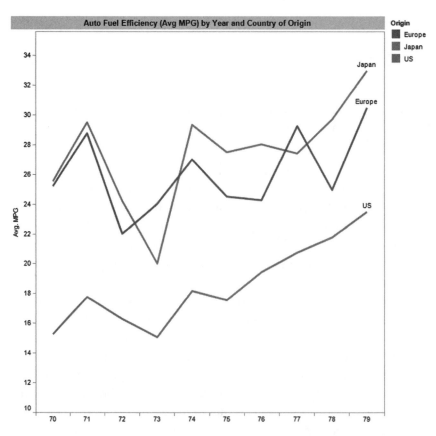

Figure 10.3. Simple visualizations of data about automobiles. Here, a quantitative value (miles per gallon) is plotted against an ordinal dimension (year), in which each line representes a nominal value (origin of car manufacturer). Trends appear clearly showing European and Japanese cars remaining on average close together and ahead of American cars, and also indicating an overall increase in MPG over time.

hand side where the heavy, fuel-inefficient cars appear. The color gradient moving from light to dark from left to right brings to light a trend of most cars becoming both heavier and more fuel efficient over time.

10.4. The Difficulties with Visualizing Nominal Data

How to do the same kind of display with text is an open question. Nominal or categorical variables are difficult to display graphically because they have no inherent ordering. Placing nominal data like words or names along an axis, unfortunately, is much like scrambling the years in a plot of change over time. Figure 10.5 shows a non-sensical graph in which

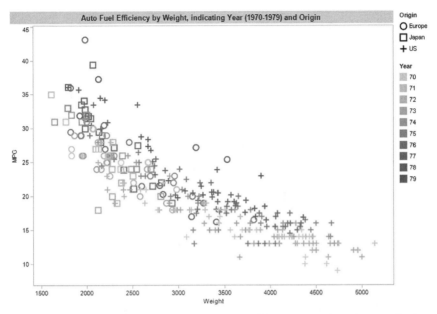

Figure 10.4. Visualization of car data using spatial layout, retinal markers, and color gradation properly applied to quantitative, ordinal, and nominal data types. (See color plate 5.)

average MPG is plotted against car model name. Although the lines have evocative peaks and valleys, these shapes are misleading, because alphabetical order of car does not have an inherent underlying meaning. Unfortunately, because text is nominal, many attempts to visualize text result in nonsensical graphs like this one.

Many text visualizations have been proposed that place icons representing documents on a 2-dimensional or 3-dimensional spatial layout; Figure 10.6 shows two examples. In Figure 10.6a, documents were clustered in an attempt to extract out common themes or topics from the very high-dimensional document space. These derived themes were then reduced down to two abstract dimensions which were used to create the x and y axes. Figure 10.6b used a similar dimension reduction, but focused on showing relationships among words rather than among documents. Adjacency on maps like these is meant to indicate semantic similarity along an abstract dimension, but this dimension does not have a spatial analog that is easily understood. Usability results for such displays tend not to be positive.

Rather than trying to convert nominal information to an abstract quantitative value, some approaches for text visualization plot quantitative values that can easily be associated with text, such as how many articles

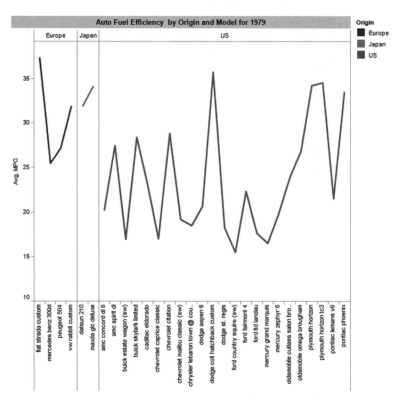

Figure 10.5. A poor graph on the same auto data, erroneously plotting a line connecting nominal values on the x-axis. The line misleadingly suggests a trend, but is meaningless because MPG is not a function of the name of car models.

in a collection contain a certain word, or the time at which the article was created or last updated. For example, the Envision visualization (Fox et al. 1993) and the GRIDL visualization (Shneiderman et al. 2003) (see Figure 10.7) used tables with graphical entries to show document information, plotting author name or paper category against date published. This may be useful for analyzing the contents of a library in order to determine what books to acquire, or comparing the publication history of academics, but is unlikely to be useful for the standard searcher. Furthermore, the graphical marks hide the information that is key for differentiating the documents: their titles and content. A usability study of educators using the GRIDL system found that they preferred a standard HTML-based view (Rose et al. 1998). When chronology is important for search results, listing of titles in chronological order works well, potentially paired with an

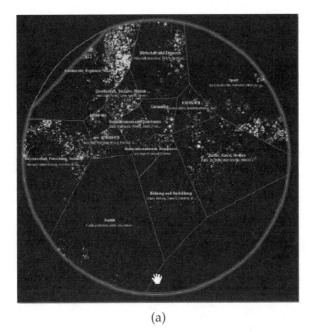

(a)

(b)

Figure 10.6. Attempts to use spatial layout for improving search. (a) Infosky, from Granitzer et al. (2004). (b) WordSpace, from Brandes et al. (2006).

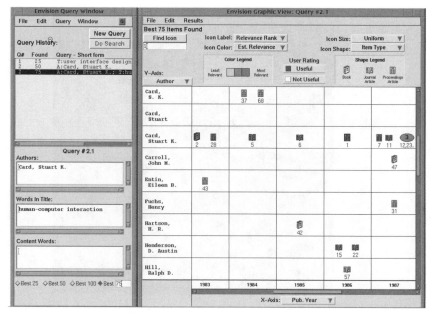

(a)

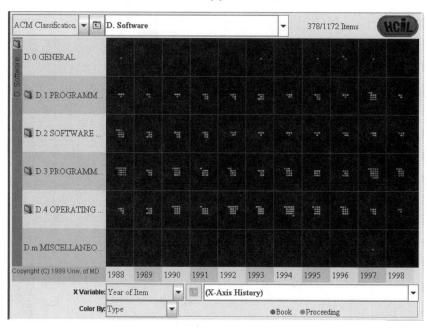

(b)

Figure 10.7. Visualizing a collection by showing its contents in a table. (a) Envision, from Fox et al. (1993). (b) GRIDL, derived from the interface available at http://www.cs.umd.edu/hcil/ and used with permission of University of Maryland Human-Computer Interaction Lab. (See color plate 4.)

option for sorting for alternative views (Cutrell et al. 2006a; Reiterer et al. 2000).

Several kinds of visualization work well with at least limited amounts of nominal data. Nodes-and-link diagrams, also called network graphs, can convey relationships among nominal variables because there is no implied ordering among the children of a node. The biggest problem with network graphs is that they do not scale well to large sizes – the nodes become unreadable and the links cross into a jumbled mess. Another potential problem with network graphs is that there is evidence that lay users are not particularly comfortable with nodes-and-links views (Viégas and Donath 2004), although there is evidence that people can understand networks in which their own social network is the focus of the visualization (Heer and Boyd 2005).

There are several common interactive methods for making large networks more understandable. One idea is to allow the user to select a node of interest and make that node the focus of the display, re-arranging the other nodes around it. This approach can be helpful for medium sized graphs (Yee et al. 2001), but quickly becomes too complex when graphs exceed about 100 nodes. Another approach is to eliminate most nodes other than those surrounding the most recently selected node. Figure 10.8a shows an example of such an approach applied to the navigation the WordNet lexical database (Fellbaum 1998). A third approach is to arrange nodes into a circle and have links crossing the center of the circle, or connecting to other nodes in the circle's center as shown in Figure 10.8b. These views are useful for exploring and understanding a dataset, but have not been shown to work well to aid the standard search process.

A number of visualizations have been proposed for displaying hierarchical information. The most familiar is the expandable directory tree browser, as seen in several forms in computer operating systems. Other approaches dynamically display network or tree graphs, such as the *hyperbolic tree browser* (Lamping et al. 1995). A popular alternative is a space-filling display known as the *treemap* (Johnson and Shneiderman 1991; Wattenberg 1999). Although its original intention was the display of hierarchical information of great depth, in practice it is used only to show two to three levels of hierarchy. Each node is represented by a rectangle r, and its child nodes are smaller rectangles embedded within r. The process continues recursively to the desired depth of hierarchy. The size of the rectangles correspond to the relative frequency or importance of the underlying node, and the rectangles are color-coded to represent either nominal or quantitative values (the latter indicated with a color gradient).

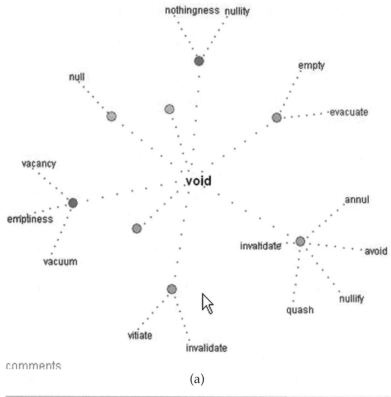

(a)

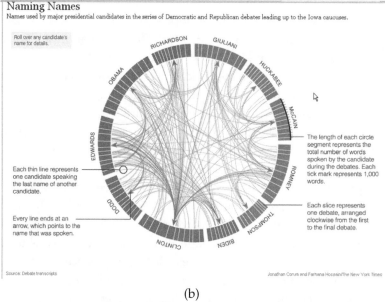

(b)

Figure 10.8. Network (nodes and links) visualizations. (a) The Visual WordNet view of the WordNet lexical thesaurus which simplifies the network by only showing nodes directly connected to the target node, from http://kylescholz.com/projects/wordnet/. (b) A circle graph visualization of who mentions whom during a debate, extracted from presidential debate transcripts, from *The New York Times*.

When designed carefully and applied to an appropriate task, the treemap can provide a useful overview of an information collection, which itself is difficult to access. However, treemaps have not been proven successful at showing textual data.

The remainder of this chapter describes attempts to use information visualization to go beyond these standard user interface visual cues to improve search. The discussion is organized around the different major components of the search process, as discussed in earlier chapters. These are: query specification, viewing of retrieval results, and query reformulation. Visualizations for search also attempt to give an overview of the contents of the collection, and this topic is also discussed below.

10.5. Visualization for Query Specification

For most search interfaces today, query specification consists of a simple entry form or combinations of entry forms, possibly aided by textual term suggestions in a query reformulation step. This section describes how researchers have attempted to innovate on query specification using information visualization techniques.

10.5.1. *Visualizing Boolean Query Specification*

As discussed in Chapter 4, full-syntax Boolean query specification is not sufficiently usable for most searchers and thus is not widely used. To remedy this, graphical depictions of Venn diagrams have been proposed several times as a way to improve Boolean query specification. Typically, a query term is associated with a circle or ring, and intersection of rings indicates conjunction of terms. The number of documents that satisfy the various conjuncts are displayed within the appropriate segments of the diagram. Several studies have found such interfaces more effective than their command-language based syntactic counterparts (Hertzum and Frokjaer 1996; Jones and McInnes 1998; Michard 1982). For example, Hertzum and Frokjaer (1996) found that a simple Venn diagram representation produced faster and more accurate results than Boolean query syntax.

However, this format imposes limitations on the complexity of the expression. Innovations have been designed to get around this problem, as seen in the VQuery system (Jones and McInnes 1998) (see Figure 10.9). In VQuery, a direct manipulation interface allowed users to assign any

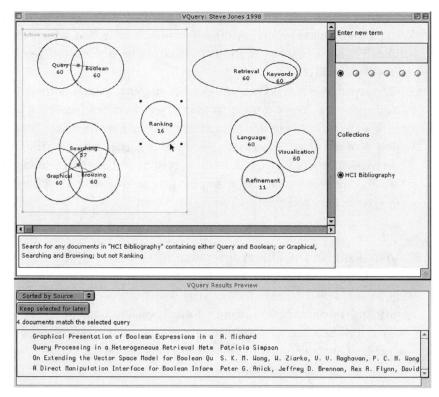

Figure 10.9. The VQuery (Jones and McInnes 1998) Venn Diagram interface for Boolean query specification.

number of query terms to ovals. If two or more ovals were placed such that they overlap with one another, and if the user selects the area of their intersection, an AND was implied among those terms. (In Figure 10.9, the term Query is conjoined with Boolean.) If the user selected outside the area of intersection but within the ovals, an OR was implied among the corresponding terms. A NOT operation is associated with any term whose oval appears in the active area of the display but which remains unselected (in the figure, NOT Ranking has been specified). An active area indicated the current query; ovals containing terms could be moved out of the active area for later use. This design was not evaluated with usability studies.

Anick et al. (1990) described another innovative direct manipulation interface for Boolean queries. The user typed a natural language query which was automatically converted to a representation in which each query term was represented by a block. The blocks were arranged into rows and columns (see Figure 10.10a). If two or more blocks appeared

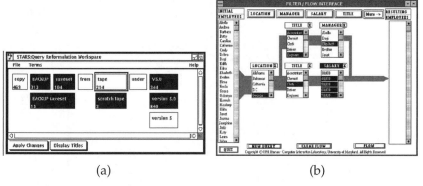

Figure 10.10. (a) A block-oriented diagram visualization for Boolean query specifi-cation, from Anick et al. (1990). (b) The filter-flow interface for Boolean query spec-ification, from Young and Shneiderman (1993). Used with permission of University of Maryland Human-Computer Interaction Lab.

along the same row they were considered to be ANDed together. Two or more blocks within the same column were ORed. Thus the user could represent a technical term in multiple ways within the same query, provid-ing a kind of faceted query interface. For example, the terms `version 5`, `version 5.0`, and `v5` might be shown in the same row. Blocks could also be activated and deactivated so users can quickly experiment with differ-ent combinations of terms and Boolean queries simply by activating and deactivating blocks. This facility also allows users to have multiple repre-sentations of the same term in different places throughout the display, thus allowing rapid feedback on the consequences of specifying various combi-nations of query terms. Informal evaluation of the system found that users were able to learn to manipulate the interface quickly and enjoyed using it. This design was not formally compared to other interaction techniques.

Young and Shneiderman (1993) found improvements over standard Boolean syntax by providing users with a direct manipulation filter-flow model. Clicking on an attribute on the left hand side caused a listbox con-taining values for those attributes to be displayed in the main portion of the screen. The user then selected which values of the attributes to let the flow go through. The number of documents that matched the query at each point was indicated by the width of the "water" flowing from one attribute to the next (see Figure 10.10b). A usability study found that fewer errors were made using the filter flow model than a standard SQL database query. However, the examples and study pertained only to data-base querying rather than to text search, since the possible query terms for full text search cannot be represented realistically in a scrollable list.

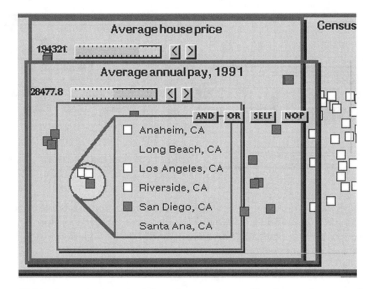

Figure 10.11. A magic lens interface for query specification, where overlapping lenses act as filters on the document set. This screenshot shows a disjunctive query that finds cities with relatively low housing prices or high annual salaries. (Courtesy of Ken Fishkin.)

Another example of a graphical approach to Boolean query specification was a technique called magic lenses. Fishkin and Stone (1995) suggested an extension to the usage of this visualization tool for the specification of Boolean queries. Information was represented as lists or icons within a 2D space. Lenses acted as filters on the document set (see Figure 10.11). For example, a word could be associated with a transparent lens. When this lens was placed over an iconic representation of a set of documents, it caused all documents that do not contain a given word to disappear. If a second lens representing another word was then laid over the first, the lenses combined to act as a conjunction of the two words with the document set, hiding any documents that did not contain both words. Additional information could be adjusted dynamically, such as a minimum threshold for how often the term occurs in the documents, or an on–off switch for word stemming.

Figure 10.11 shows an example of a disjunctive query for finding cities with relatively low housing prices or high annual salaries. One lens "calls out" a clump of southern California cities, labeling each. Above that is a lens screening for cities with average house price below $194,321 (the data is from 1990), and above this one is a lens screening for cities with average annual pay above $28,477. This approach was not evaluated in an information access setting.

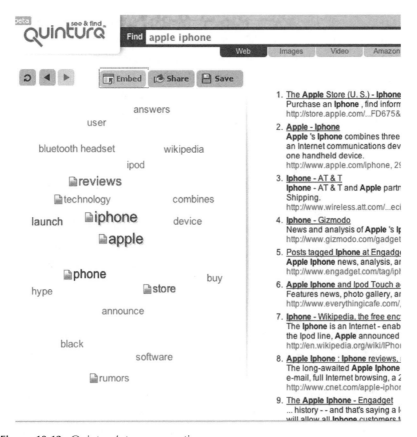

Figure 10.12. Quintura's term suggestions.

Although intriguing, these visual query specification interfaces are not usually seen in practice; interfaces that allow users to select query terms from visually depicted category labels are more successful, as discussed in Chapter 8.

10.5.2. *Visualizing Query Term Suggestions*

Chapter 4 discusses systems that automatically suggest term refinements for queries, usually by showing an orderly list of up to 8 suggestions, with hyperlinks to add them to the query. These interfaces have been found helpful, especially when a user can augment the query with a single click. The Quintura search engine shows term suggestions in a 2D map layout, or "cloud," where related terms are shown near one another but arranged somewhat arbitrarily. Mousing over a suggested term causes the others to shift away, and additional similar terms to appear nearby. For example, for the query apple iphone shown in Figure 10.12, neighboring terms include *reviews, store, wikipedia,* and *hype.* Placing the mouse over *hype* causes terms such as *sale, preview,* and *handset* to replace those that were previously visible. Selecting the term adds it to the current query. This layout has the advantage over standard views of fluidly updating in response to clicks, but the lack of predictability about where terms of different types appear, most likely resulting in long scanning times and/or confusion on the part of the user.

10.6. Visualizing Query Terms Within a Large Document

As discussed in Chapter 5, one of the most successful search interface tropes is the highlighting (in color or boldface) of query terms within retrieved documents and search results. Several approaches have been suggested for how to extend this visualization, both for individual documents (this section) and within retrieval results (next section).

The SuperBook system (Egan et al. 1989a,b; Landauer et al. 1993) (also discussed in Chapter 8) made use of the structure of a large document to display query term hits in context. The table of contents (TOC) for a book or manual were shown in a hierarchy on the left hand side of the display, and full text of a page or section was shown on the right hand side. After the user specified a query on the book, the search results are shown in the context of the table of contents hierarchy. Those sections that contain search hits are made larger and the others are compressed.

As discussed in Chapter 5, some researchers have suggested using the document scrollbar to show the location of term hits. The Read Wear/Edit Wear system (Hill et al. 1992) uses the scrollbar to indicate information such as the amount of time a reader has spent looking at a particular location in the document, or locations of query term hits. Byrd (1999) suggests applying a different color to each query term, and showing the corresponding colors to the appropriate locations within a scrollbar widget (see Figure 10.13). The ThumbBar system (Graham 1999) uses a similar scrollbar widget on the left hand side and a visualization of hits for the important terms of the document on the right hand side. This idea has been applied in the Chrome Web browser, which uses such a visualization to show where search hits occur within a searched Web page.

Hornbæk and Frøkjær (2001) conducted a study comparing a standard linear view of a document, a fisheye view, and an overview+detail view (see Figure 10.14). In the fisheye view, the idea is to reduce scrolling and help the reader focus on their task by shrinking those parts that

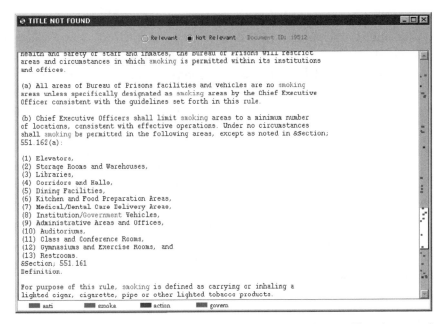

Figure 10.13. Query term hits highlighted and shown in the scrollbar, from Byrd (1999).

are estimated to be less important; they can be instantly expanded with a mouseclick. In the overview+detail view, a miniaturized view is shown alongside a standard text view; graphical lines indicate text lines and thumbnails indicate images. In both advanced views, query terms

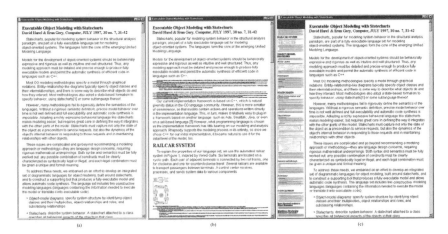

Figure 10.14. Three interface conditions compared in a study, from Hornbæk and Frøkjær (2001). The conditions are (a) linear text, (b) fisheye view, and (c) overview+detail.

are highlighted both in the text itself and in the miniaturized views. Twenty participants were asked to write essays and answer questions based on text from technical articles. All but one participant preferred the overview+detail interface and one preferred the linear interface. As has been seen in many studies, the participants did not like the fisheye view; participants also achieved higher grades using the overview+detail view, but spent more time in this view in the question answering tasks.

Similarly, as discussed in Chapter 5, Baudisch et al. (2004) experimented with several ways of showing an overview of where the query terms occur throughout a document, including an overview+context view and a fisheye view. As found by Hornbæk and Frøkjær (2001), most participants disliked the fisheye view, but preferred the overview with color keyword highlighting over a standard Web page view with color highlighting alone.

10.7. Visualizing Query Terms Within Retrieval Results

There is ample evidence that relevance judgements are aided by seeing which query terms appeared in the retrieved document, their relative proximity, and the words around them (see Chapter 5). Search results listings commonly highlight or apply boldface font to words in the results listing that match the query terms. This section discusses a number of visualizations that have been proposed that go beyond highlighting to explicitly show the locations of query terms in retrieved documents.

10.7.1. *TileBars*

An early attempt to visualize the relationship between query terms and retrieval results was the TileBars interface (Hearst 1995). At the time TileBars was introduced, search over full text (as opposed to abstracts) was relatively rare, and most ranking algorithms did not take term proximity into account. One goal of the design was to allow the searcher to see the relative length of the documents, as well as the locations and relative proximity of query terms within the retrieved documents. An algorithm called TextTiling (Hearst 1994) preprocessed the texts and subdivided them into sequential subtopic units, further allowing the user to see whether or not their query terms coincided within one logical unit of the text.

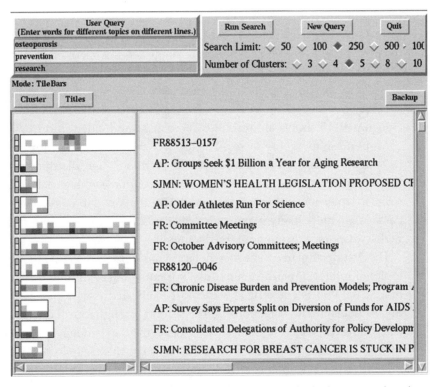

Figure 10.15. TileBars visualization (Hearst 1995) in which documents length is represented by the horizontal bar, and query occurrence is indicated by grayscale squares, one set of terms per line.

In the TileBars visualization (see Figure 10.15), an icon was shown alongside each search result hit which simultaneously showed document length and query occurrence patterns. The visualization represented each document as a rectangle whose length reflected the relative length of the document. The rectangle was further subdivided into columns, representing document segments (paragraphs, sections, or subtopical units as computed by TextTiling). Each query term was assigned its own row within the rectangle, and depth of gray scale was used to indicate the frequency of hits for each term within the subtopic. The pattern of grayscale indicated whether a term occurred as a main topic throughout the document, as a subtopic, or was just mentioned in passing. A further refinement of the idea allowed the user to optionally indicate the query as a set of facets, where each facet received its own entry form and received its own line within the graphic. Each facet of the query consisted of synonyms or related terms representing a given concept. Clicking on a "tile" brought up a view of the document scrolled to the start of the tile, with query terms highlighted in colors corresponding to the colors in the facet's query entry form. Grayscale variation was used in the glyphs instead of color because the perceptual psychological literature suggested this would lead to more accurate interpretation; however subsequent research indicates that the importance of the aesthetic preference for color outweighs the need for accuracy.

Figure 10.15 shows an example. The bar is subdivided into rows that correspond to the query facets. The top row of each TileBar corresponds to "osteoporosis," the second row to "prevention," and the third row to "research." The bar is also subdivided into columns, where each column refers to a passage within the document. Hits that overlap within the same passage are more likely to indicate a relevant document than hits that are widely dispersed throughout the document.

The first document can be seen to have considerable overlap among the topics of interest towards the middle, but not at the beginning or the end (the actual end is cut off). Thus it most likely discusses topics in addition to research into osteoporosis. The second through fourth documents, which are considerably shorter, also have overlap among all terms of interest, and so are also probably of interest. (The titles help to verify this.) The next three documents are all long, and the TileBars graphic suggests they discuss both research and prevention, but do not even touch on osteoporosis, and so probably are not of interest.

10.7.2. *Other Iconic Views of Query Term Hits*

Several alternative ways to visualize query terms in context have since been proposed. Hoeber and Yang (2006) developed a simplified version of TileBars in which only one square is shown per query term; term overlap information is not shown, nor is relative document length (see Figure 10.16). A color gradation from yellow to red was used instead of grayscale, and the query terms corresponding to each square are shown vertically at the top of the search results, thus making it easy to keep track of which square corresponds to each query term. In a study with 21 undergraduate computer science majors completing two tasks, Hoeber and Yang (2006) compared this simplified view applied to Google results (without summaries) to the standard Google interface and another design that attempted to show semantically related documents to those retrieved. No significant timing differences were found, but the visualization was

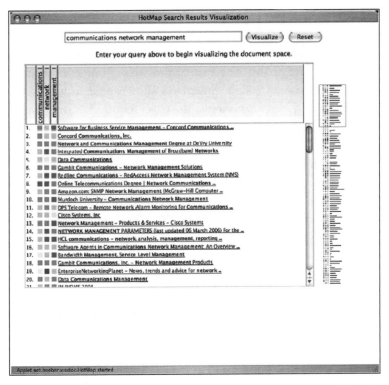

Figure 10.16. A simplified version of TileBars called HotMap, from Hoeber and Yang (2006). (See color plate 5.)

preferred to standard Google, which in turn was preferred to the semantic match algorithm.

A greatly simplified version of the idea was introduced commercially as MatchBars, part of the Xerox Pagis Pro product. A document-shaped icon showed gray-scale colored rectangles corresponding to each query term, but term overlap and document length were not shown. A similar compressed version of the visualization was proposed by Heimonen and Jhaveri (2005). In a study with computer science students, 11 of the 18 participants did not notice the graphic. Of those who did, the subjective scores indicated that participants did not find the visualization helpful for spotting useful results nor for summarizing results, but did find them useful for eliminating poor results, which is a common finding with visualizations generally.

Anderson et al. (2002) suggested showing relative query term frequencies as a color-coded pie chart beside each search result. A usability study was conducted on a very small collection of 163 documents that were

selected so that participants could not judge relevance on title and summary text alone. In addition, participants completed only two queries
each, so the results of the study should be viewed with caution. Each
of the 101 participants saw one of three conditions: a standard text results listing, a listing with pie charts shown next to text results, and a
grid view with pie charts alone. The tasks required finding an explicit answer in the full text view which used color highlighting of query terms
along with up and down arrows that made the display jump to the next
hit within the page. As seen in other studies, participants liked the color
highlighting of keywords in the full text documents and found the ability
to jump from term to term within the documents to be helpful. Detailed
subjective responses were not provided, but most participants were reported as saying that they understood the visualizations and found them
helpful.

10.7.3. *A Comparison Study of Iconic Visualizations of Retrieval Results*

Reiterer et al. (2000) built a system called Insyder that combined several
existing visualization ideas and conducted a controlled study comparing
participant performance (time and effectiveness) and preferences for three
visualizations of results listings Reiterer et al. (2005). The 40 participants
(university students and staff) each completed 12 tasks, half of which
were fact lookup, and half more intensive information-seeking tasks. The
queries were fixed in advance; participants only viewed retrieval results.

In one condition, participants could access only a standard Web-style
results listing, which acted as the baseline. In the next condition, participants could use only a sortable column view, which contained the same
information as the Web-style listing, but truncated the summary extracts
(see Figure 10.17a). The sortable view also allowed display of retrieved
documents within a frame, without replacing the results listing. The third,
fourth, and fifth conditions allowed participants to choose between one of
the three visualizations and the field-sortable column view.

For the visualizations, Reiterer et al. (2005) implemented (i) a version
of TileBars that used color for each facet rather than grayscale (Figure
10.17b), (ii) an improved version of the bar chart visualization suggested
by Veerasamy and Belkin (1996) (Figure 10.18a), and (iii) a scatter plot
view that plotted estimated relevance against date, similar to xFIND
(Andrews et al. 2001) (Figure 10.18b).

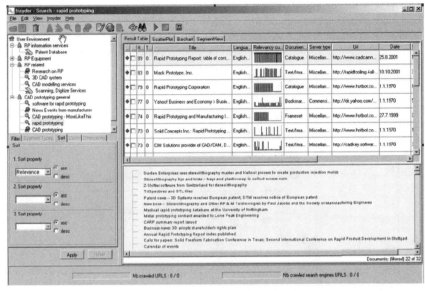

(a)

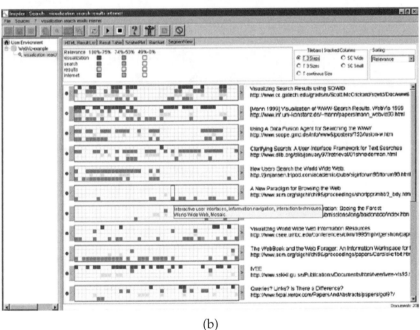

(b)

Figure 10.17. (a) Field-sortable search results view, including a sparklines-style graphic showing locations of query hits, which is a simplification of TileBars and (b) colored TileBars view, from Reiterer et al. (2005). (See color plate 6.)

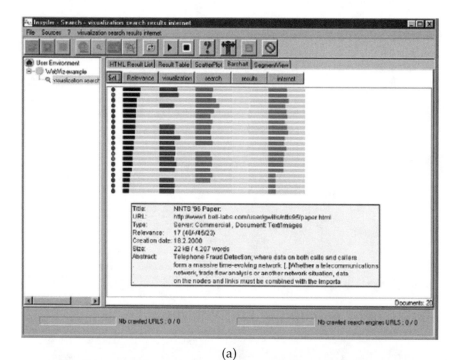

Figure 10.18. (a) Bar chart view and (b) scatter plot view, from Reiterer et al. (2005).

When asked for their favorite view, most participants ranked the field-sortable results first, followed by the TileBars, followed by the Web-style listing. The bar chart and scatter plot were not liked. Participants suggested that the visualizations should be given many of the features available in the sortable view, suggesting that using a sparklines-type view (Tufte 2006) might be useful. When compared to the Web-style listing, there were no significant differences for task effectiveness for the other conditions, except for bar charts, which were significantly worse. All conditions had significantly higher mean task times than the Web-style listing.

Despite these preference results, search results visualizations are still not commonly used for standard search, but as will be seen in Chapter 11, they are often incorporated into systems intended for analysts.

10.7.4. *Visualizing Overviews of Query Terms Hits in Retrieval Results*

Another visualization strategy is to display an overview or summary of the retrieved documents according to which subset of query terms the documents contain and share. In this kind of view, the focal icons represent query terms and the spatial positions of the documents indicate how many and which of the query terms they contain. For example, in the VIBE display (Korfhage 1991; Olsen et al. 1993), a set of documents that contain three out of five query terms are shown on an axis connecting these three terms, at a point midway between the representations of the three query terms in question (see Figure 10.19). In a study, participants did not perform better with VIBE and preferred a text-based display (Morse et al. 1998). Lyberworld (Hemmje et al. 1994) presented a 3D version of the ideas behind VIBE.

The InfoCrystal visualization showed how many documents contain each subset of query terms (Spoerri 1993), by visualizing all possible relations among N user-specified "concepts" (or Boolean keywords) in a clever extension of the Venn diagram. The goal of the Sparkler visualization (Havre et al. 2001) was to allow users to visually compare results sets for different queries on the same topic (see Figure 10.20). Glyphs representing documents were arranged along a line, where distance from the center indicates degree of relevance to the query. When there were multiple documents with the same relevance score, they were spread out horizontally from the line, forming a visualization of the distribution of relevance scores. The Sparkler for the different queries were arranged along a

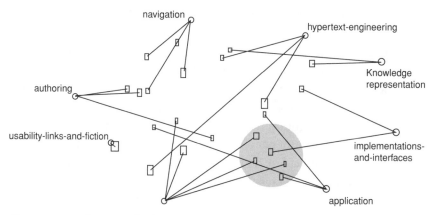

Figure 10.19. The VIBE display, in which query terms are laid out in a 2D space, and documents are arranged according to which subset of the text they share, from (Olsen et al. 1993).

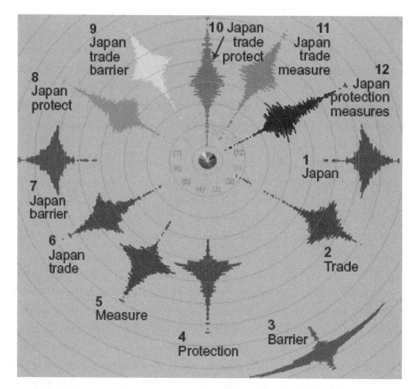

Figure 10.20. The Sparkler view in which visualizations for different queries (about trade with Japan) are arranged around an inner point. Distance from the center indicates relative degree of relevance; glyphs are spread out horizontally when multiple documents have the same relevance score. From Havre et al. (2001). (See color plate 6.)

circle, with each query's visualization assigned a different color. Selecting a document in one sparkler caused its position to be highlighted in the other Sparkler visualizations.

Several researchers have employed a graphical depiction of a mathematical lattice for the purposes of query formulation, where the query consists of a set of constraints on a hierarchy of categories (actually, semantic attributes in these systems) (Carpineto and Romano 1996; Pedersen 1993). This is one solution to the problem of displaying documents in terms of multiple attributes; a document containing terms A, B, C, and D could be placed at a point in the lattice with these four categories as parents. However, if such a representation were to be applied to retrieval results instead of query formulation, the lattice layout would in most cases be too complex to allow for readability.

10.7.5. *Showing Thumbnail Images of Documents in Search Results*

Researchers have noted that although textual summaries are compact and concise and download quickly, they require the user to read and so cannot be scanned as quickly as images. Because the visual system allows a person to "get the gist" of an entire image within 110 milliseconds or less (Woodruff et al. 2001) – the time it takes to read one or two words – researchers have often suggested that image-based search results can improve on textual summaries alone.

Image-based summaries are typically derived by creating a *thumbnail*, or miniaturized image, of the graphical appearance of the original document. Within these images, the layout and graphics can potentially give cues about the type of document and its contents. Furthermore, if a user has seen the document in the past, or one similar to it, they might be able to recognize its thumbnail image. The downside of thumbnails are that the text content in the thumbnails is difficult to see, and text-heavy pages can be difficult to distinguish from one another. Images also take longer to generate and download than text.

Many researchers have experimented with incorporating thumbnails as memory aids in browser history (Ayers and Stasko 1995; Cockburn et al. 1999; Czerwinski et al. 1999; Hightower et al. 1998; Jhaveri and Raiha 2005) (see Figure 10.21), but other efforts that attempt to use thumbnails to improve search results have not been as successful. In fact, a study by Czerwinski et al. (1999) showed that after a brief learning period, blank

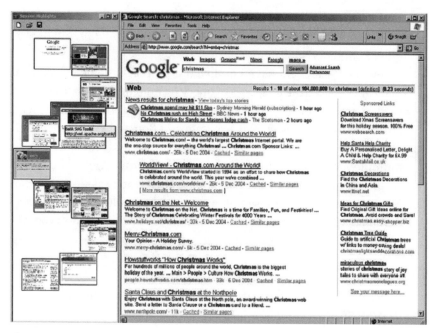

Figure 10.21. Browser history showing user-selected thumbnails, from Jhaveri and Raiha (2005). (See color plate 7.)

squares were just as effective for search results as thumbnails, although the subjective ratings for thumbnails were high. A subsequent study by Dziadosz and Chandrasekar (2002) used results listings from Microsoft Search to compare textual summaries alone, thumbnails alone, and textual plus thumbnail summaries. Thirty-five participants were given information seeking tasks such as "you need to know how to remove carpenter ants from your home" and a set of 15 retrieval results in each of the three conditions. For each result, they were asked to first judge if the result was relevant or not based on the document surrogate, and then look at the actual page, and again assess whether or not it was relevant. The participants' initial decision was considered correct if it agreed with their assessment after the page was viewed in full. Thumbnails alone were much more error-prone than the other two conditions; also, the number of errors in text alone versus text plus thumbnails was nearly identical. Additionally, showing thumbnails alongside the text made the participants much more likely to assume the document was relevant (whether in fact it was or not). As seen in other studies in which visual displays are shown alongside textual ones, scan times were longest in the combined condition and shortest in the image alone condition (but the authors did not test to see if the difference was statistically significant).

Figure 10.22. Textually enhanced thumbnails, from Woodruff et al. (2001). (See color plate 8.)

To address these issues, Woodruff et al. (2001) devised a new type of *textually enhanced thumbnail* summary that combines the strengths of the textual and the graphical approaches (see Figure 10.22). Development of the enhanced thumbnails "required significant attention to visual perception and attention management issues" (Woodruff et al. 2001). The enhanced views placed selected textual elements on a separate visual layer from the graphics of the thumbnail, using transparent color overlays to make the text stand out from the image. Since saturated colors attract visual attention, the enhanced thumbnails "washed out" the thumbnail image with a white transparent fill to desaturate its colors and make the textual highlights more prominent. In addition to enlarging the size of the called-out keywords, Woodruff et al. also slightly enlarged textual headings within the thumbnail. They found that making the headings more readable increased the usefulness of the thumbnail, but the change was so subtle that the participants were not consciously aware of the feature.

Woodruff et al. (2001) conducted a study with 18 professional researcher participants, to compare the effects of showing standard text results listings, text results augmented with thumbnail images of documents, and text results augmented with thumbnails enhanced with highlighted query term information. The study also compared four different task types: locate a picture of a given entity, locate the home page of a person not known to them, locate a consumer electronics item for purchase, and locate three or more side effects for a given drug. The timing results were strongly effected by task type. For picture search, highlighted query term thumbnails was equivalent in performance to image thumbnails alone, and both were (unsurprisingly) superior to text summaries. For finding a home page, the enhanced thumbnails tied with text summaries, and both were superior to image thumbnails. For the shopping and side-effects task, the timing differences were not significantly different. Woodruff et al. (2001) also analyzed the number of "false alarms," meaning how often the participant chose to look at the details for a page that turned out not to be relevant. The false alarm rate for enhanced thumbnails was the lowest or close to the lowest rate for all of the task types. Subjectively, 7 out of 18 participants preferred the enhanced thumbnails, and 6 others preferred them for some tasks. Hence, enhanced thumbnails may be a promising alternative to or augmentation of textual listings.

However, it may be the case that the thumbnails used in these studies were too small to show their true potential. Kaasten et al. (2002) systematically varied the sizes of web page thumbnails shown, and found participants were able to more accurately recognize web pages when larger thumbnails were shown in combination with titles, than with titles alone. When thumbnails were smaller, participants relied on color and layout to recognize the page, and could only make out text at larger image sizes. Kaasten et al. (2002) also found that in their study, 61% of the time thumbnails were seen as very good or good representations of the underlying web page, and 86% were very good, good, or satisfactory representations. The tests were done in the context of Web browser history rather than in a search context, but larger thumbnails may nonetheless change the outcome for subsequent search-based studies.

There has been experimentation in using thumbnails at commercial search engines. A VP at Google related a story in 2003 about testing thumbnails besides search engine results; after 24 hours of testing, the experiment was stopped because it was immediately detected that users were slower on the pages with the thumbnails, in part because fewer hits appeared "above the fold." The assumption was that slower was worse, without checking first to see if the user experience was better along some other metrics. More recently, the search results interface at SearchMe.com (see Figure 5.9 in Chapter 5) uses large-sized renderings of Web pages along with textual retrieval results, and also offers a "light" version in which large thumbnails are shown alongside standard search results listings. The fast rendering times of the retrieved pages may help overcome some of the timing problems experienced in earlier commercial efforts. It remains to be seen how successful this approach is in practice.

An alternative to showing image thumbnails of documents is to show figures extracted from the document, where available, as done with strong usability results in the BioText system (Hearst et al. 2007) illustrated in Chapter 1.

10.8. Visualizing Faceted Navigation

As discussed at length in Chapter 8, faceted navigation supports flexible movement within category hierarchies, seamless integration of browsing with keyword search, fluid alternation between refining and expanding, and avoidance of empty results sets. Documents within a faceted navigation system are assigned labels from multiple (optionally) hierarchical category systems called facets. Users can navigate by starting with a category from any facet hierarchy, or with a free text search. Selecting a category label from within one facet causes the retrieval results to be narrowed to only those items that are assigned that category, and furthermore causes the other facets' category labels to be updated to show how many of the categories have been assigned to the items in the result set. The user can subsequently choose another category label from any other facet and again narrow the results set, or remove a keyword or category to expand the query.

Chapter 8 discusses standard faceted navigation interfaces such as Flamenco (Hearst et al. 2002) that make use of hyperlinked Web pages and careful graphic design to clearly convey navigation choices and the context of the current search session. This kind of display attempts to maximize the amount of text that is shown while retaining as uncluttered a look as possible. This section discusses ideas that have been put forward for how to show faceted navigation more graphically.

Aduna Autofocus is an enterprise search system that has a standard textual faceted navigation interface, similar to that of Flamenco (see Figure 10.23a). It also provides a visualization interface that is a combination of VIBE (Korfhage 1991) and the Infocrystal (Spoerri 1993) (discussed

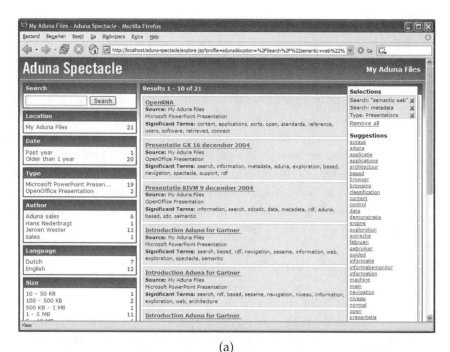

(a)

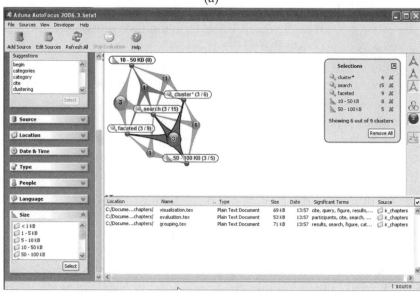

(b)

Figure 10.23. Aduna Autofocus enterprise search system. (a) A standard textual faceted navigation view. In this screenshot, the searcher has specified two query terms (`semantic web` and `metadata`) as well as selected one category from a facet *Type > Presentations*. For the 71 hits, the facets on the left have been updated to show how many of each category are represented in the retrieval results. (b) The same interface in a visualization that combines a network view of query constraints with faceted navigation.

above), in which users can both specify query terms and select values from the facets and see graphically how many documents sit at the intersection of different combinations of constraints. In Figure 10.23b, the query terms are `cluster*`, `search`, and `faceted`, and the facet categories selected are of two size ranges, *10-50KB* and *50-100KB*. The node at the intersection of `search`, `faceted`, and *10-50KB* is selected, indicating that there are 3 documents satisfying these constraints; those documents are also listed in a sortable-column view in the lower pane. Clicking on the node labeled *search* would show 15 documents there. According to the Aduna developers (Fluit 2007), most users of this system find the textual faceted navigation easy and natural to use. The visualization ends up being used primarily by those customers with analytical jobs or tasks, but works well at getting the interest of potential customers.

Much of the success of faceted navigation is due to the use of *query previews* (Plaisant et al. 1997a; Tanin et al. 2007), which give the searcher a hint of what will happen before they select a link or issue a query. In standard faceted navigation interfaces, as seen in Flamenco and in the Aduna faceted navigation shown in Figure 10.23a, the previews are indicated by simple numerical counts.

Some attempts to visualize faceted navigation focus on showing the counts for the previews in visual form. For example, the Relation Browser++ system (Zhang and Marchionini 2005) is similar to Flamenco except rather than showing the counts of each term as a number next to a text label, a graphical bar indicating relative frequency of the category is superimposed over the category label (see Figure 10.24). The white part of the bar indicates the frequency of the category in the collection, while the darker portion shows the proportion of items that match for the query term itself. In the figure, the query is `2002` and the bars show the fraction of the documents assigned to each category labels that also contains the word *2002*. A usability study found that searchers were more effective with this interface than with a standard form fill-in interface with drop-down menus. However, this approach was not compared to faceted navigation without the graphical previews.

In fact, independent research results suggest that showing the counts graphically does not improve results. Tanin et al. (2007) performed extensive studies of query previews for navigating hierarchical databases. As have other studies (Plaisant et al. 1997b), this one found that showing the searchers the number of results that fall within different attributes of the database performed better than a form fill-in interface with checkboxes. However, a study with 48 participants found there was no significant difference in timing or preference between a version of the interface

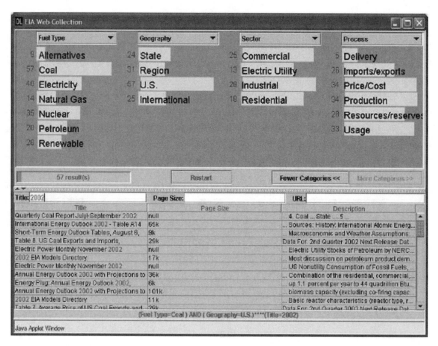

Figure 10.24. The RelationBrowser++ faceted visualization, from Zhang and Marchionini (2005).

that showed bars in addition to numbers and one that just showed the numbers.

The HIBROWSE system (Pollitt 1997) was an early graphical system that allowed users to navigate a faceted category system. Each facet was shown in a column with a portion of a Boolean query at the top. Query specification was not tightly coupled with display of category metadata; rather, navigating the categories was the focus of the system. The mSpace system (Schraefel et al. 2005) also shows facets in a sequence of columns. The user is allowed to navigate via only one category within each facet at a time, in a restricted version of faceted navigation.

Hutchinson et al. (2006), in designing a digital library interface for young children, found that the hierarchical aspects of faceted navigation were confusing for the users, and so instead showed only leaf-level categories, grouped together spatially, and arranged in a ring format surrounding a central display area (see Figure 10.25). This interface was found to be highly successful. However, because only a few choices could be shown at a time in such a display, the designers adopted a page-type view, requiring children to click to subsequent pages to see more categories choices. Only 1/3 of the children in the study noticed this

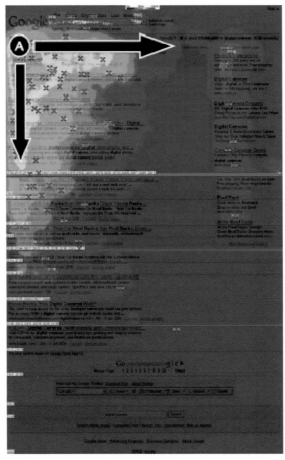

Plate 1. (Figure 1.2) Search results in the BioText system from Hearst et al. (2007), in which rich document surrogate information is shown, including figures extracted from the articles, query term highlighting and boldfacing, and an option to expand or shorten extracted document summaries. From http://biosearch.berkeley.edu.

(Figure 2.2) A heatmap showing the results of an eye-tracking study of Web page views, from Hotchkiss et al. (2007). Arrows indicate dominant directions of eye movement; "hotter" colors indicate more frequent eye fixations, and X's indicate locations of clicks. From *Search Engine Results: 2010*, by Enquiro Research.

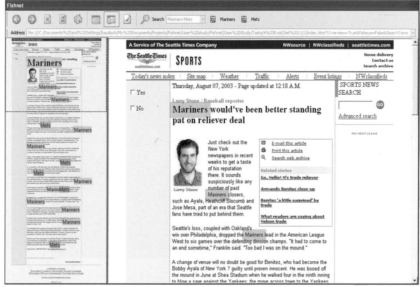

Plate 2. (Figure 5.3) Query term highlighting in the scrollbar of the Chrome browser. (Figure 5.4) Query term highlighting with overview on a Web page, from Baudisch et al. (2004).

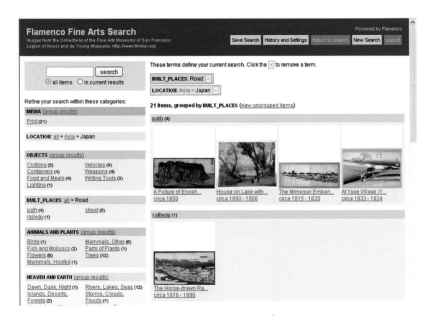

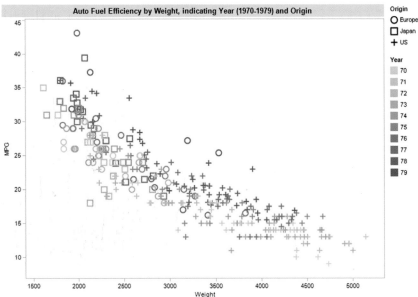

Plate 3. (Figure 8.10) Flamenco interface for browsing and search using hierarchical faceted metadata. Shown are the results after selecting *Location > Asia > Japan* and *Built Places > Road* and grouping by the subcategories of *Road*. Image credits shown in the Appendix.

(Figure 10.4) Visualization of car data using spatial layout, retinal markers, and color gradation properly applied to quantitative, ordinal, and nominal data types.

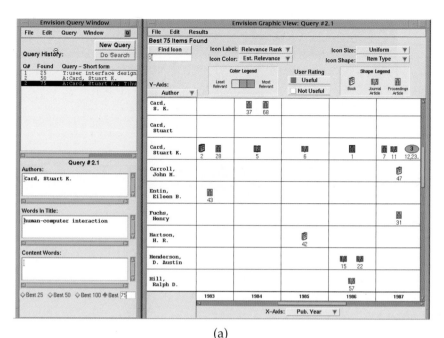

(a)

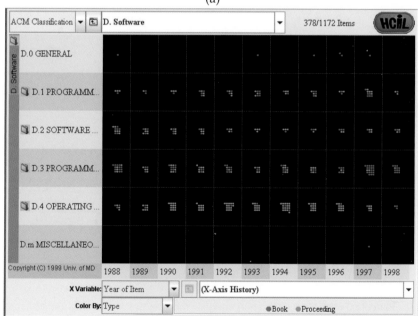

(b)

Plate 4. (Figure 10.7) Visualizing a collection by showing its contents in a table. (a) Envision, from Fox et al. (1993). (b) GRIDL, derived from the interface available at http://www.cs.umd.edu/hcil/ and used with permission of University of Maryland Human-Computer Interaction Lab.

(a)   (b)

Plate 5. (Figure 10.16) A simplified version of TileBars called HotMap, from Hoeber and Yang (2006).
(Figure 10.17) (a) Field-sortable search results view, including a sparklines-style graphic showing locations of query hits, which is a simplification of TileBars and (b) colored TileBars view, from Reiterer et al. (2005).

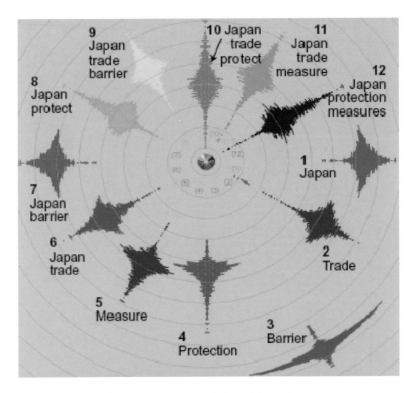

Plate 6. (Figure 10.20) The Sparkler view in which visualizations for different queries (about trade with Japan) are arranged around an inner point. Distance from the center indicates relative degree of relevance; glyphs are spread out horizontally when multiple documents have the same relevance score. From Havre et al. (2001). (Figure 10.21) Browser history showing user-selected thumbnails, from Jhaveri and Raiha (2005).

Plate 7. (Figure 10.22) Textually enhanced thumbnails, from Woodruff et al. (2001). (Figure 10.26) The Fathumb faceted navigation interface for small screens, from Karlson et al. (2006).

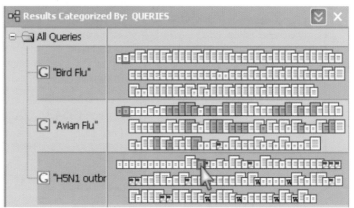

Plate 8. (Figure 11.3) The BETA system for exploring document collections from Meredith and Pieper (2006), showing results listings for the query `web fountain` on the right, augmented with TileBars, and entity frequency information plotted along the left hand side.

(Figure 11.4) (b) TRIST search results, from Proulx et al. (2006), allowing the analyst to contrast the results of three different queries. Gray document icons represent those already viewed by the analyst. Icon size indicates relative document size and other colors indicate document file type. The green border shows where the selected document appears in all three result sets.

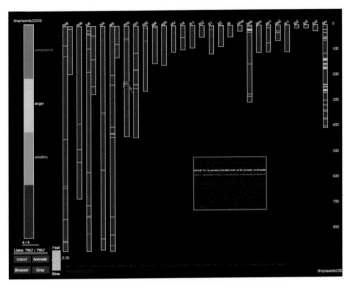

Plate 9. (Figure 11.6) The SeeSoft visualization for query hits within a large document, in this case The New Testament, from Eick (1994).
(Figure 11.8) The DocuBurst visualization of hierarchical links between words, described in (Collins 2006). In this case, "idea" was chosen as the root of the visualization; occurrences of subconcepts of "idea" appear as wedges in concentric circles. The size of the wedge reflects the number of times the indicated word appeared in the collection; gold colored nodes indicate words in which the first two characters match "pl." (Courtesy of Christopher Collins.)

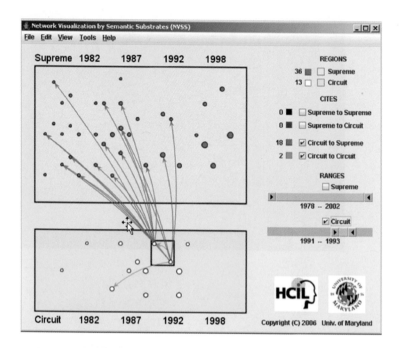

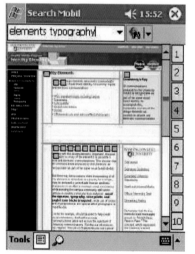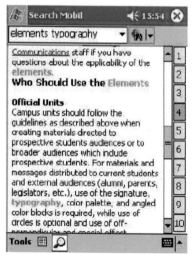

Plate 10. (Figure 11.15) Legal citation analysis visualization, from Shneiderman and Aris (2006). Used with permission of University of Maryland Human-Computer Interaction Lab.

(Figure 12.4) Search hits displayed in the SearchMobil interface, from Rodden et al. (2003). Yellow squares in each region in the view on the left indicate the number of query term hits within that region. Numbered tabs indicate the rank order of the corresponding search result.

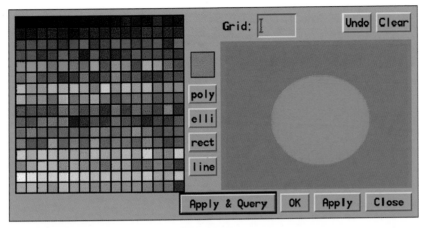

(a)

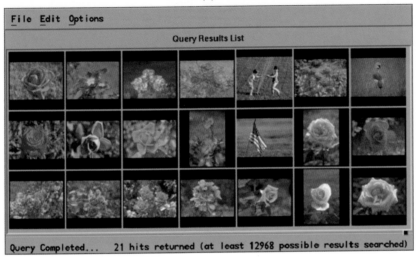

(b)

Plate 11. (Figure 12.6) An example of query-by-example for images in the QBIC system from Flickner et al. (1995), in which the user specifies desired colors and corresponding shapes in the query (a) and retrieved images are shown in a grid view (b). (Courtesy of Myron Flickner.)

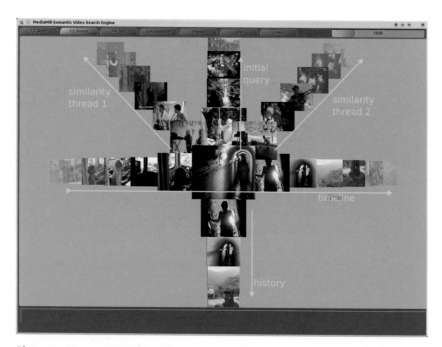

Plate 12. (Figure 12.9) The ForkBrowser visualization for scanning video search results in the MediaMill system (de Rooij et al. 2008). The center "tine" of the fork shows the results of a keyword query; the horizontal tine shows the temporal sequence images from one video segment; the diagonal tines show sequences of shots that are semantically or visually similar to the center image, and the "stem" of the fork shows the browse history. (Courtesy of Ork de Rooij.)

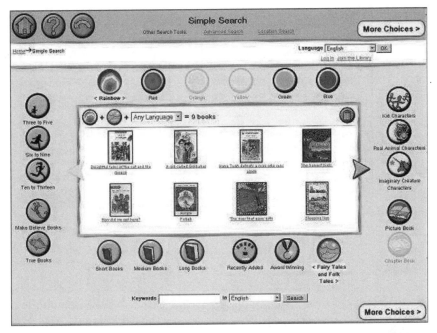

Figure 10.25. A simplified faceted navigation interface, designed for young children, from Hutchinson et al. (2006).

button, and so in effect the interface works with only a limited number of facets.

The Fathumb (Karlson et al. 2006) interface uses visualization to aid in showing faceted navigation on a small screen, such as for a mobile device (see Figure 10.26). Each facet is represented by a position within a 3×3 grid. Pressing a number on the keypad selects and enlarges the associated facet category; internal tree nodes drill down to the next hierarchical level, while leaf nodes expand to occupy the entire navigation region. Transitions are indicated with animation, and small graphic touches suggest which categories are leaf nodes (solid purple) and a graphical grid indicates where in a facet hierarchy a particular label is. A usability study with 17 participants found strong positive subjective responses for the faceted graphical navigation, and a preference for it over a text entry system on most dimensions. However, participants did not notice the graphic icons embedded within the facets' rectangles (Karlson 2006).

Visualization of faceted selectors is taken to a playful extreme in the WeFeelFine interface, as shown in Figure 10.27. The goal of this Web site is to graphically express emotions that have been expressed textual throughout the blogosphere, and so the query specification is equally whimsical.

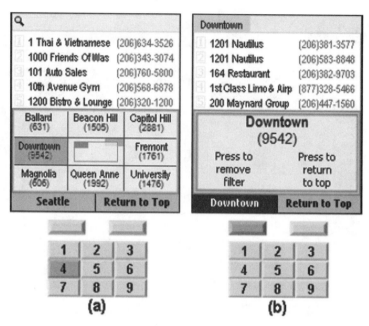

Figure 10.26. The Fathumb faceted navigation interface for small screens, from Karlson et al. (2006). (See color plate 7.)

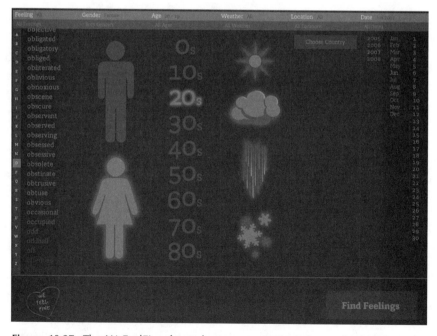

Figure 10.27. The WeFeelFine faceted query constraint selector. In this view, the selections are *Gender > Female, Age > 20's, Date > 2000 > June.*

The Cat-a-Cone system (Hearst and Karadi 1997) showed a category hierarchy in 3D with a link to Web pages displayed in a 3D book representation. When a user selected one category, the Web pages containing that category were shown in the book. The category hierarchy was subsequently modified to show the other categories contained within those retrieval results, retaining their original positions within the hierarchy. However, as discussed in the section on 3D visualization below, this is probably not the most successful way to show this kind of navigation.

10.9. Visualizing Search Results as Clusters and "Starfields"

Chapter 8 describes attempts to use document clustering to improve search interfaces. Many researchers have proposed using text clustering to map documents from their high dimensional representation in document space into a 2D or 3D visual overview. The goal is to derive thematic groups or topics from the text and display them graphically. In most of these views, each document is represented as a small glyph or icon laid out within an abstract space, where proximity suggests thematic closeness or similarity. The layout in these systems make use of "negative space" to help emphasize the areas of concentration where the clusters occur. The functions for transforming the data into the lower-dimensional space differ, but the net effect is that each document is placed at one point in a "starfield"-like representation. These visualizations are intended to help searchers get oriented with an initial overview of the contents of the collection, to discern themes or clusters in the arrangement of the glyphs, and to find important documents that might otherwise be missed.

Attempts to employ such graphical displays include BEAD (Chalmers and Chitson 1992), the Galaxy of News (Rennison 1994), IN-Spire (Hetzler and Turner 2004; Whiting and Cramer 2002; Wise et al. 1995) which includes both 2D and 3D cluster views (see Figures 10.28 and 10.29a), xFIND (Andrews et al. 2001), WebRat (Granitzer et al. 2003), and InfoSky (Granitzer et al. 2004). Lin et al. (Chen et al. 1998; Lin et al. 1991) used Kohonen's feature map algorithm to create maps that graphically characterize the overall content of a document collection or subcollection (see Figure 10.29b).

A big part of the appeal of visualizing clusters is that the algorithm can be fully automated, and the results can be initially visually striking. Although very frequently proposed, these kinds of graphical overviews of

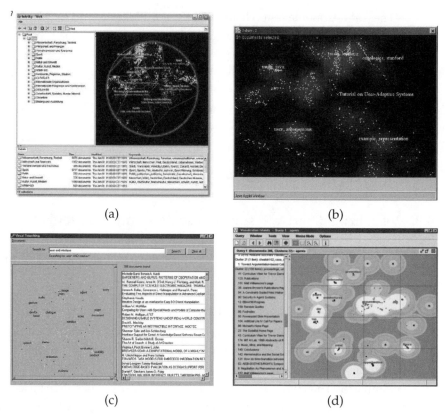

(a)   (b)

(c)   (d)

Figure 10.28. The idea of representing documents as a 2D or 3D mapping of glyphs has been proposed many times. Four examples are shown here: (a) InfoSky, from Granitzer et al. (2004); (b) the Galaxy view, from Whiting and Cramer (2002); (c) a thematic map studied in Hornbæk and Frøkjær (1999); and (d) xFIND's VisIslands, from Andrews et al. (2001).

large document spaces have yet to be shown to be useful and understandable for users. In fact, evaluations that have been conducted so far provide negative evidence as to their usefulness. This is not surprising, since as discussed in Chapter 8, text clustering has a number of drawbacks limiting its usability. One of the biggest problems is the imposition of a single organization upon the entire collection, when information represented in text usually is best understood in terms of multi-faceted overlapping concepts or categories. These problems are compounded in visualizations that do not show the titles or text of the documents, thus making it harder still to understand the meanings of the glyphs.

An early study by Kleiboemer et al. (1996) compared textual, 2D, and 3D clustering interfaces, finding that for non-experts the results of clustering were difficult to use, and that graphical depictions (representing

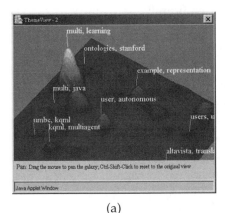

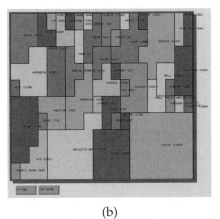

(a)   (b)

Figure 10.29. (a) The ThemeView interface (formerly Themescapes) showing an overview of the document collection retrieved in response to a query on ontologies and software agents, from Whiting and Cramer (2002). (b) A two-dimensional overview created using a Kohonen feature map learning algorithm on Web pages having to do with the topic Entertainment, from Chen et al. (1998).

clusters with circles and lines connecting documents) were much harder to use than textual representations (for example, showing titles and topical words, as in Scatter/Gather (Cutting et al. 1992)), because documents' contents are difficult to discern without actually reading some text. The 3D version was the most difficult for the participants.

Russell et al. (2006) compared a scatter plot-like view, with 300 documents organized according to an Latent Semantic Indexing (LSI)-based layout, to a bound collection of paper documents. Twelve participants completed an in-depth analysis task; participants were faster and more accurate with the paper.

Hornbæk and Frøkjær (1999) compared a thematic map view (see Figure 10.28c) to a Boolean command line interface. In this small study, the six participants used both interfaces on 8 different tasks, conducted over a small collection of HCI research articles (presumably the participants had scientific backgrounds). Multidimensional scaling was used to create a two-dimensional layout of the documents, based on cosine similarity. The most discriminating terms were computed and also shown on the map, placed by computing their midpoint between all the documents on the map in which they occurred. For interaction, all icons for documents and terms that matched a query were highlighted in yellow.

There were no significant effects for number of documents marked as relevant between the two interfaces and no difference in an approximated relevance score. Participants took significantly more time with the visual interface and spent more time shifting between interaction types (querying, scanning titles, reading full text, and viewing the map). Participants assumed adjacency on the map suggested similarity and relevancy, which caused problems when adjacency was not meaningful, and they sometimes got lost and browsed aimlessly. On the positive side, a think-aloud protocol revealed that ideas for query terms came from the map 11% of the time, suggesting that the discriminating terms were useful even if the document cluster-based layout was not (and potentially supports the ideas behind the Quintura term suggestions layout, described above). In subjective responses, the thematic map was favored over the Boolean search by 4 out of 6 participants, who found it more fun and providing inspiration for terms. However, half of the participants expressed difficulty in understanding the map, and this proportion might increase if non-scientists are used in such a study. In addition, the collection was very small and it may be the case that a larger document collection would produce a more difficult to understand map.

More recently, Granitzer et al. (2004) compared the InfoSky visualization (see Figure 10.28a) against a standard tree-style navigation browser. The tree browser significantly outperformed the starfield display for timing on 5 tasks with 8 participants. They then substantially revised the interface, making it easier to see titles and improving the zooming capabilities. They performed a second study with 6 tasks and 9 participants, this time revising the tasks to better suit the visualization at the expense of realism for search tasks (e.g., count the number of documents contained within a subcollection) and still found the tree browser to be faster than the cluster visualization. They did not collect subjective responses.

As noted above, Lin et al. (1991) used Kohonen's feature map algorithm to create an overview of a document collection, to be used in search and navigation (see Figure 10.29b). The regions of the 2D map vary in size and shape corresponding to how frequently documents assigned to the corresponding themes occur within the collection. Regions are characterized by single words or phrases, and adjacency of regions is meant to reflect semantic relatedness of the themes within the collection. A cursor moved over a document region causes the titles of the documents most strongly associated with that region to be displayed in a pop-up window. Documents can be associated with more than one region.

A study by Chen et al. (1998) compared navigation of the Yahoo textual hyperlinked category directory to a visualization of clustering results produced by Kohonen learning algorithm. For one of the tasks, participants were asked to find an "interesting" Web page within the entertainment category of Yahoo and of an organization of the same Web pages into a Kohonen map layout. The experiment varied whether participants started in the hyperlinked category directory or in the graphical map. After completion of the browsing task, participants were asked to attempt to repeat the browse using the other tool. For the participants that began with the Kohonen map visualization, 11 out of 15 found an interesting page within 10 minutes. Eight of these were able to find the same page using Yahoo. Of the participants who started with Yahoo, 14 out of 16 were able to find interesting home pages. However, only 2 of the 14 were able to find the page in the graphical map display. This is strong evidence against the navigability of the display and certainly suggests that the simple label view provided by Yahoo is more useful. However, the map display may be more useful if the system is modified to tightly integrate querying with browsing. Many found the single-term labels to be misleading, in part because they were ambiguous (one region called "BILL" was thought to correspond to a person's name rather than currency).

The participants did prefer some aspects of the map representation. In particular, some liked the ease of being able to jump from one area to another without having to back up as is required in a hierarchical directory, and some liked the fact that the maps have varying levels of granularity. Some participants expressed a desire for a visible hierarchical organization, others wanted an ability to zoom in on a subarea to get more detail, and some users disliked having to look through the entire map to find a theme, desiring an alphabetical ordering instead. Most of these desired but missing features are met by faceted navigation systems.

Another variation on visualizing the results of clustering is to place the documents for each cluster into nested sets of circles; selecting a circle navigates in to subclusters, as done in the Grokker system (see Figure 10.30). Grokker hides the text and shows only graphics initially, so users must first decide which cluster to explore, and since there is very little text in the visualization. In a study comparing it to a textually represented clustering system (Vivisimo), Rivadeneira and Bederson (2003) found that participants did not like the Grokker interface and preferred that of Vivisimo, although there we no significant differences in terms of speed and accuracy. They observed an advantage of the textual display: participants could look at search results before exploring the clusters, so they could decide when clusters would be useful; this was seen to be a useful feature in a study by Käki (2005b) as well (see Chapter 8).

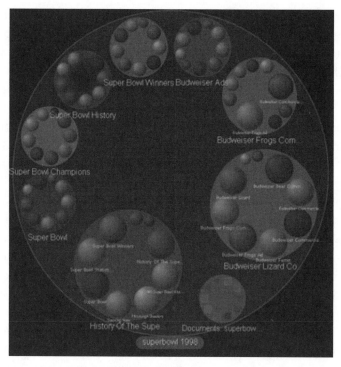

Figure 10.30. The Grokker visualization, from Rivadeneira and Bederson (2003).

Another common way to attempt to show inter-document is to show retrieved documents in node-and-link networks based on inter-document similarity (Fowler et al. 1991; Swan and Allan 1998; Thompson and Croft 1989). Swan and Allan (1998) implement a version of this idea in which documents are laid out according to a spring embedding algorithm based on similarity within a vector space measure. Results of a usability study were not positive (Swan and Allan 1998); for subjective responses, although librarians preferred the traditional system, general users preferred the experimental visualization system. Other systems display inter-document similarity hierarchically (Allen et al. 1993; Maarek and Wecker 1994).

10.10. 3D Visualization in Search

Several researchers have experimented with 3D views of information spaces. Typically in such displays, the view can be rotated and the image can be viewed from all angles. Some interfaces described as 3D are better labeled as "2-and-a-half-D," since they cannot be moved around in all dimensions, but instead use perspective and other techniques to make them look less flat than standard 2D.

It may be the case that 3D interfaces will become more successful as the technology improves, but for information processing tasks, 3D has been found to be inferior, or at best equivalent to 2D or textual interfaces when usability comparisons are done. For example, Tory et al. (2007) compared point-based displays (like scatter plots) to 2D and 3D information "landscapes" representations for visual search tasks on non-spatial information, such as ThemeViews shown above in Figure 10.29. They found that point-based spatializations were superior to landscapes, and 2D landscapes were superior to 3D landscapes. Westerman and Cribbin (2000) compared 2D and 3D representations of document space and found that "for the purposes of information search, the amount of additional semantic information that can be conveyed by a three-dimensional solution does not outweigh the associated additional cognitive demands."

Sebrechts et al. (1999) asked 15 participants to complete 32 search tasks using one of three interfaces. The first was a textual interface depicting document titles organized into clusters labeled with concept names and marked with colors. The second was a 2D interface in which the clusters were shown as bar charts in rows and columns along latitude and longitude lines. The third was a 3D rendering of the second. The tasks were not standard search tasks; rather they were artificial tasks designed to benefit a visual interface, such as marking a specific article with a color, finding articles marked earlier, or finding specific clusters. Despite this, the study found that the textual view was significantly faster than the other two, and that 2D was faster than 3D. As participants became more familiar with the system and the collection, the times became more similar, and those participants who had a lot of computer experience did as well with 3D as with text. The color marking indicating cluster identity was the most often used visual component, making use of the preattentive property of color matching. One problem with the visual displays was the lack of legibility of the text. As seen in all studies of this kind, it is important to be able to read the text in order to make sense of the contents behind the icons.

Cockburn and McKenzie (2000) compared an 3D file browser interface to a 2D standard file browser for file location efficiency, finding that the 3D participants took substantially longer to find files, and that performance worsened as the size of the hierarchy increased. However, they saw some evidence that participants got a better overview using the 3D display. In a followup study, Cockburn and McKenzie (2001) compared what they called 2D and 3D versions of document management systems and found that participants were faster at storing and retrieving using the 2D display, but not significantly so. In this case, subjective assessments favored the 3D display. However, in this study the 3D display was more like an enhanced 2D display. To address this discrepancy, they repeated the study, this time using physical cards that participants manipulated along either a flat plane or in three dimensions, and using virtual versions of the display that varied from 2D to 2.5D to a more realistic 3D display (Cockburn and McKenzie 2002). Time taken to retrieve pages significantly increased from 2D to 2.5D to 3D in both physical and virtual conditions, and subjective assessment became less favorable as the dimensions increased.

10.11. Conclusions

This chapter has described attempts to use information visualization to go beyond the standard user interface visual cues to improve search. It began with a brief exposition on principles of information visualization and the human perceptual system, and a summary of interactive techniques that are often used in visualization interfaces. This was followed by a discussion of the effects of data type on design choices that can be made for visualizing information, and a discussion of why it is so difficult to present nominal (textual) data graphically. The rest of the chapter discussed the application of visualization techniques to different aspects of the search process, including query specification, retrieval results, and getting an overview of the collection. Another topic was visualization of search results organization, including its application to faceted navigation and clustering techniques. Finally, efforts to use 3D in search interfaces were touched on.

As stated in the introduction to this chapter, information visualization has not yet proven itself for search interfaces. It may be that the best uses have not yet been discovered, or it may be the case that the nominal nature of textual information renders visualization problematic for this particular application. The next chapter describes the application of visualization to text for more analytical purposes, where it seems to be better suited, if only for a small audience of users.

11 Information Visualization for Text Analysis

As discussed in the previous chapter, visualization when applied to text seems to be most effective for specialists doing data analysis. Although this is an exciting field, it is not what most people think of when one talks about search interfaces. Unfortunately, some researchers working on visualization of text conflate search tasks with data analysis tasks. For example, Veerasamy and Heikes (1997) critique one interface for making it "more difficult than in our tool to gain an overall picture of the query word distribution for a whole set of documents in one glance." It is unclear why a searcher would want to see such a distribution, even though such a view may be of great interest to a computational linguist.

This chapter describes ideas that have been put forward for understanding the contents of text collections from a more analytical point of view. The first section discusses applications in the field of Text Mining, which usually involve visualizing connections among entities within and across documents. The next section discusses methods for visualization occurrences of words or phrases within documents, in what have classically been called concordances. The final section discusses various attempts to visualize relationships between words in their usage in language and in lexical ontologies.

11.1. Visualization for Text Mining

There is great interest in the field of text mining, which can be defined as the discovery by computer of new, previously unknown information, by automatically extracting information from different written resources (Feldman and Sanger 2006; Hearst 1999a).

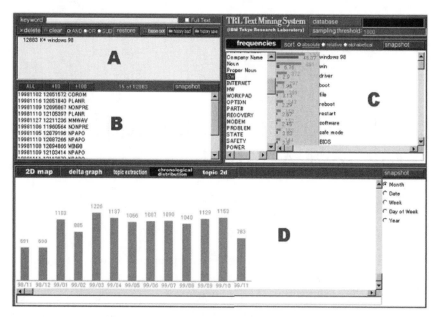

Figure 11.1. The TAKMI text mining interface. Frame A shows the number of documents returned by the search, B shows titles of relevant documents, C shows the distribution of concepts that have been extracted from these documents, and D shows statistics computed across these concepts, from Nasukawa and Nagano (2001).

One of the most common strategies used in text mining is to identify important entities within the text and attempt to show connections among those entities. For example, Figure 11.1 shows a screenshot from the TAKMI text mining system (Nasukawa and Nagano 2001; Uramoto et al. 2004), in which text from call center complaints were analyzed to help staff members determine which problems with a product receive increasing numbers of complaints over time. The interface shows the distribution of entity mentions over time, using the brushing-and-linking technique to connect selected topics to bar charts. The authors state that this system was used enthusiastically by call center staff (a more advanced version of this interface is now part of IBM's OmniFind Analytics product). Other dashboard-like text analysis tools have been developed in this vein, such as FeatureLens (Don et al. 2007).

Similarly, the Jigsaw system (Gorg et al. 2007) was designed to allow intelligence analysts to examine relationships among entities mentioned in a document collection and phone logs. Among other things, the display included a sortable-column view that shows multiple reorderable lists of entities (see Figure 11.2) and a node-and-link diagram displaying connections between entities.

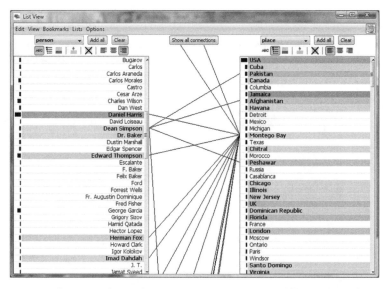

Figure 11.2. Showing relationships among entities extracted from text in the Jigsaw system, described in (Gorg et al. 2007). Selected entities are shown in yellow and connected entities are indicated by lines and orange shading; darker shading represents stronger connections. (Courtesy of John Stasko.)

The BETA system, part of the IBM Web Fountain project (Meredith and Pieper 2006), also had the goal of facilitating exploration of data within dimensions automatically extracted from text. Figure 11.3 shows the results of a query on `ibm webfountain`. The search results list on the right hand side was augmented with a TileBars display (Hearst 1995) showing the location of term hits in color and the relative lengths of the documents. Along the left hand side was shown a 3D bar chart of occurrences of entity names plotted against Web domains, as well as a sorted bar chart showing frequency of entity names across domains. Entity occurrence information can also be plotted across time in this interface. The system was not formally evaluated.

The TRIST information "triage" system (Jonker et al. 2005; Proulx et al. 2006) attempted to address many of the deficiencies of standard search for information analysts' tasks. Search results were represented as document icons; thousands of documents can be viewed in one display, and the system supports multiple linked dimensions that allow for finding characteristics and correlations among the documents (see Figure 11.4).

TRIST used document icons, in combination with visual grouping, to allow the analyst to compare and contrast the documents that were returned for different queries. Figure 11.4b shows an example of an

Figure 11.3. The BETA system for exploring document collections (Meredith and Pieper 2006), showing results listings for the query web fountain on the right, augmented with TileBars, and entity frequency information plotted along the left hand side. (See color plate 10.)

epidemiological analysis of avian flu, contrasting the results of three related queries (Avian Flu, Bird Flu, and H5N1 outbreak). Icon color was used to show the user which documents they have already viewed, and icon size and shape show the length and type of the document, respectively. TRIST also used entity extraction to identify the people, places, and organizations that occur within the retrieved documents. Entities of interest could be dragged to the workspace below the search results, while retaining the links to the search results from which they came.

The document icons could also be organized using Country and Time dimensions, to produce a quick trend analysis of where and when the disease has occurred, without opening any of the search result documents.

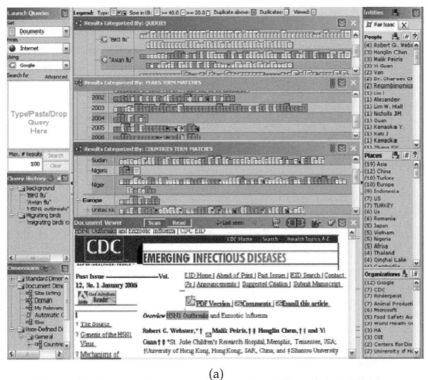

(a)

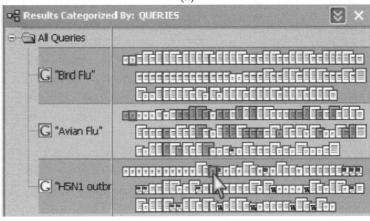

(b)

Figure 11.4. (a) The full TRIST interface shown responding to queries related to Avian Flu, from Proulx et al. (2006). Left column: Launch Queries, Query History, and Dimensions panes. Middle column: Displayed dimensions with categorized results and Document Viewer. Right column: Entities pane. (b) TRIST search results, also from (Proulx et al. 2006), allowing the analyst to contrast the results of three different queries. Gray document icons represent those already viewed by the analyst. Icon size indicates relative document size and other colors indicate document file type. The green border shows where the selected document appears in all three result sets. (See color plate 10.)

The document icons were linked across the different views, so, for example, selecting all the documents from the Nigeria dimension shows the distribution of the dates mentioned in those documents (see Figure 11.4a). The documents could also be grouped by clustering or automated categorization; in Figure 11.4b the *animals* category suggests that cats, not just birds, are mentioned, which may be an interesting avenue to explore given the suspicions about the role of birds in this scenario. The tool also allowed the entities extracted from the documents to be organized according to automatically detected relations, such as work relation (works with, subordinate of) and family relation.

TRIST, when used along with sensemaking tools (see Chapter 7) seems to be an effective tool, as it enabled its designers to win the IEEE Visual Analytics Science and Technology (VAST) contest (Grinstein et al. 2006) for two years running. However, because each system was tested by its implementors, the TRIST system may have performed better in part because its designers had training in intelligence analysis while most other participants did not.

11.2. Visualizing Document Concordances and Word Frequencies

In the field of literature analysis it is commonplace to analyze a text or a collection of texts by extracting a *concordance*: an alphabetical index of all the words in a text, showing those words in the contexts in which they appear. The standard way to view the concordance is to place the word of interest in the center of the view with "gutters" on either side, and then sort the surrounding text in some way (see Figure 11.5).

This is similar to the notion of showing keywords in context (KWIC) summaries for search results, as discussed in Chapter 5. The difference is that concordance analysis is intended for understanding properties of language or for analyzing the structure and content of a document for its own sake, rather than for search. This section discusses a number of visualizations of this type.

The SeeSoft visualization (Eick 1994) represented text in a manner resembling columns of newspaper text, with one "line" of text on each horizontal line of the strip (see Figure 11.6.) The representation is compact and aesthetically pleasing. Graphics are used to abstract away the details, providing an overview showing the amount and shape of the text. Color highlighting was used to pick out various attributes, such as where a

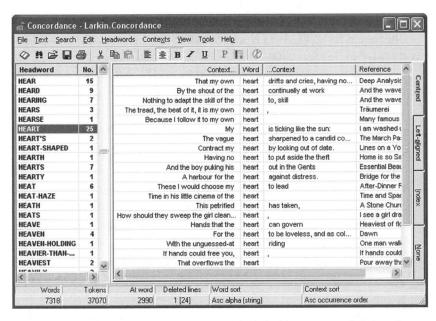

Figure 11.5. A typical document concordance, from Concordance software, http://www.concordancesoftware.co.uk/.

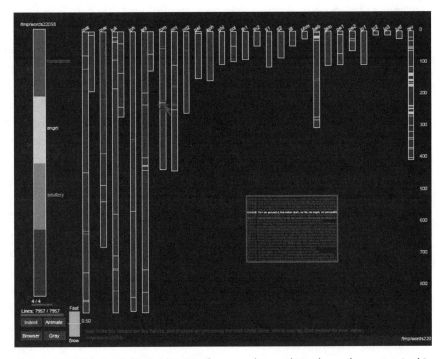

Figure 11.6. The SeeSoft visualization for query hits within a large document, in this case The New Testament, from Eick (1994). (See color plate 11.)

particular word appears in the text. Details of a smaller portion of the display could be viewed via a pop-up window; the overview shows more of the text but in less detail.

SeeSoft was originally designed for software development, in which a line of text is a meaningful unit of information. The visualization showed attributes relevant to the programming domain, such as which lines of code were modified by which programmer, how often particular lines have been modified, and how many days have elapsed since the lines were last modified. The SeeSoft developers then experimented with applying this idea to the display of text, although this was not integrated into an information access system. Color highlighting was used to show which characters appear where in a book of fiction, and which passages of the Bible contain references to particular people and items. Note that an entire line is used to represent a single word such as a character's name (even though this might obscure a tightly interwoven conversation between two characters).

The TextArc visualization (Paley 2002) is similar to SeeSoft, but arranged the lines of text in a spiral and placed frequently occurring words within the center of the spiral. Selecting one of the central words drew lines radiating out to connect to every line of text that contain that word (see Figure 11.7). Clicking on the word showed the contexts in which it occurred within the document, so it acts as a kind of visual concordance tool. In a similar vein, the DocuBurst visualization (Collins 2006) used a coxcomb-type radial visualization to show words from a document in terms of their hypernym (ISA) links (see Figure 11.8). And the Word Tree (Wattenberg and Viégas 2008) shows a visualization of a document concordance, allowing the user to view which words and phrases commonly precede or follow a given word, thus showing the contexts in which the words appear (see Figure 11.9).

Some Web sites have used *tag clouds* as a way to show the frequency of term occurrences, but without the context that concordance views provide. Figure 11.10 shows an example from the Many Eyes social visualization Web site (Viégas et al. 2007). In this case, the source of the words is the text of three early paragraphs from Chapter 10. However, usability results (Halvey and Keane 2007; Rivadeneira et al. 2007) suggest that tag clouds are inferior to straightforward lists both for finding individual items and for getting the gist of a site, and are more effective as a signaler of social activity (Hearst and Rosner 2008). Figure 11.11 is an example of an more aesthetically pleasing variation of these "word clouds," called

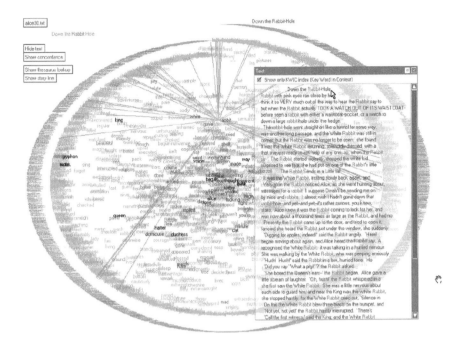

Figure 11.7. The TextArc visualization of the contents of a document, in this case, *Alices Adventures in Wonderland* by Lewis Carroll. The screenshot shows a KWIC display for the selected word (Paley 2002).

a Wordle; usability studies have not been conducted on this representation.

Standard data graphics can be an effective tool for understanding frequencies of usage of terms within documents. Figure 11.12 from *The New York Times* shows an analysis of uses of different words across the texts of the U.S. president's annual "State of the Union" address, showing which terms are used how often as the national situation changes. On the left, a SeeSoft-style visualization of the text is linked to the search box, and a table showing frequency of term usage graphically across time is shown on the right. Note the use of time as a meaningful dimension for an analysis task such as this one, showing how topics ebb and flow as the concerns of the day change. The diagram is useful for seeing gaps in the data – for example, for seeing which terms do not occur frequently as well as for which do.

As discussed in Chapter 10, nominal or categorical variables are difficult to display graphically because they have no inherent ordering. The

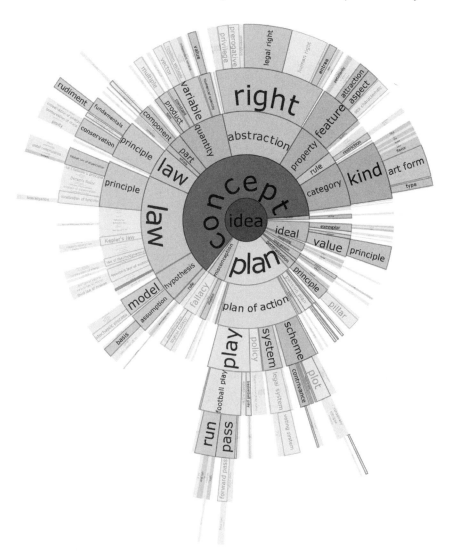

Figure 11.8. The DocuBurst visualization of hierarchical links between words, described in (Collins 2006). In this case, "idea" was chosen as the root of the visualization; occurrences of subconcepts of "idea" appear as wedges in concentric circles. The size of the wedge reflects the number of times the indicated word appeared in the collection; gold colored nodes indicate words in which the first two characters match "pl." (Courtesy of Christopher Collins.) (See color plate 11.)

categorical nature of text, and its very high dimensionality, make it very challenging to display graphically. However, certain carefully designed tools manage to work within these constraints successfully. For example, The NameVoyager visualization (Wattenberg and Kriss 2006) shows

Search hope
Back
Forward
Start
End
Occurrence Order
Clicks Will Zoom
10 hits
hope
for in a child .
?
.
john edwards calls on us to hope .
i'm not talking about blind optimism here — the almost willful ignorance that thinks un
of
slaves sitting around a fire singing freedom songs ; the hope of immigrants setting ou
immigrants setting out for distant shores ; the hope of a young naval lieutenant brave
a
young naval lieutenant bravely patrolling the mekong delta ; the hope of
millworker's son who dares to defy the odds ; the hope of a skinny kid wi
skinny kid with a funny name who believes that america has a place for
!

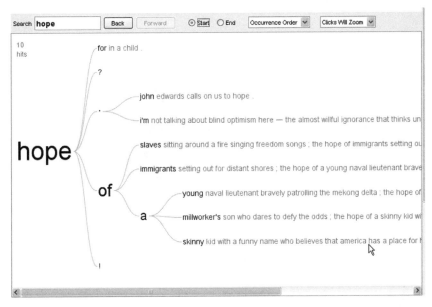

Figure 11.9. The Word Tree visualization (Wattenberg and Viégas 2008), showing the phrases that follow the word hope in the document (in this case, Barack Obama's speech to the Democratic National Convention in 2004). (Courtesy of Martin Wattenberg.)

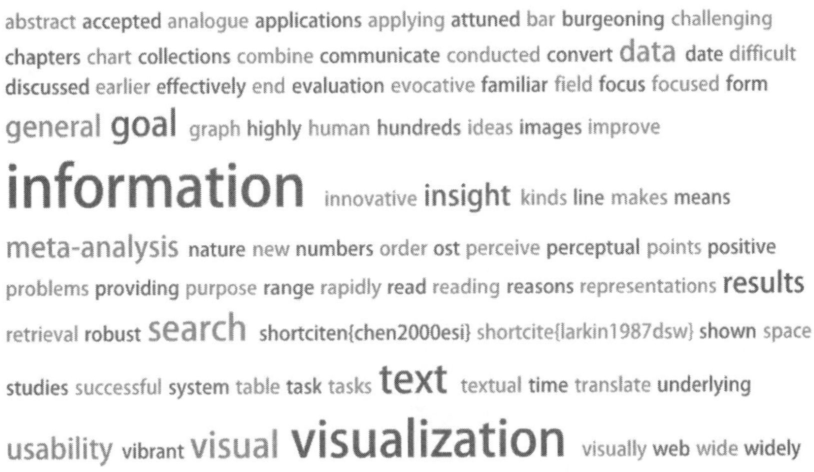

abstract accepted analogue applications applying attuned bar burgeoning challenging
chapters chart collections combine communicate conducted convert data date difficult
discussed earlier effectively end evaluation evocative familiar field focus focused form
general goal graph highly human hundreds ideas images improve
information innovative insight kinds line makes means
meta-analysis nature new numbers order ost perceive perceptual points positive
problems providing purpose range rapidly read reading reasons representations results
retrieval robust search shortciten{chen2000esi} shortcite{larkin1987dsw} shown space
studies successful system table task tasks text textual time translate underlying
usability vibrant visual visualization visually web wide widely

Figure 11.10. Tag cloud visualization of most frequently occurring words, using as data three paragraphs of text from this book, built using software from the Many Eyes project (Viégas et al. 2007).

Figure 11.11. A word cloud, or "wordle," using as data three paragraphs of text from this book, using software from www.wordle.net. (Courtesy of Jonathan Feinberg.)

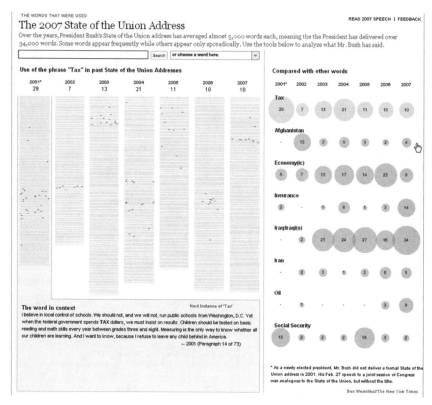

Figure 11.12. Depiction of word usages in the U.S. president's annual "State of the Union" speech across time. On the left, a visualization of the text is linked to the search box, and on the right, areas of circles show the relative frequency of word usage across time. From the New York Times.

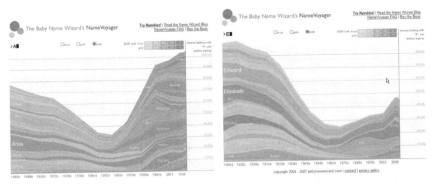

Figure 11.13. A visualization of the relative popularity of U.S. baby names across time, using a stacked line graph, showing the dip in midcentury in the popularity of names starting with vowels (a and e are shown), followed by a subsequent increase in popularity in the 1990s. From babynameswizard.com.

frequencies of baby names for U.S. children across time. The user types in the first few letters of a name, and a stacked bar graph is shown in which all matching names are shown, in alphabetical order, with the frequency for a given year determining how much space lies between the line for that name and the name below it. The naming frequency changes over time, producing an impression of undulating waves.

It appears from these graphs that fashion in naming of children tends to be correlated with the way names sound (Wattenberg and Kriss 2006); it may be that naming is influenced by a psychological principle called *phonesthesia*, in which vocal sounds suggest hints of meaning (Pinker 2007, p. 301). For example, users of this tool discovered that names beginning with vowels were popular at the end of the 19th century, dropped precipitiously in midcentury, and then grew popular again starting in the 1990s (see Figure 11.13). If there were no phonesthetic effects, strong patterns like this would probably not appear in the data.

The ThemeRiver visualization uses a similar view to show frequencies of mentions of topics in text over time (Havre et al. 2002). Despite the popularity of the NameVoyager interface, stacked bar graphs are problematic because the shape of any given line is determined in part by the shapes of the lines below it, thus potentially misleading the interpretation of the graph's values.

Numerous visualizations have been proposed for showing relationships among words, both within documents and within lexical ontologies. One strategy is to show words in a 2D layout, as done in the Word Space (Brandes et al. 2006) visualization described in Chapter 10. As a more readable alternative, several systems use an animated nodes-and-links layout to progressively and dynamically show relationships among words, as seen in Visual WordNet, seen above in Figure 10.8.

11.3. Visualizing Literature and Citation Relationships

Closely related to both text mining and text concordance analysis is the broader field of literary analysis and citation analysis. Hundreds of research papers have been written analyzing how the authors of articles in the scientific literature refer to or cite one another. This information is used to assess the importance of the authors, the papers, and the topics in the field, and how these measures change over time. (Document citation patterns are also used in Web ranking algorithms to help identify high quality pages.) As discussed above, relationships among nominal categories are easier to visualize than those nominal categories themselves, and nodes-and-links graphs are the most popular for showing connections between documents and authors. One of the more innovative views of such graphs was created by Small (1999) and emphasizes relations among scientific disciplines (see Figure 11.14).

Some more recent approaches have moved away from nodes-and-links in order to break the interesting relationships into pieces and show their connections via brushing-and-linking interactions. As one example, Shneiderman and Aris (2006) show citations between court cases by breaking the nodes up into different meaningful regions and showing the connections between or within the regions. Users are given control of which links' connections are shown at any given time (see Figure 11.15). The PaperLens visualization (Lee et al. 2005) analyzes the papers that have appeared within an academic conference over eight years (see Figure 11.16). The data is broken into different views including year by year top 10 cited papers/authors, popularity of topic by year, degrees of separation among selected authors, as well as an alphabetical list of all authors and their citation frequency within the collection. Brushing and linking is used heavily; selecting a paper or author in one view shows where it appears in the other views. Even more elaborate visualizations of citation patterns have been developed, such as the Butterfly visualization for asynchronously downloading documents that have been cited by other documents (Mackinlay et al. 1995).

Another topic within the domain of literary analysis is the problem of author identification; Keim and Oelke (2007) took standard stylistics

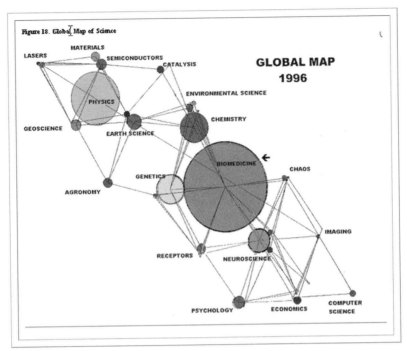

Figure 11.14. Citation analysis graph showing relationships among scientific disciplines, from Small (1999).

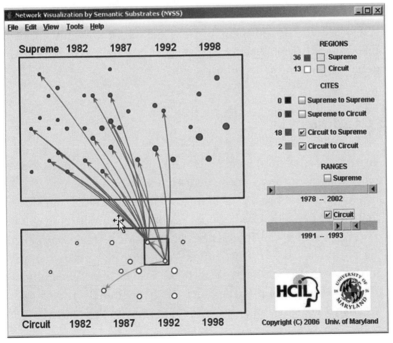

Figure 11.15. Legal citation analysis visualization, from (Shneiderman and Aris 2006). Used with permission of University of Maryland Human-Computer Interaction Lab. (See color plate 12.)

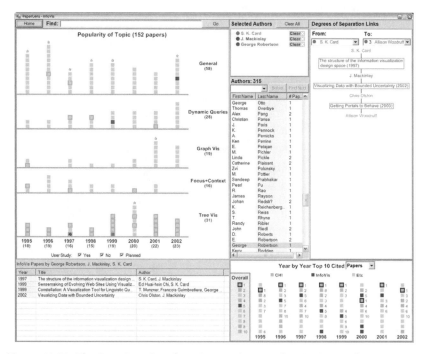

Figure 11.16. The PaperLens interface (Lee et al. 2005) for citation analysis.

statistics and mapped them into a visual display reminiscent of TileBars. Plaisant et al. (2006) used visualization to try to help literary scholars understand patterns in an author's work.

11.4. Conclusions

Visualization is a promising tool for the analysis and understanding of text collections, including semi-structured text as found in citation collections, and for applications such as literary analysis. Although not shown in this chapter, visualization has also been applied to online conversations and other forms of social interaction which have textual components. With the advent of social visualization Web sites like IBM's manyeyes.com, and other tools that continue to make visualization generally accessible to users who are not programmers, it is likely that the use of visualization for analysis of text will only continue to grow in popularity.

12 Emerging Trends in Search Interfaces

This chapter describes several areas that are gaining in importance and are likely to play a significant role in search interfaces in the future. These predictions come primarily from extrapolating out from emerging trends. The areas that seem most likely to be important, and so demand changes in search interface technology, are: mobile search, multimedia search, social search, and a hybrid of natural language and command-based queries in search. Each is discussed in detail below.

12.1. Mobile Search Interfaces

Mobile communication devices are becoming increasingly popular as information access tools. A recent survey of more than 1,000 technology leaders and other stakeholders said they expect that mobile devices will be the primary connection tool to the Internet for most people in the world in 2020 (Rainie 2008). They also predict that voice recognition and touch user interfaces will be more prevalent and accepted by 2020. Usable interfaces for search on mobile devices are only now beginning to emerge, but this area will most certainly undergo rapid development and innovation in the next few years.

Until recently, mobile devices had small screens, awkward text input devices, and relatively low bandwidth, which pose challenges for information-rich applications like search. However, bandwidth is increasing, and the recent appearance of personal digital assistants (PDAs) with relatively large, high-resolution screens, such as the Apple iPhone, are making search on mobile platforms feel more like desktop-based Web search.

The following sections discuss how mobile search interfaces differ from those of desktop search, including how mobile query intent differs from general Web queries, specialized techniques for query specification, and techniques for viewing retrieval results that have been developed for mobile devices.

12.1.1. *Mobile Search Usage Patterns*

Researchers and technologists have suspected that, for mobile devices, the context of use may strongly influence the kinds of information seeking tasks the user is likely to engage in. For example, it has often been proposed that temporal and geolocation information can be used to better anticipate mobile users' information needs (Kaasinen 2003; Sohn et al. 2008). A standard example is a query such as "Find a reservation for one half hour from now at a restaurant that is less than one mile from where I am standing." Route-finding tasks, planning tasks, and informational queries relevant to the current location have been predicted to be more likely than other kinds of queries for users of mobile devices, and mobile search interfaces have become tailored towards these anticipated modes of use. The studies of mobile information usage described below support these hypotheses.

To address the question of how information seeking from small portable devices differs from desktop search, Kamvar and Baluja (2006) studied a set of more than 1 million page view requests to the Google mobile search engine (see Figure 12.1) from cell phones and PDAs during a one month period in 2005. Among other things, they found that average query length was less for cell phones than PDAs, and both of these were shorter than desktop-based search queries on average. They also found less variation in queries issued on small devices. When they looked at a random sample of 50,000 queries, the most frequent 1,000 queries for the cell phone searchers comprised 22% of all the queries, whereas the most frequent 1,000 desktop (personal information) queries accounted for only 6% of all desktop queries. They also classified queries into topics, finding that "adult" queries were the most frequent for cell phones at greater than 20%, but were about 5% for the PDA queries, which is similar to Web search today. Since Web search has seen a rapid decline in adult queries as a proportion of all queries over time (Spink et al. 2002), they speculate that the prevalence of adult queries in cell phones reflects both their

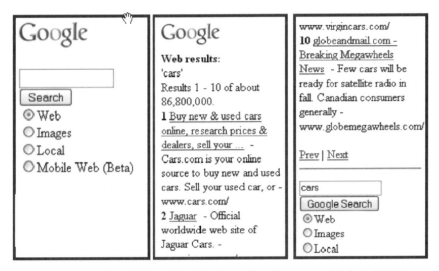

Figure 12.1. Google Mobile XHTML interface, from Kamvar and Baluja (2006).

novelty and their perception as personal, private devices. This is in contrast with PDAs which are often used in a business context.

Kamvar and Baluja (2006) also examined properties of session usage and clickthrough, finding that both PDA and cell phone sessions had significantly fewer page views per query than desktop search. For cell phone queries, they found that 28% of queries within a 5 minute session window were reformulations, 14% were responses to spelling suggestions, and 32% were repetitions of the original query. Thus in most cases, users came to the system with a specific information need and did not stray or explore other topics. These results are not surprising given the relatively slow bandwidth of mobile devices at the time and the fact that some services charge according to the number of bytes transmitted.

Sohn et al. (2008) conducted a diary study in which they asked 20 people to record their information needs while mobile over a two week period. Participants were asked to send a text message to a special email address whenever they felt a desire to acquire some information, regardless of whether or not they knew how to obtain that information. Sohn et al. (2008) created a taxonomy of information needs, the most common of which were "trivia" (answering questions that came up in conversation, such as "What did Bob Marley die of and when?"), directions, points of interest ("tell me about a place and then give me directions to it"), information about friends, business hours, shopping, and phone numbers. In total, 72% of the information needs were contextual in nature, where context can be defined as current activity, location, time, and conversation. Thus this study lends further support to the idea that mobile search benefits from using personal and contextual information.

12.1.2. *Query Entry on Mobile Devices*

For the smallest mobile devices, text entry is accomplished by 12-key input devices requiring up to three clicks per letter. Larger handhelds such as Blackberry devices allow for "thumb typing" on small physical keyboards, and more recently touch-screen interfaces such as that seen on the Apple iPhone allow for tapping on a virtual keyboard on the screen. Nevertheless, these techniques are slower than typing on a full keyboard. The techniques described below can help improve query entry.

Dynamic Term Suggestions: One way to speed up text entry is to use previously popular queries to generate statistics for auto-completion of query terms (Buyukkokten et al. 2000) (also known as dynamic term suggestions). Yahoo OneSearch provides this functionality on some mobile phones, showing suggested queries to complete what the user has typed so far (see Figure 12.2). (See Chapter 4 for a discussion of auto-completion of query terms in non-mobile interfaces.)

Anticipate Common Queries: Another way to simplify query entry is to know the kind of query that might be asked in advance. This can be used to reduce typing by allowing for abbreviated, command-like queries for a limited set of commonly executed actions. In the Google SMS text messaging system, users can send a short command and receive a text message in response with a short answer. For example, a query such as "pizza 10003" returns short descriptions of nearby restaurants based on the zip code, and "price ipod 20g" shows competitive price information while shopping (Schusteritsch et al. 2005). Yahoo OneSearch supports similar kinds of queries, but focuses on providing "instant answers" – specially formatted answers to questions, rather than standard results listings, using the graphical display available on advanced handheld devices. Thus, a search on ping pong returns a vertical listing divided into main categories including *products, images, Web sites, news articles, Wikipedia,* and *Yahoo Answers* (see Figure 12.2). A few hits from each category is shown along with a link to see more. A link that appears at the top of the additional listings page allows the user to return back to the main results page.

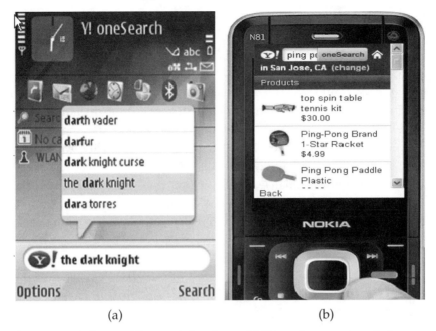

(a)   (b)

Figure 12.2. Yahoo mobile search interfaces. (a) Dynamic query completion suggestions (called "Search assist") help speed up entry of queries on a Nokia phone interface by matching against letters typed so far. (b) Specially formatted search results for a query on `ping` on a mobile device. Shown in the figure are product hits; scrolling below these shows hits for images, Web pages, Wikipedia articles, Yahoo Answers, and other kinds of information. (Reproduced with permission of Yahoo! Inc. ©2009 Yahoo! Inc. YAHOO! and the YAHOO! logo are registered trademarks of Yahoo! Inc.)

Spoken Queries: Voice-controlled computers have been a dream of technology developers and users for many years, and very recently, the major search engines have introduced mobile phone-based voice-entered query terms. These work for answer-based or command-like queries discussed above, including searching for local information such as nearby restaurants, looking up current airline flight information, zip codes, and video search, but are also used for general keyword queries and Web results. In these interfaces, the user indicates they are starting a query by, in the case of Yahoo on Nokia, holding a special *Talk* button on the phone, or more recently, in the case of Google Mobile on the iPhone, using motion sensors on the phone to activate the speech recognition technology when the phone is moved from the user's waist-level up to their ear. Usually in these interfaces, search results are shown as text on the screen, although some specialized queries show tailored results displays. For instance, Tellme's mobile search (now owned by Microsoft), uses GPS mechanisms on the phone to sense the user's current location, so that a query on `coffee` returns a map showing nearby coffee shops. Travel directions, movie listings, sports scores, and other context-sensitive information are shown in response to simple voice commands such as `movies`. The accuracy of the voice recognition for entered queries has not yet been reported, but benefits by being trained on many millions of queries from query logs (Markoff 2008). As more people use the voice interfaces, more training data will accumulate on the voice data itself, and the interfaces will further improve.

As a more radical, but less scalable alternative, the ChaCha.com search system employs human experts to answer user's questions, entered either as text messages or voice questions. The user must wait a few minutes to receive an answer, which is looked up by a human using an online search system and is sent via text message.

12.1.3. *Presenting Retrieval Results on Mobile Devices*

Web pages designed for large screens do not necessarily translate well to small screens, and considerable research has gone into developing alternative methods of presenting the content of Web pages themselves to better accommodate the small screens and slow bandwidth commonly experienced in mobile computing (Bickmore and Schilit 1997; Björk et al. 2000; Buyukkokten et al. 2000; Lam and Baudisch 2005; MacKay et al. 2004; Wobbrock et al. 2002; Xiao et al. 2009). For example, MacKay and Watters (2003) analyzed four methods of transforming information content from large to small devices: direct migration, data modification, data suppression, and data overview. They analyzed the impact of each method on browsing, reading, and comparing information.

Despite the work in content transformation, to date mobile search interfaces vary little from that of desktop search (Church et al. 2006), although the formatting for instant answers as shown in Figure 12.2 is an advance. Commercially, Apple's Safari browser has been optimized to work well with small screens such as that of the iPhone.

Interfaces for search results display are a different matter. Some research papers address how to improve search for small devices, but most of this work focuses on experiments attempting to determine how much information should be displayed in search results for small devices. Sweeney and Crestani (2006) conducted a controlled experiment to determine the effect of smaller screen sizes on search results interpretation. They compared what they call micro displays (mobile phones, smart phones), small

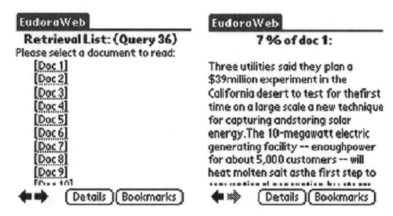

Figure 12.3. Screenshots from a PDA view showing only ranked documents, and first 7% of the document's contents, from Sweeney and Crestani (2006). Conditions showing title only and first 15% and first 30% are not shown.

displays (PDAs, Pocket PCs), and normal sized displays (desktop PCs and tablet PCs). In their between-subjects study design, each participant worked with only one device, and had to make a relevance judgement for each document presented for each pre-specified query. The participant first was shown the title of the document, and then could choose to expand the surrogate to include the first 7% of content, then the first 15%, and then the first 30% (see Figure 12.3).

The authors hypothesized that larger screens would lead to higher accuracy, and while they did see a decline in accuracy with decline in screen size, the differences among device sizes were not significant. The authors also hypothesized that participants using larger screens would choose to see more content, and that more content would produce better results. They did find that larger screens resulted in more requests for content, but they also found that more content did not produce better results. Participants, regardless of device, performed better on precision and recall measures with smaller amounts of context. The title alone achieved the highest precision scores, while title plus the first 7% of the document was best for recall. Increasing to 15% or 30% of content did not help with the relevance assessments. It should be noted, however, that the evaluation was performed with TREC queries, which tend to be complex and are probably not representative of what people want to query on while mobile. The authors also noted that the participants seemed to be much better at excluding irrelevant documents than they were at picking out the truly relevant documents, as recall was very low.

Two recent papers describe the benefits of converting the format of the content to better reflect search results. Xie et al. (2005) experimented with four different representations of Web page content for search result presentation on smart phones and Pocket PCs. They applied an algorithm that decomposes a Web page into blocks that are labeled according to three levels of importance: main content; useful information but not central to the main points of the page, including navigation bars; and unimportant information such as ads, copyright declarations, and decorations. They then evaluated four conditions: (1) The original page. (2) A thumbnail view which showed the original page but divided into blocks, each of which can be navigated to, selected, and its contents then shown in a zoomed-in view. The predicted importance of each block is indicated by showing graphically the number of query terms in each block and color coded according to predicted importance level. (3) An optimized one-column view that sorts the blocks in descending order of importance and then reformats them to avoid horizontal scrolling, and (4) A main content view which just shows the contents of the most important blocks, formatted to avoid horizontal scroll.

Twenty-five participants performed searches in a within-subjects design. Both task and interface affected the search time. The main content view was the fastest, averaging 9.4 seconds per query on the Pocket PC, followed by the optimized one column view (11.0 s/q), the standard view (31.3 s/q) and the thumbnail view (33.3 s/q). The subjective scores also favored the one-column views. The authors speculate that the thumbnail view suffered from a complicated interface and that the overview approach may hold merit despite these results.

In a similar study, Rodden et al. (2003) compared a standard mobile search interface in which the user sees a version of the Web page that mimics that seen in a standard browser, thus requiring horizontal and vertical scrolling, with an alternative that segments the page and graphically shows the number of query term hits within each segment. After some pilot studies, they decided to use two yellow squares to indicate the region of a page with the most query term hits, while all other regions with at least one hit received one yellow square. An interesting innovation is the display of numbered tabs on the right hand side that correspond to the top 10 search results (see Figure 12.4).

They conducted a usability study to examine participants' ability to spot the answer to a question on a single retrieved page. They intentionally designed some questions to perform well in their interface, while other tasks were expected to perform poorly on their design (for example, placing

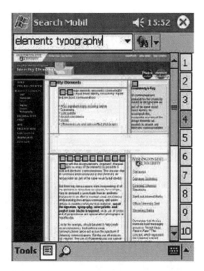 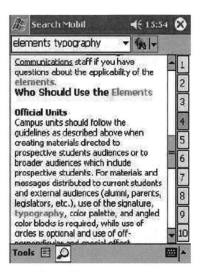

Figure 12.4. Search hits displayed in the SearchMobil interface, from Rodden et al. (2003). Yellow squares in each region in the view on the left indicate the number of query term hits within that region. Numbered tabs indicate the rank order of the corresponding search result. (See color plate 12.)

the answer far enough down the view that it would require scrolling). They found no main effect of browser type, but did observe significant effects between browser and task type, reflecting the relative appropriateness of each browser. Subjective reactions strongly favored the segmented approach.

In a similar finding, Lam and Baudisch (2005) found that preserving the screen layout in a thumbnail view while highlighting terms important to the information need resulted in faster times for finding specific information within a Web page than with a single-column view or a standard thumbnail.

Moving from search to navigation, the Fathumb (Karlson et al. 2006) interface uses faceted categories and information visualization for a navigation-based method for accessing an information space, such as a travel guide (see Figure 10.26 in Chapter 10). Each facet is represented by a position within a 3×3 grid. Pressing a number on the keypad selects and enlarges the associated facet category; internal tree nodes drill down to the next hierarchical level, while leaf nodes expand to occupy the entire navigation region. Bainbridge et al. (2008) created a browsing interface for the Apple iPod music player, which has very limited interaction controls and no keyboard (physical or virtual). They converted a digital library to a hierarchical structure and made it navigable using the thumbwheel control that characterizes the iPod (see Figure 12.5).

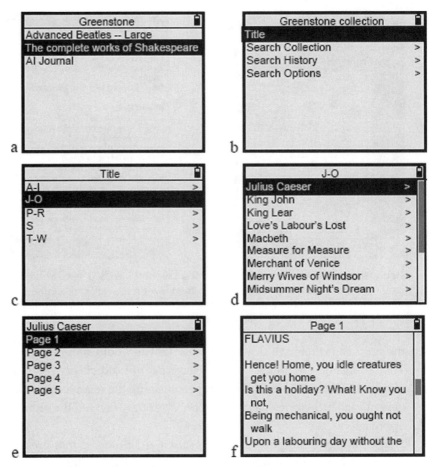

Figure 12.5. An interface for browsing a digital library on the Apple iPod, from Bainbridge et al. (2008).

As mentioned previously, another way that search results display is changing is by showing specialized interfaces for particular question types, such as showing maps with locations of restaurants in response to a query on restaurant location. Specialized site search, such as Powerset's interface for viewing Wikipedia encyclopedia search results, are being well-received for larger-screen mobile devices like the iPhone.

12.2. Multimedia Search Interfaces

Images, video, and audio information objects are increasingly important to the information landscape. The ease of creation, storage, and distribution of digital video and audio over the last few years has created a boom in their use. A Pew Research survey conducted during January 2008 reported that 48% of Internet users had used a video-sharing site such as YouTube, and 15% said they had used such a site on the previous day (Pew 2008a). A media executive reported that email offering podcasts of conferences was opened about 20% more frequently than traditional marketing email (Ranie 2006).

Although this book focuses primarily on user interfaces for searching textual information, it is highly likely that audio, video, and image search will take on an increasingly important role in the coming decade. With improvements in spoken language recognition, it may become the case in future that keyboard typing will disappear entirely, with text being entered exclusively by voice. Video over the Internet now supplements the U.S. President's weekly radio address. Movies have replaced books as cultural touchstones. And people in the developing world may skip textual literacy altogether in favor of video literacy.

However, the technology for search over multimedia lags far behind that of text for its creation, storage, and distribution. This is primarily because automatic image recognition is still a largely unsolved problem. Automatic speech recognition is greatly improved, which allows for the new spoken-query input techniques described in the previous section on mobile search, but more advances are needed to achieve universal transcription of long spoken audio documents. Furthermore, the text that is associated with video is often not particularly descriptive of its contents. Hauptmann et al. (2006) write:

> Despite a flurry of recent research in video retrieval, objectively demonstrable success in searching video has been limited, especially when contrasted with text retrieval. Most of the mean average precision in standard evaluations can be attributed to text transcripts associated with the video, with small additional benefit derived from video analysis.

Nonetheless, given the growing importance of this form of interface, it is likely that improvements will be made over the next few years. The following sections briefly describe the state of the art in user interface development for multimedia search.

12.2.1. *Image Search Interfaces*

Image search techniques that attempt retrieval based on the bits representing image or video data are referred are to in that field as *content-based retrieval*, to stand in contrast with keyword retrieval. One of the

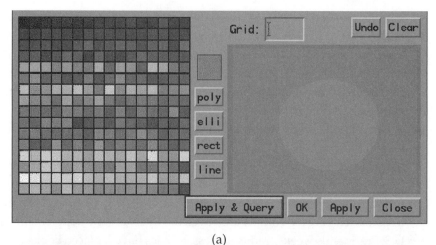

(a)

File Edit Options

Query Results List

Query Completed... 21 hits returned (at least 12968 possible results searched)

(b)

Figure 12.6. An example of query-by-example for images in the QBIC system (Flickner et al. 1995), in which the user specifies desired colors and corresponding shapes in the query (a) and retrieved images are shown in a grid view (b). (Courtesy of Myron Flickner.) (See color plate 8.)

best-known early image retrieval systems, QBIC, represented images by color histograms; that is, a count was made of how many pixels in the image contained each color, using a color space representation such as Munsell color coordinates (Flickner et al. 1995). A query could consist of an image, and other images with similar color distributions would be retrieved. Alternatively, a user could select a set of colors from a color palette, and indicate the desired percentage. QBIC also allowed querying against texture samples and general shapes. Figure 12.6 shows an example in which the user has painted a magenta circular area on a green background using standard drawing tools, and query results are shown below in a grid view (Flickner et al. 1995). For a query specifying both color and shape, the matching algorithm tries to find images with a centered magenta shape surrounded by a green background, such a roses in a field. QBIC also allowed for search over image stills derived from video content.

One drawback of query-by-example for images is that it requires the searcher to know a great deal about the visual property of the image they are searching for, which can be helpful for known-item search but is usually not the case when looking for new images. Another drawback is that it can be quite difficult to successfully specify the colors and shapes in order to retrieve the desired object.

Relevance feedback techniques (see Chapter 6) have been applied to image and video search (Rui et al. 1998). Users are asked to scan a grid of images and mark those that new retrieved images should be similar to (and in some cases, different from). The image retrieval algorithm computes similarity of the marked images to other images in the collection, using a weighted combination of attributes of the image, such as color, texture, and shape.

A commercial Web site, Like.com, provides everyday users with the facility to search for products based on similarity to visual properties, within a faceted navigation framework. The user can draw a rectangle around a portion of a selected product's image and choose to refine the query by either the represented shape, color, or both (see Figure 12.7). This kind of visual relevance feedback sometimes works well, but often brings back unexpected or confusing results. As in text search, relevance feedback tends to work better when the user selects multiple objects as being relevant, as well as indicating which objects are not relevant. But more generally, image retrieval using purely visual measures has so far had limited success (Rodden et al. 2001). Rather, as discussed in Chapter 8, faceted navigation works well for image navigation and search when the appropriate category labels and textual descriptions are available, and is the preferred method for image navigation and retrieval today, along with keyword search used in Web image search interfaces (described below).

There have been numerous interfaces developed for browsing of small personal image collections (Bederson 2001; Graham et al. 2002; Kang and Shneiderman 2000), including many attempts at using image clustering as an organizational framework (Cai et al. 2004; Platt et al. 2003) (which has been shown to be confusing in usability studies (Rodden et al. 2001)) as well as some work on aiding in the automated annotation of image and video collections (Abowd et al. 2003; Shneiderman and Kang 2000).

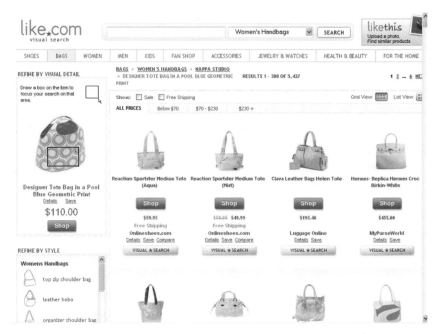

Figure 12.7. Image similarity technology commercially applied in the apparel shopping Web site Like.com.

12.2.2. *Video Search Interfaces*

For video retrieval, the data is first segmented into higher-level story units or scenes, and then into *shots*, where a shot is a video sequence that consists of continuous video frames for one camera action (Zhang et al. 2003). From within the shot, one or more *key frames* is selected to represent the shot in search interfaces and for matching purposes. If text is associated with the video segments, as in a spoken transcript for television news, the text is indexed to correspond with the temporal aspects of the shots.

Until recently, most of the innovation in video retrieval was focused on the underlying algorithms for analyzing, storing, and efficiently retrieving the data, with less emphasis on the search interfaces. However, the TREC Video track and its successor, the TRECVID competition (Smeaton et al. 2004), have brought more attention to the interface aspects of video retrieval. Figure 12.8 shows the query and retrieval interface for an interactive video search system (Adcock et al. 2008).

There has recently been a realization that the algorithms cannot do as well as interactive systems that allow users to quickly scan a large number of images and select among those. This differs from text retrieval in that

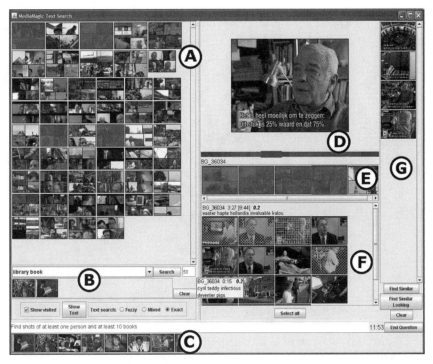

Figure 12.8. An interactive interface for video search, over a collection of Dutch television (Adcock et al. 2008). (A) Search results area with story key frame summaries. (B) Search text and image entry. (C) Search topic and example media. (D) Media player and keyframe zoom. (E) Story timeline. (F) Shot keyframes. (G) Relevant shot list. (Courtesy of John Adcock.)

people can scan images much more quickly than they can read lines of text. Hauptmann et al. (2006) write:

> Interactive system performance...appears strongly correlated with the system's ability to allow the user to efficiently survey many candidate video clips (or keyframes) to find the relevant ones. The best interactive systems allow the user to type in a text query, look at the results, drill deeper if appropriate, choose relevant shots for color, texture and/or shape similarity match and iterate in this by reformulating or modifying the query.

Hauptmann et al. (2006) also note the increasing popularity of what is known as *Rapid Serial Visual Presentation* (RSVP) techniques, in which the user is presented with a series of images, one replacing the next in the same place on the screen, to eliminate the need for eye movement, and so make scanning of images faster (Spence 2002) (This approach is also being investigated for mobile interfaces (Öquist and Goldstein 2003).) Researchers are exploring many variations on the RSVP browsing technique in which images travel in a path across the screen and images in addition

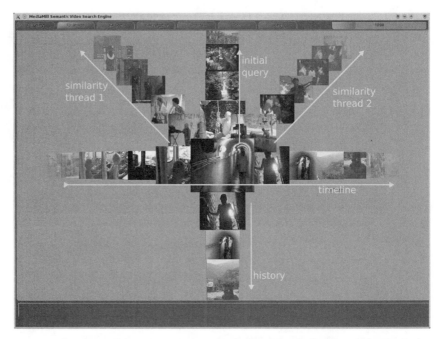

Figure 12.9. The ForkBrowser visualization for scanning video search results in the MediaMill system (de Rooij et al. 2008). The center "tine" of the fork shows the results of a keyword query; the horizontal tine shows the temporal sequence images from one video segment; the diagonal tines show sequences of shots that are semantically or visually similar to the center image, and the "stem" of the fork shows the browse history. (Courtesy of Ork de Rooij.) (See color plate 9.)

to the focus image are shown (Wittenburg et al. 2003). Another mechanism for laying out video shot search results is seen in the ForkBrowser interface (Snoek et al. 2007; de Rooij et al. 2008), which was found to reduce the number of steps needed and increase the number of relevant shots viewed in a small usability study (see Figure 12.9).

Relevance feedback is a popular method for experimental video retrieval systems, but it has been shown that simply retrieving shots that are temporally near shots that are already marked relevant can be nearly as effective (Hauptmann et al. 2006).

12.2.3. *Audio Search Interfaces*

Audio in search can be used both as an input modality, as in spoken queries, and as a media type to search over. Kohler et al. (2008) note a "renaissance" in speech retrieval in the last few years, due both to the increased availability of podcasts and other audio and video collections, and to the maturing of speech recognition technology. Although much of the audio retrieval research has been done on broadcast news, the availability of digitally stored casual speech in the form of interviews, lectures, debates, radio talk show archives, and educational podcasts is increasingly available. However, searching conversational speech poses additional challenges over professional speech (Maybury 2007). Music retrieval is also an active area of research (Downie 2003; Mandel et al. 2006; McNab et al. 1996; Vignoli and Pauws 2005).

Because spoken language audio can be converted with some degree of accuracy to text, audio retrieval interfaces can be closer to those of text retrieval than image and video data, although in some cases, such as voice-mail retrieval, the nuances in spoken language are the important part of an audio message, and for these text transcripts are insufficient (Whittaker et al. 1998). Nonetheless, some researchers have experimented with creating visual interfaces to speech archives. For example, the SCAN (Speech Content Based Audio Navigator) system (Whittaker et al. 1999) provided a scannable interface for searching an archive of the audio of broadcast news (see Figure 12.10). In a study with 12 participants, participants were more successful and preferred an interface with a visual component showing location of query term hits, even though they were searching over audio content.

Tombros and Crestani (2000), in a study with 10 participants, compared retrieval results presented as text on a screen versus read aloud by a human in person, read by a human over the phone, and read by a speech synthesizer over the phone. The phone-based systems were significantly slower than the on-screen system, and less accurate as well. They found that precision, recall, and time taken for the last query when hearing information over the phone was significantly slower than for the first query in that condition, but did not find this in the screen reading condition.

Some researchers have focused on speaker recognition algorithms and interfaces to show who is speaking at different points of time in a meeting or other group situation (see Figure 12.11) (Kimber and Wilcox 1997). Many efforts in this domain are multi-modal, meaning that audio, text, and video are interlinked and cues from each are used to segment and recognize different attributes from each media type (Bett et al. 2000; Maybury 2007; Oviatt and Darrell 2004; Oviatt et al. 1997).

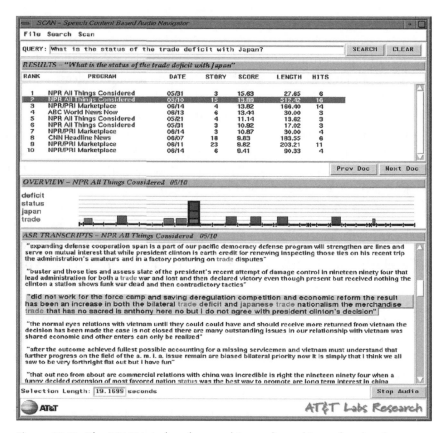

Figure 12.10. The SCAN interface for searching audio archives of spoken language, from Whittaker et al. (1999). Search hits are shown visually, similar to TileBars (Hearst 1995).

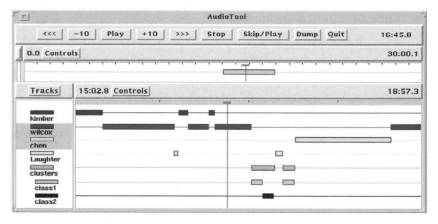

Figure 12.11. Interface for browsing spoken language by different speakers participating in a panel discussion at a conference, from Kimber and Wilcox (1997).

12.2.4. *Multimedia Search on Web Search Engines*

Web search engines have long offered search over images as well as text, and more recently have begun offering video search as well. Most search engines offer multimedia search as an explicit search starting point, activated when the user selects a tab or a link from the main search page. Thus if a user selected *Image Search* and typed in rainbow, the results would look much different than querying on the same keyword in Web search. Additionally, for many years, if the user included image or pic as part of the query, the search results would suggest that the user switch over to image search. When implemented this way, the multimedia search is referred to as a *vertical* search, meaning search over a specialized or limited collection.

Recently the major search engines have introduced what they call *blended results* or *universal search*, in which hits on images, videos, news, and other kinds of specialized content are interwoven with the Web page hits in the search results listing. (But only those queries that the algorithm determines should have such hits; many queries bring up only Web page hits.) A survey by iProspect of 2,404 adults found that when multimedia search is offered as a vertical that requires changing the search interface, a large proportion of users either do not use it (35%) or else do not recall clicking on a link after using it (25%). Of those who have used vertical search, 26% recall having clicked on an image result, 17% on a news result, and only 10% on a video result. However, in the approximately six-month period between when blended results were introduced by the major search engines and when the survey was conducted, 81% of users reported having clicked on these specialized links in the blended results, with news results being the most popular (iProspect 2008). Eye-tracking results also indicate that including an image within the search results page tends to alter the scanning pattern (Hotchkiss 2007a).

For Web search engines, image search is primarily keyword search, based on text labels derived from anchor text and/or the text surrounding the images on the Web pages in which they appear. Image search engines can also make use of human-assigned tags, as used in the Flickr photo sharing Web site. In most cases, the user enters a query into a search form, and the images are shown in a grid, labeled with some metadata. Microsoft image search uses an "endless scroll" grid interface, meaning that rather than breaking the results up into pages of 10, 30, or 50 images, all the images are shown in one continuously growing Web page, progressively appearing in the grid as they are retrieved. Image analysis

Figure 12.12. Keyword-and-tag search over metadata describing the contents of the Prelinger video collection, from the Internet Archive.

technology is used to allow the user to refine by certain attributes that can be easily computed, such as image size, aspect ratio, color versus black and white, and photograph vs. illustration. The system also runs a face recognizer so users can refine images to those that contain people. Flickr also allows search over images according to manually assigned geographic location tags, showing the locations of resulting images on a map.

Video search on the Web is also based on text, but currently primarily based on titles assigned to the video. It currently is not possible in most cases to search by director or creator of the video. On more curated video search sites, such as the Prelinger collection at the Internet Archive, videos have been labeled with metadata, and so keyword searches can be refined by creator, date, and viewer ratings (see Figure 12.12). The video's content is suggested by a series of thumbnail still images extracted from the video. The commercial video search site Blinkx claims to use speech recognition and video analysis in addition to searching the text of the metadata.

A simple form of audio search is offered by Yahoo, but not the other major Web search engines. There are podcast search services offered online such as Podscope that appear to use speech recognition technology to extract terms to search over.

12.3. Social Search

In physical libraries, librarians have traditionally acted as a mediator between a client with an information need and the physical or computer catalog system (and now some libraries offer online chat services with a librarian during working hours). With the arrival of automation, the focus of search engine development shifted to individuals searching on their own, and most interfaces discussed in this book are designed for an individual user. However, with the rise of the interactive Web ("Web 2.0"), in which people interact with one another, variations on what might be called *social search* are becoming increasingly popular and promise to play an important role in the future of search. The following subsections describe three manifestations of this phenomenon: social ranking, collaborative search, and human-powered question answering. These all have in common the use of the thoughts and efforts of multiple people to improve search or the search experience.

12.3.1. *Social Ranking*

As mentioned in Chapter 9, an increasingly popular way for people to find information serendipitously is through Web sites like Digg.com and StumbleUpon.com that use the "wisdom of crowds," record people's recommendations, and show the most popular information items at the top of the list. Social bookmarking sites, like Delicious.com and Furl.com, in which people record items they want to use later, also act as recommendation services. The use of social tagging and social bookmarks to improve ranking has begun to been explored (Heymann et al. 2008; Yanbe et al. 2007).

Also as discussed in Chapter 9, user clickthrough is being used by Web search engines today to adjust their ranking algorithms. This is a kind of implicit feedback, in that users click on the links because they think they are relevant, but not with the purpose of influencing the ranking algorithm in future. A related idea that has been investigated numerous times is that of allowing users to explicitly comment on or change the ranking produced by the search engine. This is akin to relevance feedback (see Chapter 6), but the difference is that the preferences indicated affect

Figure 12.13. The Google SearchWiki system which allows the user to move a search hit to the top of the rankings (the up-arrow icon), remove it from the rankings (the X icon; the item is moved to the bottom of the results page), and comment on the link (the cloud icon). The down-arrow icon moves the result back to its original position. The rank order is retained for the next time the same query is issued.

rankings shown in future for the user in question, and also potentially affect the search engine's algorithms for all users. Microsoft Research proposed a system called U Rank which allows users to move the rank position of hits, and Google has recently introduced SearchWiki which allows the user to move a search hit to the top of the rankings, remove it from the rankings, and comment on the link, and the actions are visible to other users of the system (see Figure 12.13). Experimental results on this kind of system have not be strongly positive in the past (Teevan et al. 2005b), but have not been tried on a large scale in this manner.

Another variation on the idea of social ranking is to promote Web pages that people in one's social network have rated highly in the past, as seen in the Yahoo MyWeb system mentioned in Chapter 9. Small studies have suggested that using a network of one's peers can act as a kind of personalization to bias some search results to be more effective (Joachims 2002; Mislove et al. 2006).

12.3.2. *Multi-Person and Collaborative Search*

There is an increasing trend in HCI to examine how to better support collaboration among users of software systems, and this has recently extended to collaborative or cooperative search. At least three studies suggest that people often work together when performing searches, despite the limitations of existing software (Evans and Chi 2008; Morris 2008; Twidale et al. 1997). Morris (2008), from a survey of 204 workers at a large U.S. technology company, found that 53.4% answered "yes" to the question "Have you ever cooperated with other people to search the Web?" and of those who said "no," 10.5% indicated that they had "needed/wanted to cooperate with other people to search the Web and had been unable to effectively do so." The most common collaborative search strategies were to watch over someone's shoulder as they searched the Web and suggest alternative query terms, and to email links to share the results of a Web search. (The Ariadne system (Twidale and Nichols 1998), discussed in Chapter 7, attempted to make the "sharing the screen" aspect of collaboration more visual.)

Of the 109 survey respondents in Morris (2008) who collaborated with others, the most common tasks involving collaboration were:

- Travel planning (28%)
- General shopping (26%)
- Literature search (20%)
- Technical information search (17%)
- Fact finding (17%)
- Social planning (13%)
- Medical information search (6%)
- Real estate search (6%)

It is interesting, but not surprising, that, with the exception of fact finding, these are complex information seeking tasks that require comparisons and synthesis. This task list suggests that richer tasks benefit from collaborative search. This meshes with the results of Pickens et al. (2008) (described below) that found much greater gains in collaboration on difficult tasks than on simple ones.

There have been a few attempts to design search interfaces specifically for collaborative search. Foley et al. (2005) designed a collaborative video search system in which still images of retrieved videos are shown on a computerized table display. Searchers were seated across from one another at the table while working on shared retrieval tasks. Foley et al. (2005) compared two versions of the search interface, with eight pairs of participants. In one design, searchers had to drag the images into a centralized location in order to activate the video, and when they did so, a sound was played, thus increasing the awareness of their partners of what they are doing. The second design utilized more efficient interaction: to activate a retrieved video, the searcher double-tapped on the image, which was a subtle action that might not be noticed by the search partner. The study found that searchers performed better in terms of precision and recall when using the first design in which they were made aware of what their partner was doing.

Amershi and Morris (2008) built and tested a tool to make interactions with other searchers a collaborative activity. The main idea was to make the queries and results from one user's search visible to other users who had joined a search task. Their usability study asked groups of three people to complete search tasks, in each of three conditions: they each had their own computer, they all shared one computer with one participant acting as "driver," or they all shared one computer, but with special software called CoSearch that allowed the two observers to contribute using mobile devices. Participants did best with, and preferred, the shared computer condition, and did nearly as well with CoSearch. There was also significantly higher perceived communication and collaboration in the shared conditions.

Pickens et al. (2008) took this idea further. They note that in other work the search algorithm does not respond to the fact that multiple queries are being issued to achieve the same goals. They assume that ideally the ranking algorithm should allow people to work at their own pace, but be influenced in real-time by the different teammates' search activities. But the different searchers should not step on one another's toes: if one searcher decides to issue a new query, others should not be interrupted in their trains of thought.

Pickens et al. (2008) describe an algorithm that combines multiple interactions of queries from multiple searchers during a single search session, by using two weighting variables called "relevance" and "freshness," where both are functions of the ranked list of documents returned for a given query. Freshness is higher for lists of documents that contain many not yet seen documents. Relevance is higher for documents that closely match the query. The two factors are combined to counter-balance each other, and are continuously updated based on new queries and searcher-specified relevance judgements.

Pickens et al. (2008) assume a team of two people collaborating, and assign one the role of Prospector, who is in charge of issuing new queries to explore new parts of the information space, while the other acts as Miner, whose job is to look deeply into the retrieved results to determine which are relevant. Documents that have not yet been looked at are queued up for the Miner interface according to the freshness/relevance weighted scores. The Prospector is shown new query term suggestions based on difference from queries already issued, and also based implicitly on the relevance judgements being made by the Miner. Each role has its own distinct interface, but a third computer screen is used to show continually updating information about the queries that have been issued, the documents that have been marked as relevant, and system-suggested query terms based on the actions of both users.

In a study with four two-person teams, Pickens et al. (2008) compared results of the system in which the relevant documents were collaboratively determined versus a condition in which the queries were sent to a standard ranking algorithm that did not alter its behavior based on the activities of the two participants, but did produce a merged list of results. They found that collaborative search consistently outperformed the post hoc merging of the queries issued by the two participants. This result was especially strong for queries for which it was difficult to find relevant results.

12.3.3. *Massive-Scale Human Question Answering*

A relatively recent and quite surprising search interface phenomenon is the rise of human question answering sites, in which people enter questions, and thousands of other people suggest answers in nearly real time. The question–answer pairs are retained over time, and members are allowed to vote on the quality of the answers, so that the better answers move to more prominent positions.

In the Korean search market, human question answering is more popular than standard Web search (Ihlwan et al. 2006), perhaps in part because there is less information available online in the Korean languages than in English. However, the launch of Yahoo Answers was very successful in the English-speaking world, with more that 160 million answers after one year of service. One reason for the popularity seems to be the community-oriented aspects of these sites, allowing individuals to converse with one another. Another reason is the integration of user-generated answers into Yahoo and Google's search results. Some question the quality of the answers, finding them uneven, although there is evidence that community-supplied answers can be valuable (Agichtein et al. 2008).

A contrast is seen in the rent-an-expert approach in which experts answer difficult questions for a fee, as seen in the now-defunct Google

Answers. The ChaCha.com Search service, in which human experts answer a user's question free of charge, has not become popular on the Web, but is experiencing growth as a service for mobile device users. And companies continue to experiment with models of charging for online answers, as is currently available at the Mahalo.com Web site.

12.4. A Hybrid of Command and Natural Language Search

As mentioned several times throughout this book, Web search engine algorithms are becoming more sophisticated in handling long queries as well as in attempting to discern the intent that underlies cryptic keyword queries. Right now they work by eliding some stopwords, and in some cases doing synonym substitution. As longer queries become more successful, people may try more "teleporting" queries more often – stating their full information need in the expectation that the search engine can process it successfully. There are also a number of startup companies claiming to do natural language processing and "semantic" search. Some of these take a syntax-based approach to language interpretation, as seen in Powerset, while others attempt to achieve more deep semantics, as seen in Cognition.

A related trend is the use of using a flexible command syntax to create quasi-natural language interfaces. Norman (2007b) writes that "[S]earch engines have become answer engines, controlled through a modern form of command line interface." Norman notes that their syntax at major Web search is idiosyncratic and their coverage is spotty, but points out their virtues over command languages of old: "tolerant of variations, robust, and they exhibit slight touches of natural language flexibility."

The Inky and Chickenfoot projects have implemented what they refer to as "sloppy commands" (Little and Miller 2006; Miller et al. 2008), meaning the user has a lot of flexibility in how they express the command, and so memorization is not required to make use of them. The Enso system has implemented this idea in a robust manner for all operating systems. The Quicksilver application for Apple operating systems supports a hybrid command/GUI interface. They use continuous feedback to whittle down the available choices to include what the user has typed so far and that still matches available commands. The continuous feedback aids in the discoverability, lessening memory load.

It is likely that this hybrid between improved language analysis and command languages, making use of structured knowledge bases such as

Metaweb's FreeBase, will be paired with clever uses of interaction, to lead to more intelligent interfaces and an expansion of dialogue-like interaction.

12.5. Conclusions

This chapter has discussed several areas that are likely to have a big impact on, or play a big role in, search in the future. The emphasis in this chapter is on mobile search, multimedia search, social search, and an increase in importance of natural language queries, at the expense of keyword search. Also worth mentioning are advances in search of verticals, such as travel information, health care information, government information, and blogs (Hearst et al. 2008), all of which can most likely be better served by specialized algorithms and interfaces. Search over intranets can still use improvement. Multilingual search, although sophisticated algorithmically, is not yet interesting from an interface perspective, but this may change with time. Local, or geographic information is being incorporated into many interfaces generally, including search, and especially into those for mobile applications.

Just as some displays are getting smaller, large displays with both projected views and touch-screen interaction will become cheaper and more prevalent. These will help facilitate collaborative information access as well as better support complex information analysis activities and visualization. Touch-screen displays may also change the dynamics of how people interact with search systems, and displays that project images onto tabletops or even into the air may enhance multi-person search efforts.

Of course, there is always the unexpected, unanticipated new development, and it will be exciting to see what that future brings to search user interfaces.

Appendix: Additional Copyright Notices

For images appearing in Figures 8.8, 8.9, 8.10, and 8.11, the following credit information applies:

T. Tokuhara (Japanese, active late 19th century)
House on Lake with Boy and Man in Foreground, ca. 1890–1900
Albumen silver print with hand coloring
21 × 27.1 cm (image)
Fine Arts Museums of San Francisco, Gift of James H. Soong, 1989.3.25

Hiroshige (Japanese, 1797–1858)
At Yase Village (Yase no sato), from the series Famous Places in Kyoto
(Kyoto meisho no uchi), ca. 1833–1834
Color woodcut
21.9 × 35.5 cm (sheet)
Fine Arts Museums of San Francisco, Gift of Jane Scribner, 1982.1.92

Eisen (Japanese, 1790–1848)
The Mimeguri Embankment of the Sumida River, ca. 1815–1820
Color woodcut surimono
17.6 × 47.1 cm (sheet)
Fine Arts Museums of San Francisco, Gift of Katherine Ball to the DeYoung
Museum, transferred to AFGA, 1964.141.970

Eishi (Japanese, 1756–1829)
The Courtesan Takigawa of the Tamaya with Attendants (a Shinzo
and Her Two Kamuro, Chidori and Namiji) (Tamaya no uchi Takigawa,
Chidori, Namiji), ca. 1788–1790
Color woodcut
37.1 × 25.6 cm (image)
Fine Arts Museums of San Francisco, Gift of Miss Carlotta Mabury, 54755.32

Eishi (Japanese, 1756–1829)
Kneeling Woman Showing a Miniature Plum Tree to a Child in Its Mother's
Artms, from the series Children's Pastimes in the Four Seasons (Shiki
warabe asobi), ca. 1794–1796

325

Bibliography

Aalbersberg, I. (1992). Incremental relevance feedback. In *Proceedings of the 15th Annual International ACM SIGIR Conference on Research and Development in Information Retrieval (SIGIR'92)*. Interaction in Information Retrieval, 11–22.

Abowd, G., Gauger, M., and Lachenmann, A. (2003). The Family Video Archive: An annotation and browsing environment for home movies. In *Proceedings of the 5th ACM SIGMM International Workshop on Multimedia Information Retrieval*. ACM New York, NY, USA, 1–8.

Adar, E. (2007). User 4xxxxx9: Anonymizing query logs. In *Proceedings of the 16th International Conference on World Wide Web (WWW'07) Workshop on Query Log Analysis: Social and Technological Challenges*.

Adcock, J., Cooper, M., and Pickens, J. (2008). Experiments in interactive video search by addition and subtraction. In *Proceedings of the 2008 International Conference on Content-Based Image and Video Retrieval*. ACM Press, New York, NY, USA, 465–474.

Adomavicius, G., and Tuzhilin, A. (2005). Toward the next generation of recommender systems: A survey of the state-of-the-art and possible extensions. *IEEE Transactions on Knowledge and Data Engineering 17*, 6, 734–749.

Agichtein, E., Brill, E., and Dumais, S. (2006a). Improving Web search ranking by incorporating user behavior information. In *Proceedings of the 29th Annual International ACM SIGIR Conference on Research and Development in Information Retrieval (SIGIR'06)*.

Agichtein, E., Brill, E., Dumais, S., and Ragno, R. (2006b). Learning user interaction models for predicting Web search result preferences. In *Proceedings of the 29th Annual International ACM SIGIR Conference on Research and Development in Information Retrieval (SIGIR'06)*.

Agichtein, E., Castillo, C., Donato, D., Gionis, A., and Mishne, G. (2008). Finding high-quality content in social media. In *Proceedings of the International Conference on Web Search and Web Data Mining (WSDM'08)*. ACM Press, New York, NY, USA, 183–194.

Ahn, J.-S., Brusilovsky, P., He, D., and Syn, S. (2007). Open user profiles for adaptive news systems: Help or harm? In *Proceedings of the 16th International Conference on World Wide Web (WWW'07)*.

Allan, J. (1995). Relevance feedback with too much data. In *Proceedings of the 18th Annual International ACM SIGIR Conference on Research and Development in Information Retrieval (SIGIR'95)*. Feedback Methods, 337–343.

Allan, J. (2005). HARD Track overview in TREC 2004 high accuracy retrieval from documents. In *Proceedings of the Thirteenth Text REtrieval Conference (TREC'04)*.

Allen, B. (1992). Cognitive differences in end user searching of a CD-ROM index. In *Proceedings of the 15th Annual International ACM SIGIR Conference on Research and Development in Information Retrieval (SIGIR'92)*. ACM Press, New York, NY, USA, 298–309.

Allen, B. (1994). Perceptual speed, learning and information retrieval performance. In *Proceedings of the 17th Annual International ACM SIGIR Conference on Research and Development in Information Retrieval (SIGIR'94)*, 71–80.

Allen, B. (2000). Individual differences and the conundrums of user-centered design: Two experiments. *Journal of the American Society for Information Science 51*, 6, 508–520.

Allen, R. B., Obry, P., and Littman, M. (1993). An interface for navigating clustered document sets returned by queries. In *Proceedings of ACM COOCS: Conference on Organizational Computing Systems*.

Alonso, O., Rose, D., and Stewart, B. (2008). Crowdsourcing for relevance evaluation. *ACM SIGIR Forum 42*, 2, 9–15.

Amento, B., Terveen, L., and Hill, W. (2000). Does "authority" mean quality? predicting expert quality ratings of Web documents. In *Proceedings of the 23rd Annual International ACM SIGIR Conference on Research and Development in Information Retrieval*. ACM Press, New York, NY, USA, 296–303.

Amershi, S., and Morris, M. (2008). CoSearch: A system for co-located collaborative Web search. In *Proceedings of the SIGCHI Conference on Human Factors in Computing Systems (CHI'08)*. ACM Press, New York, NY, USA.

Anderson, T., Hussam, A., Plummer, B., and Jacobs, N. (2002). Pie charts for visualizing query term frequency in search results. In *Proceedings of the Fifth International Conference on Asian Digital Library*, 440–451.

Andrews, K., Gütl, C., Moser, J., Sabol, V., and Lackner, W. (2001). Search result visualisation with xFIND. In *Proceedings of User Interfaces to Data Intensive Systems (UIDIS 2001)*, 50–58.

Androutsopoulos, I., Ritchie, G., and Thanisch, P. (1995). Natural language interfaces to databases – An introduction. *Journal of Natural Language Engineering 1*, 29–81.

Anick, P. (1994). Adapting a full-text information retrieval system to the computer troubleshooting domain. In *Proceedings of the 17th Annual International ACM SIGIR Conference on Research and Development in Information Retrieval (SIGIR'94)*, 349–358.

Anick, P. (2003). Using terminological feedback for Web search refinement: A log-based study. In *Proceedings of the 26th Annual International ACM SIGIR Conference on Research and Development in Information Retrieval (SIGIR'03)*, 88–95.

Anick, P., Brennan, J., Flynn, R., Hanssen, D., Alvey, B., and Robbins, J. (1990). A direct manipulation interface for Boolean information retrieval via natural language query. In *Proceedings of the 13th Annual International ACM SIGIR Conference on Research and Development in Information Retrieval (SIGIR'90)*, 135–150.

Anick, P., and Kantamneni, R. (2008). A longitudinal study of real-time search assistance adoption. In *Proceedings of the 31st Annual International ACM SIGIR*

Conference on Research and Development in Information Retrieval (SIGIR'08). ACM Press, New York, NY, USA, 701–702.

Aula, A. (2004). Enhancing the readability of search result summaries. *Proceedings of HCI 2004*, 6–10.

Aula, A. (2005). Studying user strategies and characteristics for developing web search interfaces. Ph.D. Dissertation, Dissertations in Interactive Technology, Number 3, University of Tampere, Finland.

Aula, A., Jhaveri, N., and Käki, M. (2005a). Information search and re-access strategies of experienced web users. In *Proceedings of the 14th International Conference on World Wide Web (WWW'05)*, 583–592.

Aula, A., and Käki, M. (2005). Less is more in Web search interfaces for older adults. *First Monday 10*, 5.

Aula, A., Majaranta, P., and Räihä, K. (2005b). Eye-tracking reveals the personal styles for search result evaluation. In *Proceedings of Human-Computer Interaction (INTERACT'05)*.

Aula, A., and Siirtola, H. (2005). Hundreds of folders or one ugly pile: Strategies for information search and re-access. In *Proceedings of Human-Computer Interaction (INTERACT'05)*, 954–957.

Ayers, E., and Stasko, J. (1995). Using graphic history in browsing the World Wide Web. In *Proceedings of the 4th International Conference on World Wide Web (WWW'95b)*.

Bainbridge, D., Jones, S., McIntosh, S., Jones, M., and Witten, I. (2008). Portable digital libraries on an ipod. In *Proceedings of the 8th ACM/IEEE-CS Joint Conference on Digital Libraries*. ACM Press, New York, NY, USA, 333–336.

Balabanović, M., and Shoham, Y. (1997). Fab: Content-based, collaborative recommendation. *Communications of the ACM 40*, 3, 66–72.

Baldonado, M., and Winograd, T. (1997). Sensemaker: An information-exploration interface supporting the contextual evolution of a user's interests. In *Proceedings of the SIGCHI Conference on Human Factors in Computing Systems (CHI'97).* ACM, Vancouver.

Baldonado, M., and Winograd, T. (1998). Hi-cites: Dynamically-created citations with active highlighting. In *Proceedings of the SIGCHI Conference on Human Factors in Computing Systems (CHI'98).* ACM, Los Angeles, CA.

Bar-Ilan, J. (2007). Position paper: Access to query logs – An academic researcher's point of view. In *Proceedings of the 16th International Conference on World Wide Web (WWW'07) Workshop on Query Log Analysis: Social and Technological Challenges*.

Barreau, D., and Nardi, B. (1995). Finding and reminding: File organization from the desktop. *ACM SIGCHI Bulletin 27*, 3, 39–43.

Basu, C., Hirsh, H., and Cohen, W. (1998). Recommendation as classification: Using social and content-based information in recommendation. In *Proceedings of 15th Annual Conference on Artificial Intelligence (AAAI 98)*, 714–720.

Bates, M. (1979). Information search tactics. *Journal of the American Society for Information Science 30*, 4, 205–214.

Bates, M. (1988). How to use controlled vocabularies more effectively in online searching. *Online 12*, 6, 45–56.

Bates, M. (1989). The design of browsing and berrypicking techniques for the online search interface. *Online Review 13*, 5, 407–431.

Bates, M. (1990). Where should the person stop and the information search interfaces start? *Information Processing and Management 26*, 5.

Baudisch, P., Lee, B., and Hanna, L. (2004). Fishnet, a fisheye web browser with search term popouts: A comparative evaluation with overview and linear view. In *Proceedings of the Working Conference on Advanced Visual Interfaces (AVI'04)*, 133–140.

Beaudouin-Lafon, M., and Mackay, W. (2003). Prototyping tools and techniques. In *Human-Computer Interaction Handbook*. Lawrence Erlbaum Associates, Hillsdale, NJ.

Bederson, B. (2001). PhotoMesa: A zoomable image browser using quantum treemaps and bubblemaps. In *Proceedings of the 14th Annual ACM Symposium on User Interface Software and Technology*. ACM Press, New York, NY, USA, 71–80.

Belkin, N., Kelly, D., Kim, G., Kim, J.-Y., Lee, H.-J., Muresean, G., Tang, M.-C., Yuan, X.-J., and Cool, C. (2003). Query length in interactive information retrieval. In *Proceedings of the 26th Annual International ACM SIGIR Conference on Research and Development in Information Retrieval (SIGIR'03)*, 205–212.

Belkin, N., Marchetti, P. G., and Cool, C. (1993). Braque – Design of an interface to support user interaction in information retrieval. *Information Processing and Management 29*, 3, 325–344.

Belkin, N., Oddy, R., and Brooks, H. (1982). ASK for information retrieval: Part I. Background and theory. *Journal of Documentation 38*, 2, 61–71.

Bell, D., and Ruthven, I. (2004). Searchers' assessments of task complexity for Web searching. In *Proceedings of the 26th European Conference on Information Retrieval*, 57–71.

Ben-Bassat, T., Meyer, J., and Tractinsky, N. (2006). Economic and subjective measures of the perceived value of aesthetics and usability. *ACM Transactions on Computer-Human Interaction (TOCHI) 13*, 2, 210–234.

Bergman, O., Beyth-Marom, R., Nachmias, R., Gradovitch, N., and Whittaker, S. (2008). Improved search engines and navigation preference in personal information management. *ACM Transactions on Information Systems (TOIS) 26*, 4, 1–24.

Bertin, J. (1983). *Semiology of Graphics*. University of Wisconsin Press, Madison, WI.

Bett, M., Gross, R., Yu, H., Zhu, X., Pan, Y., Yang, J., and Waibel, A. (2000). Multimodal meeting tracker. In *Proceedings of RIAO2000*.

Bickmore, T., and Schilit, B. (1997). Digestor: Device-independent access to the World Wide Web. *Proceedings of the 6th International Conference on World Wide Web (WWW'97) 29*, 8–13, 1075–1082.

Bilal, D. (2000). Children's use of the Yahooligans! Web search engine. I. Cognitive, physical, and affective behaviors on fact-based search tasks. *Journal of the American Society for Information Science 51*, 7, 646–665.

Bilal, D. (2002). Children's use of the Yahooligans! Web search engine. III. Cognitive and physical behaviors on fully self-generated search tasks. *Journal of the American Society for Information Science and Technology 53*, 13, 1170–1183.

Björk, S., Redström, J., Ljungstrand, P., and Holmquist, L. (2000). POWERVIEW: Using information links and information views to navigate and visualize information on small displays. In *Proceedings of the 2nd International Symposium on Handheld and Ubiquitous Computing*, 46–62.

Blair, D., and Maron, M. (1985). An evaluation of retrieval effectiveness for a full-text document-retrieval system. *Communications of the ACM 28*, 3.

Boren, M., and Ramey, J. (2000). Thinking aloud: Reconciling theory and practice. *IEEE Transactions on Professional Communication 43*, 3, 261.

Borgman, C. (1996). Why are online catalogs still hard to use? *Journal of the American Society for Information Science 47, 7,* 493–503.

Boyle, J., Ogden, W., Uhlir, S., and Wilson, P. (1984). Qmf usability: How it really happened. In *Proceedings of IFIP INTERACT'84: Human-Computer Interaction,* 877–882.

Brandes, U., Hoefer, M., and Lerner, J. (2006). WordSpace: Visual summary of text corpora. *Proceedings of SPIE 6060,* 212–223.

Broder, A. (2002). A taxonomy of web search. *SIGIR Forum 36,* 2, 3–10.

Broder, A., Fontoura, M., Gabrilovich, E., Joshi, A., Josifovski, V., and Zhang, T. (2007). Robust classification of rare queries using web knowledge. In *Proceedings of the 30th Annual International ACM SIGIR Conference on Research and Development in Information Retrieval (SIGIR'07).*

Bruza, P., and Dennis, S. (1997). Query reformulation on the Internet: Empirical data and the hyperindex search engine. In *Proceedings of the Riao Conference: Intelligent Text and Image Handling,* 488–499.

Bruza, P., Mcarthur, R., and Dennis, S. (2000). Interactive Internet search: Keyword, directory and query reformulation mechanisms compared. In *Proceedings of the 23th Annual International ACM SIGIR Conference on Research and Development in Information Retrieval (SIGIR'00),* 280–287.

Buchanan, G., Cunningham, S., Blandford, A., Rimmer, J., and Warwick, C. (2005). Information seeking by humanities scholars. In *Proceedings of the European Conference on Digital Libraries (ECDL'05).*

Buckley, C. (2004). Why current IR engines fail. *Proceedings of the 27th Annual International ACM SIGIR Conference on Research and Development in Information Retrieval (SIGIR'04),* 584–585.

Buckley, C., Salton, G., and Allan, J. (1994). The effect of adding relevance information in a relevance feedback environment. In *Proceedings of the 17th Annual International ACM SIGIR Conference on Research and Development in Information Retrieval (SIGIR'94),* 292–300.

Buckley, C., and Walz, J. (2000). The TREC-8 Query Track. In *Proceedings of the Eighth Text REtrieval Conference (TREC-8),* 65–75.

Burke, R., Hammond, K., Kulukin, V., Lytinen, S., Tomuro, N., and Schoenberg, S. (1997). Experiences with the FAQ system. *AI Magazine 18,* 2, 57–66.

Buyukkokten, O., Garcia-Molina, H., and Paepcke, A. (2000a). Focused Web searching with PDAs. *Computer Networks 33,* 1–6, 213–230.

Buyukkokten, O., Garcia-Molina, H., Paepcke, A., and Winograd, T. (2000b). Power browser: Efficient Web browsing for PDAs. In *Proceedings of the SIGCHI Conference on Human Factors in Computing Systems (CHI'00),* 430–437.

Byrd, D. (1999). A scrollbar-based visualization for document navigation. In *Proceedings of the Fourth ACM International Conference on Digital Libraries.*

Cai, D., He, X., Li, Z., Ma, W., and Wen, J.-R. (2004). Hierarchical clustering of WWW image search results using visual, textual and link information. In *Proceedings of the 12th Annual ACM International Conference on Multimedia.* ACM Press, New York, NY, USA, 952–959.

Card, S., Robertson, G., and Mackinlay, J. (1991). The information visualizer, an information workspace. In *Proceedings of the SIGCHI Conference on Human Factors in Computing Systems (CHI'91),* 181–188.

Card, S., Robertson, G., and York, W. (1996). The webbook and the web forager: An information workspace for the world-wide web. In *Proceedings of the SIGCHI Conference on Human Factors in Computing Systems (CHI'96).*

Carpineto, C., and Romano, G. (1996). Information retrieval through hybrid navigation of lattice representations. *International Journal of Human-Computer Studies 45*, 5, 553–578.

Catledge, L., and Pitkow, J. (1995). Characterizing browsing strategies in the World-Wide Web. *Proceedings of the 4th International Conference on World Wide Web (WWW'95b) 27*, 6, 1065–1073.

Chalmers, M., and Chitson, P. (1992). Bead: Explorations in information visualization. In *Proceedings of the 15th Annual International ACM SIGIR Conference on Research and Development in Information Retrieval (SIGIR'92)*, 330–337.

Chang, S.-J., and Rice, R. E. (1993). Browsing: A multidimensional framework. *Annual Review of Information Science and Technology 28*, 231–276.

Chaudhri, V., Cheyer, A., Guili, R., Jarrold, B., Myers, K., and Niekrasz, J. (2006). A case study in engineering a knowledge base for an intelligent personal assistant. In *Proceedings of the 2006 Semantic Desktop Workshop*.

Chen, C. (2000). Individual differences in a spatial-semantic virtual environment. *Journal of the American Society for Information Science 51*, 6, 529–542.

Chen, C., and Yu, Y. (2000). Empirical studies of information visualization: A meta-analysis. *International Journal of Human-Computers Studies 53*, 5, 851–866.

Chen, H., Houston, A. L., Sewell, R. R., and Schatz, B. R. (1998). Internet browsing and searching: User evaluations of category map and concept space techniques. *Journal of the American Society for Information Sciences 49*, 7.

Chen, M., and Hearst, M. (1998). Presenting web site search results in context: A demonstration. In *Proceedings of the 21st Annual International ACM SIGIR Conference on Research and Development in Information Retrieval (SIGIR'98)*.

Chen, M., Hearst, M., Hong, J., and Lin, J. (1999). Cha-Cha: A system for organizing Intranet search results. In *Proceedings of the 2nd Conference on USENIX Symposium on Internet Technologies and Systems*, 11–14.

Chen, M., Lapaugh, A., and Singh, J. (2002). Predicting category accesses for a user in a structured information space. In *Proceedings of the 25th Annual International ACM SIGIR Conference on Research and Development in Information Retrieval (SIGIR'02)*, 65–72.

Chin, J., Diehl, V., and Norman, K. (1988). Development of an instrument measuring user satisfaction of the human-computer interface. In *Proceedings of the SIGCHI Conference on Human Factors in Computing Systems (CHI'88)*. ACM Press, New York, NY, USA, 213–218.

Christos, F., Christos, K., Eleftherios, P., Nikolaos, T., and Nikolaos, A. (2007). Remote usability evaluation methods and tools: A survey. In *Proceedings of the 11th Panhellenic Conference in Informatics (PCI 2007)*.

Church, K., Smyth, B., and Keane, M. (2006). Evaluating interfaces for intelligent mobile search. In *Proceedings of the 2006 International Cross-Disciplinary Workshop on Web Accessibility (W4A): Building the Mobile Web: Rediscovering Accessibility?*, 69–78.

Clarke, C., Agichtein, E., Dumais, S., and White, R. (2007). The influence of caption features on clickthrough patterns in web search. In *Proceedings of the 30th Annual International ACM SIGIR Conference on Research and Development in Information Retrieval (SIGIR'07)*. ACM Press, New York, NY, USA, 135–142.

Clarke, C., Cormack, G., and Burkowski, F. (1996). Shortest substring ranking (multitext experiments for TREC-4). In D. Harman, ed., *Proceedings of the Fifth Text REtrieval Conference (TREC-5)*.

Claypool, M., Gokhale, A., Miranda, T., Murnikov, P., Netes, D., and Sartin, M. (1999). Combining content-based and collaborative filters in an online newspaper. In *Proceedings of the 22nd Annual International ACM SIGIR Conference on Research and Development in Information Retrieval (SIGIR'99) Workshop on Recommender Systems*.

Cleveland, W. (1985). *The Elements of Graphing Data*. Wadsworth, Belmont, CA.

Cleveland, W., and McGill, R. (1984). Graphical perception: Theory, experimentation, and application to the development of graphical methods. *Journal of the American Statistical Association 79*, 387, 531–554.

Cockburn, A., Greenberg, S., McKenzie, B., Jasonsmith, M., and Kaasten, S. (1999). WebView: A graphical aid for revisiting Web pages. *Proceedings of OZCHI 99*, 15–22.

Cockburn, A., and McKenzie, B. (2000). An evaluation of cone trees. *People and Computers XIV-Usability Or Else! British Computer Society Conference on Human Computer Interaction 2000*, 425–436.

Cockburn, A., and McKenzie, B. (2001). 3D or not 3D?: Evaluating the effect of the third dimension in a document management system. In *Proceedings of the SIGCHI Conference on Human Factors in Computing Systems (CHI'01)*, 434–441.

Cockburn, A., and McKenzie, B. (2002). Evaluating the effectiveness of spatial memory in 2D and 3D physical and virtual environments. In *Proceedings of the SIGCHI Conference on Human Factors in Computing Systems (CHI'02)*, 203–210.

Collins, C. (2006). DocuBurst: Document content visualization using language structure. In *Proceedings of IEEE Symposium on Information Visualization, Poster Session*.

Combs, T., and Bederson, B. (1999). Does zooming improve image browsing? In *Proceedings of the fourth ACM Conference on Digital Libraries*, 130–137.

Cooper, A. (1995). *About Face: The Essentials of User Interface Design*. IDG Books, Foster city, CA.

Cooper, A. (2008). A survey of query log privacy-enhancing techniques from a policy perspective. *ACM Transactions on the Web (TWeb) 2*, 4.

Cooper, A., Reimann, R., and Cronin, D. (2007). *About Face 3: The Essentials of User Interface Design*. Wiley, IN.

Cousins, S. (1992). In their own words: An examination of catalogue users' subject queries. *Journal of Information Science 18*, 5, 329.

Cousins, S. (1997). Reification and affordances in a user interface for interacting with heterogeneous distributed applications. Ph.D. thesis, Stanford University, Stanford, CA.

Cousins, S., Paepcke, A., Winograd, T., Bier, E., and Pier, K. (1997). The digital library integrated task environment. In *Proceedings of the ACM Conference on Digital Libraries*. ACM, Philadelphia, PA.

Cowley, P., Nowell, L., and Scholtz, J. (2005). Glass box: An instrumented infrastructure for supporting human interaction with information. In *Proceedings of the 38th Annual Hawaii International Conference on System Sciences (HICSS'05)*, 296c–296c.

Croft, W., Cronen-Townsend, S., and Larvrenko, V. (2001). Relevance feedback and personalization: A language modeling perspective. In *Delos Workshop: Personalisation and Recommender Systems in Digital Libraries*.

Croft, W. B., and Wei, X. (2005). Context-based topic models for query modification. IR 424, University of Massachusetts.

Cronen-Townsend, S., Zhou, Y., and Croft, W. (2004). A language modeling framework for selective query expansion. Technical Report IR-338, Center For Intelligent Information Retrieval, University of Massachusetts, Amherst, MA.

Cucerzan, S., and Brill, E. (2004). Spelling correction as an iterative process that exploits the collective knowledge of Web users. In *Proceedings of Conference on Empirical Methods in Natural Language Processing (Emnlp'04)*, 293–300.

Cucerzan, S., and Brill, E. (2005). Extracting semantically related queries by exploiting user session information. Technical Report, Microsoft Research, Cambridge, MA.

Cui, H., Wen, J.-R., Nie, J., and Ma, W. (2003). Query expansion by mining user logs. *IEEE Transactions on Knowledge and Data Engineering 15*, 4, 829–839.

Cutrell, E., Dumais, S., and Teevan, J. (2006a). Searching to eliminate personal information management. *Communications of the ACM 49*, 1, 58–64.

Cutrell, E., and Guan, Z. (2007). What are you looking for?: An eye-tracking study of information usage in Web search. In *Proceedings of the SIGCHI Conference on Human Factors in Computing Systems (CHI'07)*. ACM Press, New York, NY, USA, 407–416.

Cutrell, E., Robbins, D., Dumais, S., and Sarin, R. (2006b). Fast, flexible filtering with Phlat. In *Proceedings of the SIGCHI Conference on Human Factors in Computing Systems (CHI'06)*, 261–270.

Cutting, D., Karger, D., and Pedersen, J. (1993). Constant interaction-time scatter/gather browsing of very large document collections. In *Proceedings of the 16th Annual International ACM SIGIR Conference on Research and Development in Information Retrieval (SIGIR'93)*, 126–135.

Cutting, D., Pedersen, J., Karger, D., and Tukey, J. (1992). Scatter/Gather: A cluster-based approach to browsing large document collections. In *Proceedings of the 15th Annual International ACM SIGIR Conference on Research and Development in Information Retrieval (SIGIR'92)*, 318–329.

Czerwinski, M., van Dantzich, M., Robertson, G., and Hoffman, H. (1999). The contribution of thumbnail image, mouse-over text and spatial location memory to web page retrieval in 3D. *Proceedings of Human-Computer Interaction (INTERACT'99) 99*, 163–170.

Dakka, W., and Ipeirotis, P. (2008). Automatic extraction of useful facet hierarchies from text databases. In *IEEE 24th International Conference on Data Engineering (ICDE'08)*. 466–475.

Das, A., Datar, M., Gang, A., and Rajaram, S. (2007). Google news personalization: Scalable online collaborative filtering. In *Proceedings of the 16th International Conference on World Wide Web (WWW'07)*.

de Rooij, O., Snoek, C. G. M., and Worring, M. (2008). Mediamill: Fast and effective video search using the ForkBrowser. In *Proceedings of the ACM International Conference on Image and Video Retrieval*, 561–561.

Dearman, D., Kellar, M., and Truong, K. (2008). An examination of daily information needs and sharing opportunities. In *Proceedings of the ACM 2008 Conference on Computer Supported Cooperative Work (CSCW'08)*. ACM Press, New York, NY, USA, 679–688.

Dempsey, L. (2006). Libraries and the long tail: Some thoughts about libraries in a network age. *D-Lib Magazine 12*, 4.

Dennis, S., Mcarthur, R., and Bruza, P. (1998). Searching the World Wide Web made easy? The cognitive load imposed by query refinement mechanisms. In *Proceedings of the Australian Document Computing Conference*, 65–71.

Deshpande, M., and Karypis, G. (2004). Selective Markov models for predicting Web page accesses. *ACM Transactions on Internet Technology (Toit) 4,* 2, 163–184.

Dialog, Inc. (2002a). *DialogWeb Command Search Tutorial.* Dialog LLC, Morrisville, NC. www.dialog.com. http://support.dialog.com/techdocs/dialogweb_command_tutorial.pdf.

Dialog, Inc. (2002b). *DialogWeb Guided Search Tutorial.* Thomson, Philadelphia, PA. http://support.dialog.com/techdocs/dialogweb_guided_tutorial.pdf.

Dialog, Inc. (2006). *Dialog Command Language Pocket Guide.* Dialog LLC, Morrisville, NC. www.dialog.com. http://support.dialog.com/searchaids/dialog/pocketguide/pktgde.pdf.

Dinet, J., Favart, M., and Passerault, J. (2004). Searching for information in an online public access catalogue(OPAC): The impacts of information search expertise on the use of Boolean operators. *Journal of Computer Assisted Learning 20,* 5, 338–346.

Divoli, A., Hearst, M., and Wooldridge, M. (2008). Evidence for showing gene/protein name suggestions in bioscience literature search interfaces. *Pacific Symposium on Biocomputing 568,* 79.

Don, A., Zheleva, E., Gregory, M., Tarkan, S., Auvil, L., Clement, T., Shneiderman, B., and Plaisant, C. (2007). Discovering interesting usage patterns in text collections: Integrating text mining with visualization. In *Proceedings of the Sixteenth International Conference on Information and Knowledge Management (CIKM'07).*

Doncheva, M., Drucker, S., Wade, G., Salesin, D., and Cohen, M. (2006). Collecting and organizing Web content. In *Proceedings of the 29th Annual International ACM SIGIR Conference on Research and Development in Information Retrieval (SIGIR'06) Workshop on Personal Information Management.*

Dou, Z., Song, R., and Wen, J.-R. (2007). A large-scale evaluation and analysis of personalized search strategies. In *Proceedings of the 16th International Conference on World Wide Web (WWW'07).*

Downie, J. (2003). Music information retrieval. *Annual Review of Information Science and Technology 37,* 1, 295–340.

Draper, S., and Dunlop, M. (1997). New IR-new evaluation: The impact of interactive multimedia on information retrieval and its evaluation. *The New Review of Hypermedia and Multimedia 3,* 107–122.

Dumais, S., Banko, M., Brill, E., Lin, J., and Ng, A. (2002). Web question answering: Is more always better? In *Proceedings of the 25th Annual International ACM SIGIR Conference on Research and Development in Information Retrieval (SIGIR'02),* 291–298.

Dumais, S., Cutrell, E., Cadiz, J., Jancke, G., Sarin, R., and Robbins, D. (2003). Stuff I've seen: A system for personal information retrieval and re-use. In *Proceedings of the 26th Annual International ACM SIGIR Conference on Research and Development in Information Retrieval (SIGIR'03),* 72–79.

Dumais, S., Cutrell, E., and Chen, H. (2001). Optimizing search by showing results in context. In *Proceedings of the SIGCHI Conference on Human Factors in Computing Systems (CHI'01),* 277–284.

Dumais, S., and Nielsen, J. (1992). Automating the assignment of submitted manuscripts to reviewers. In *Proceedings of the 15th Annual International ACM SIGIR Conference on Research and Development in Information Retrieval (SIGIR'92),* 233–244.

Dziadosz, S., and Chandrasekar, R. (2002). Do thumbnail previews help users make better relevance decisions about Web search results. In *Proceedings of the*

25th Annual International ACM SIGIR Conference on Research and Development in Information Retrieval (SIGIR'02), 365–366.

Eastman, C., and Jansen, B. (2003). Coverage, relevance, and ranking: The impact of query operators on Web search engine results. *ACM Transactions on Information Systems (TOIS) 21*, 4, 383–411.

Egan, D., Remde, J., Gomez, L., Landauer, T., Eberhardt, J., and Lochbaum, C. (1989a). Formative design evaluation of SuperBook. *Transaction on Information Systems 7*, 1.

Egan, D., Remde, J., Landauer, T., Lochbaum, C., and Gomez, L. (1989b). Behavioral evaluation and analysis of a hypertext browser. In *Proceedings of the SIGCHI Conference on Human Factors in Computing Systems (CHI'89)*, 205–210.

Eick, S. G. (1994). Graphically displaying text. *Journal of Computational and Graphical Statistics 3*, 2, 127–142.

Ekstrom, R., French, J., Harman, H., and Dermen, D. (1976). *Kit of Factor-Referenced Cognitive Tests*. Educational Testing Service, Princeton, NJ.

Ellis, D. (1989). A behavioural model for information retrieval system design. *Journal of Information Science 15*, 237–247.

English, J., Hearst, M., Sinha, R., Swearingen, K., and Yee, K.-P. (2001). Examining the usability of web site search. Unpublished manuscript, http://flamenco.berkley.edu/papers/epicurious-study.pdf.

Evans, B., and Chi, E. H. (2008). Towards a model of understanding social search. In *Proceedings of the 2008 ACM Conference on Computer Supported Cooperative Work (CSCW'08)*, 485–494.

Eysenbach, G., and Kohler, C. (2002). How do consumers search for and appraise health information on the world wide web? Qualitative study using focus groups, usability tests, and in-depth interviews. *British Medical Journal 324*, 7337, 573–577.

Fass, A., Forlizzi, J., and Pausch, R. (2002). MessyDesk and MessyBoard: Two designs inspired by the goal of improving human memory. In *Proceedings of the 4th Conference on Designing Interactive Systems: Processes, Practices, Methods, and Techniques*. ACM Press, New York, NY, USA, 303–311.

Feldman, R., and Sanger, J. (2006). *The Text Mining Handbook*. Cambridge University Press, Boston, MA.

Fellbaum, C. E. (1998). *WordNet: An Electronic Lexical Database*. MIT Press, Cambridge, MA.

Few, S. (2009). *Show Me the Numbers: Designing Tables and Graphs to Enlighten*. Analytics Press, Oakland, CA.

Few, S. (2009). *Information Dashboard Design: The Effective Visual Communication of Data*. O'Reilly, Sebastopol, CA.

Fischer, G. (2001). User modeling in human–computer interaction. *User Modeling and User-Adapted Interaction 11*, 1, 65–86.

Fishkin, K., and Stone, M. C. (1995). Enhanced dynamic queries via movable filters. *Proceedings of the SIGCHI Conference on Human Factors in Computing Systems (CHI'95) 1*, 415–420.

Flickner, M., Sawhney, H., Niblack, W., Ashley, J., Huang, Q., Dom, B., Gorkhani, M., Hafner, J., Lee, D., Petkovic, D., Steele, D., and Yanker, P. (1995). Query by image and video content: The QBIC System. *IEEE Computer 28*, 9, 23–32.

Fluit, C. (2007). Personal Communication. May 2, 2007.

Fogg, B., Swani, P., Treinen, M. et al. (2001). What makes Web sites credible?: A report on a large quantitative study. In *Proceedings of the SIGCHI Conference on Human Factors in Computing Systems (CHI'01)*, 61–68.

Foley, C., Gurrin, C., Jones, G., Lee, H., McGivney, S., O'Connor, N., Sav, S., Smeaton, A. F., and Wilkins, P. (2005). TRECVid 2005 experiments at Dublin City University. In *Proceedings of the Fourteenth Text REtrieval Conference (TREC'05) TREC Video Retrieval Evaluation Online Proceedings (TRECVID)*.

Fowler, R. H., Fowler, W. A. L., and Wilson, B. A. (1991). Integrating query, thesaurus, and documents through a common visual representation. In *Proceedings of the 14th Annual International ACM SIGIR Conference on Research and Development in Information Retrieval (SIGIR'91)*, 142–151.

Fox, E. A., Hix, D., Nowell, L. T., Brueni, D. J., Wake, W. C., Heath, L. S., and Rao, D. (1993). Users, user interfaces, and objects: Envision, a digital library. *Journal of the American Society for Information Science 44*, 8, 480–491.

Fox, S., Karnawat, K., Mydland, M., Dumais, S., and White, T. (2005). Evaluating implicit measures to improve Web search. *ACM Transactions on Information Systems (Tois) 23*, 2, 147–168.

Franzen, K., and Karlgren, J. (2000). Verbosity and interface design. Technical Report T2000, Swedish Institute of Computer Science, Stockholm.

Furnas, G. (1997). Effective view navigation. In *Proceedings of the SIGCHI Conference on Human Factors in Computing Systems (CHI'97)*, 367–374.

Furnas, G., Landauer, T., Gomez, L., and Dumais, S. (1987). The vocabulary problem in human-system communication. *Communications of the ACM 30*, 11, 964–971.

Gauch, S. (2003). Ontology-based personalized search and browsing. *Web Intelligence and Agent Systems 1*, 3, 219–234.

Goldstein, J., Kantrowitz, M., Mittal, V., and Carbonell, J. (1999). Summarizing text documents: Sentence selection and evaluation metrics. In *Proceedings of the 22nd Annual International ACM SIGIR Conference on Research and Development in Information Retrieval (SIGIR'99)*. ACM Press, New York, NY, USA, 121–128.

Gorg, C., Liu, Z., Parekh, N., Singhal, K., and Stasko, J. (2007). Visual analytics with jigsaw. In *Proceedings of the IEEE Symposium on Visual Analytics Science and Technology (VAST'07)*, 201–202.

Graham, A., Garcia-Molina, H., Paepcke, A., and Winograd, T. (2002). Time as essence for photo browsing through personal digital libraries. In *Proceedings of the 2nd ACM/IEEE-CS Joint Conference on Digital Libraries*. ACM Press, New York, NY, USA, 326–335.

Graham, J. (1999). The reader's helper: A personalized document reading environment. In *Proceedings of the SIGCHI Conference on Human Factors in Computing Systems (CHI'99)*, 481–488.

Granitzer, M., Kienreich, W., Sabol, V., Andrews, K., and Klieber, W. (2004). Evaluating a system for interactive exploration of large, hierarchically structured document repositories. In *Proceedings of the IEEE Symposium on Information Visualization (INFOVIS'04)*, 127–133.

Granitzer, M., Kienreich, W., Sabol, V., and Dosinger, G. (2003). WebRat: Supporting agile knowledge retrieval through dynamic, incremental clustering and automatic labelling of Web search result sets. In *Proceedings of the Twelfth International Workshop on Enabling Technologies: Infrastructure for Collaborative Enterprises (WETICE'03)*, 296–301.

Granka, L., Joachims, T., and Gay, G. (2004). Eye-tracking analysis of user behavior in WWW search. In *Proceedings of the 27th Annual International ACM SIGIR Conference on Research and Development in Information Retrieval (SIGIR'04)*, 478–479.

Greene, S., Marchionini, G., Plaisant, C., and Shneiderman, B. (2000). Previews and overviews in digital libraries: designing surrogates to support visual information seeking. *Journal of the American Society for Information Science 51*, 4, 380–393.

Greene, S. L., Devlin, S., Cannata, P., and Gomez, L. (1990). No ifs, ands, or ors: A study of database querying. *International Journal of Man [sic] – Machine Studies 32*, 3, 303–326.

Grimes, C., Tang, D., and Russell, D. (2007). Query logs alone are not enough. In *Proceedings of the 16th International Conference on World Wide Web (WWW'07)*.

Grinstein, G., O'Connell, T., Laskowski, S., Plaisant, C., Scholtz, J., and Whiting, M. (2006). VAST 2006 Contest – A tale of Alderwood. In *Proceedings of the IEEE Symposium on Visual Analytics Science and Technology (VAST'06)*, 215–216.

Guan, Z., and Cutrell, E. (2007). An eye tracking study of the effect of target rank on web search. In *Proceedings of the SIGCHI Conference on Human Factors in Computing Systems (CHI'07)*. ACM Press, New York, NY, USA, 417–420.

Halvey, M., and Keane, M. (2007). An assessment of tag presentation techniques. In *Proceedings of the 16th International Conference on World Wide Web (WWW'07)*, 1313–1314.

Hanani, U., Shapira, B., and Shoval, P. (2001). Information filtering: Overview of issues, research and systems. *User Modeling And User-Adapted Interaction 11*, 3, 203–259.

Hansell, S. (2007). Google keeps tweaking its search engine. *The New York Times*, June 3, 2007.

Harabagiu, S., Pasca, M., and Maiorano, S. (2000). Experiments with open-domain textual question answering. In *Proceedings of the 18th Conference on Computational Linguistics (ACL'00)*, 292–298.

Hargittai, E. (2002). Beyond logs and surveys: In-depth measures of people's Web use skills. *Journal of the American Society for Information Science and Technology 53*, 14, 1239–1244.

Hargittai, E. (2004). Classifying and coding online actions. *Social Science Computer Review 22*, 2, 210–227.

Hargittai, E. (2006). Hurdles to information seeking: Spelling and typographical mistakes during users' online behavior. *Journal of the Association for Information Systems 7*, 1, 52–67.

Harman, D. (1992). Relevance feedback revisited. In *Proceedings of the 15th Annual International ACM SIGIR Conference on Research and Development in Information Retrieval (SIGIR'92)*, 1–10.

Harman, D. (1993). Overview of the first text retrieval conference. In *Proceedings of the 16th Annual International ACM SIGIR Conference on Research and Development in Information Retrieval (SIGIR'93)*, 36–38.

Hassenzahl, M. (2004). The interplay of beauty, goodness, and usability in interactive products. *Human-Computer Interaction 19*, 4, 319–349.

Hauptmann, A., Lin, W., Yan, R., Yang, J., and Chen, M. (2006). Extreme video retrieval: Joint maximization of human and computer performance. In *Proceedings of the 14th Annual ACM International Conference on Multimedia*. ACM Press, New York, NY, USA, 385–394.

Haveliwala, T. (2003). Topic-sensitive pagerank: A context-sensitive ranking algorithm for Web search. *IEEE Transactions on Knowledge and Data Engineering 15*, 4, 784–796.

Havre, S., Hetzler, E., Perrine, K., Jurrus, E., and Miller, N. (2001). Interactive visualization of multiple query results. In *Proceedings of the IEEE Symposium on Information Visualization (INFOVIS'01)*, 105–112.

Havre, S., Hetzler, E., Whitney, P., and Nowell, L. (2002). ThemeRiver: Visualizing thematic changes in large document collections. *IEEE Transactions on Visualization and Computer Graphics*, 9–20.

He, D., and Goker, A. (2000). Detecting session boundaries from Web user logs. In *Proceedings of the 22nd Annual Colloquium on Information Retrieval Research*, 5–7.

Healy, C. (1993). Visualization of multivariate data using preattentive processing. M.Sc. thesis, University of British Columbia, Canada. http://www.csc.ncsu.edu/faculty/healey/download/masters.pdf.

Hearst, M. (1994). Multi-paragraph segmentation of expository text. In *Proceedings of the 32nd Meeting of the Association for Computational Linguistics (ACL'94)*, 9–16.

Hearst, M. (1995). TileBars: Visualization of term distribution information in full text information access. In *Proceedings of the SIGCHI Conference on Human Factors in Computing Systems (CHI'95)*.

Hearst, M. (1996). Improving full-text precision using simple query constraints. In *Proceedings of the Fifth Annual Symposium on Document Analysis and Information Retrieval (SDAIR'96)*.

Hearst, M. (1998). The use of categories and clusters in organizing retrieval results. In T. Strzalkowski, ed., *Natural Language Information Retrieval*. Kluwer Academic Publishers, Boston, MA.

Hearst, M. (1999a). Untangling text data mining. In *Proceedings of the 37th Meeting of the Association for Computational Linguistics (ACL'99)*, 3–10.

Hearst, M. (1999b). User interfaces and visualization. In *Modern Information Retrieval*. Addison-Wesley, MA, 257–324.

Hearst, M. (2000). Next generation Web search: Setting our sites. *IEEE Data Engineering Bulletin 23*, 3, 38–48.

Hearst, M. (2006a). Clustering versus faceted categories for information exploration. *Communcations of the ACM 49*, 4, 59–61.

Hearst, M. (2006b). Design recommendations for hierarchical faceted search interfaces. In *Proceedings of the 29th Annual International ACM SIGIR Conference on Research and Development in Information Retrieval (SIGIR'06) Workshop on Faceted Search*.

Hearst, M., Divoli, A., Guturu, H. et al. (2007). BioText Search Engine: Beyond abstract search. *Bioinformatics 23*, 16, 2196.

Hearst, M., English, J., Sinha, R., Swearingen, K., and Yee, K.-P. (2002). Finding the flow in web site search. *Communications of the ACM 45*, 9.

Hearst, M., Hurst, M., and Dumais, S. (2008). What should blog search look like? *Proceedings of the Seventeenth International Conference on Information and Knowledge Management (CIKM'08) Workshop on Search and Social Media*.

Hearst, M., and Karadi, C. (1997). Cat-a-cone: An interactive interface for specifying searches and viewing retrieval results using a large category hierarchy. In *Proceedings of the 20th Annual International ACM SIGIR Conference on Research and Development in Information Retrieval (SIGIR'97)*.

Hearst, M., and Pedersen, J. (1996). Reexamining the cluster hypothesis: Scatter/gather on retrieval results. In *Proceedings of the 19th Annual International ACM SIGIR Conference on Research and Development in Information Retrieval (SIGIR'96)*, 76–84.

Hearst, M., Pedersen, J., Pirolli, P., Schütze, H., Grefenstette, G., and Hull, D. (1998). Xerox site report: Four TREC-4 tracks. In *Text Retrieval Conference, 4th*.

Hearst, M., and Rosner, D. (2008). Tag clouds: Data analysis tool or social signaller? In *Proceedings of the 41st Annual Hawaii International Conference on System Sciences (HICSS'08)*.

Hearst, M., Smalley, P., and Chandler, C. (2006). Chi course on faceted metadata for information architecture and search. http://flamenco.berkley.edu/talks/chi_course06.pdf.

Heer, J., and Boyd, D. (2005). Vizster: Visualizing online social networks. In *Proceedings of the IEEE Symposium on Information Visualization (INFOVIS'05)*, 5–5.

Heer, J., and Chi, E. (2002). Separating the swarm: Categorization methods for user sessions on the Web. In *Proceedings of the SIGCHI Conference on Human Factors in Computing Systems (CHI'02)*, 243–250.

Heer, J., and Robertson, G. (2007). Animated transitions in statistical data graphics. *Proceedings of the IEEE Symposium on Information Visualization (INFOVIS'07) 13, 6*, 1240–1247.

Heimonen, T., and Jhaveri, N. (2005). Visualizing query occurrence in search result lists. In *Proceedings of the IEEE Symposium on Information Visualization (INFOVIS'05)*, 877–882.

Helft, M. (2008). Changing that home page? Take baby steps. *The New York Times*, October 17, 2008.

Hembrooke, H., Granka, L., Gay, G., and Liddy, E. (2005). The effects of expertise and feedback on search term selection and subsequent learning. *Journal of the American Society for Information Science and Technology 56, 8*, 861–871.

Hemmje, M., Kunkel, C., and Willett, A. (1994). LyberWorld – A visualization user interface supporting fulltext retrieval. In *Proceedings of the 17th Annual International ACM SIGIR Conference on Research and Development in Information Retrieval (SIGIR'94)*, 249–259.

Hendry, D., and Harper, D. (1997). An informal information-seeking environment. *Journal of the American Society for Information Science 48*, 11, 1036–1048.

Herlocker, J., Konstan, J., Terveen, L., and Riedl, J. (2004). Evaluating collaborative filtering recommender systems. *ACM Transactions on Information Systems (Tois) 22*, 1, 5–53.

Hert, C., Jacob, E., and Dawson, P. (2000). A usability assessment of online indexing structures in the networked environment. *Journal of the American Society for Information Science 51*, 11, 971–988.

Hertzum, M., and Frokjaer, E. (1996). Browsing and querying in online documentation: A study of user interfaces and the interaction process. *ACM Transactions on Computer-Human Interaction (ToCHI) 3*, 2, 136–161.

Hetzler, E., and Turner, A. (2004). Analysis experiences using information visualization. *IEEE Computer Graphics and Applications 24*, 5, 22–26.

Heymann, P., Koutrika, G., and Garcia-Molina, H. (2008). Can social bookmarking improve web search? In *Proceedings of the International Conference on Web Search and Web Data Mining*. ACM Press, New York, NY, USA, 195–206.

Hightower, R. R., Ring, L. T., Helfman, J. I., Bederson, B. B., and Hollan, J. D. (1998). Grapical multiscale web histories: A study of padprints. In *Proceedings of the Ninth ACM Conference on Hypertext*.

Hildreth, C. (1989). OPAC research: Laying the groundwork for future OPAC design. *The Online Catalogue: Development and Directions*, 1–24.

Hill, W., Hollan, J., Wroblewski, D., and McCandless, T. (1992). Edit wear and read wear. *Proceedings of the SIGCHI Conference on Human Factors in Computing Systems (CHI'92) 92*, 3–9.

Hoeber, O., and Yang, X. D. (2006). A comparative user study of web search interfaces: HotMap, Concept Highlighter, and Google. In *IEEE/WIC/ACM International Conference on Web Intelligence*.

Hölscher, C., and Strube, G. (2000). Web search behavior of Internet experts and newbies. *Computer Networks 33*, 1–6, 337–346.

Hornbæk, K., and Frøkjær, E. (1999). Do thematic maps improve information retrieval. *Human-Computer Interaction (INTERACT'99)*, 179–186.

Hornbæk, K., and Frøkjær, E. (2001). Reading of electronic documents: The usability of linear, fisheye, and overview + detail interfaces. In *Proceedings of the SIGCHI Conference on Human Factors in Computing Systems (CHI'01)*, 293–300.

Hornbæk, K., and Hertzum, M. (2007). Untangling the usability of fisheye menus. *ACM Transactions on Computer-Human Interaction (ToCHI) 14*, 2.

Hornbæk, K., and Law, E. (2007). Meta-analysis of correlations among usability measures. In *Proceedings of the SIGCHI Conference on Human Factors in Computing Systems (CHI'07)*. ACM Press, New York, NY, USA, 617–626.

Horvitz, E., Breese, J., Heckerman, D., Hovel, D., and Rommelse, K. (1998). The Lumiere project: Bayesian user modeling for inferring the goals and needs of software users. In *Proceedings of the Fourteenth Conference on Uncertainty in Artificial Intelligence*, 256–265.

Hotchkiss, G. (September 21, 2007a). Eye tracking on universal and personalized search. Technical Report, Enquiro Research, British Columbia, Canada. http://searchengineland.com/eye-tracking-on-universal-and-personalized-search-12233.

Hotchkiss, G. (2007b). Just behave: Google's marissa mayer on personalized search. http://searchengineland.com/070223-090000.php.

Hotchkiss, G. (2007c). Q&A with marissa mayer, Google VP, search products & user experience. http://searchengineland.com/070126-124723.php.

Hotchkiss, G., Sherman, T., Tobin, R., Bates, C., and Brown, K. (August 16, 2007). Search engine results: 2010. Technical Report, Enquiro Research, British Columbia, Canada.

Huang, X., Peng, F., An, A., and Schuurmans, D. (2004). Dynamic Web log session identification with statistical language models. *Journal of the American Society for Information Science and Technology 55*, 14, 1290–1303.

Hurst, M. (2002). Interview: Marissa mayer, product manager, Google. http://www.goodexperience.com/blog/archives/000066.php.

Hutchings, D., and Stasko, J. (2002). QuickSpace: New operations for the desktop metaphor. In *Proceedings of the SIGCHI Conference on Human Factors in Computing Systems (CHI'02)*, 802–803.

Hutchinson, H., Bederson, B., and Druin, A. (2006). The evolution of the international children's digital library searching and browsing interface. *Interaction Design and Children*, 105–112.

Ihlwan, M., Woyke, E., and Elgin, B. (2006). NHN: The little search engine that could. Korea's NHN thumps Google at home, and it's teaching the big dogs a new trick. *BusinessWeek Online*.

iProspect. (2008). *iProspect Blended Search Results Study*. iProspect. http://www.iprospect.com/about/researchstudy_2008_blendedsearchresults.htm.

ISO 9241-11. (1998). Ergonomic requirements for office work with visual display terminals (VDTs) – Part 11: Guidance on usability.

Ittycheriah, A., Franz, M., and Roukos, S. (2001). IBM's statistical question answering system – TREC 10. In *Proceedings of the Tenth Text REtrieval Conference (TREC'01)*.

Jacobson, T., and Fusani, D. (1992). Computer, system, and subject knowledge in novice searching of a full-text, multifile database. *Library and Information Science Research 14*, 1, 97–106.

Jameson, A. (2003). Adaptive interfaces and agents. In J. A. Jacko and A. Sears, eds., *Human-Computer Interaction Handbook*. Erlbaum, Mahwah, NJ, 305–330.

Jansen, B., and Spink, A. (2006). How are we searching the World Wide Web? A comparison of nine search engine transaction logs. *Information Processing and Management 42*, 1, 248–263.

Jansen, B., Spink, A., Bateman, J., and Saracevic, T. (1998). Real life information retrieval: A study of user queries on the Web. *SIGIR Forum 32*, 1, 5–17.

Jansen, B., Spink, A., Blakely, C., and Koshman, S. (2007a). Defining a session on Web search engines. *Journal of the American Society for Information Science and Technology 58*, 6, 862–871.

Jansen, B., Spink, A., and Koshman, S. (2007b). Web searcher interaction with the Dogpile.com metasearch engine. *Journal of the American Society for Information Science and Technology 58*, 5, 744–755.

Jansen, B., Spink, A., and Pedersen, J. (2005). A temporal comparison of AltaVista Web searching. *Journal of the American Society for Information Science and Technology 56*, 6, 559–570.

Jarvelin, K., and Ingwersen, P. (2004). Information seeking research needs extension towards tasks and technology. *Information Research 10*, 1, 10–1.

Järvelin, K., and Kekäläinen, J. (2000). IR evaluation methods for retrieving highly relevant documents. In *Proceedings of the 23rd Annual International ACM SIGIR Conference on Research and Development in Information Retrieval*. ACM Press, New York, NY, USA, 41–48.

Jeffries, R., Miller, J., Wharton, C., and Uyeda, K. (1991). User interface evaluation in the real world: A comparison of four techniques. In *Proceedings of the SIGCHI Conference on Human Factors in Computing Systems (CHI'91)*, 119–124.

Jenkins, C., Corritore, C., and Wiedenbeck, S. (2003). Patterns of information seeking on the Web: A qualitative study of domain expertise and Web expertise. *IT & Society 1*, 3, 64–89.

Jhaveri, N., and Raiha, K.-J. (2005). The advantages of a cross-session web workspace. In *Proceedings of the SIGCHI Conference on Human Factors in Computing Systems (CHI'05)*.

Joachims, T. (2002). Optimizing search engines using clickthrough data. In *Proceedings of the Eighth ACM SIGKDD International Conference on Knowledge Discovery and Data Mining (Kdd'02)*, 133–142.

Joachims, T., Freitag, D., and Mitchell, T. (1997). Webwatcher: A tour guide for the World Wide Web. In *Proceedings of 15th International Joint Conference on Artificial Intelligence (IJCAI'97)*.

Joachims, T., Granka, L., Pan, B., Hembrooke, H., and Gay, G. (2005). Accurately interpreting clickthrough data as implicit feedback. In *Proceedings of the 28th Annual International ACM SIGIR Conference on Research and Development in Information Retrieval (SIGIR'05)*, 154–161.

Johnson, B., and Shneiderman, B. (1991). Tree-Maps: A space-filling approach to the visualization of hierarchical information structures. In *Proceedings of the IEEE Symposium on Information Visualization (INFOVIS'91)*, 284–291.

Jones, R., Kumar, R., Pang, B., and Tomkins, A. (2007). "I know what you did last summer": Query logs and user privacy. In *Proceedings of the Sixteenth International Conference on Information and Knowledge Management (CIKM'07)*. ACM Press, New York, NY, USA, 909–914.

Jones, R., Rey, B., Madani, O., and Greiner, W. (2006). Generating query substitutions. In *Proceedings of the 15th International Conference on World Wide Web (WWW'06)*. ACM Press, New York, NY, USA, 387–396.

Jones, S., and McInnes, S. (1998). Graphical query specification and dynamic result previews for a digital library. In *Proceedings of the 11th Annual ACM Symposium on User Interface Software and Technology (UIST'98)*.

Jones, W., Bruce, H., and Dumais, S. (2001). Keeping found things found on the Web. In *Proceedings of the Tenth International Conference on Information and Knowledge Management (CIKM'01)*, 119–126.

Jones, W., Dumais, S., and Bruce, H. (2002). Once found, what then? A study of "keeping" behaviors in the personal use of Web information. *Proceedings of the American Society for Information Science and Technology 39*, 1, 391–402.

Jonker, D., Wright, W., Schroh, D., Proulx, P., and Cort, B. (2005). Information triage with TRIST. In *Proceedings of the International Conference on Intelligence Analysis*.

Kaasinen, E. (2003). User needs for location-aware mobile services. *Personal and Ubiquitous Computing 7*, 1, 70–79.

Kaasten, S., Greenberg, S., and Edwards, C. (2002). How People Recognise Previously Seen Web Pages from Titles, URLs and Thumbnails. *PEOPLE AND COMPUTERS*, 247–266.

Kaisser, M., Hearst, M., and Lowe, J. (2008). Improving search results quality by customizing summary lengths. In *Proceedings of the 46th Annual Meeting of the Association for Computational Linguistics: Human Language Technologies (ACL-HLT'08)*.

Käki, M. (2005a). Enhancing Web search result access with automatic categorization. Ph.D. Dissertation, Dissertations in Interactive Technology, Number 2, University of Tampere, Finland.

Käki, M. (2005b). Findex: Search result categories help users when document ranking fails. In *Proceedings of the SIGCHI Conference on Human Factors in Computing Systems (CHI'05)*, 131–140.

Käki, M. (2005c). Optimizing the number of search result categories. In *Proceedings of the SIGCHI Conference on Human Factors in Computing Systems (CHI'05)*, 1517–1520.

Käki, M., and Aula, A. (2008). Controlling the complexity in comparing search user interfaces via user studies. *Information Processing and Management 44*, 1, 82–91.

Kamba, T., Bharat, K., and Albers, M. C. (1995). The krakatoa chronicle: An interactive, personalized newspaper on the web. In *Proceedings of the 4th International Conference on World Wide Web (WWW'95b)*.

Kamvar, M., and Baluja, S. (2006). A large scale study of wireless search behavior: Google mobile search. In *Proceedings of the SIGCHI Conference on Human Factors in Computing Systems (CHI'06)*, 701–709.

Kang, H., and Shneiderman, B. (2000). Visualization methods for personal photo collections: Browsing and searching in the PhotoFinder. In *IEEE International Conference on Multimedia and Expo (III)*, 1539–1542.

Kanungo, T., and Orr, D. (2009). Predicting the readability of short Web summaries. In *Proceedings of the International Conference on Web Search and Web Data Mining (WSDM'09)*. ACM Press, New York, NY, USA.

Karlson, A. (2006). Personal Communication.

Karlson, A., Robertson, G., Robbins, D., Czerwinski, M., and Smith, G. (2006). FaThumb: A facet-based interface for mobile search. In *Proceedings of the SIGCHI Conference on Human Factors in Computing Systems (CHI'06)*, 711–720.

Keim, D., and Oelke, D. (2007). Literature fingerprinting: A new method for visual literary analysis. In *IEEE Symposium on Visual Analytics Science and Technology, 2007. VAST 2007*, 115–122.

Kekäläinen, J. (2005). Binary and graded relevance in IR evaluations – Comparison of the effects on ranking of IR systems. *Information Processing and Management 41*, 5, 1019–1033.

Kellar, M., Watters, C., and Shepherd, M. (2006). A goal-based classification of Web information tasks. In *Proceedings of American Society for Information Science and Technology Conference*.

Kelly, D., and Cool, C. (2002). The effects of topic familiarity on information search behavior. In *Proceedings of the Second ACM/IEEE-CS Joint Conference on Digital Libraries*, 74–75.

Kelly, D., Dollu, V., and Fu, X. (2005). The loquacious user: A document-independent source of terms for query expansion. In *Proceedings of the 28th Annual International ACM SIGIR Conference on Research and Development in Information Retrieval (SIGIR'05)*, 457–464.

Keppel, G., Saufley, W., and Tokunaga, H. (1992). *Introduction to Design and Analysis*. Freeman and Company, New York.

Kickmeier, M., and Albert, D. (2003). The effects of scanability on information search: An online experiment. *Proceedings of HCI 2003 2*, 33–36.

Kim, J., Oard, D., and Romanik, K. (2001). User modeling for information access based on implicit feedback. In *3rd Symposium of ISKO – France, Information Filtering and Automatic Summarisation in Networds*.

Kimber, D., and Wilcox, L. (1997). Acoustic segmentation for audio browsers. *Computing Science and Statistics*, 295–304.

Kleiboemer, A., Lazear, M., and Pedersen, J. (1996). Tailoring a retrieval system for naive users. In *Proceedings of the Fifth Annual Symposium on Document Analysis and Information Retrieval (SDAIR '96)*.

Koenemann, J., and Belkin, N. (1996). A case for interaction: A study of interactive information retrieval behavior and effectiveness. *Proceedings of the SIGCHI Conference on Human Factors in Computing Systems (CHI'96) 1*, 205–212.

Kohavi, R., Henne, R., and Sommerfield, D. (2007). Practical guide to controlled experiments on the web: Listen to your customers not to the hippo. In *Proceedings of the 13th ACM SIGKDD International Conference on Knowledge Discovery and Data Mining (KDD'07)*. ACM Press, New York, NY, USA, 959–967.

Kohavi, R., Longbotham, R., Sommerfield, D., and Henne, R. (2008). Controlled experiments on the Web: Survey and practical guide. *Data Mining and Knowledge Management*.

Kohavi, R., Mason, L., Parekh, R., and Zheng, Z. (2004). Lessons and challenges from mining retail E-commerce data. *Machine Learning 57*, 1, 83–113.

Kohler, J., Larson, M., de Jong, F., Kraaij, W., and Ordelman, R. (2008). Spoken content retrieval: Searching spontaneous conversational speech. *ACM SIGIR Forum 42*, 2, 66–75.

Korfhage, R. R. (1991). To see or not to see – Is that the query? In *Proceedings of the 14th Annual International ACM SIGIR Conference on Research and Development in Information Retrieval (SIGIR'91)*, 134–141.

Kozierok, R., and Maes, P. (1993). A learning interface agent for scheduling meetings. In *Proceedings of the 1993 International Workshop on Intelligent User Interfaces*, 81–88.

Kuhlthau, C. (1991). Inside the search process: Information seeking from the user's perspective. *Journal of the American Society for Information Science 42*, 5, 361–371.

Kukich, K. (1992). Techniques for automatically correcting words in text. *ACM Computing Surveys 24*, 4.

Kules, B., and Shneiderman, B. (2008). Users can change their web search tactics: Design guidelines for categorized overviews. *Information Processing and Management 44*, 2, 463–484.

Kummamuru, K., Lotlikar, R., Roy, S., Singal, K., and Krishnapuram, R. (2004). A hierarchical monothetic document clustering algorithm for summarization and browsing search results. In *Proceedings of the 13th International Conference on World Wide Web (WWW'04)*, 658–665.

Kuniavsky, M. (2003). *Observing the User Experience: A Practitioner's Guide to User Research*. Morgan Kaufmann, San Francisco, CA.

Kupiec, J. (1993). MURAX: A robust linguistic approach for question answering using an on-line encyclopedia. In *Proceedings of the 16th Annual International ACM SIGIR Conference on Research and Development in Information Retrieval (SIGIR'93)*, 181–190.

Kupiec, J., Pedersen, J., and Chen, F. (1995). A trainable document summarizer. In *Proceedings of the 18th Annual International ACM SIGIR Conference on Research and Development in Information Retrieval (SIGIR'95)*, 68–73.

Kushmerick, N., and Lau, T. (2005). Automated email activity management: An unsupervised learning approach. In *Proceedings of the 10th International Conference on Intelligent User Interfaces (IUI'05)*, 67–74.

Kwok, K. L. (2005). An attempt to identify weakest and strongest queries. In *Proceedings of the 28th Annual International ACM SIGIR Conference on Research and Development in Information Retrieval (SIGIR'05) Workshop on Predicting Query Difficulty*.

Kwok, K. L., Grunfeld, L., and Lewis, D. D. (1995). Trec-3 ad-hoc, routing retrieval and thresholding experiments. In *Proceedings of the Fourth Text REtrieval Conference (TREC-4)*.

Lake, M. (1998). Desperately seeking Susan OR Suzie NOT Sushi. *The New York Times*, September 3, 1998.

Lam, H., and Baudisch, P. (2005). Summary thumbnails: Readable overviews for small screen web browsers. In *Proceedings of the SIGCHI Conference on Human Factors in Computing Systems (CHI'05)*, 681–690.

Lamping, J., Rao, R., and Pirolli, P. (1995). A focus+context technique based on hyperbolic geometry for visualizing large hierarchies. In *Proceedings of the SIGCHI Conference on Human Factors in Computing Systems (CHI'95)*, 401–408.

Landauer, T., Egan, D., Remde, J., Lesk, M., Lochbaum, C., and Ketchum, D. (1993). Enhancing the usability of text through computer delivery and formative evaluation: The superbook project. In C. McKnight, A. Dillon, and J. Richardson, eds., *Hypertext: A Psychological Perspective*. Ellis Horwood, Chichester, UK, 71–136.

Larkin, J., and Simon, H. (1987). Why a diagram is (sometimes) worth 10,000 words. *Cognitive Science 11*, 1, 65–99.

Larson, R. (1991). The decline of subject searching: Long-term trends and patterns of index use in an online catalog. *Journal of the American Society for Information Science 42*, 3, 197–215.

Lazonder, A., Biemans, H., and Wopereis, I. (2000). Differences between novice and experienced users in searching information on the World Wide Web. *Journal of the American Society for Information Science 51*, 6, 576–581.

Lee, B., Czerwinski, M., Robertson, G., and Bederson, B. (2005). Understanding research trends in conferences using paperLens. In *Proceedings of the SIGCHI Conference on Human Factors in Computing Systems (CHI'05)*, 1969–1972.

Lesk, M. (1997). *Practical Digital Libraries; Books, Bytes, & Bucks*. Morgan Kaufmann, San Francisco, CA.

Li, M., Zhu, M., Zhang, Y., and Zhou, M. (2006). Exploring distributional similarity based models for query spelling correction. In *Annual Meeting-Association for Computational Linguistics (ACL'06)*.

Lieberman, H. (1995). Letizia: An agent that assists web browsing. In *Proceedings of 14th International Joint Conference on Artificial Intelligence (IJCAI'95)*, 924–929.

Lin, J., DiCuccio, M., Grigoryan, V., and Wilbur, W. (2008). Navigating information spaces: A case study of related article search in PubMed. *Information Processing and Management 44*, 5, 1771–1783.

Lin, J., Quan, D., Sinha, V., Bakshi, K., Huynh, D., Katz, B., and Karger, D. R. (2003). What makes a good answer? The role of context in question answering. In *Proceedings of Human-Computer Interaction (INTERACT'03)*.

Lin, J., and Wilbur, W. (2007). PubMed related articles: A probabilistic topic-based model for content similarity. *BMC Bioinformatics 8*, 1, 423.

Lin, X., Soergel, D., and Marchionini, G. (1991). A self-organizing semantic map for information retrieval. In *Proceedings of the 14th Annual International ACM SIGIR Conference on Research and Development in Information Retrieval (SIGIR'91)*, 262–269.

Linden, G. (2006). Marissa mayer at web 2.0. http://glinden.blogspot.com/2006/11/marissa-mayer-at-web-20.html.

Linden, G., Smith, B., and York, J. (2003). Amazon. com recommendations: Item-to-item collaborative filtering. *IEEE Internet Computing 7*, 1, 76–80.

Lindgaard, G., and Chattratichart, J. (2007). Usability testing: What have we overlooked? In *Proceedings of the SIGCHI Conference on Human Factors in Computing Systems (CHI'07)*.

Lindgaard, G., and Dudek, C. (2003). What is this evasive beast we call user satisfaction? *Interacting with Computers 15*, 3, 429–452.

Little, G., and Miller, R. (2006). Translating keyword commands into executable code. In *Proceedings of the 19th Annual ACM Symposium on User Interface Software and Technology (UIST'06)*. ACM Press, New York, NY, USA, 135–144.

Liu, F., Yu, C., and Meng, W. (2002). Personalized Web search by mapping user queries to categories. In *Proceedings of the Eleventh International Conference on Information and Knowledge Management (CIKM'02)*, 558–565.

Luhn, H. (1959). *Keyword-in-Context Index for Technical Literature (KWIC Index)*. International Business Machines Corp., Advanced Systems Development Division, New York.

Lynch, C. (1992). The next generation of public access information retrieval systems for research libraries – Lessons from 10 years of the melvyl system. *Information Technology and Libraries 11*, 4, 405–415.

Maarek, Y. S., and Wecker, A. (1994). The librarian's assistant: Automatically assembling books into dynamic bookshelves. In *Proceedings of RIAO '94; Intelligent Multimedia Information Retrieval Systems and Management*.

MacKay, B., and Watters, C. (2003). The impact of migration of data to small screens on navigation. *Information Technology and Society 1*, 3, 90–101.

MacKay, B., Watters, C., and Duffy, J. (2004). Web page transformation when switching devices. In *Proceedings of Sixth International Conference on Human Computer Interaction with Mobile Devices and Services (Mobile HCI'04)*.

Mackinlay, J. (1986). Automating the design of graphical presentations of relational information. *ACM Transactions on Graphics 5*, 2.

Mackinlay, J., Rao, R., and Card, S. (1995). An organic user interface for searching citation links. In *Proceedings of the SIGCHI Conference on Human Factors in Computing Systems (CHI'95)*, 67–73.

Malone, T. (1983). How do people organize their desks?: Implications for the design of office information systems. *ACM Transactions on Information Systems (TOIS) 1*, 1, 99–112.

Manber, U., Patel, A., and Robison, J. (2000). Experience with personalization of Yahoo! *Communications of the ACM 43*, 8, 35–39.

Mandel, M., Poliner, G., and Ellis, D. (2006). Support vector machine active learning for music retrieval. *Multimedia Systems 12*, 1, 3–13.

Maple, A. (1995). Faceted access: A review of the literature. *Music Library Association Annual Meeting 10*. http://library.music.indiana.edu/tech_s/mla/facacc.rev.

Marchionini, G. (1989). Information-seeking strategies of novices using a full-text electronic encyclopedia. *Journal of the American Society for Information Science 40*, 1, 54–66.

Marchionini, G. (1995). *Information Seeking in Electronic Environments*. Cambridge University Press, New York.

Marchionini, G., Geisler, G., and Brunk, B. (2000). Agileviews: A human-centered framework for interfaces to information spaces. *Proceedings of the American Society for Information Science Annual Meeting 37*, 271–280.

Marchionini, G., and Levi, M. (2003). Digital government information services: The Bureau of Labor Statistics Case. *Interactions 10*, 4, 18–27.

Marchionini, G., and Shneiderman, B. (1988). Finding facts vs. browsing knowledge in hypertext systems. *Computer 21*, 1, 70–80.

Marchionini, G., and White, R. (2008). Find what you need, understand what you find. *Journal of Human-Computer Interaction 23*, 3, 205–237.

Markoff, J. (2008). Google, iPhone, and the future of machines that listen. *The New York Times*, November 18, 2008.

Marshall, C., Halasz, F., Rogers, R., and Janssen, Jr., W. (1991). Aquanet: A hypertext tool to hold your knowledge in place. In *Proceedings of the Third Annual ACM Conference on Hypertext*, 261–275.

Marshall, C., Shipman, III, F., and Coombs, J. (1994). VIKI: Spatial hypertext supporting emergent structure. In *Proceedings of the 1994 ACM European Conference on Hypermedia Technology*, 13–23.

Martzoukou, K. (2004). A review of web information seeking research: Considerations of method and foci of interest. *Information Research 10*, 2, 10–12.

Maybury, M. (2007). Searching conversational speech. In *Proceedings of the 30th Annual International ACM SIGIR Conference on Research and Development in Information Retrieval (SIGIR'07) Workshop on Searching Spontaneous Conversational Speech*.

Mayhew, D. (1999). *The Usability Engineering Lifecycle: A Practitioner's Handbook for User Interface Design*. ACM Press, New York, NY, USA.

McFadden, E., Hager, D., Elie, C., and Blackwell, J. (2002). Remote usability evaluation: Overview and case studies. *International Journal of Human-Computer Interaction 14*, 3–4, 489–502.

McNab, R., Smith, L., Witten, I., Henderson, C., and Cunningham, S. (1996). Towards the digital music library: Tune retrieval from acoustic input. In *Proceedings of the First ACM International Conference on Digital Libraries*. ACM Press, New York, NY, USA, 11–18.

McNee, S., Albert, I., Cosley, D., Gopalkrishnan, P., Lam, S. K., Rashid, A. M., Konstan, J., and Riedl, J. (2002). On the recommending of citations for research papers. In *Proceedings of the 2002 ACM Conference on Computer Supported Cooperative Work (CSCW'02)*, 116–125.

McNee, S., Kapoor, N., and Konstan, J. (2006). Don't look stupid: Avoiding pitfalls when recommending research papers. In *Proceedings of the 2006 20th Anniversary Conference on Computer Supported Cooperative Work (CSCW'06)*, 171–180.

McSherry, D. (2003). Explanation of retrieval mismatches in recommender system dialogues. In *Proceedings of the ICCBR-03 Workshop on Mixed-Initiative Case-Based Reasoning*, 191–199.

Meadow, C., Cerny, B., Borgman, C., and Case, D. (1989a). Online access to knowledge: System design. *Journal of the American Society for Information Science 40*, 2, 86–98.

Meadow, C., Cerny, B., Borgman, C., and Case, D. (1989b). Online access to knowledge: System design. *Journal of the American Society for Information Science 40*, 2, 86–98.

Meredith, D., and Pieper, J. (2006). Beta: Better extraction through aggregation. In *Proceedings of the 29th Annual International ACM SIGIR Conference on Research and Development in Information Retrieval (SIGIR'06) Workshop on Faceted Search*.

Michard, A. (1982). Graphical presentation of Boolean expressions in a database query language: Design notes and an ergonomic evaluation. *Behaviour and Information Technology 1*, 3.

Milic-Frayling, N., Jones, R., Rodden, K., Smyth, G., Blackwell, A., and Sommerer, R. (2004). Smartback: Supporting users in back navigation. In *Proceedings of the 13th International Conference on World Wide Web (WWW'04)*, 63–71.

Millen, D., Feinberg, J., and Kerr, B. (2006). Dogear: Social bookmarking in the enterprise. In *Proceedings of the SIGCHI Conference on Human Factors in Computing Systems (CHI'06)*, 111–120.

Miller, R., Chou, V., Bernstein, M., Little, G., Van Kleek, M., and Karger, D. (2008). Inky: A sloppy command line for the web with rich visual feedback. In *Proceedings of the 21st Annual ACM Symposium on User Interface Software and Technology (UIST'08)*. ACM Press, New York, NY, USA, 131–140.

Mislove, A., Gummadi, K., and Druschel, P. (2006). Exploiting social networks for Internet search. In *Proceedings of the 5th Workshop on Hot Topics in Networks (HotNets-V), Irvine, CA, November 2006*.

Mitchell, T., Wang, S., Huang, Y., and Cheyer, A. (2006). Extracting knowledge about users' activities from raw workstation contents. In *Proceedings of the Twenty-First National Conference on Artificial Intelligence (AAAI'06)*.

Mitra, M., Singhal, A., and Buckley, C. (1998). Improving automatic query expansion. In *Proceedings of the 21st Annual International ACM SIGIR Conference on Research and Development in Information Retrieval (SIGIR'98)*, 206–214.

Morita, M., and Shinoda, Y. (1994). Information filtering based on user behavior analysis and best match text retrieval. In *Proceedings of the 17th Annual International ACM SIGIR Conference on Research and Development in Information Retrieval (SIGIR'94)*, 272–281.

Morris, M. (2008). A survey of collaborative web search practices. In *Proceedings of the SIGCHI Conference on Human Factors in Computing Systems (CHI'08)*. ACM Press, New York, NY, USA.

Morse, E., Lewis, M., Korfhage, R., and Olsen, K. (1998). Evaluation of text, numeric and graphical presentations for information retrieval interfaces: User preference and task performance measures. *IEEE International Conference on Systems, Man, and Cybernetics 1.*

Morville, P., and Rosenfeld, L. (2006). *Information Architecture for the World Wide Web.* O'Reilly, Cambridge, MA.

Muramatsu, J., and Pratt, W. (2001). Transparent queries: Investigation users' mental models of search engines. In *Proceedings of the 24th Annual International ACM SIGIR Conference on Research and Development in Information Retrieval (SIGIR'01),* 217–224.

Nakarada-Kordic, I., and Lobb, B. (2005). Effect of perceived attractiveness of web interface design on visual search of web sites. In *Proceedings of the 6th ACM SIGCHI New Zealand Chapter's International Conference on Computer-Human Interaction: Making CHI Natural,* 25–27.

Nardi, B. A. (1993). *A Small Matter of Programming: Perspectives on End User Computing.* MIT Press, Cambridge, MA.

Nasukawa, T., and Nagano, T. (2001). Text analysis and knowledge mining system. *IBM Systems Journal 40,* 4, 967–984.

Nation, A. (1997). Visualizing websites using a hierarchical table of contents browser: Webtoc. In *Proceedings of the Third Conference on Human Factors and the Web.*

Newman, M., and Landay, J. (2000). Sitemaps, storyboards, and specifications: A sketch of Web site design practice. In *Proceedings of the 3rd Conference on Designingc Interactive Systems: Processes, Practices, Methods, and Techniques.* ACM Press, New York, NY, USA, 263–274.

Nielsen, J. (1989a). The matters that really matter for hypertext usability. In *Proceedings of the Second Annual ACM Conference on Hypertext,* 239–248.

Nielsen, J. (1989b). Usability engineering at a discount. In *Proceedings of the Third International Conference on Human-Computer Interaction.* Elsevier Science, New York, NY, USA, 394–401.

Nielsen, J. (1992). Finding usability problems through heuristic evaluation. In *Proceedings of the SIGCHI Conference on Human Factors in Computing Systems (CHI'92),* 373–380.

Nielsen, J. (1993). *Usability Engineering.* Academic Press, Boston, MA.

Nielsen, J. (1994). Guerilla HCI: Using discount usability engineering to penetrate the intimitation barrier. In *Cost-Justifying Usability.* Academic Press, Boston, MA, 245–272. http://www.Useit.Com/Papers/Guerilla_Hci.html.

Nielsen, J. (1998). Personalization is over-rated. http://www.useit.com/alertbox/981004.html.

Nielsen, J. (2000). Why you only need to test with 5 users. http://www.useit.com/alertbox/20000319.html.

Nielsen, J. (2003a). Information foraging: Why Google makes people leave your site faster. http://www.useit.com/alertbox/20030630.html.

Nielsen, J. (2003b). Usability 101. http://www.useit.com/alertbox/20030825.html.

Nielsen, J. (2004a). Deceivingly strong information scent costs sales. http://www.useit.com/alertbox/20040801.html.

Nielsen, J. (2004b). When search engines become answer engines. http://www.useit.com/alertbox/20040816.html.

Nielsen, J. (2007). Breadcrumb navigation increasingly useful. http://www.useit.com/alertbox/breadcrumbs.html.

Nielsen, J., and Landauer, T. (1993). A mathematical model of the finding of usability problems. In *Proceedings of the INTERCHI Conference on Human Factors in Computing Systems (CHI'93),* 206–213.

Nielsen, J., and Loranger, H. (2006). *Prioritizing Web Usability*. New Riders, Berkeley, CA.

Nielsen, J., and Pernice, K. (2009). *Eyetracking Web Usability*. New Riders, Berkeley, CA.

Norman, D. (1988). *The Psychology of Everyday Things*. Basic Books, New York.

Norman, D. (2004). *Emotional Design: Why We Love (or Hate) Everyday Things*. Basic Books, New York.

Norman, D. (2007a). *The Design of Future Things*. Basic Books, New York.

Norman, D. (2007b). The next UI breakthrough: Command lines. *Interactions 14*, 3, 44–45.

O'Day, V. L., and Jeffries, R. (1993). Orienteering in an information landscape: How information seekers get from here to there. In *Proceedings of the INTERCHI Conference on Human Factors in Computing Systems (CHI'93)*. IOS Press, Amsterdam.

Oddy, R. (1977). Information retrieval through man-machine dialogue. *Journal Documentation 33*, 1–14.

O'Hara, K., and Sellen, A. (1997). A comparison of reading paper and on-line documents. In *Proceedings of the SIGCHI Conference on Human Factors in Computing Systems (CHI'97)*.

Olsen, K., Korfhage, R., Sochats, K., Spring, M., and Williams, J. (1993). Visualization of a document collection with implicit and explicit links – The vibe system. *Scandinavian Journal of Information Systems 5*, 79–95.

Olson, T. (2007). Utility of a faceted catalog for scholarly research. *Library Hi Tech 25*, 4, 550–561.

Öquist, G., and Goldstein, M. (2003). Towards an improved readability on mobile devices: Evaluating adaptive rapid serial visual presentation. *Interacting with Computers 15*, 4, 539–558.

Oviatt, S., and Darrell, T. (2004). Multimodal interfaces that flex, adapt, and persist. *Communications of the ACM 47*, 1, 31.

Oviatt, S., DeAngeli, A., and Kuhn, K. (1997). Integration and synchronization of input modes during multimodal human-computer interaction. In *Proceedings of the SIGCHI Conference on Human Factors in Computing Systems*. ACM Press, New York, NY, USA, 415–422.

Paek, T., Dumais, S., and Logan, R. (2004). WaveLens: A new view onto internet search results. In *Proceedings of the SIGCHI Conference on Human Factors in Computing Systems (CHI'04)*, 727–734.

Page, L., Brin, S., Motwani, R., and Winograd, T. (1998). The PageRank citation ranking: Bringing order to the Web. Tech. rep., Stanford Digital Library Technologies Project.

Paley, W. (2002). TextArc: Showing word frequency and distribution in text. *Proceedings of the IEEE Symposium on Information Visualization (INFOVIS'02) Poster presentation 2002*.

Parikh, N., and Sundaresan, N. (2008). Inferring semantic query relations from collective user behavior. *Proceedings of the Seventeenth International Conference on Information and Knowledge Management (CIKM'08)*.

Parush, A., Nadir, R., and Shtub, A. (1998). Evaluating the layout of graphical user interface screens: Validation of a numerical computerized model. *International Journal of Human-Computer Interaction 10*, 4.

Patterson, E., Roth, E., and Woods, D. (2001). Predicting vulnerabilities in computer-supported inferential analysis under data overload. *Cognition, Technology & Work 3*, 4, 224–237.

Pazzani, M., Billsus, D., and Muramatsu, J. (1996). Syskill & webert: Identifying interesting web sites. In *Proceedings of the Thirteenth Annual National Conference on Artificial Intelligence (AAAI'96)*.

Pedersen, G. S. (1993). A browser for bibliographic information retrieval, based on an application of lattice theory. In *Proceedings of the 16th Annual International ACM SIGIR Conference on Research and Development in Information Retrieval (SIGIR'93)*, 270–279.

Pedersen, J., Cutting, D., and Tukey, J. (1991). Snippet search: A single phrase approach to text access. In *Proceedings of the 1991 Joint Statistical Meetings*.

Peterson, R. (1997). Eight Internet search engines compared. *First Monday 2*, 2.

Pew. (2008a). Pew Internet project data memo, video sharing Websites. http://www.pewinternet.org/pdfs/Pew_Videosharing_memo_Jan08.pdf.

Pew. (2008b). Tracking survey. http://www.pewinternet.org/trends/Internet_Activities_7.22.08.htm.

Pickens, J., Golovchinsky, G., Shah, C., Qvarfordt, P., and Back, M. (2008). Algorithmic mediation for collaborative exploratory search. In *Proceedings of the 31st Annual International ACM SIGIR Conference on Research and Development in Information Retrieval (SIGIR'08)*. ACM Press, New York, NY, USA, 315–322.

Pierrakos, D., Paliouras, G., Papatheodorou, C., and Spyropoulos, C. (2003). Web usage mining as a tool for personalization: A survey. *User Modeling and User-Adapted Interaction 13*, 4, 311–372.

Pinker, S. (2007). *The stuff of thought: Language as a window into human nature*. Viking.

Piontek, S., and Garlock, K. (1996). Creating a World Wide Web resource collection. *Internet Research: Electronic Networking Applications and Policy 6*, 4, 20–26.

Pirolli, P. (2007). *Information Foraging Theory*. Oxford University Press, New York.

Pirolli, P., and Card, S. (1999). Information foraging. *Psychological Review 106*, 4, 643–675.

Pirolli, P., and Card, S. (2005). The sensemaking process and leverage points for analyst technology as identified through cognitive task analysis. In *Proceedings of the 2005 International Conference on Intelligence Analysis*.

Pirolli, P., Card, S., and Van Der Wege, M. (2003). The effects of information scent on visual search in the hyperbolic tree browser. *ACM Transactions on Computer-Human Interaction (TOCHI) 10*, 1, 20–53.

Pirolli, P., Schank, P., Hearst, M., and Diehl, C. (1996). Scatter/gather browsing communicates the topic structure of a very large text collection. In *Proceedings of the SIGCHI Conference on Human Factors in Computing Systems (CHI'96)*. ACM, Vancouver, Canada.

Pitkow, J., and Pirolli, P. (1999). Mining longest repeating subsequences to predict WWW surfing. In *Proceedings of the 1999 Usenix Annual Technical Conference*, 139–150.

Pitkow, J., Schütze, H., Cass, T., Turnbull, D., Edmonds, A., and Adar, E. (2002). Personalized search. *Communications of the ACM 45*, 9, 50–55.

Plaisant, C., Bruns, T., Shneiderman, B., and Doan, K. (1997a). Query previews in networked information systems: The case of EOSDIS. *Proceedings of the SIGCHI Conference on Human Factors in Computing Systems (CHI'97) 2*, 202–203.

Plaisant, C., Marchionini, G., Bruns, T., Komlodi, A., and Campbell, L. (1997b). Bringing treasures to the surface: Iterative design for the Library of Congress National Digital Library Program. In *Proceedings of the SIGCHI Conference on Human Factors in Computing Systems (CHI'97)*, 518–525.

Plaisant, C., Rose, J., Yu, B., Auvil, L., Kirschenbaum, M. G., Smith, M. N., Clement, T., and Lord, G. (2006). Exploring erotics in Emily Dickinson's correspondence with text mining and visual interfaces. In *Proceedings of the 6th ACM/IEEE-CS Joint Conference on Digital Libraries*, 141–150.

Plaisant, C., Shneiderman, B., Doan, K., and Bruns, T. (1999). Interface and data architecture for query preview in networked information systems. *ACM Transactions on Information Systems (TOIS) 17*, 3, 320–341.

Platt, J., Czerwinski, M., and Field, B. (2003). PhotoTOC: Automatic clustering for browsing personal photographs information, communications and signal processing. In *Proceedings of the Fourth IEEE Pacific-Rim Conference on Multimedia*.

Plumlee, M., and Ware, C. (2006). Zooming versus multiple window interfaces: Cognitive costs of visual comparisons. *ACM Transactions on Computer-Human Interaction (TOCHI) 13*, 2, 179–209.

Pollitt, A. (1997). Interactive information retrieval based on faceted classification using views. In *Proceedings of the 6th International Study Conference on Classification (FID/CR)*.

Pollock, A., and Hockley, A. (1997). What's wrong with Internet searching. *D-Lib Magazine*. www.dlib.org.

Pratt, W., Hearst, M., and Fagan, L. (1999). A knowledge-based approach to organizing retrieved documents. In *Proceedings of 16th Annual Conference on Artificial Intelligence (AAAI 99)*.

Proulx, P., Tandon, S., Bodnar, A., Schroh, D., Harper, R., and Wright, W. (2006). Avian flu case study with nSpace and GeoTime. In *Proceedings of the IEEE Symposium on Visual Analytics Science and Technology (VAST'06)*. IEEE, Baltimore, MA.

Pu, H., Chuang, S., and Yang, C. (2002). Subject categorization of query terms for exploring Web users' search interests. *Journal of the American Society for Information Science and Technology 53*, 8, 617–630.

Qiu, F., and Cho, J. (2006). Automatic identification of user interest for personalized search. In *Proceedings of the 15th International Conference on World Wide Web (WWW'06)*, 727–736.

Rainie, L. (2008). The future of the Internet III. http://www.pewinternet.org/pdfs/PIP_FutureInternet3.pdf.

Ramakrishnan, G., and Paranjpe, D. (2004). Is question answering an acquired skill? In *Proceedings of the 13th International Conference on World Wide Web (WWW'04)*, 111–120.

Ranganathan, S. (1933). *Colon Classification, Basic Classification*. Asia Publishing House, New York.

Ranie, L. (2006). Digital "natives" invade the workplace. http://pewresearch.org/pubs/70/digital-natives-invade-the-workplace.

Rao, R., Card, S., Jellinek, H., MacKinlay, J., and Robertson, G. (1992). The information grid: A framework for building information retrieval and retrieval-centered applications. In *Proceedings of the ACM Symposium on User Interface Software and Technology*. ACM Press, New York, USA.

Rao, R., Card, S., Johnson, W., Klotz, L., and Trigg, R. (1994). Protofoil: Storing and finding the information worker's paper documents in an electronic file cabinet. In *Proceedings of the SIGCHI Conference on Human Factors in Computing Systems (CHI'94)*, 180–185.

Rao, R., Pedersen, J., Hearst, M., MacKinlay, J., Card, S., Masinter, L., Halvorsen, P.-K., and Robertson, G. (1995). Rich interaction in the digital library. *Communications of the ACM 38*, 4, 29–39.

Ravichandran, D., and Hovy, E. (2001). Learning surface text patterns for a question answering system. In *Proceedings of the 40th Annual Meeting on Association for Computational Linguistics (ACL'01)*, 41–47.

Reiterer, H., Mußler, G., Mann, T., and Handschuh, S. (2000). INSYDER – An information assistant for business intelligence. In *Proceedings of the 23th Annual International ACM SIGIR Conference on Research and Development in Information Retrieval (SIGIR'00)*, 112–119.

Reiterer, H., Tullius, G., and Mann, T. (2005). Insyder: A content-based visual-information-seeking system for the web. *International Journal on Digital Libraries 5*, 1, 25–41.

Rennison, E. (1994). Galaxy of news: An approach to visualizing and understanding expansive news landscapes. In *Proceedings of the 7th Annual ACM Symposium on User Interface Software and Technology (UIST'94)*, 3–12.

Resnick, P., and Varian, H. (1997). Introduction: Special issue on collaborative filtering. *Communications of the ACM 40*, 3, 56–58.

Rettig, M. (1994). Prototyping for tiny fingers. *Communications of the ACM 37*, 4.

Rieh, S. (2002). Judgment of information quality and cognitive authority in the Web. *Journal of the American Society for Information Science and Technology 53*, 2, 145–161.

Rivadeneira, A., Gruen, D., Muller, M., and Millen, D. (2007). Getting our head in the clouds: Toward evaluation studies of tagclouds. In *Proceedings of the SIGCHI Conference on Human Factors in Computing Systems (CHI'07)*.

Rivadeneira, W., and Bederson, B. (2003). A study of search result clustering interfaces: Comparing textual and zoomable user interfaces. Technical Report HCIL-2003-36, CS-TR-4682, University of Maryland, College Park, MD.

Robertson, G., Card, S., and MacKinlay, J. (1993). Information visualization using 3D interactive animation. *Communications of the ACM 36*, 4, 56–71.

Robertson, G., Czerwinski, M., Larson, K., Robbins, D., Thiel, D., and van Dantzich, M. (1998). Data mountain: Using spatial memory for document management. In *Proceedings of the 11th Annual ACM Symposium on User Interface Software and Technology (UIST'98)*, 153–162.

Robertson, S., and Hull, D. (2001). The Trec-9 filtering track final report. In *Proceedings of the Tenth Text REtrieval Conference (TREC'01)*, 25–40.

Rodden, K., Basalaj, W., Sinclair, D., and Wood, K. R. (2001). Does organisation by similarity assist image browsing? In *Proceedings of the SIGCHI Conference on Human Factors in Computing Systems (CHI'01)*, 190–197.

Rodden, K., Milic-Frayling, N., Sommerer, R., and Blackwell, A. (2003). Effective Web searching on mobile devices. In *Proceedings of the 17th Annual Conference on Human-Computer Interaction (HCI 2003)*, 281–296.

Rogers, L., and Chapparo, B. (2003). Breadcrumb navigation: Further investigation of usage. *Usability News, Wichita Software Usability Research Laboratory 5*.

Rose, A., Ding, W., Marchionini, G., Beale, Jr., J., and Nolet, V. (1998). Building an electronic learning community: From design to implementation. In *Proceedings of the SIGCHI conference on Human factors in computing systems*. ACM Press/Addison-Wesley Publishing Co. New York, NY, USA, 203–210.

Rose, D. (2004). Why is Web search so hard . . . to evaluate? *Journal of Web Engineering 3*, 3–4, 171–181.

Rose, D. (2006). Reconciling information-seeking behavior with search user interfaces for the Web. *Journal of the American Society of Information Science and Technology 57*, 6, 797–799.

Rose, D., and Levinson, D. (2004). Understanding user goals in Web search. In *Proceedings of the 13th International Conference on World Wide Web (WWW'04)*, 13–19.

Rose, D., Mander, R., Oren, T., Ponceleon, D., Salomon, G., and Wong, Y. (1993). Content awareness in a file system interface: Implementing the "pile" metaphor for organizing information. In *Proceedings of the 13th Annual International ACM SIGIR Conference on Research and Development in Information Retrieval (SIGIR'90)*, 260–269.

Rose, D., Orr, D., and Kantamneni, R. (2007). Summary attributes and perceived search quality. In *Proceedings of the 16th International Conference on World Wide Web (WWW'07)*. ACM Press, New York, NY, USA, 1201–1202.

Rui, Y., Huang, T., Ortega, M., and Mehrotra, S. (1998). Relevance feedback: A power tool for interactive content-based image retrieval. *IEEE Transactions on Circuits and Systems for Video Technology 8*, 5, 644–655.

Russell, D. (2006). How do Google searchers behave? Improving search by divining intent. Lecture. http://hci.stanford.edu/cs547/abstracts/05-06/060310-russell.html.

Russell, D., Slaney, M., Qu, Y., and Houston, M. (2006). Being literate with large document collections: Observational studies and cost structure tradeoffs. In *Proceedings of the 39th Annual Hawaii International Conference on System Sciences (HICSS'06)*.

Russell, D., Stefik, M., Pirolli, P., and Card, S. (1993). The cost structure of sensemaking. In *Proceedings of the INTERCHI Conference on Human Factors in Computing Systems (CHI'93)*. Conceptual Analysis of Users and Activity, 269–276.

Ruthven, I., and Lalmas, M. (2003). A survey on the use of relevance feedback for information access systems. *The Knowledge Engineering Review 18*, 2, 95–145.

Sahami, M., Yusufali, S., and Baldonado, M. Q. W. (1998). SONIA: A service for organizing networked information autonomously. In *Proceedings of the Third Annual Conference on Digital Libraries*, 200–209.

Sakagami, H., and Kamba, T. (1997). Learning personal preferences on online newspaper articles from user behaviors. *Proceedings of the 16th International Conference on World Wide Web (WWW'07) 29*, 8–13, 1447–1455.

Salton, G. (1989). *Automatic Text Processing: The Transformation, Analysis, and Retrieval of Information by Computer*. Addison-Wesley, Reading, MA.

Salton, G., and Buckley, C. (1990). Improving retrieval performance by relevance feedback. *Journal of the American Society for Information Science 41*, 4, 288–297.

Saracevic, T. (1997). The stratified model of information retrieval interaction: Extension and applications. *Proceedings of the American Society for Information Science 34*, 2, 313–27.

Saracevic, T. (2007). Relevance: A review of the literature and a framework for thinking on the notion in information science. Part III: Behavior and effects of relevance. *Journal of the American Society for Information Science and Technology 58*, 13, 2126–2144.

Sarwar, B., Konstan, J., Herlocker, J., Miller, B., and Riedl, J. (1998). Using filtering agents to improve prediction quality in the GroupLens research collaborative filtering system. In *Proceedings of the 1998 ACM Conference on Computer Supported Cooperative Work (CSCW'98)*, 345–354.

Schacter, J., Chung, G., and Dorr, A. (1998). Children's internet searching on complex problems: Performance and process analyses. *Journal of the American Society for Information Science 49*, 9, 840–849.

Schraefel, M., Smith, D., Owens, A., Russell, A., and Harris, C. (2005). The evolving mSpace platform: Leveraging the semantic Web on the trail of the Memex. In *Proceedings of the 16th ACM Conference on Hypertext and Hypermedia*, 6–9.

Schusteritsch, R., Rao, S., and Rodden, K. (2005). Mobile search with text messages: Designing the user experience for google SMS. In *Proceedings of the SIGCHI Conference on Human Factors in Computing Systems (CHI'05)*, 1777–1780.

Schütze, H., and Pedersen, J. (1994). A cooccurrence-based thesaurus and two applications to information retrieval. In *Proceedings of the Riao Conference: Research in Intelligent Multimedia Information Retrieval Systems and Management*, 266–274.

Sebastiani, F. (2002). Machine learning in automated text categorization. *ACM Computing Surveys (CSUR) 34*, 1, 1–47.

Sebrechts, M., Vasilakis, J., Miller, M., Cugini, J., and Laskowski, S. (1999). Visualization of search results: A comparative evaluation of text, 2D and 3D interfaces. In *Proceedings of the 22nd Annual International ACM SIGIR Conference on Research and Development in Information Retrieval (SIGIR'99)*, 3–10.

Sharanand, U., and Maes, P. (1995). Social information filtering: Algorithms for automating word of mouth. In *Proceedings of the SIGCHI Conference on Human Factors in Computing Systems (CHI'95)*.

Shen, D., Pan, R., Sun, J., Pan, J. J., Wu, K., Yin, J., and Yang, Q. (2005a). Q2C@UST: Our winning solution to query classification in KDDCUP 2005. *ACM SIGKDD Explorations Newsletter 7*, 2, 100–110.

Shen, X., Tan, B., and Zhai, C. (2005b). Context-sensitive information retrieval using implicit feedback. In *Proceedings of the 28th Annual International ACM SIGIR Conference on Research and Development in Information Retrieval (SIGIR'05)*, 43–50.

Sherman, C. (2001). Google goes for stop words. http://searchenginewatch.com/2158311.

Shipman, F., Marshall, C., and Moran, T. (1995). Finding and using implicit structure in human-organized spatial layouts of information. *Proceedings of the SIGCHI Conference on Human Factors in Computing Systems (CHI'95) 1*, 346–353.

Shneiderman, B. (1994). Dynamic queries for visual information seeking. *IEEE Software 11*, 6, 70–77.

Shneiderman, B. (2008). Personal Communication. December.

Shneiderman, B., and Aris, A. (2006). Network visualization by semantic substrates. *IEEE Transactions on Visualization and Computer Graphics 12*, 5.

Shneiderman, B., Byrd, D., and Croft, W. (1997). Clarifying search: A user-interface framework for text searches. *DL Magazine*.

Shneiderman, B., Byrd, D., and Croft, W. (1998). Sorting out searching: A user-interface framework for text searches. *Communications of the ACM 41*, 4, 95–98.

Shneiderman, B., Feldman, D., Rose, A., and Grau, X. (2003). Visualizing digital library search results with categorical and hierarchical axes. In *The Craft of Information Visualization: Readings and Reflections*.

Shneiderman, B., and Kang, H. (2000). Direct annotation: A drag-and-drop strategy for labeling photos. In *Proceedings of the International Conference on Information Visualisation (IV'00)*.

Shneiderman, B., and Maes, P. (1997). Direct manipulation vs. interface agents. *Interactions 4*, 6, 42–61.

Shneiderman, B., and Plaisant, C. (2004). *Designing the User Interface: Strategies for Effective Human-Computer Interaction, 4th edn*. Addison-Wesley, Reading, MA.

Shneiderman, B., and Plaisant, C. (2006). Strategies for evaluating information visualization tools: Multi-dimensional in-depth long-term case studies. In

Proceedings of the 2006 Conference Advanced Visual Interfaces (AVI'04), Workshop on Beyond Time and Errors: Novel Evaluation Methods for Information Visualization, 1–7.

Sihvonen, A., and Vakkari, P. (2004). Subject knowledge, Thesaurus-assisted query expansion and search success. In *Proceedings of the Riao Conference: Research in Intelligent Multimedia Information Retrieval Systems and Management*, 393–404.

Silverstein, C., Henzinger, M., Marais, H., and Moricz, M. (1999). Analysis of a very large web search engine query log. *SIGIR Forum 33*, 1, 6–12.

Singh, S., Murthy, H., and Gonsalves, T. (2008). Determining User's Interest in Real Time. *Proceedings of the 17th International Conference on World Wide Web (WWW'08) Poster Session*.

Sinha, R. (2005). Google's pragmatic, data-driven approach to user interface design. http://rashmisinha.com/2005/01/13/googles-pragmatic-data-driven-approach-to-user-interface-design/.

Small, H. (1999). Visualizing science by citation mapping. *Journal of the American Society for Information Science 50*, 9, 799–813.

Smeaton, A., Over, P., and Kraaij, W. (2004). TRECVID: Evaluating the effectiveness of information retrieval tasks on digital video. In *Proceedings of the 12th Annual ACM International Conference on Multimedia*. ACM Press, New York, NY, USA, 652–655.

Snoek, C., Everts, I., van Gemert, J., Geusebrock, J. M., Huurnink, B., Koelma, D. C., van Liempt, M., de Rooij, O., van de Sande, K. E. A., Smeulders, A. W. M., Vijlings, J. R. R., and Worring, M. (2007). The MediaMill TRECVID 2007 semantic video search engine. In *Proceedings of the 5th TRECVID Workshop, November 2007*.

Snow, R., O'Connor, B., Jurafsky, D., and Ng, A. (2008). Cheap and fast but is it good? Evaluating non-expert annotations for natural language tasks. In *Proceedings of the Conference on Empirical Methods in Natural Language Processing (EMNLP 2008)*.

Sohn, T., Li, K. A., Griswold, W. G., and Hollan, J. D. (2008). A diary study of mobile information needs. In *Proceedings of the SIGCHI Conference on Human Factors in Computing Systems (CHI'08)*.

Song, R., Luo, Z., Wen, J.-R., Yu, Y., and Hon, H.-W. (2007). Identifying ambiguous queries in web search. In *Proceedings of the 16th International Conference on World Wide Web (WWW'07) Poster Session*.

Spence, R. (2002). Rapid, serial and visual: A presentation technique with potential. *Information Visualization 1*, 1, 13–19.

Spink, A., Greisdorf, H., and Bateman, J. (1998). From highly relevant to not relevant: Examining different regions of relevance. *Information Processing and Management 34*, 5, 599–621.

Spink, A., Jansen, B., Wolfram, D., and Saracevic, T. (2002). From e-sex to e-commerce: Web search changes. *IEEE Computer 35*, 3, 107–109.

Spoerri, A. (1993). InfoCrystal: A visual tool for information retrieval & management. In *Proceedings of the Second International Conference on Information and Knowledge Management (CIKM'93)*.

Spool, J. (2002). Usability beyond common sense. http://www.bcs-hci.org.uk/talks/Spool/UIE-BeyondCommonSense.pdf.

Spool, J. (2007). Scent of a web page: Getting users to what they want. In *Proceedings of the SIGCHI Conference on Human Factors in Computing Systems (CHI'07) Course Notes*.

Spool, J., and Schroeder, W. (2001). Testing web sites: Five users is nowhere near enough. In *Proceedings of the SIGCHI Conference on Human Factors in Computing Systems (CHI'01)*, 285–286.

Stadnyk, I., and Kass, R. (1992). Modeling users' interests in information filters. *Communications of the ACM 35*, 12, 49–50.

Stanfill, C., and Kahle, B. (1986). Toward memory-based reasoning. *Communications of the ACM 29*, 12, 1213–1228.

Steinberg, S. (1996). Seek and ye shall find (maybe). *Wired 4*, 5, 108–114.

Stockburger, D. W. (1998). *Introductory Statistics: Concepts, Models, and Applications* [Online]. http://www.psychstat.missouristate.edu/sbk00.htm.

Stoica, E., Hearst, M., and Richardson, M. (2007). Automating creation of hierarchical faceted metadata structures. In *Human Language Technologies: The Annual Conference of the North American Chapter of the Association for Computational Linguistics (NAACL-HLT 2007)*, 244–251.

Sugiura, A., and Koseki, Y. (1998). Internet scrapbook: Automating Web browsing tasks by demonstration. In *Proceedings of the 11th Annual ACM Symposium on User Interface Software and Technology (UIST'98)*. ACM Press, New York, NY, USA, 9–18.

Sugiyama, K., Hatano, K., and Yoshikawa, M. (2004). Adaptive web search based on user profile constructed without any effort from users. In *Proceedings of the 13th International Conference on World Wide Web (WWW'04)*, 675–684.

Sutcliffe, A., and Ennis, M. (1998). Towards a cognitive theory of information retrieval. *Interacting with Computers 10*, 321–351.

Swan, R., and Allan, J. (1998). Aspect windows, 3-D visualizations, and indirect comparisons of information retrieval systems. In *Proceedings of the 21st Annual International ACM SIGIR Conference on Research and Development in Information Retrieval (SIGIR'98)*, 173–181.

Sweeney, S., and Crestani, F. (2006). Effective search results summary size and device screen size: Is there a relationship? *Information Processing and Management 42*, 4, 1056–1074.

Tabatabai, D., and Shore, B. (2005). How experts and novices search the Web. *Library & Information Science Research 27*, 2, 222–248.

Tan, B., Shen, X., and Zhai, C. (2006). Mining long-term search history to improve search accuracy. In *Proceedings of the 12th ACM SIGKDD International Conference on Knowledge Discovery and Data Mining (KDD'06)*, 718–723.

Tanin, E., Shneiderman, B., and Xie, H. (2007). Browsing large online data tables using generalized query previews. *Information Systems 32*, 3, 402–423.

Tao, T., and Zhai, C. (2007). An exploration of proximity measures in information retrieval. In *Proceedings of the 30th Annual International ACM SIGIR Conference on Research and Development in Information Retrieval (SIGIR'07)*. ACM Press, New York, NY, USA, 295–302.

Teevan, J., Adar, E., Jones, R., and Potts, M. (2006). History repeats itself: Repeat queries in Yahoo's logs. In *Proceedings of the 29th Annual International ACM SIGIR Conference on Research and Development in Information Retrieval (SIGIR'06)*, 703–704.

Teevan, J., Adar, E., Jones, R., and Potts, M. (2007). Information re-retrieval: Repeat queries in Yahoo's logs. In *Proceedings of the 30th Annual International ACM SIGIR Conference on Research and Development in Information Retrieval (SIGIR'07)*. ACM Press, New York, NY, USA, 151–158.

Teevan, J., Alvarado, C., Ackerman, M., and Karger, D. (2004). The perfect search engine is not enough: A study of orienteering behavior in directed search. In *Proceedings of the 27th Annual International ACM SIGIR Conference on Research and Development in Information Retrieval (SIGIR'04)*, 415–422.

Teevan, J., Dumais, S., and Horvitz, E. (2005a). Beyond the commons: Investigating the value of personalizing Web search. In *Proceedings of the Workshop on New Technologies for Personalized Information Access (Pia)*.

Teevan, J., Dumais, S., and Horvitz, E. (2005b). Personalizing search via automated analysis of interests and activities. In *Proceedings of the 28th Annual International ACM SIGIR Conference on Research and Development in Information Retrieval (SIGIR'05)*, 449–456.

Teevan, J., Dumais, S. T., and Liebling, D. J. (2008). To personalize or not to personalize: Modeling queries with variation in user intent. In *Proceedings of the 31st Annual International ACM SIGIR Conference on Research and Development in Information Retrieval (SIGIR'08)*. ACM Press, New York, NY, USA, 163–170.

Teevan, J., Jones, W., and Bederson, B. B. (2006). Special issue on personal information management. *Communications of the ACM 49*, 1.

Thies, W., Prevost, J., Mahtab, T., Cuevas, G., Shakhshir, S., Artola, A., Vo, B., Litvak, Y., Chan, S., Henderson, S., Halsey, M., Levison, L., and Amarasinghe, S. (2002). Searching the World Wide Web in low-connectivity communities. In *Proceedings of the 11th International Conference on World Wide Web (WWW'02)*.

Thompson, P., Turtle, H., Yang, B., and Flood, J. (1995). Trec-3 ad-hoc retrieval and routing experiments using the win system. In *Proceedings of the Fourth Text REtrieval Conference (TREC-4)*.

Thompson, R., and Croft, B. (1989). Support for browsing in an intelligent text retrieval system. *International Journal of Man [sic] – Machine Studies 30*, 6, 639–668.

Tombros, A., and Sanderson, M. (1998). Advantages of query biased summaries in information retrieval. In *Proceedings of the 21st Annual International ACM SIGIR Conference on Research and Development in Information Retrieval (SIGIR'98)*, 2–10.

Tombros, T., and Crestani, F. (2000). Users' perception of relevance of spoken documents. *Journal of the American Society for Information Science 51*, 10, 929–939.

Tory, M., Sprague, D., Wu, F., So, W., and Munzner, T. (2007). Spatialization design: Comparing points and landscapes. *Transactions on Visualization and Computer Graphics 13*, 6, 1262–1269.

Triesman, A. (1985). Preattentive processing in vision. *Computer Vision, Graphics and Image Processing 31*, 156–177.

Tufte, E. (1983). *The Visual Display of Quantitative Information*. Graphics Press, Chelshire, CT.

Tufte, E. (1990). *Envisioning Information*. Graphics Press, Cheshire, CT.

Tufte, E. R. (2006). *Beautiful Evidence*. Graphics Press, LLC.

Twidale, M., and Nichols, D. (1998). Designing interfaces to support collaboration in information retrieval. *Interacting with Computers 10*, 2, 177–193.

Twidale, M., Nichols, D., and Paice, C. (1997). Browsing is a collaborative process. *Information Processing and Management 33*, 6, 761–783.

Uramoto, N., Matsuzawa, H., Nagano, T., Murakami, A., Takeuchi, H., and Takeda, K. (2004). A text-mining system for knowledge discovery from biomedical documents. *IBM Systems Journal 43*, 3, 516–533.

Vakkari, P. (2000a). Cognition and changes of search terms and tactics during task performance: A longitudinal case study. In *Riao 2000 Content-Based Multimedia Information Access*, 12–14.

Vakkari, P. (2000b). Relevance and contributing information types of searched documents in task performance. In *Proceedings of the 23th Annual International ACM SIGIR Conference on Research and Development in Information Retrieval (SIGIR'00)*, 2–9.

Vakkari, P., and Hakala, N. (2000). Changes in relevance criteria and problem stages in task performance. *Journal of Documentation 56*, 5, 540–562.

van der Heijden, H. (2003). Factors influencing the usage of websites: The case of a generic portal in the Netherlands. *Information & Management 40*, 6, 541–549.

van Schaik, P., and Ling, J. (2005). Five psychometric scales for online measurement of the quality of human–computer interaction in Web sites. *International Journal of Human-Computer Interaction 18*, 3, 309–322.

Varadarajan, R., and Hristidis, V. (2006). A system for query-specific document summarization. In *Proceedings of the Fifteenth International Conference on Information and Knowledge Management (CIKM'06)*. ACM Press, New York, NY, USA, 622–631.

Veerasamy, A., and Belkin, N. (1996). Evaluation of a tool for visualization of information retrieval results. In *Proceedings of the 19th Annual International ACM SIGIR Conference on Research and Development in Information Retrieval (SIGIR'96)*, 85–92.

Veerasamy, A., and Heikes, R. (1997). Effectiveness of a graphical display of retrieval results. In *Proceedings of the 20th Annual International ACM SIGIR Conference on Research and Development in Information Retrieval (SIGIR'97)*, 236–245.

Viégas, F., and Donath, J. (2004). Social network visualization: Can we go beyond the graph. *Proceedings of the 2006 20th Anniversary Conference on Computer Supported Cooperative Work (CSCW'06), Workshop on Social Networks 4*, 6–10.

Viégas, F., Wattenberg, M., van Ham, F., Kriss, J., and McKeon, M. (2007). Many eyes: A site for visualization at Internet scale. *IEEE Transactions on Visualization and Computer Graphics 13*, 6, 1121–1128.

Vignoli, F., and Pauws, S. (2005). A music retrieval system based on user-driven similarity and its evaluation. In *Proceedings of the International Conference on Music Information Retrieval (ISMIR'05)*.

Virzi, R., Sokolov, J., and Karis, D. (1996). Usability problem identification using both low-and high-fidelity prototypes. In *Proceedings of the SIGCHI Conference on Human Factors in Computing Systems (CHI'96)*, 236–243.

Voorhees, E. (1994). Query expansion using lexical-semantic relations. In *Proceedings of the 17th Annual International ACM SIGIR Conference on Research and Development in Information Retrieval (SIGIR'94)*, 61–69.

Voorhees, E. (1999). The TREC-8 question answering track report. *Proceedings of the Eighth Text REtrieval Conference (TREC-8) 8*, 77–82.

Voorhees, E. (2003). Overview of the TREC 2003 question answering track. In *Proceedings of the Twelfth Text REtrieval Conference (TREC'03)*.

Voorhees, E. (2004). Overview of the TREC 2004 robust track. In *Proceedings of the Thirteenth Text REtrieval Conference (TREC'04)*.

Voorhees, E., and Harman, D. (2000). Overview of the sixth text retrieval conference (TREC-6). *Information Processing and Management 36*, 1, 3–35.

Wærn, A. (2004). User involvement in automatic filtering: An experimental study. *User Modeling and User-Adapted Interaction 14*, 2, 201–237.

Ware, C. (2004). *Information Visualization: Perception for Design*. Morgan Kaufmann, San Francisco, CA.

Waterworth, J., and Chignell, M. (1991). A model of information exploration. *Hypermedia 3*, 1, 35–58.

Wattenberg, M. (1999). Visualizing the stock market. In *Proceedings of the SIGCHI Conference on Human Factors in Computing Systems (CHI'99) Extended Abstracts*, 188–189.

Wattenberg, M., and Fernand Viégas, B. (2008). The word tree, an interactive visual concordance. *Visualization and Computer Graphics, IEEE Transactions on 14*, 6, 1221–1228.

Wattenberg, M., and Kriss, J. (2006). Designing for social data analysis. *IEEE Transactions on Visualization and Computer Graphics 12*, 4, 549–557.

Wen, J.-R., Nie, J., and Zhang, H. (2002). Query clustering using user logs. *ACM Transactions on Information Systems (TOIS) 20*, 1, 59–81.

West, R., and Lehman, K. (2006). Automated summative usability studies: An empirical evaluation. In *Proceedings of the SIGCHI Conference on Human Factors in Computing Systems (CHI'06)*. ACM Press, New York, NY, USA, 631–639.

Westerman, S., and Cribbin, T. (2000). Mapping semantic information in virtual space: Dimensions, variance and individual differences. *International Journal of Human-Computers Studies 53*, 5, 765–787.

White, R., Bilenko, M., and Cucerzan, S. (2007). Studying the use of popular destinations to enhance Web search interaction. In *Proceedings of the 30th Annual International ACM SIGIR Conference on Research and Development in Information Retrieval (SIGIR'07)*.

White, R., Jose, J., and Ruthven, I. (2003a). A task-oriented study on the influencing effects of query-biased summarisation in web searching. *Information Processing and Management 39*, 5, 707–733.

White, R., Jose, J., and Ruthven, I. (2003b). Using top-ranking sentences for Web search result presentation. In *Proceedings of the 12th International Conference on World Wide Web (WWW'03)*.

White, R., and Marchionini, G. (2007). Examining the effectiveness of real-time query expansion. *Information Processing and Management 43*, 3.

White, R., and Morris, D. (2007). Investigating the querying and browsing behavior of advanced search engines users. In *Proceedings of the 30th Annual International ACM SIGIR Conference on Research and Development in Information Retrieval (SIGIR'07)*.

White, R., Ruthven, I., and Jose, J. (2005). A study of factors affecting the utility of implicit relevance feedback. In *Proceedings of the 28th Annual International ACM SIGIR Conference on Research and Development in Information Retrieval (SIGIR'05)*, 35–42.

Whiting, M., and Cramer, N. (2002). WebTheme: Understanding Web information through visual analytics. In *Proceedings of the First International Semantic Web Conference (ISWC'02)*. Springer-Verlag, London, UK, 460–468.

Whittaker, S., and Hirschberg, J. (2001). The character, value, and management of personal paper archives. *ACM Transactions on Computer-Human Interaction (TOCHI) 8*, 2, 150–170.

Whittaker, S., Hirschberg, J., Choi, J., Hindle, D., Pereira, F., and Singhal, A. (1999). SCAN: Designing and evaluating user interfaces to support retrieval from speech archives. In *Proceedings of the 22nd Annual International ACM SIGIR Conference on Research and Development in Information Retrieval (SIGIR'99)*. ACM Press, New York, NY, USA, 26–33.

Whittaker, S., Hirschberg, J., and Nakatani, C. (1998). All talk and all action: Strategies for managing voicemail messages. In *Conference on Human Factors in Computing Systems*. ACM Press, New York, NY, USA, 249–250.

Whitworth, B. (2005). Polite computing. *Behaviour & Information Technology 24*, 5, 353–363.

Wildemuth, B. (2004). The effects of domain knowledge on search tactic formulation. *Journal of the American Society for Information Science and Technology 55*, 3, 246–258.

Willett, P. (1988). Recent trends in hierarchical document clustering: A critical review. *Information Processing and Management 24*, 5, 577–597.

Wilson, T. (1981). On user studies and information needs. *Journal of Librarianship 37*, 1, 3–15. http://informationr.net/tdw/publ/papers/1981infoneeds.htm.

Wise, J. A., Thomas, J. J., Pennock, K., Lantrip, D., Pottier, M., and Schur, A. (1995). Visualizing the non-visual: Spatial analysis and interaction with information from text documents. In *Proceedings of the IEEE Symposium on Information Visualization (INFOVIS'95)*. IEEE Computer Society Press, Washington, DC, 51–58.

Wittenburg, K., Forlines, C., Lanning, T., Esenther, A., Harada, S., and Miyachi, T. (2003). Rapid serial visual presentation techniques for consumer digital video devices. In *Proceedings of the 16th Annual ACM Symposium on User Interface Software and Technology (UIST'03)*. ACM Press, New York, NY, USA, 115–124.

Wittenburg, K., and Sigman, E. (1997). Integration of browsing, searching, and filtering in an applet for web information access. In *Proceedings of the SIGCHI Conference on Human Factors in Computing Systems (CHI'97)*. ACM Press, New York, NY, USA.

Wobbrock, J., Forlizzi, J., Hudson, S., and Myers, B. (2002). WebThumb: Interaction techniques for small-screen browsers. In *Proceedings of the 15th Annual ACM Symposium on User Interface Software and Technology (UIST'02)*, 205–208.

Woodruff, A., Faulring, A., Rosenholtz, R., Morrison, J., and Pirolli, P. (2001). Using thumbnails to search the Web. In *Proceedings of the SIGCHI Conference on Human Factors in Computing Systems (CHI'01)*, 198–205.

Wright, W., Schroh, D., Proulx, P., Skaburskis, A., and Cort, B. (2006). The sandbox for analysis–concepts and methods. In *Proceedings of the SIGCHI Conference on Human Factors in Computing Systems (CHI'06)*. ACM Press, New York, NY, USA.

Wroblewski, L. (2006). Granular bucket testing. http://www.lukew.com/ff/entry.asp?372.

Wu, Y., Shankar, L., and Chen, X. (2003). Finding more useful information faster from web search results. In *Proceedings of the Twelfth International Conference on Information and Knowledge Management (CIKM'03)*, 568–571.

Xiao, X., Luo, Q., Hong, D., Fu, H., Xie, X., and Ma, W.-Y. (2009). Facilitating hierarchical browsing on small displays. *ACM Transactions on the Web (TWeb)*. To appear.

Xie, X., Miao, G., Song, R., Wen, J.-R., and Ma, W. (2005). Efficient browsing of Web search results on mobile devices based on block importance model. In *Proceedings of the Third IEEE International Conference on Pervasive Computing and Communications (PERCOM'05)*, 17–26.

Xiong, L., and Agichtein, E. (2007). Towards privacy-preserving query log publishing. In *Proceedings of the 16th International Conference on World Wide Web (WWW'07) Workshop on Query Log Analysis: Social and Technological Challenges*.

Xu, J., and Croft, W. (1996). Query expansion using local and global document analysis. In *Proceedings of the 19th Annual International ACM SIGIR Conference on Research and Development in Information Retrieval (SIGIR'96)*, 4–11.

Yan, T., and Garcia-Molina, H. (1995). SIFT – A tool for wide-area information dissemination. *Proceedings of the 1995 USENIX Technical Conference 186*.

Yanbe, Y., Jatowt, A., Nakamura, S., and Tanaka, K. (2007). Towards improving Web search by utilizing social bookmarks. *Lecture Notes in Computer Science 4607*, 343.

Yang, B., and Jeh, G. (2006). Retroactive answering of search queries. In *Proceedings of the 15th International Conference on World Wide Web (WWW'06)*, 457–466.

Yee, K.-P., Fisher, D., Dhamija, R., and Hearst, M. (2001). Animated exploration of dynamic graphs with radial layout. In *Proceedings of the IEEE Symposium on Information Visualization (INFOVIS'01)*, 43–50.

Yee, K.-P., Swearingen, K., Li, K., and Hearst, M. (2003). Faceted metadata for image search and browsing. In *Proceedings of the SIGCHI Conference on Human Factors in Computing Systems (CHI'03)*. ACM Press, New York, NY, USA, 401–408.

Young, D., and Shneiderman, B. (1993). A graphical filter/flow model for Boolean queries: An implementation and experiment. *Journal of the American Society for Information Science 44*, 6, 327–339.

Zamir, O., and Etzioni, O. (1999). Grouper: A dynamic clustering interface to Web search results. *Proceedings of the 8th International Conference on World Wide Web (WWW'99) 31*, 11–16, 1361–1374.

Zhang, C., Chen, S., and Shyu, M. (2003). PixSO: A system for video shot detection. In *Proceedings of the Fourth IEEE Pacific-Rim Conference on Multimedia*, 1–5.

Zhang, J., and Marchionini, G. (2005). Evaluation and evolution of a browse and search interface: Relation browser. In *Proceedings of the 2005 National Conference on Digital Government Research*, 179–188.

Zhang, X., Anghelescu, H., and Yuan, X. (2005). Domain knowledge, search behaviour, and search effectiveness of engineering and science students: An exploratory study. *Information Research 10*, 2.

Zhu, Y., Modjeska, D., Wigdor, D., and Zhao, S. (2002). Hunter gatherer: Interaction support for the creation and management of within-web-page collections. In *Proceedings of the 11th International Conference on World Wide Web (WWW'02)*. ACM Press, New York, NY, USA, 172–181.

Index

3D, 170, 178, 261, 273, 275, 278–280, 283, 285, 287, 292–293, 297

A/B testing. *See* bucket testing
abraham lincoln, 110, 114
abstracts. *See* summaries
adaptive filtering, 216, 226
Adobe Labs, 132
ads, xv
Aduna, 269, 280
advertisements, xv, 28, 135, 158
advice seeking queries, 84
aesthetics, 26–28, 45–46
agileviews, 164, 171
alerts, 214–215, 221–222, 224–225, 231–232
Alices Adventures in Wonderland, 286, 300
AltaVista, 17, 53, 84, 85, 112, 117, 141, 146, 147
Amazon, 44, 131, 136, 220, 231
ambiguous queries, 87, 134, 141, 150, 156, 204, 209, 214, 220
AMIT, 185, 193
Amway, 96
analysis. *See* sensemaking
analytical tasks, 235, 245
anchoring, 79, 142, 147
AND-based ranking, *see* conjunction-based queries
animation, 238, 248
answer types, 98, 101
AOL, 110, 114
Apple, 300, 302, 305, 316, 319, 322, 323, 341
apple, 177, 185
Aquanet, 169, 177
Ariadne, 165, 173
art history collection, 190–193, 199–201

Ask, 12, 95, 97, 105, 109
audio collections, 313, 330
audio search, 312–313, 329–332
auto-suggest. *See* dynamic term suggestions
Autofocus, 269, 280
automobile data collection, 239–240, 249–251

baby naming, 293, 307
bandwidth, 297, 313
bar charts, 234, 244, 258, 273
BEAD, 273, 287
Berkeley, 21
berry-picking, 67–69
BETA, 283, 297
between-participants design, 41, 51
bibliographic systems, 4, 92, 94, 107, 112, 159–160, 165–167, 173, 190, 199
big dog, 110, 114
bike, 182, 190
Bill, 277, 290
bioscience collection, 16, 19, 148, 154, 161, 186, 194, 207, 217
BioText, 10, 148, 154, 267
Blackberry, 23, 300, 316
blackberry, 23
blended results, 134, 141, 315, 333
blind relevance feedback, 153, 160
Blinkx, 316, 334
blogs, 323, 341
bookmarks, 158, 164
Boolean syntax, 3, 4, 72, 99–103, 107–114, 119, 163, 170, 275, 288
  + operator, 112, 117
  "all the words", 111, 116
  "any of the words", 111, 116
  adjacency operator, 108, 112

Boolean syntax (*Cont.*)
  conjunction operator, 108, 112
  difficulties of, 3, 108–109, 112–113
  disjunction operator, 108, 112
  double-quote operator, 110, 114
  faceted queries, 111, 115
  filters, 111, 116
  form-based interfaces, 111, 116
  mandatory operator, 112, 117
  morphological analysis, 110, 114
  NEAR operator, 110, 114
  post-coordinate queries, 110, 114
  query term proximity, 110, 114
  question mark operator, 108, 112
  visualizations, 247–251, 258–262
  Web forms, 111, 116
  wildcard operators, 109, 114
breadcrumbs, 19, 163–164, 170–171, 193,
    196, 203, 205
browsing. *See* navigation
brushing and linking, 238, 247, 286, 300
bucket testing, 49–52

camera price, 24
card sorting, 25
cards, 165, 173
Cat-a-Cone, 273, 285
categories, 20, 75, 77, 174–198, 208, 224–225,
    234–235
  faceted, 21, 174, 182, 188–196, 205,
    208–210, 217–221, 267–273, 279–285
  flat, 21, 174–190
  hierarchical, 21, 174, 182, 187–188,
    195–196, 224, 234, 247, 256
cats, 207, 217
cats dogs fish mice, 110, 115
Cha-Cha, 54, 185, 193
ChaCha, 302, 318, 322, 340
charge for use, 4
checkboxes, 149, 154
Chickenfoot, 322, 341
child searchers, 59, 95, 97, 270, 283
Chrome, 19, 104, 106, 129, 134, 158, 164, 252,
    263
chronological order, 245, 253
chronological ordering, 16, 47, 109, 113, 136,
    141
citation analysis, 129, 134, 294–296, 309–311
clavical surgery, 16
click logs. *See* clickthrough; query logs
clickthrough, 87, 133, 139, 225–228, 235–238,
    318, 336
clickthrough inversion, 122, 126
clustering, 175, 183, 199–210, 221, 273–278,
    285–292

monothetic, 200, 203–206, 210, 214–217
  polythetic, 200–203, 210–213
Clusty, 207, 217
Co-op, 159, 165, 177, 184, 208, 218
cognitive abilities, 57, 235, 245
collaborative filtering, 218–221, 229–231
collaborative search, 318–321, 336–339
collection characteristics, 4, 158, 165
collections
  art history, 190, 199
  audio, 313, 330
  bioscience, 16, 19, 148, 154, 161, 186, 194,
    207, 217
  Cranfield, 61
  email, 11, 136, 141, 181, 188, 230, 240
  images, 190, 199, 307, 324
  news, 4, 228, 238
  personal information, 181, 188
  sports collections, 175, 183
  TREC, 31
  video, 310, 327
color coding, 237, 247, 263, 274, 284, 298
color highlighting, 9, 129, 134, 252, 263
command languages, 4, 91, 94, 114–124,
    322–323, 340–341
  difficulties of, 3
  sequences of queries, 115, 120
  shortcuts, 117, 122
  Web forms, 116, 122
concordances, 286–288, 300–303
conjunction-based queries, 16, 93–94, 96–97
controlled experiments. *See* formal usability
    studies
cooperative search. *See* collaborative search
cost structure analysis. *See* foraging theory
cover flow, 139, 144
Cranfield collection, 61
crowdsourcing, 44
curation, 158, 165
customization, 213, 224

Data Mountain, 170, 178
database systems, xv, 95, 98, 112, 118
DCG. *See* discounted cumulative gain
deep links. *See* sitelinks
DeepDyve, 99, 102
Delicious, 218, 228, 317, 335
dependent variables, 40
design guidelines, 6–28
  aesthetics, 26–28
  balance user control, 14–18
  feedback, 7–14
  reduce errors, 23–25
  reduce memory load, 18–21
  shortcuts, 22–23

small details, 25–26
transparency, 14–18, 101, 103
design process, 5–6
  iterative design, 6
  needs assessment, 6
  task analysis, 6
design space, 6
Dewey Decimal System, 190, 199
Dialog, 108, 112, 115, 120, 163, 170
dialogue interfaces, 162, 169, 323, 341
Digg, 218, 228, 317, 335
digital libraries, 165, 173, 270, 283
directories, 158, 165, 178, 186, 187, 195
discount usability testing, 6, 34
discounted cumulative gain, 34
distortion-based techniques, 238, 248
diversity, 87, 132, 134, 137, 141
DLITE, 165–168, 173–176
Docuburst, 288, 303
document summaries. *See* summaries
document surrogates. *See* surrogates
DOE OSTI, 11
Dogpile, 85, 93, 95, 150, 156
dogs and cats, 108, 113
drop-down menus, 11, 19, 101, 111, 158, 163, 189, 269
Dynacat, 186, 194
dynamic term suggestions, 12, 105–112, 300, 317

e-commerce sites, 214, 224
eBay, 105, 109, 110, 115, 181, 188
  eBay Express, 195–196, 204–205
ecological validity, 46
economic vs. exhaustive scanning, 139, 144
effectiveness, 5, 30
efficiency, 5, 30
elderly searchers, 2
Ella Fitzgerald, 196, 205
email collections, 11, 136, 141, 181, 188, 230, 240
empty results, 24, 113, 118, 167, 174, 189, 197
Enso, 322, 341
entry forms, 91, 94, 101–104, 108
  color, 103, 106
  faceted queries, 111, 116
  grayed-out instructions, 18, 21, 103, 106
  hints, 103, 106
  length, 101–104
  size, 103, 106
  wording, 103, 104
ERIC, 111, 116
ESPN, 175, 183
ESPN, 213, 224
evaluation, 29–63

experiment design, 40–43
guidelines, 52–63
  encourage participant motivation, 53–54
  experimenter bias, 53
  experts, 57
  individual differences, 54–57
  novices, 57
  participants' cognitive abilities, 57
  participants' knowledge, 55
  participants' search experience, 56
  strong baseline, 62
  task differences, 57–60
  test collections, 60–61
  timing, 61–62
informal usability testing, 34–36
number of participants, 36
number of tasks, 36
query and task bias, 60
query logs, 47–52
query variability, 59
questionnaires, 44–45
stardard IR evaluation, 30–34
task variability, 58–59
experiment design, 40–43
expert searchers, 5, 57, 82, 95, 98, 114, 115, 119, 120
extracts. *See* summaries
eye movement, 236, 246, 312, 329
eye tracking, 37, 136–139, 141–144, 315, 333

F-measure, 32
faceted navigation, 188–196, 205, 208–210, 217–221, 267–273, 279–285, 305, 323
faceted queries, 111, 115
fact finding, 89
FAQ Finder, 97, 99
Fathumb, 271, 284, 305, 323
FeatureLens, 282, 295
field studies, 36
filter-flow model, 249, 260
filtering, 180–182, 188–190, 214, 216, 225, 226
Findex, 203–205, 214–216
Firefox, 129, 134
fisheye views, 130, 135, 238, 248, 254, 265
Flamenco, 54, 189–195, 197–204, 267, 280
Flickr, 316, 333
focus-plus-context, 183, 191
foraging theory, 73–74
  information consumption, 74
  information patches, 74, 76
  information scent, 76–77
ForkBrowser, 312

Forkbrowser, 329
formal usability studies, 36–46
    aesthetics, 45–46
    balancing condition order, 39–43
    between-participants design, 41
    blocking, 40
    consent forms, 37
    dependent variables, 40
    experiment design, 40–43
    hypotheses, 40
    independent variables, 40
    Latin Square, 41–43
    learning effects, 39
    pilot testing, 39
    remote usability testing, 39
    within-participants design, 41
FreeBase, 323, 341
full-sentence queries. *See* natural language
    queries
full text, 4, 92, 94, 98, 101
Furl, 218, 228, 317, 335

Galaxy of News, 273, 287
geographic information, 323, 341
Gestalt principles, 237, 247
giants, 179, 187
golden parachute, 96
Google, 1, 16, 17, 23, 26, 28, 110, 114, 118,
        123, 124, 130, 131, 136, 159, 165, 177,
        184, 208, 214, 218, 228, 238, 299, 300,
        314, 317, 318, 322, 336, 340
Google Alerts, 215, 225
Google Answers, 322, 340
Google toolbar, 129, 134
Greco-Latin Square. *See* Latin Square
greyed-out text, 18
Grokker, 277, 291
Grouper, 205, 216
grouping, 177–180, 185–188
guided navigation, 189, 197
gulf of evaluation/execution, 67
gutters, 286, 300

Hakia, 134, 141
Halloween, 97
harry potter, 142, 148
HCI, 5
heuristic evaluation, 36
HIBROWSE, 270, 283
high-fidelity design, 35
highlighting, 124, 128–130, 134–135, 183,
        192, 237, 238, 246, 247, 252–261,
        263–274
    boldface, 128, 134
    color highlighting, 128, 134, 258, 270

query terms, 9, 254, 265
    reverse video, 128, 134, 183, 192
history. *See* search history
hits, 120, 126
how to prevent cheese from
        molding, 123, 130
human question answering, 321–322,
        339–340
Human–Computer Interaction, 5
Hunter Gatherer, 170, 177
hyperbolic tree browser, 247, 256
hyperlinks, 23, 72, 75, 77, 79, 133, 139, 149,
        151, 154, 158, 165, 252, 263, 267, 280

IBM, 282, 283, 295, 297
iBoogie, 207, 217
icons, 131, 137, 241, 253, 284, 286, 298,
        300
image collections, 307, 324
image search, 307–309, 324–326
immediate accuracy, 34
incremental search. *See* dynamic term
        suggestions
independent variables, 40
Infocrystal, 263, 269, 274, 280
Infogrid, 164, 172
informal usability testing, 34–36
information architecture, 76
information canvas, 170, 177
information foraging theory. *See* foraging
        theory
information gathering, 89
information needs, 65, 82–91, 94, 123,
        130
information quality, 158, 165
information scent, 76–77
information seeking, 64–90
information structure, 76
Information Visualizer, 170, 178
informational queries, 84, 137, 144
Infoseek, 1
InfoSky, 273, 276, 287, 289
Inky, 322, 341
instant answers, 300, 317
Insyder, 258–261, 270–273
intellectual property concerns, 124, 130
intelligence analysts, 80–82, 283–286,
        297–300
intermediaries. *See* librarians
Internet Archive, 316, 334
Internet Scrapbook, 170, 177
iPhone, 300, 306, 316, 323
iPod, 305, 323
ipod, 97
iterative design, 6

Japan, 192, 200
jets, 134, 141, 150, 156
Jigsaw, 282, 296
Joe McCarthy, 158, 165
journalists, 4, 180, 187

kayaking, 188, 196
key frames, 310, 327
keyword queries, 1, 2, 20, 24, 91–95, 98, 112,
    117, 192, 201
keyword removal, 13, 217, 228
keyword-in-context. *See* KWIC
kittens, 134, 141
Kohenen's feature maps, 273, 276–277, 287,
    289–291
Korean search, 321, 340
KWIC, 122–130, 135, 286, 300

lab study. *See* formal usability studies
laboratory. *See* usability testing
labrador retrievers, 132, 137
labs, 132, 137
large-scale log-based usability testing.
    See bucket testing
Latent Semantic Indexing, 275, 287
Latin Square, 41–43
lattice views, 263, 275
legal cases, 4, 168, 176
LexisNexis, 160, 167
librarians, 4, 158, 165, 190, 199, 278, 292, 317,
    334
Likert scales, 44–45
line graphs, 234, 244
literature analysis, 286, 294–296, 300,
    309–311
long queries, 80, 97, 100, 322, 340
longitudinal studies, 46–47, 182, 190, 205,
    216, 232, 241
low-fi design, 34–35
low-fidelity prototypes. *See* low-fi design
LSI. *See* Latent Semantic Indexing
Lyberworld, 261, 273

machine learning, 128, 133, 216, 226
Madagascar, 4
magic lenses, 250, 261
Mahalo, 159, 165
mandatory operator, 112, 117
Many Eyes, 289
MAP score, 32
Marilyn Monroe, 96
Markov models, 223, 233
MatchBars, 257, 269
mean average precision. *See* MAP score
media players, 310, 327

MediaMill, 312, 329
mental models, 66
meta-analysis, 235, 244
metadata, 4, 120, 126, 177, 185, 189, 197, 317,
    334
Metaweb, 323, 341
Microsoft, 17, 28, 97, 100, 104, 108, 134, 141,
    150, 156, 170, 177, 302, 316, 318, 333,
    336
misspellings. *See* spelling
    corrections/suggestions
mobile search, 297–306, 313–323
Moby Dick, 92, 94
models of search
    anchoring, 79
    berry-picking, 67–69
    browsing, 74–76
    cognitive model, 66–67
    cost structure analysis, 73–74
    dynamic model, 67–69
    emotional response, 69
    foraging theory, 73–74
    gulf of evaluation/execution, 67
    incremental feedback, 77
    information scent, 76–77
    information seeking cycle, 65
    mental models, 66
    monitoring, 72
    navigability proposition, 76
    Norman's model, 66–67
    orienteering, 77–80
    recognition over recall, 74
    seeking in stages, 69–71
    sensemaking, 66, 80–82, 168–173, 176–179
    standard model, 64–66
    stop conditions, 72
    strategies, 65, 71–80
    tactics, 71–73
    teleporting, 79
    thrashing, 79
    triggers, 72
monitoring, 72
more like this. *See* related articles
morphological analysis, 17, 99–103
motivation, 53–54
MovieLens, 219, 230
MSN/Foxsports, 175, 183
mSpace, 270, 283
MTurk, 44
multilingual search, 323, 341
multimedia search, 91, 94, 135, 141, 306–317,
    323–334
    audio search, 312–313, 329–332
    image search, 307–309, 324–326
    video search, 310–312, 326–329

multi-person search. *See* collaborative
    search
Murax, 96, 99
MyWeb, 218, 228, 318, 336
MyYahoo, 213, 224

NAFTA, 189, 197
Name Voyager, 293, 307
narrowing, 175–177, 183–185
narwhales, 92, 94
natural language queries, 91, 94–95, 97–98,
    322–323, 340–341
navigability proposition, 76
navigation, 20–21, 74–76, 89, 91, 94, 174–210,
    221, 305, 323
navigation paths, 223, 233
navigation structure, 20, 75, 76, 210,
    221
navigational queries, 84, 137, 144
needs assessment, 6
network views. *See* nodes-and-links views
New York Times, 18, 289, 305
news collection, 4, 228, 238
NFL depression concessions, 95, 98
nodes-and-links views, 245, 253, 278, 282,
    292, 294, 296, 308
Nokia, 302, 318
nominal data types, 239–247, 249, 251–256,
    293, 306
non-sensical graph, 241, 252
novice searchers, 3, 57, 82, 94–95, 97–98, 209,
    220
null results. *See* empty results

Obama, 288
Obama, 139, 144
ODP. *See* Open Directory Project
older search systems, 3–5, 9, 107, 112, 115,
    120
Omnifind Analytics, 282, 295
OneNote, 170, 177
OneSearch, 300, 317
Open Directory Project, 86, 180, 187, 195,
    224, 234
ordinal data types, 239, 249
organic results, 135
orienteering, 77–80
osteoporosis, 256, 268
overviews, 130, 135, 164, 171, 254, 261, 265,
    273

PageRank, 16, 224, 234
  topic-based, 224, 234
Pagis Pro, 257, 269
panning, 238, 247

paper prototypes. *See* low-fi design
paragraph-length queries, 15, 98–99,
    101–102
paralegals, 4
parallel flights. *See* bucket testing
parametric search, 189, 197
participants, 34, 43–44
  recruiting, 43–44
perceptual system, 234, 244
peripheral views, 164, 171
personal information, 181, 188, 229–232,
    239–241, 299, 314
personalization, 211–233, 243, 318, 336
  combined explicit and implicit, 229–231,
    239–240
  explicit methods, 213–221, 224–231
  implicit methods, 221–229, 231–239
Phlat, 104, 108, 181–182, 188–190
phonesthesia, 293, 307
pie charts, 258, 270
ping pong, 300, 317
pizza, 300, 317
podcasts, 307, 313, 323, 330
Podscope, 317, 334
popular destination suggestions, 151–152,
    157–159
popularity measure, 16
pornography queries, 85, 299, 314
post-coordinate queries, 110, 114
Powerset, 97, 100, 306, 323
preattentiveness, 236, 246
precision, 9, 16, 32
  alternative measures, 34
  average precision, 32
  immediate accuracy, 34
  MAP score, 32
  precision-at-k, 32
Prelinger, 316, 334
previews, 21, 24, 131, 137, 164, 171
Prisma, 145–147, 151–153
productivity of language. *See* vocabulary
    problem
profiles, 214–217, 224–228, 236–238
Protofoil, 164, 172
prototyping, 6
proximity of query terms, 9, 94, 97, 101, 103,
    128, 134, 237, 247, 254, 266
proximity of terms, 16
pseudo-relevance feedback, 153, 160
PubMed, 19, 154, 161, 163, 170

qualified search speed, 62
quantitative data types, 239, 245, 249,
    253
query box length. *See* entry forms

query classification
  automated, 85–86
  manual, 83–85, 88–90
query history, 19
query intent, 83–88
query length, 93, 95
query logs, 47–52, 83–88, 120–122, 126–128,
      141, 145–147, 150–151, 153, 156–158,
      221–222, 225–229, 231–232, 235–239
  bucket testing, 49–52
  session boundaries, 48–49
  user identity, 49
query operators, 107–114, 119
query previews, 21, 24, 192, 200
query reformulation. *See* reformulation
query specification, 65, 91–119, 125,
      247–252, 258–263
query taxonomies, 83–86
  advice seeking queries, 84
  ambiguous queries, 87
  browsing, 89
  fact finding, 89
  information gathering, 89
  informational queries, 84
  mobile queries, 300, 315
  navigational queries, 84
  pornography queries, 85
  resource queries, 84
  topical queries, 85
  transactional queries, 84
  transactions, 89
query term expansions. *See* query term
      suggestions
query term highlighting. *See* highlighting
query term suggestions, 11, 71, 144–151,
      157, 177, 185, 252, 263
query terms, 252–261, 263–273
query transformations, 16–18, 99, 102
query-oriented summaries, 122–130, 135
  fragments vs. sentences, 127–128, 133
  highlighting, 128–130, 134–135
  sentence selection, 125, 130
  summary length, 125–127, 131–132
question answering, 95–98, 101, 321–322,
      339–340
questionnaires, 44–45
Quicksilver, 322, 341
quorum-level ranking, 110, 114

rabbit, 286, 300
rainbow, 315, 333
Rapid Serial Visual Presentation, 312, 329
re-access. *See* revisitation
re-ranking, 225–228, 235–238
Read Wear/Edit Wear, 129, 134, 252, 263

real-time query expansion, 106, 110
recall, 32, 93, 96, 98, 101
recognition over recall, 20, 74
recommender systems, 217–221, 228–231,
      317, 335
  content-based, 214, 220, 225, 230
  item-based, 220, 230
  user-similarity-based, 218, 229
reformulation, 72, 104, 108, 136, 141–156,
      216, 226
related articles, 154–155, 161–163
RelationBrowser++, 269, 283
relevance, 31–32, 128, 131, 134, 137
  judgements, 31, 34
  non-binary judgements, 34
  relevance judgements, 215–216, 222,
      225–226, 232
  relevance scores shown graphically, 131,
      137
relevance feedback, 152–154, 159–161, 215,
      222, 225, 232, 310, 318, 327, 336
  pseudo-relevance feedback, 153, 160
remote usability testing, 39
resource queries, 84
response variables. *See* dependent variables
results diversity. *See* diversity
results evaluation. *See* search results
      presentations
results listings. *See* search results
      presentations
retinal variables, 237, 247
retrieval results. *See* search results
      presentations
revisitation, 19, 87, 158, 164, 231,
      241
routing, 214, 225
RSVP, 312, 329

Safari, 302, 319
Sally Ride, 107, 112
Sandbox, 170–173, 178–179
satisfaction, 5, 30
scanning, 139, 144, 236, 246, 263, 264, 275,
      276, 312, 315, 329, 333
scatter plots, 258, 273, 275, 279, 287, 292
Scatter/Gather, 200–203, 210–213, 275, 287
screen size, 297, 302, 313, 319
scrollbars, 129, 134, 252, 263
scrolling, 304, 321
  endless scroll, 316, 333
search engine optimization, xv
search history, 19, 158, 162–164, 170–171,
      222–225, 232–235
search hits. *See* search results presentations
search process interfaces, 164–168, 171–176

search results ordering effects, 135–139, 141–144
search results presentations, 8–11, 120–140, 146, 302–306, 319–323
search within, 18
SearchMe, 139, 144, 267, 278
SearchMobil, 303
SearchWiki, 318, 336
SeeSoft, 288, 289, 301, 305
sensemaking, 66, 80–82, 168–173, 176–179, 286, 300
SEO, xv
SERP. *See* search results presentations
server logs. *See* query logs
sessions, 48–49, 151, 158, 222–224, 232–234
    session boundaries, 48–49
    session trails, 151, 158
shortcuts, 117, 122, 133, 139
shots, 310, 327
sitelinks, 23, 133, 139
SketchTrieve, 170, 178
SMS, 300, 317
Snap, 131, 137
Snap Shot, 131
Snapshot, 137
snippets. *See* summaries
social bookmarking, 196–198, 205–208, 218, 228, 317, 335
social ranking, 317–318, 334–336
social search, 317–322, 334–340
social tagging, 196–198, 205–208, 316, 317, 333, 335
    tag clouds, 289, 304
sortable column views, 11, 181, 188, 258, 270
sorting, 180–182, 188–190
    sortable columns, 11, 181, 188, 258, 270
    stable sorting, 181, 188
source selection, 157, 159, 164, 165
Sparkler, 263, 274
sparklines, 238, 249, 261, 273
spatial position, 237, 240, 247, 251
speech. *See* spoken queries
spelling corrections/suggestions, 11, 18, 24, 142–144, 148–150
split testing. *See* bucket testing
spoken queries, 302, 307, 313, 318, 324, 330
sports sites, 175, 183
standing queries, 214, 225
starfields, 273, 285
starting points, 157–162, 164–169
State of the Union Address, 289, 305
statistical data, 160, 167
statistical ranking, 15, 93, 96, 99, 101, 107, 112

stemming
    seemorphological analysis, 17
Steve Jobs, 97
stopwords, 17, 99–103
Stuff I've Seen, 232, 241
StumbleUpon, 317, 335
summaries, 8, 16, 120, 122, 123, 126, 128
    summary length, 9
SuperBook, 182–183, 190–193, 252, 263
surrogates, 8, 91–92, 94–95, 101, 103, 106, 107, 110, 112, 120–123, 126–128, 130
sweet spot, 28, 196, 205
synthesis. *See* sensemaking

table-of-contents views, 123, 182–187, 190–195, 200
tabular views, 245, 253
tag clouds, 289, 304
tagging. *See* social tagging
TAKMI, 282, 295
tamoxifen, 159, 165, 177, 184
task analysis, 6
taste, 219
taxonomies. *See* query taxonomies
tea or coffee, 108, 113
teleporting, 79
TellMe, 302, 318
term expansions, 11, 25, 99–103. *See* query term suggestions
    suffix term expansion, 101, 103
term order variation, 101, 103
text analysis, 281–296, 312
text classification, 99, 102, 199, 208, 215, 225
text messages, 302, 318
text mining, 281–286, 295–300
TextArc, 288, 303
thematic maps, 273–278, 285–292
ThemeRiver, 293, 308
ThemeScapes, 273, 287
thrashing, 79, 142, 147
three dimensional. *See* 3D
thumb typing, 300, 316
Thumbar, 129
ThumbBar, 134, 252, 263
thumbnails, 19, 139, 144, 158, 163–165, 170, 173, 263–267, 275–278, 304, 305, 321, 322
    textually enhanced, 265, 277
TileBars, 254–261, 266–273
timing
    in evaluation, 61–62
    qualified search speed, 62
    response time, 14, 131, 136
    scan times, 252, 263, 264, 276
titles, 115, 116, 120, 122, 126, 245, 253

to be or not to be, 17
TOC. *See* table-of-contents views
Toshagu Shrine, 192, 201
transactional queries, 84, 89
travel sites, 214, 224
TREC, 31–33, 96, 99, 223, 233, 310, 327
    ad hoc track, 31, 33, 99, 101, 123,
        130
    critiques, 32–33
    hard track, 153, 160
    interactive track, 33
    question answering track, 96,
        99
    routing track, 216, 226
    video track, 310, 327
TRECVID, 310, 327
treemaps, 245–247, 256
triage, 283, 297
TRIST, 283–286, 297–300
trucks, 189, 197

U Rank, 318, 336
universal search, 315, 333
URLs, 2, 9, 122, 126
USA Today, 175, 183
usability, 5, 29–30
usability measures
    effectiveness, 5, 30
    efficiency, 5, 30
    errors, 5, 30
    memorability, 5, 30
    satisfaction, 30, 222, 233
    subjective responses, 5, 30
usability testing
    discount testing, 6
    formal studies, 6
    informal studies, 6
    usability laboratory, 37
user modeling, 214, 225
user satisfaction. *See* satisfaction
user-centered design, 5, 34

Valentina Tereshkova, 107, 112
VAST, 286, 300
Venn Diagrams, 247, 259
vertical sites, 163, 170, 175, 183, 315, 323,
        333, 341
VIBE, 261, 269, 273, 280
video collections, 310, 327
video search, 310–312, 326–329
VIKI, 169, 177
virtual keyboard, 300, 316
Visual WordNet, 294, 308

visualization, 14, 130, 131, 135, 137, 139, 144,
        234–280, 294
    Boolean queries, 247–251, 262
    data types, 238–247, 249–256
    faceted navigation, 267–273, 279–285
    nominal data types, 239–247, 249,
        251–256, 293, 306
    principles, 235–247, 256
    query specification, 247–252, 258–263
    query term suggestions, 252, 263
    query terms, 252–261, 263–273
    text analysis, 281–296, 312
    thumbnails, 263–267, 275–278
visualization, 218, 228
Vivisimo, 207, 217, 277, 291
vocabulary problem, 24–25
voice queries. *See* spoken queries
VQuery, 248, 259

weather in Berkeley, 133, 139
Web 2.0, 317, 334
Web Book, 139, 144
Web browsers, 19, 104, 106, 158, 163, 164,
        170
    address bar, 2, 104, 106
    Chrome, 19, 104, 106, 129, 134
    Firefox, 129, 134
    Safari, 302, 319
Web Forager, 139, 144, 170, 178
Web Fountain, 283, 297
WebRat, 273, 287
WebTOC, 185, 193
WeFeelFine, 271, 284
Wikipedia, 306, 323
Windows XP, 104, 108
wisdom of crowds, 218, 228, 317, 335
within-participants design, 41
word clouds. *See* tag clouds
Word Space, 294, 308
Word Tree, 288, 303
Wordle, 289, 304

Xerox, 257, 269
xFIND, 273, 287

Yahoo, 11, 13, 23, 28, 151, 157, 158, 165,
        187–188, 195–196, 213, 218, 224, 228,
        300, 302, 317, 318, 321, 334, 336, 340
Yahoo Alerts, 215, 225
Yahoo Answers, 321, 340

zooming, 171, 179, 238, 247, 304, 321
zvents, 21

Author Index

Aalbersberg, I., 154
Abowd, G., 309
Ackerman, M., 77, 79, 80, 87, 158
Adar, E., 19, 49, 88, 211, 232
Adcock, J., 310, 311
Adomavicius, G., 214
Agichtein, E., 9, 49, 94, 121, 122, 321
Ahn, J.-S., 13, 216, 217
Albers, M. C., 214
Albert, D., 9
Albert, I., 220
Allan, J., 153, 235, 277, 278
Allen, B., 25, 57, 235
Allen, R. B., 278
Alonso, O., 44
Alvarado, C., 77, 79, 80, 87, 158
Alvey, B., 248, 249
Amarasinghe, S., 14, 154
Amento, B., 158
Amershi, S., 320
An, A., 48
Anderson, T., 257
Andrews, K., 8, 243, 258, 273, 274, 276
Androutsopoulos, I., 95
Anghelescu, H., 56
Anick, P., 11–13, 48, 77, 105, 144, 145, 149, 151, 248, 249
Aris, A., 294, 295
Artola, A., 14, 154
Ashley, J., 308, 309
Aula, A., 2, 9, 33, 41, 42, 56, 60, 62, 75, 113, 127
Auvil, L., 282, 296
Ayers, E., 263

Back, M., 33, 319–321
Bainbridge, D., 305, 306

Bakshi, K., 9, 98, 127
Balabanović, M., 220
Baldonado, M., 165
Baldonado, M. Q. W., 128, 230
Baluja, S., 298, 299
Banko, M., 97
Bar-Ilan, J., 49
Barreau, D., 231
Basalaj, W., 209, 309
Basu, C., 220
Bateman, J., 55, 92, 93, 154
Bates, C., 38, 134
Bates, M., 68, 71, 73, 77, 190
Baudisch, P., 58, 129, 130, 238, 254, 302, 305
Beaudouin-Lafon, M., 34
Bederson, B., 235, 270, 271, 277, 278, 294, 296, 309
Bederson, B. B., 231, 263
Belkin, N., 64, 75, 102, 103, 152, 162, 217, 258
Bell, D., 59
Ben-Bassat, T., 27, 46
Bergman, O., 79, 231
Bernstein, M., 322
Bertin, J., 237
Bett, M., 313
Beyth-Marom, R., 79, 231
Bharat, K., 214
Bickmore, T., 302
Biemans, H., 56
Bier, E., 165, 166
Bilal, D., 3, 59, 94
Bilenko, M., 11, 13, 131, 147, 149, 151
Billsus, D., 230
Björk, S., 302
Blackwell, A., 19, 231, 304, 305
Blackwell, J., 39

Blair, D., 61, 98
Blandford, A., 53
Bodnar, A., 171, 172, 283, 285
Boren, M., 35
Borgman, C., 68, 69, 92
Boyd, D., 245
Boyle, J., 108
Brandes, U., 243, 293
Breese, J., 230
Brennan, J., 248, 249
Brill, E., 97, 142–144
Brin, S., 16
Broder, A., 65, 66, 83, 84, 86, 90
Brooks, H., 64
Brown, K., 38, 134
Bruce, H., 19, 231
Brueni, D. J., 242, 244
Brunk, B., 71, 164
Bruns, T., 21
Brusilovsky, P., 13, 216, 217
Bruza, P., 11, 144, 145
Buchanan, G., 53
Buckley, C., 58, 59, 153, 154
Burke, R., 97
Burkowski, F., 9, 15, 109, 110
Buyukkokten, O., 300, 302
Byrd, D., 6, 13, 64, 65, 83, 129, 252, 253

Cadiz, J., 16, 19, 47, 182, 231
Cai, D., 309
Cannata, P., 108
Carbonell, J., 125
Card, S., 57, 73, 80, 81, 123, 139, 164, 165,
    168–170, 238, 294
Carpineto, C., 263
Cass, T., 211
Castillo, C., 321
Catledge, L., 48
Chalmers, M., 273
Chan, S., 14, 154
Chandler, C., 196
Chandrasekar, R., 139, 264
Chang, S.-J., 75
Chapparo, B., 163
Chattratichart, J., 35, 58
Chaudari, V., 231
Chen, C., 57, 234, 235
Chen, F., 123
Chen, H., 178, 179, 202, 205, 208, 273, 275,
    276
Chen, M., 48, 54, 133, 183, 185, 224, 307, 311,
    312
Chen, S., 310
Chen, X., 205
Cheyer, A., 231

Chi, E., 222
Chi, E. H., 319
Chignell, M., 75, 77
Chin, J., 44
Chitson, P., 273
Cho, J., 224, 232
Choi, J., 313, 314
Chou, V., 322
Christos, F., 39
Christos, K., 39
Chuang, S., 86
Chung, G., 3, 94
Church, K., 302
Clarke, C., 9, 15, 94, 109, 110, 121, 122
Claypool, M., 220
Clement, T., 282, 296
Cleveland, W., 237
Cockburn, A., 263, 279, 280
Cohen, M., 169
Cohen, W., 220
Collins, C., 288, 290
Combs, T., 235
Cool, C., 55, 75, 102, 103, 162
Coombs, J., 169, 170
Cooper, A., 7, 49, 167
Cooper, M., 310, 311
Cormack, G., 9, 15, 109, 110
Corritore, C., 56
Cort, B., 81, 82, 170, 171, 283
Cosley, D., 220
Cousins, S., 68, 92, 107, 165–167
Cowley, P., 80
Cramer, N., 273–275
Crestani, F., 57, 302, 303, 313
Cribbin, T., 279
Croft, B., 277
Croft, W., 6, 13, 64, 65, 83, 144, 153, 154, 214,
    216
Croft, W. B., 232
Cronen-Townsend, S., 153, 154, 214, 216
Cronin, D., 7
Cucerzan, S., 11, 13, 131, 142–144, 147, 149,
    151
Cuevas, G. T., 14, 154
Cugini, J., 235, 279
Cui, H., 144
Cunningham, S., 53, 313
Cutrell, E., 9, 16, 19, 47, 126, 137, 178, 179,
    182, 205, 208, 231
Cutting, D., 123, 165, 199, 274
Czerwinski, M., 139, 169, 170, 235, 263, 271,
    272, 294, 296, 305, 309

Dakka, W., 199
Darrell, T., 313

Das, A., 99, 228, 229
Datar, M., 99, 228, 229
Dawson, P., 189
de Jong, F., 312
de Rooij, O., 312
DeAngeli, A., 313
Dearman, D., 83
Dempsey, L., 159, 208
Dennis, S., 11, 144, 145
Dermen, D., 57
Deshpande, M., 222
Devlin, S., 108
Dhamija, R., 245
Dialog, Inc 107
DiCuccio, M., 155
Diehl, C., 200
Diehl, V., 44
Dinet, J., 108
Divoli, A., 9–11, 147, 148, 267
Doan, K., 21
Dollu, V., 153
Dom, B., 308, 309
Don, A., 282
Donath, J., 245
Donato, D., 321
Doncheva, M., 169
Dorr, A., 3, 94
Dosinger, G., 273
Dou, Z., 224, 226–228
Downie, J., 313
Draper, S., 29, 34
Drucker, S., 169
Druin, A., 270, 271
Druschel, P., 225, 318
Dudek, C., 27, 45
Duffy, J., 302
Dumais, S., 9, 16, 19, 24, 25, 47, 53, 94, 97,
    99, 121, 122, 126, 154, 178, 179, 182, 205,
    208, 211, 213, 222, 223, 227, 231, 232, 318,
    323
Dumais, S. T., 232
Dunlop, M., 29, 34
Dziadosz, S., 139, 264

Eastman, C., 114
Edmonds, A., 211
Egan, D., 9, 75, 123, 128, 183, 184
Eick, S. G., 286, 287
Ekstrom, R., 57
Eleftherios, P., 39
Elgin, B., 321
Elie, C., 39
Ellis, D., 69, 313
English, J., 21, 54, 159, 190, 194, 267
Ennis, M., 53, 64, 65, 82

Esenther, A., 312
Etzioni, O., 180, 205, 206
Evans, B., 319
Everts, I., 312
Eysenbach, G., 77

Fagan, L., 186, 208, 210
Fang, N., 158
Fass, A., 169
Faulring, A., 58, 139, 263, 265, 266
Favart, M., 108
Feinberg, J., 198
Feldman, D., 242
Feldman, R., 281
Fellbaum, C. E., 245
Fernanda, B., 288, 291
Few, S., 235–237
Field, B., 309
Fischer, G., 214, 232
Fisher, D., 245
Fishkin, K., 250
Flickner, M., 308, 309
Flood, J., 153
Fluit, C., 269
Flynn, R., 248, 249
Fogg, B., 158
Foley, C., 319
Fontoura, M., 86
Forlines, C., 312
Forlizzi, J., 169, 302
Fowler, R. H., 277
Fowler, W. A. L., 277
Fox, E. A., 242, 244
Fox, S., 222
Franz, M., 97
Franzen, K., 25, 101
Freitag, D., 230
French, J., 57
Frokjær, E., 8, 238, 252–254, 274, 275
Fu, H., 302
Fu, X., 153
Furnas, G., 24, 25, 76
Fusani, D., 55

Gabrilovich, E., 86
Gang, A., 99, 228, 229
Garcia-Molina, H., 214, 300, 302, 309, 317
Garlock, K., 158
Gauch, S., 86, 224
Gauger, M., 309
Gay, G., 26, 55, 80, 122, 136, 137, 139, 225
Geisler, G., 71, 164
Geusebroek, J., 312
Gionis, A., 321
Goker, A., 48

Gokhale, A., 220
Goldstein, J., 125
Goldstein, M., 311
Golovchinsky, G., 33, 319–321
Gomez, L., 24, 25, 108
Gopalkrishnan, P., 220
Gorg, C., 282, 283
Gorkani, M., 308, 309
Gradovitch, N., 79, 231
Graham, A., 309
Graham, J., 129, 252
Granitzer, M., 8, 243, 273, 274, 276
Granka, L., 26, 55, 80, 122, 136, 137, 139, 225
Grau, X., 242
Greenberg, S., 263
Greene, S., 14
Greene, S. L., 108
Grefenstette, G., 164
Gregory, M., 282
Greiner, W., 144
Greisdorf, H., 55, 154
Grigoryan, V., 155
Grimes, C., 36
Grinstein, G., 286
Griswold, W. G., 298, 299
Gross, R., 313
Gruen, D., 288
Grunfeld, L., 153
Guan, Z., 9, 126, 137
Gummadi, K., 225, 318
Gurrin, C., 319
Gütl, C., 258, 273, 274
Guturu, H., 9, 10, 267

Hafner, J., 308, 309
Hager, D., 39
Hakala, N., 55, 154
Halasz, F., 169
Halsey, M., 14, 154
Halvey, M., 288
Halvorsen, P., 164, 165
Hammond, K., 97
Hanani, U., 214
Handschuh, S., 164, 258
Hanna, L., 58, 129, 130, 238, 254
Hansell, S., 95
Hanssen, D., 248, 249
Harabagiu, S., 97
Harada, S., 312
Hargittai, E., 2, 103, 143, 144
Harman, D., 31, 33, 58, 59, 61, 153
Harman, H., 57
Harper, D., 68, 170
Harper, R., 171, 172, 283, 285
Harris, C., 270

Hassenzahl, M., 27, 45
Hatano, K., 229
Hauptmann, A., 307, 311, 312
Haveliwala, T., 224
Havre, S., 261, 262, 293
He, D., 13, 48, 216, 217
He, X., 309
Healy, C., 236
Hearst, M., 9–11, 14, 15, 21, 40, 44, 54, 98,
   109, 111, 124, 127, 133, 147, 148, 159,
   163–165, 183, 185, 186, 190, 194, 196,
   199–202, 208–210, 245, 254, 255, 267, 271,
   281, 283, 288, 314, 323
Heath, L. S., 242, 244
Heckerman, D., 230
Heer, J., 222, 238, 245
Heikes, R., 281
Heimonen, T., 257
Helfman, J. I., 263
Helft, M., 52
Hembrooke, H., 26, 55, 80, 122, 136, 137, 225
Hemmje, M., 261
Henderson, C., 313
Henderson, S., 14, 154
Hendry, D., 68, 170
Henne, R., 37, 40, 43, 50–52
Henzinger, M., 48, 92, 93
Herlocker, J., 218, 220, 229
Hert, C., 189
Hertzum, M., 75, 79, 108, 142, 238, 247
Hetzler, E., 261, 262, 273, 293
Heymann, P., 317
Hightower, R. R., 263
Hildreth, C., 108
Hill, W., 129, 158, 252
Hindle, D., 313, 314
Hirschberg, J., 169, 313, 314
Hirsh, H., 220
Hix, D., 242, 244
Hockley, A., 3, 94, 95, 187
Hoeber, O., 256, 257
Hoefer, M., 243, 293
Hoffman, H., 139, 263
Hollan, J., 129, 252
Hollan, J. D., 263, 298, 299
Holmquist, L., 302
Hölscher, C., 56
Hon, H.-W., 87
Hong, D., 302
Hong, J., 54, 133, 183
Hornbæk, K., 8, 30, 44–46, 238, 252–254, 274,
   275
Horvitz, E., 53, 154, 211, 213, 222, 223, 227,
   230, 232, 318
Hotchkiss, G., 27, 38, 134, 233, 315

Houston, A. L., 202, 273, 275, 276
Houston, M., 25, 53, 275
Hovel, D., 230
Hovy, E., 97
Hristidis, V., 125
Huang, Q., 308, 309
Huang, T., 309
Huang, X., 48
Huang, Y., 231
Hudson, S., 302
Hull, D., 164, 215
Hurst, M., 26, 233, 323
Hussam, A., 257
Hutchings, D., 172
Hutchinson, H., 270, 271
Huurnink, B., 312
Huynh, D., 9, 98, 127

Ihlwan, M., 321
Ingwersen, P., 64
Ipeirotis, p., 199
iProspect 133, 315
ISO 9241-11 29
Ittycheriah, A., 97

Jacob, E., 189
Jacobs, N., 257
Jacobson, T., 55
Jameson, A., 230, 232
Jancke, G., 16, 19, 47, 182, 231
Jansen, B., 80, 85, 92, 93, 113, 114, 141, 150, 298
Janssen, Jr., W., 169
Jarvelin, K., 64
Jasonsmith, M., 263
Jatowt, A., 317
Jeffries, R., 36, 68, 69, 72, 77, 81
Jeh, G., 215, 221
Jellinek, H., 164
Jenkins, C., 56
Jhaveri, N., 257, 263, 264
Joachims, T., 26, 80, 122, 136, 137, 139, 225, 226, 230, 318
Johnson, B., 245
Johnson, W., 123, 164
Jones, G., 319
Jones, M., 305, 306
Jones, R., 19, 49, 88, 144, 231, 232
Jones, S., 247, 248, 305, 306
Jones, W., 19, 231
Jonker, D., 82, 171, 283
Jose, J., 9, 56, 123, 125, 128, 154, 216, 233
Joshi, A., 86
Josifovski, V., 86

Jurafsky, D., 44
Jurrus, E., 261, 262

Kaasinen, E., 298
Kaasten, S., 263
Kahle, B., 230
Kaisser, M., 9, 44, 98, 127
Käki, M., 2, 33, 47, 60, 62, 180, 203–205, 209, 277
Kamba, T., 214, 229
Kamvar, M., 298, 299
Kang, H., 309
Kantamneni, R., 9, 12, 13, 105, 128, 151
Kantrowitz, M., 125
Kanungo, T., 128
Kapoor, N., 220
Karadi, C., 271
Karger, D., 9, 77, 79, 80, 87, 98, 127, 158, 165, 199, 274, 322
Karis, D., 34
Karlgren, J., 25, 101
Karlson, A., 271, 272, 305
Karnawat, K., 222
Karypis, G., 222
Kass, R., 214
Katz, B., 9, 98, 127
Keane, M., 288, 302
Keim, D., 294
Kekäläinen, J., 33
Kellar, M., 83, 88, 89
Kelly, D., 55, 102, 103, 153
Keppel, G., 37, 40, 42
Kerr, B., 198
Ketchum, D., 9, 75, 123, 128, 183, 184
Kickmeier, M., 9
Kienreich, W., 8, 243, 273, 274, 276
Kim, G., 102, 103
Kim, J., 102, 103
Kimber, D., 313, 314
Kirschenbaum, M., 296
Kleiboemer, A., 209, 274
Klieber, W., 8, 243, 273, 274, 276
Klotz, L., 123, 164
Koelma, D., 312
Koenemann, J., 152, 217
Kohavi, R., 37, 40, 43, 50–52
Kohler, C., 77
Kohler, J., 312
Konstan, J., 218, 220, 229
Korfhage, R., 261, 262
Korfhage, R. R., 261, 267
Koseki, Y., 169
Koshman, S., 150
Koutrika, G., 317
Kozierok, R., 230

Kraaij, W., 310, 312
Krishnapuram, R., 200, 203
Kriss, J., 288, 290, 291, 293
Ksikes, A., 9, 10, 267
Kuhlthau, C., 64, 69
Kuhn, K., 313
Kukich, K., 142
Kules, B., 179, 205, 208
Kulukin, V., 97
Kumar, R., 49
Kummamuru, K., 200, 203
Kuniavsky, M., 6, 25, 34
Kunkel, C., 261
Kupiec, J., 96, 123
Kushmerick, N., 230
Kwok, K. L., 59, 153

Lachenmann, A., 309
Lackner, W., 258, 273, 274
Lake, M., 15, 93
Lalmas, M., 152–154, 216
Lam, H., 302, 305
Lam, S., 220
Lamping, J., 245
Landauer, T., 9, 24, 25, 34, 75, 123, 128, 183, 184
Landay, J., 76
Lanning, T., 312
Lantrip, D., 273
Lapaugh, A., 48, 224
Laraki, O., 158
Larkin, J., 234
Larson, K., 169, 170, 235
Larson, M., 312
Larson, R., 189
Larvrenko, V., 153, 154, 214, 216
Laskowski, S., 235, 279, 286
Lau, T., 230
Law, E., 30, 44–46
Lazear, M., 209, 274
Lazonder, A., 56
Lee, B., 58, 129, 130, 238, 254, 294, 296
Lee, D., 308, 309
Lee, H., 102, 103, 319
Lehman, K., 39
Lerner, J., 243, 293
Lesk, M., 9, 75, 123, 128, 183, 184
Levi, M., 77, 78
Levinson, D., 60, 83–85, 90
Levison, L., 14, 154
Lewis, D. D., 153
Lewis, M., 261
Li, K., 21, 40, 54, 194, 208
Li, K. A., 298, 299
Li, M., 142, 143

Li, Z., 309
Liddy, E., 55
Lieberman, H., 222, 230
Liebling, D. J., 232
Lin, J., 9, 54, 97, 98, 127, 133, 155, 183
Lin, W., 307, 311, 312
Lin, X., 273, 276
Linden, G., 131, 220
Lindgaard, G., 27, 35, 45, 58
Ling, J., 45
Little, G., 322
Littman, M., 278
Litvak, Y., 14, 154
Liu, F., 224
Liu, Z., 282, 283
Ljungstrand, P., 302
Lobb, B., 27, 45
Lochbaum, C., 9, 75, 123, 128, 183, 184
Logan, R., 126
Longbotham, R., 43, 51
Loranger, H., 7, 35
Lord, G., 296
Lotlikar, R., 200, 203
Lowe, J., 9, 44, 98, 127
Luhn, H., 124
Luo, Q., 302
Luo, Z., 87
Lynch, C., 114
Lytinen, S., 97

Ma, W., 144, 304, 309
Maarek, Y. S., 278
MacKay, B., 302
Mackay, W., 34
Mackinlay, J., 164, 165, 170, 237, 238, 294
Madani, O., 144
Maes, P., 219, 230, 233
Mahtab, T., 14, 154
Maiorano, S., 97
Malone, T., 169
Manber, U., 213
Mandel, M., 313
Mander, R., 169
Mann, T., 14, 131, 164, 258–260
Maple, A., 190
Marais, H., 48, 92, 93
Marchetti, P. G., 75, 162
Marchionini, G., 9, 14, 64, 66, 71, 75, 77, 78, 94, 106, 107, 120, 128, 154, 164, 269, 270, 273, 276
Markoff, J., 302
Maron, M., 61, 98
Marshall, C., 169, 170
Marshall, J., 158
Martzoukou, K., 59

Masinter, L., 164, 165
Mason, L., 51
Matsuzawa, H., 282
Maybury, M., 313
Mayhew, D., 6, 34
Mcarthur, R., 11, 145
McCandless, T., 129, 252
McFadden, E., 39
McGill, R., 237
McGivney, S., 319
McInnes, S., 247, 248
McIntosh, S., 305, 306
McKenzie, B., 263, 279, 280
McKeon, M., 288, 291
McNab, R., 313
McNee, S., 220
McSherry, D., 162
Meadow, C., 110, 114
Mehrotra, S., 309
Meng, W., 224
Meredith, D., 14, 283, 284
Meyer, J., 27, 46
Miao, G., 304
Michard, A., 108, 247
Milic-Frayling, N., 19, 231, 304,
  305
Millen, D., 198, 288
Miller, B., 220, 229
Miller, J., 36
Miller, M., 235, 279
Miller, N., 261, 262
Miller, R., 322
Miranda, T., 220
Mishne, G., 321
Mislove, A., 225, 318
Mitchell, T., 230, 231
Mitra, M., 153, 154
Mittal, V., 125
Miyachi, T., 312
Modjeska, D., 169
Moran, T., 169
Moricz, M., 48, 92, 93
Morita, M., 222
Morris, D., 113
Morris, M., 319, 320
Morrison, J., 58, 139, 263, 265, 266
Morse, E., 261
Morville, P., 76
Moser, J., 258, 273, 274
Motwani, R., 16
Mußler, G., 164, 258
Muller, M., 288
Munzner, T., 279
Murakami, A., 282
Muramatsu, J., 2, 93, 99, 150, 230

Muresan, G., 102, 103
Murnikov, P., 220
Mydland, M., 222
Myers, B., 302

Nachmias, R., 79, 231
Nadir, R., 26, 27
Nagano, T., 282
Nakamura, S., 317
Nakarada-Kordic, I., 27, 45
Nakatani, C., 313
Nakov, P., 9, 10, 267
Nardi, B., 231
Nardi, B. A., 169
Nasukawa, T., 282
Nation, A., 185
Netes, D., 220
Newman, M., 76
Ng, A., 44, 97
Niblack, W., 308, 309
Nichols, D., 17, 165, 166, 319
Nie, J., 87, 144
Nielsen, J., 5–7, 29, 34–37, 54, 55, 57, 60, 73,
  74, 77, 99, 133, 163, 233
Nikolaos, A., 39
Nikolaos, T., 39
Norman, D., 27, 66, 67, 233, 322
Norman, K., 44
Nowell, L., 80, 293
Nowell, L. T., 242, 244

Obry, P., 278
O'Connell, T., 286
O'Connor, B., 44
O'Connor, N., 319
O'Day, V. L., 68, 69, 72, 77, 81
Oddy, R., 64, 162
Oelke, D., 294
Ogden, W., 108
O'Hara, K., 81
Olsen, K., 261, 262
Öquist, G., 311
Ordelman, R., 312
Olson, T., 159
Oren, T., 169
Orr, D., 9, 128
Ortega, M., 309
Osipovich, A., 158
Over, P., 310
Oviatt, S., 313
Owens, A., 270

Paek, T., 126
Paepcke, A., 165, 166, 300, 302,
  309

Page, L., 16
Paice, C., 319
Paley, W., 288, 289
Paliouras, G., 213
Pan, B., 26, 80, 122, 136, 137, 225
Pan, Y., 313
Pang, B., 49
Papatheodorou, C., 213
Paranjpe, D., 97
Parekh, N., 282, 283
Parekh, R., 51
Parikh, N., 144
Parush, A., 26, 27
Pasca, M., 97
Passerault, J., 108
Patel, A., 213
Patterson, E., 81
Paul, J., 158
Pausch, R., 169
Pauws, S., 313
Pazzani, M., 230
Pedersen, G. S., 263
Pedersen, J., 80, 93, 113, 123, 141, 144, 164, 165, 199, 201, 202, 209, 274
Peng, F., 48
Pennock, K., 273
Pereira, F., 313, 314
Pernice, K., 37
Perrine, K., 261, 262
Peterson, R., 17
Petkovic, D., 308, 309
Pew 4, 307
Pickens, J., 33, 310, 311, 319–321
Pieper, J., 14, 283, 284
Pier, K., 165, 166
Pierrakos, D., 213
Piontek, S., 158
Pirolli, P., 57, 58, 73, 76, 80, 81, 139, 164, 168, 169, 200, 222, 245, 263, 265, 266
Pitkow, J., 48, 211, 222
Plaisant, C., 5, 14, 21, 29, 37, 44, 46, 282, 286, 296
Platt, J., 309
Plumlee, M., 238
Plummer, B., 257
Poliner, G., 313
Pollitt, A. S., 270
Pollock, A., 3, 94, 95, 187
Ponceleon, D., 169
Pottier, M., 273
Potts, M., 19, 88, 232
Pratt, W., 2, 93, 99, 150, 186, 208, 210
Prevost, J., 14, 154
Proulx, P., 81, 82, 170–172, 283, 285
Pu, H., 86

Qiu, F., 224, 232
Qu, Y., 25, 53, 275
Quan, D., 9, 98, 127
Qvarfordt, P., 33, 319–321

Raiha, K.-J., 263, 264
Rainie, L., 297
Rajaram, S., 99, 228, 229
Ramakrishnan, G., 97
Ramey, J., 35
Ranganathan, S., 190
Rangnekar, A., 158
Ranie, L., 307
Rao, D., 242, 244
Rao, R., 123, 164, 165, 245, 294
Rao, S., 300
Ravichandran, D., 97
Redström, J., 302
Reimann, R., 7
Reiterer, H., 14, 131, 164, 258–260
Remde, J., 9, 75, 123, 128, 183, 184
Rennison, E., 273
Resnick, P., 218
Rettig, M., 34
Rey, B., 144
Rice, R. E., 75
Richardson, M., 199
Riedl, J., 218, 220, 229
Rieh, S., 158
Rimmer, J., 53
Ring, L. T., 263
Ritchie, G., 95
Rivadeneira, A., 288
Rivadeneira, W., 277, 278
Robbins, D., 16, 19, 47, 169, 170, 182, 231, 235, 271, 272, 305
Robbins, J., 248, 249
Robertson, G., 139, 164, 165, 169, 170, 235, 238, 263, 271, 272, 294, 296, 305
Robertson, S., 215
Robison, J., 213
Rodden, K., 19, 209, 231, 300, 304, 305, 309
Rogers, L., 163
Rogers, R., 169
Romano, G., 263
Rommelse, K., 230
Rose, A., 242
Rose, D., 9, 44, 53, 60, 62, 83–85, 90, 107, 128, 169
Rose, J., 296
Rosenfeld, L., 76
Rosenholtz, R., 58, 139, 263, 265, 266
Rosner, D., 288
Roth, E., 81
Roukos, S., 97

Roy, S., 200, 203
Rui, Y., 309
Russell, A., 270
Russell, D., 25, 36, 53, 73, 79, 80, 142–144, 168, 169, 275
Ruthven, I., 9, 56, 59, 123, 125, 128, 152–154, 216, 233

Sabol, V., 8, 243, 258, 273, 274, 276
Sahami, M., 230
Sakagami, H., 229
Salesin, D., 169
Salomon, G., 169
Salton, G., 64, 110, 153
Sanderson, M., 9, 16, 123
Sanger, J., 281
Saracevic, T., 31, 64, 85, 92, 93, 113, 298
Sarin, R., 16, 19, 47, 182, 231
Sartin, M., 220
Sarwar, B., 220, 229
Saufley, W., 37, 40, 42
Sav, S., 319
Sawhney, H., 308, 309
Schacter, J., 3, 94
Schank, P., 200
Schatz, B. R., 202, 273, 275, 276
Schilit, B., 302
Schoenberg, S., 97
Scholtz, J., 80, 286
Schraefel, M., 270
Schroeder, W., 35
Schroh, D., 81, 82, 170–172, 283, 285
Schur, A., 273
Schusteritsch, R., 300
Schütze, H., 144, 164, 211
Schuurmans, D., 48
Sebastiani, F., 99, 199, 208, 215
Sebrechts, M., 235, 279
Sellen, A., 81
Sewell, R. R., 202, 273, 275, 276
Shah, C., 33, 319–321
Shakhshir, S., 14, 154
Shankar, L., 205
Shapira, B., 214
Sharanand, U., 219
Shen, D., 85–87
Shen, X., 223, 228
Shepherd, M., 88, 89
Sherman, C., 17
Sherman, T., 38, 134
Shinoda, Y., 222
Shipman, F., 169
Shipman III, F., 169, 170
Shneiderman, B., 5, 6, 13, 14, 21, 29, 37, 44, 46, 64, 65, 82, 83, 105, 108, 131, 154, 179,

205, 208, 233, 242, 245, 249, 269, 282, 294, 295, 309
Shoham, Y., 220
Shore, B., 56, 82
Shoval, P., 214
Shtub, A., 26, 27
Shyu, M., 310
Sigman, E., 133, 185
Sihvonen, A., 55, 144
Siirtola, H., 113
Silverstein, C., 48, 92, 93
Simon, H., 234
Sinclair, D., 209, 309
Singal, K., 200, 203
Singh, J., 48, 224
Singh, S., 224
Singhal, A., 153, 154, 313, 314
Singhal, K., 282, 283
Sinha, R., 21, 26, 52, 54, 159, 190, 194, 267
Sinha, V., 9, 98, 127
Skaburskis, A., 81, 170
Slaney, M., 25, 53, 275
Small, H., 294, 295
Smalley, P., 196
Smeaton, A., 310, 319
Smeulders, A., 312
Smith, B., 220
Smith, D., 270
Smith, G., 271, 272, 305
Smith, L., 313
Smith, M., 296
Smyth, B., 302
Smyth, G., 19, 231
Snoek, C., 312
Snoek, C. G. M., 312
Snow, R., 44
So, W., 279
Sochats, K., 261, 262
Soergel, D., 273, 276
Sohn, T., 298, 299
Sokolov, J., 34
Sommerer, R., 19, 231, 304, 305
Sommerfield, D., 37, 40, 43, 50–52
Song, R., 87, 224, 226–228, 304
Spence, R., 311
Spink, A., 55, 80, 85, 92, 93, 113, 141, 150, 154, 298
Spoerri, A., 261, 267
Spool, J., 35, 53, 54, 77
Sprague, D., 279
Spring, M., 261, 262
Spyropoulos, C., 213
Stadnyk, I., 214
Stanfill, C., 230
Stasko, J., 172, 263, 282, 283

Stefik, M., 73, 80, 168, 169
Steinberg, S., 158
Stewart, B., 44
Stockburger, D. W., 42
Stoica, E., 199
Stone, M. C., 250
Strube, G., 56
Sugiura, A., 169
Sugiyama, K., 229
Sundaresan, N., 144
Sutcliffe, A., 53, 64, 65, 82
Swan, R., 235, 277, 278
Swani, P., 158
Swearingen, K., 21, 40, 54, 159, 190, 194, 208, 267
Sweeney, S., 302, 303
Syn, S., 13, 216, 217

Tabatabai, D., 56, 82
Takeda, K., 282
Takeuchi, H., 282
Tan, B., 223, 228
Tanaka, K., 317
Tandon, S., 171, 172, 283, 285
Tang, D., 36
Tang, M., 102, 103
Tanin, E., 131, 269
Tao, T., 9, 109
Tarkan, S., 282
Teevan, J., 19, 53, 77, 79, 80, 87, 88, 154, 158, 211, 213, 222, 223, 227, 231, 232, 318
Terveen, L., 158, 218
Thanisch, P., 95
Thiel, D., 169, 170, 235
Thies, W., 14, 154
Thomas, J. J., 273
Thompson, P., 153
Thompson, R., 277
Tobin, R., 38, 134
Tokunaga, H., 37, 40, 42
Tombros, A., 9, 16, 123
Tombros, T., 57, 313
Tomkins, A., 49
Tomuro, N., 97
Tory, M., 279
Tractinsky, N., 27, 46
Treinen, M., 158
Triesman, A., 236
Trigg, R., 123, 164
Truong, K., 83
Tufte, E., 235, 261
Tukey, J., 123, 165, 199, 274
Tullius, G., 14, 131, 258–260
Turnbull, D., 211
Turner, A., 273

Turtle, H., 153
Tuzhilin, A., 214
Twidale, M., 17, 165, 166, 319

Uhlir, S., 108
Uramoto, N., 282
Uyeda, K., 36

Vakkari, P., 55, 70, 144, 154
van Dantzich, M., 139, 169, 170, 235, 263
van de Sande, K., 312
van der Heijden, H., 27, 45
Van Der Wege, M., 57
van Gemert, J., 312
van Ham, F., 288, 291
Van Kleek, M., 322
van Liempt, M., 312
van Schaik, P., 45
Varadarajan, R., 125
Varian, H., 218
Varma, C., 158
Vasilakis, J., 235, 279
Veerasamy, A., 258, 281
Viégas, F., 245, 288, 291
Vignoli, F., 313
Virzi, R., 34
Vo, B. D., 14, 154
Voorhees, E., 31, 33, 58, 59, 95, 144

W-Y., M., 302
Wade, G., 169
Wærn, A., 214, 216, 221
Waibel, A., 313
Wake, W. C., 242, 244
Walz, J., 58, 59
Wang, S., 231
Ware, C., 236, 238
Warwick, C., 53
Waterworth, J., 75, 77
Wattenberg, M., 245, 288, 290, 291, 293
Watters, C., 88, 89, 302
Wecker, A., 278
Wei, X., 232
Wen, J.-R., 87, 144, 224, 226–228, 304, 309
West, R., 39
Westerman, S., 279
Wharton, C., 36
White, R., 9, 11, 13, 56, 94, 106, 107, 113, 120–123, 125, 128, 131, 147, 149, 151, 154, 216, 233
White, T., 222
Whiting, M., 273–275, 286
Whitney, P., 293
Whittaker, S., 79, 169, 231, 313, 314
Whitworth, B., 233

Wiedenbeck, S., 56
Wigdor, D., 169
Wilbur, W., 155
Wilcox, L., 313, 314
Wildemuth, B., 55
Wilkins, P., 319
Willett, A., 261
Willett, P., 60, 200
Williams, J., 261, 262
Wilson, B. A., 277
Wilson, P., 108
Wilson, T., 83
Winograd, T., 16, 128, 165, 166, 302, 309
Wise, J. A., 273
Witten, I., 305, 306, 313
Wittenburg, K., 133, 185, 312
Wobbrock, J., 302
Wolfram, D., 85, 113, 298
Wong, Y., 169
Wood, K. R., 209, 309
Woodruff, A., 58, 139, 263, 265, 266
Woods, D., 81
Wooldridge, M., 9–11, 147, 148, 267
Wopereis, I., 56
Worring, M., 312
Woyke, E., 321
Wright, W., 81, 82, 170–172, 283, 285
Wroblewski, D., 129, 252
Wu, F., 279
Wu, Y., 205

Xiao, X., 302
Xie, H., 131, 269
Xie, X., 302, 304
Xiong, L., 49
Xu, J., 144

Yan, R., 307, 311, 312
Yan, T., 214
Yanbe, Y., 317
Yang, B., 153, 215, 221
Yang, C., 86
Yang, J., 307, 311–313
Yang, X. D., 256, 257
Ye, j., 9, 10, 267
Yee, K.-P., 21, 40, 54, 159, 190, 194, 208, 245, 267
York, J., 220
York, W., 139, 170
Yoshikawa, M., 229
Young, D., 108, 249
Yu, B., 296
Yu, C., 224
Yu, H., 313
Yu, Y., 87, 234, 235
Yuan, X., 56, 102, 103
Yusufali, S., 230

Zamir, O., 180, 205, 206
Zhai, C., 9, 109, 223, 228
Zhang, C., 310
Zhang, H., 87
Zhang, J., 269, 270
Zhang, T., 86
Zhang, X., 56
Zhang, Y., 142, 143
Zhao, S., 169
Zheleva, E., 282
Zheng, Z., 51
Zhou, M., 142, 143
Zhou, Y., 154
Zhu, M., 142, 143
Zhu, X., 313
Zhu, Y., 169